The debates and proceedings of the British House of Commons, during the third, fourth and fifth sessions of the third Parliament of His late Majesty George II : Held in the year 1743, 1744, 1745, and 1746 Volume v.7

Almon, John, 1737-1805, publisher,
Bladon, Samuel, d. 1799, bookseller

Nabu Public Domain Reprints:

You are holding a reproduction of an original work published before 1923 that is in the public domain in the United States of America, and possibly other countries. You may freely copy and distribute this work as no entity (individual or corporate) has a copyright on the body of the work. This book may contain prior copyright references, and library stamps (as most of these works were scanned from library copies). These have been scanned and retained as part of the historical artifact.

This book may have occasional imperfections such as missing or blurred pages, poor pictures, errant marks, etc. that were either part of the original artifact, or were introduced by the scanning process. We believe this work is culturally important, and despite the imperfections, have elected to bring it back into print as part of our continuing commitment to the preservation of printed works worldwide. We appreciate your understanding of the imperfections in the preservation process, and hope you enjoy this valuable book.

THE
DEBATES
AND
PROCEEDINGS
OF THE
British House of Commons,

From 1765 to 1768.

LONDON:
Printed in the Year MDCCLXXII.

CONTENTS

Of VOL. VII.

FOURTH SESSION.

KING's speech and address	Page 1
Debate on general warrants	9
Supplies and ways and means for 1765	11
Foundation of the American stamp act, with observations	20
Motion relative to informations in the King's Bench	39
Bargain for the Isle of Man	40
King's speech on proposing a regency	42
Regency bill brought into the House of Commons, debated and altered	46
Acts passed and King's speech	50

FIFTH SESSION.

King's speech	57
Debate on the address, with Mr. Pitt's speech proposing a repeal of the American stamp act	61 to 77
Copies of papers relative to the disturbances in America	79
Petitions against the American stamp act	100
Examination of Dr. Franklin	106
Stamp act repealed, and division upon it	140
Resolutions and acts relative to America	147 to 156
Bill establishing free ports in Dominica, &c.	156
Excise on cyder, &c. repealed	157
Supplies and ways and means for 1766	159
Mr. Calvert's humourous speech	181
Resolutions on the prices of corn	181
General warrants condemned	182
Acts passed, and King's speech	186

Sixth

CONTENTS.

SIXTH SESSION.

King's speech	191
State of facts relative to a proclamation prohibiting the exportation of corn	195
Speech against the suspending and dispensing prerogative, &c.	196
Supplies and ways and means for 1767	258
Bargain with the East India Company	279
Land tax reduced to 3s. in the pound, and division	282
Petition of the half pay lieutenants in the navy, supported by Commodore Hervey	296
Assembly of New York suspended	301
Petition from New York	315
Acts passed and King's speech	322

SEVENTH SESSION.

King's speech	327
Debate on the address	329
Petition from the City of London respecting the prices of provisions	339
Supplies and ways and means for 1768	342
Magistrates of Oxford reprimanded, with remarks	356
Division on the motion for a bill to quiet the possessions of the subject	365
Acts passed, King's speech, and parliament dissolved	370 to 373

THE HISTORY

OF THE

Proceedings and Debates

OF THE HONOURABLE

HOUSE of COMMONS

OF THE

FOURTH SESSION

OF THE

Twelfth Parliament of *Great-Britain*.

This Session was opened at Westminster, *on the 10th Day of January* 1765, *by his Majesty, with the following Speech from the Throne.*

My Lords and Gentlemen,

"THE situation of affairs both at home and abroad, has enabled me to allow you that recess, which has been usual in times of public tranquillity.

"I have now the satisfaction to inform you, that I have agreed with my good brother the king of *Denmark*, to cement the union which has long subsisted between the two crowns, by the marriage of the Prince Royal of *Denmark* with my sister the Princess *Caroline Matilda*, which is to be solemniz'd as soon as their respective ages will permit." [The Prince Royal of *Denmark*, Christian,

The King's speech.

Vol. VII.   B

tian, was born *January* 29, 1746; and the Princess *Caroline Matilda, July* 22, 1751.

'I observe with pleasure, that the events which
' have happened in the course of the last year,
' give us reason to hope for the duration of that
' peace, which has been so happily established,
' and which it is my resolution strictly to maintain.
' The courts of *France* and *Spain* have given me
' fresh assurances of their good dispositions. The
' future quiet of the empire has been confirmed
' by the unanimous choice of a successor to the im-
' perial dignity; and the peaceable election of
' the King of *Poland*, has prevented those fatal
' consequences, which, upon similar occasions,
' have so frequently been destructive to the repose
' of *Europe*. I am happy, therefore, to meet my
' parliament at a time when no foreign disturb-
' ances interrupt their consultations, for the inter-
' nal good order and prosperity of my kingdoms.

Gentlemen of the House of Commons.

' I shall ask of you, for the current service of
' the year, no other supplies, than such as are
' necessary for those establishments, which have
' already met with your approbation; and I will
' order the proper estimates for this purpose to be
' laid before you.
' I must, however, earnestly recommend to you
' the continuance of that attention, which you
' have hitherto shewn, for the improvement of the
' public revenue, and the diminution of the nati-
' onal debt. For these desirable and necessary
' ends, I am persuaded, that you will pursue e-
' very proper measure, which the state of my
' dominions, and the circumstances of the times
' may require.

My Lords and Gentlemen,

'The experience which I have had of your former conduct makes me rely on your wisdom, and firmness, in promoting that obedience to the laws, and respect to the legislative authority of this kingdom, which is essentially necessary for the safety of the whole; and in establishing such regulations, as may best connect and strengthen every part of my dominions, for their mutual benefit and support.

'The affection which I bear to my people, excites my earnest wishes, that every session of parliament may be distinguished by some plans for the public advantage, and for their relief from those difficulties, which an expensive war has brought upon them. My concurrence and encouragement shall never be wanting where their welfare is concerned: And I trust, that for the attainment of that great object, you will proceed with temper, unanimity, and dispatch.'

The Commons agreed unanimously to the following Address.

Most gracious Sovereign,

'We, your Majesty's most dutiful and loyal subjects, the Commons of *Great Britain*, in Parliament assembled, beg leave to return your Majesty the most humble thanks of this House, for your most gracious speech from the throne.

'Permit us, at the same time, to offer to your Majesty our dutiful congratulations upon the marriage agreed to be solemnized, between the Prince Royal of *Denmark* and her Royal Highness the Princess *Caroline Matilda*, as soon as their respective ages will permit; which happy union could not but be most pleasing to your

'faithful

'faithful Commons, as it must tend to cement
'and strengthen the ancient alliance between
'the Crowns of *Great Britain* and *Denmark*, and
'thereby add security to the Protestant religion.

'We beg leave also to declare our satisfaction
'at those events of the last year, which promised
'the continuance of the peace, so happily esta-
'blished and maintained by your Majesty's wise and
'steady conduct; and to express our hopes, that
'the fresh assurances, which have been given by
'the Courts of *France* and *Spain*, of their good
'disposition, the unanimous choice of a successor
'to the Imperial throne, and the undisturbed
'election of the king of *Poland*, will secure and
'confirm the general tranquillity of *Europe*. In
'this situation, we think it our duty to give our
'particular attention to such regulations, as will
'most effectually promote the internal good or-
'der and prosperity of these kingdoms.

'Your Majesty may be assured that we will with
'chearfulness and dispatch, raise such supplies as
'shall be found necessary for the current service of
'the year: And being thoroughly sensible of your
'Majesty's paternal concern for the relief and wel-
'fare of your people, in recommending to us
'the improvement of the public revenue, and
'the diminution of the national debt, on which
'the future safety of *Great Britain* must depend;
'we will apply ourselves with the utmost zeal and
'assiduity, to carry into execution every proper
'measure which may contribute to these great and
'salutary purposes, and which the state of his Ma-
'jesty's dominions, and the circumstances of the
'times require.

'We acknowledge, with the liveliest gratitude,
'the gracious expressions of your Majesty's tender
'affection, and of your constant care, for the mu-
'tual benefit and support of all your subjects.
'And we assure your Majesty, that, animated with
'these

'these sentiments, we will endeavour to deserve
'the confidence which your Majesty is pleased to
'repose in us, by pursuing every plan which shall
'appear to us to be calculated for the public ad-
'vantage; and will proceed therein with that tem-
'per and firmness, which will best conciliate and
'ensure due submission to the laws, and reverence
'to the legislative authority of *Great Britain.*

Mr. Speaker acquainted the House, that he had on *Tuesday*, the 28th day of that instant *January*, received from Vice-admiral *Cornish* the following letter, in return to the thanks of the House, signified to him by Mr. Speaker, in obedience to their commands of the 19th of *April*, 1763.

To the Right Hon. Sir John Cust, *Bart. Speaker of the Honourable House of Commons.*

'SIR,
'The honour of your letter, inclosing the most
'valuable testimony of the honourable House of
'Commons, in favour of my conduct, in assist-
'ing the reduction of *Manila*, and the *Philippine*
'islands, with his Majesty's forces under my com-
'mand, was not received till the 15th of *August*
'last; it did not reach *India* till after my depar-
'ture, and consequently could not come to my
'hand, but by being sent back to *England.*

'But this delay has no power to diminish the
'satisfaction which every honest man must receive
'from the approbation of that honourable House,
'which represents the Commons of *Great Britain.*
'I can pretend only to the merit of intending
'well, and in that intention I hope this illustri-
'ous distinction will encourage me to persevere.
'—To you, Sir, I shall always acknowledge my
'obligations for your kind attention, and hope,
'always to retain the honour of being,

'Sir, Your most obliged, most
'obedient, and most humble servant

Parliament-street, Jan. 8. 1765. 'S. CORNISH.

On the 11th it was resolved, that an humble address be presented to his Majesty, that he would be graciously pleased to give directions for laying before the House an account of such proceedings as have been had since the 26th of *March*, 1764, in pursuance of so much of an act of parliament passed in the 12th year of the reign of King *George* I. intitled, 'An act for the improvement of his Majesty's revenues of the customs, excise, and inland duties, as impowered the Lord High Treasurer, or the Commissioners of the Treasury for the time being, to treat with the proprietors of the *Isle of Man*, for the absolute purchase or sale, release or surrender, of the said isle to the Crown.'

On the 14th, Mr. Speaker reported to the House, that his Majesty, having been attended on Saturday last with their address, was pleased to give this most gracious answer:

'*Gentlemen,*

'I return you my thanks for this very dutiful and affectionate address; and I receive with the greatest pleasure your congratulations on the marriage agreed to be solemnised between the Prince Royal of *Denmark* and my sister the Princess *Caroline Matilda*. My constant endeavour shall be employed to preserve the public tranquillity, to secure the rights, and promote the happiness of my people.'

On the 15th, Mr. Chancellor of the Exchequer acquainted the House, that he had a message from his Majesty and signed by him; and he presented the same to the House; and it was read by Mr. Speaker, and is as followeth, viz.

'GEORGE

A. 1765.   DEBATES.

'GEORGE R.

'His Majesty, having received from the ambassador of the Most Christian King, a declaration, made by order of his Court, containing a proposal for the more speedy settlement of the accounts concerning the subsistence and maintenance of prisoners of war, and for the discharge of the balance due thereon, is desirous, as the Parliament is now sitting, to know the sense of his faithful Commons, before he takes his final resolution upon this subject; and has therefore ordered a copy of the abovementioned declaration, together with the accounts referred to therein, to be laid before the House of Commons.'

Then Mr. Chancellor of the Exchequer presented to the House, by his Majesty's command,

Copy of a declaration, made by order of his Most Christian Majesty, containing a proposal for the more speedy settlement of the accounts concerning the subsistence and maintenance of prisoners of war; and for the discharge of the balance due thereon, dated the 5th of *January*, 1765, and translation; and also,

Copy of an account delivered by order of his Most Christian Majesty, being a state of the expence for the maintenance and subsistence of *English* prisoners of war, who were detained in *France* during the late war; and at *Martinico* and *Guadaloupe*, during the year 1765; and translation; and also,

A paper, intitled, 'Articles whereon the charge of 121,990*l*. 1*s*. 1*d*. mentioned in the general abstract of subsisting *French* prisoners of war, to the 11th of *November*, 1762, was incurred;' and also

Account, shewing the charge of maintaining and supporting *French* prisoners of war, in his Majesty's dominions at home and abroad, between the 14th of *October* 1755, and 11th of *November*, 1762, distinguishing the expences of subsisting those confined in prisons, in hospitals, and on parole respectively, and the number who have been subsisted daily on an average in each year, during the time above-mentioned; with an abstract of the total charge, and the estimated expence of maintaining and supporting for one week, or one day, the number of prisoners remaining in *England* at the time this account ends.

On the 16th, it was resolved, *nem. con.* that an humble address be presented to his Majesty, to return the unfeigned thanks of the House for his most gracious message of the 15th; and to represent to his Majesty, that, having taken into their consideration the state and nature of the accounts communicated to the House by his Majesty, and the difficulties and delay which must necessarily attend a complete liquidation of them, they were humbly of opinion, that it would be most adviseable for his Majesty to accept the proposal contained in the declaration made by the *French* ambassador, for the more speedy satisfaction of his Majesty's demand, upon account of the subsistence and maintenance of the *French* prisoners of war.

On the 22d it was resolved, that the laws relating to the poor are, in many respects defective.

That the present method of regulating the poor by annual parochial officers, in separate parishes and townships, is, in general, ineffectual for their proper relief and employment.

That the present methods of applying the sums raised for the relief of the poor are, in general, grievous to their respective parishes, and of pernicious effects to the public.

That the employment of the able poor, in such works as may be suited to their strength and capacity, will be very beneficial to the kingdom.

That the appointment of a competent number of districts, throughout *England* and *Wales*, by authority

thority of Parliament, with proper powers for uniting and incorporating the several parishes, townships, and places, in each; and the establishing a proper hospital, workhouse, and house of correction, in each district, under the management of governors, directors, or trustees, to be specially chosen for that purpose, will be the most easy and effectual method for relieving the impotent, employing the industrious, and reforming the vicious poor.

On the 23d. Mr. Chancellor of the Exchequer reported to the House, that their address of the 21st (to return the unfeigned thanks of the House, for his Majesty's most gracious message, &c.) had been presented to his Majesty; and that his Majesty was pleased to receive the same very graciously, and to say he would give the proper orders for signifying to the court of *France* his acceptance of the proposal contained in the *French* ambassador's declaration.

On the 29th of *January* the question relating to *General Warrants* was resumed. Sir *William Meredith* moved to resolve,

' That a General Warrant for apprehending the
' authors, printers, or publishers of a libel, toge-
' ther with their papers, is not warranted by law,
' and is an high violation of the liberty of the
' subject.'

It was supported with the same arguments as before, with some retort upon the administration; that the question was not now *sub judice* in the action brought by Mr. *Wilkes* against Lord *Halifax*; for Mr. *Wilkes* being outlawed, that action could not be tried. The ministry, however, still insisted that the question was *sub judice*; particularly in the cases between the printers and the messengers, where bills of exceptions had been brought, and which were not yet argued. There was fallacy in this argument; as those bills of exceptions

ceptions did not touch the legality of the warrant. It is true, the court of King's Bench did, several months afterwards, when some of those bills of exceptions came to be argued, solemnly condemn the warrant; but that question was not strictly before them, and they need not have done it, had they not been so inclined. The Ministry likewise insisted, that the delay in obtaining this determination in the courts below, was entirely owing to the solicitor for the prosecutors; and they dwelt particularly, upon the impropriety, as they called it, of one House of Parliament only, coming to a resolution upon a point of law; that such resolution was no security to liberty, that it was ineffectual as to the purpose intended, and that it would be nugatory in a pleading in *Westminster-Hall*, the judges there being bound to follow the law as made by the three estates, and not the sentiments of the House of Commons alone. In the course of the debate Dr. *Hay* narrowed the question, by proposing the following amendment; 'That in the particular case 'of libels, it is proper and necessary to fix, by a 'vote of this House only, what ought to be deem-'ed the law, in respect of General Warrants; and 'for that purpose, at the time when the determi-'nation of the legality of such warrants, in the 'instance of a most seditious and treasonable libel, 'is actually depending before the courts of law, 'for this House to declare that a General War-'rant for apprehending the authors, printers or 'publishers, of a libel, together with their pa-'pers, is not warranted by law, and is an high 'violation of the liberty of the subject;' which occasioned a long debate. At length the question was put, whether the amendment should be prefixed to the question. The House divided, 224 for it, and 184 against it.

The

The question so amended was then put, and without a second division passed in the negative. This debate lasted till 5 o' clock in the morning. Mr. *Pitt* was not able to attend it, being confined to his bed by a severe fit of the gout.

Resolutions of the Committee of supply, agreed to by the House.

January 22.

	l.	s.	d.

1. That 16000 men be employed for sea service for 1765, including 4287 marines
2. That a sum not exceeding 4l. per man per month be allowed for maintaining them, including ordnance for sea service — — — — 832000 0 0

January 24.

1. That a number of land-forces, including 2628 invalids, amounting to 17421 effective men, commission and non-commission officers included, be employed for 1765
2. That for defraying the charge of this number of effective men, for guards, garrisons, and other his Majesty's land-forces in *Great Britain*, *Guernsey* and *Jersey*, for 1765, there be granted to his Majesty a sum not exceeding   608130 10 7
3. For maintaining his Majesty's forces and garrisons in the plantations, including those in garrison at *Minorca* and *Gibraltar*, and for provisions for the forces in *North America*,

ca, *Nova Scotia*, *Newfoundland*, *Gibraltar*, and the ceded islands for 1765 — 387502 *l.* 3 *s.* 11½ *d.*

4. For defraying the charge of the difference of pay between the *British* and *Irish* establishments of five regiments of foot, serving at *Gibraltar*, *Minorca*, and the ceded islands for 1465 — 6346 3 5

5. For the pay of the general and general staff-officers in *Great Britain* for 1765 — 11291 8 6

6. To enable his Majesty to defray the charge of the subsidies due to the duke of *Brunswick*, pursuant to treaties, for 1765 — 10343 16 9

7. Upon account towards defraying the charge of out-pensioners of *Chelsea* Hospital, for 1765 — 109107 18 4

8. For the paying of pensions to the widows of such reduced officers of the land-forces and marines as died upon the establishment of half-pay in *Great Britain*, and who were married to them before 25th *December* 1716, for 1765 — 1664 0 0

9. Upon account of the reduced officers of the land-forces and marines, for 1765 — 135606 12 6

10. For defraying the charge for allowances to the several officers and private gentlemen of the two troops of horse guards, and regiment of horse reduced, and to the superannuated

	l.	s.	d.
nuated gentlemen of the four troops of horse guards, for 1765	2361	14	2
11. For the charge of the office of ordnance for land service, for 1765	174673	15	10
12. For defraying the expence of services performed by the office of ordnance for land service, and not provided for in 1764	55519	10	7
	1502547	14	8 2/12

January 28.

1. For the ordnary of the navy, including half pay to sea and marine officers, for 1765	407734	11	3
2. Upon account to be applied by the governors of *Greenwich* hospital for the support and relief of seamen worn out and become decrepit in the service of their country, who shall not be provided for within said hospital	5000	0	0
3. Towards the buildings, rebuildings, and repairs of the navy, for 1765	200000	0	0
	612734	11	3

February 5.

For defraying the extraordinary expences of the land-forces and other services incurred between the 24th of *December* 1763, and the 25th of *December* 1764, and not provided for	404496	7	6

PARLIAMENTARY A. 1765.

	l.	s.	d.

March 12.
Towards discharging bills payable in course of the navy and victualling offices, and for transports — 1500000 0 0

March 18.
1. For paying off and discharging the exchequer bills made out by an act of the preceding session, and charged upon the first aids to be granted in this session — 800000 0 0

2. To be applied towards finishing and compleating the works for improving, widening and enlarging the passage over and through *London* bridge — 7000 0 0

807000 0 0

March 19.
1. Upon account, for defraying the charge of the pay and cloathing of the militia, for one year, beginning the 25th of *March* 1765 — 80000 0 0

2. To replace to the sinking fund, the like sum paid out of the same, to make good the deficiency, on the 5th of *July* 1764, of the several rates and duties upon offices and pensions, and upon houses, and upon windows or lights, which were made a fund, by an act of the thirty-first of his late Majesty, for paying annuities at the bank, in respect

	l.	s.	d.

of five millions borrowed, towards the supply of 1758 — 48176 1 11

3. To replace to ditto, the like sum paid out of the same, to make good the deficiency, on the 10th of *October* 1764, of the several additional duties upon wines imported, and certain duties upon cyder and perry, which were made a fund, by an act of the third of his Majesty, for paying annuities in respect of 3500000*l.* borrowed towards the supply of 1763. — 497442, 1 2¼

4. To replace to ditto, the like sum issued thereout, for paying annuities after the rate of 4*l. per cent.* for the year ending the 29th of *September* 1764, granted in respect of certain navy, victualling and transport bills, and ordnance debentures, delivered in and cancelled, pursuant to act of the third of his present Majesty. — 139342 3 4

——————
317260 5 6
——————

March 26.

1. To make good the deficiency of the grants for 1764 — 249660 4 10

2. On account towards assisting his Majesty to grant a reasonable succour in money to the Landgrave of *Hesse Cassel*, pursuant to treaty — 50000 0 0

3. On account, for maintaining and supporting the civil

	l.	s.	d.
vil establishment of *Nova Scotia*, for 1765	4911	14	11
4. Upon account of sundry expences for the service of *Nova Scotia* in the years 1750, 1751, 1752, 1762, 1763, and not provided for	7000	0	0
5. Upon account for defraying the charges of the civil establishment of *Georgia*, and other incidental expences attending the same, from 24 *June* 1764, to 24 *June* 1765	3966	0	0
6. Upon account, for defraying the charges of the civil establishment of *East Florida*, and other incidental expences attending the same, from 24 *June* 1764, to 24 *June* 1765	5200	0	0
7. Upon account, for defraying the charges of the civil establishment of *West Florida*, and other incidental expences attending the same, from 24 *June* 1764, to 24 *June* 1765	5200	0	0
8. Upon account, for defraying the expence attending general surveys of his Majesty's dominions in *North America*, for 1765	1601	14	0
9. Towards building a Lazaret	5000	0	0
	332539	13	9

March 28.

1. That one fourth part of the capital stock of annuities, after

A. 1765.   DEBATES.   17

after the rate of 4*l. per cent. per ann.* granted in respect of certain navy, victualling, and transport bills, and ordnance debentures, delivered in and cancelled, pursuant to an act of the third of his present Majesty's reign, be redeemed and paid off on the 25th of *December* next, after discharging the interest then payable in respect of the same.

 2. For enabling his Majesty to redeem and pay off one fourth part of the capital stock of the said annuities   870888 5 5¼

  April 2.

 1. Upon account, towards discharging such unsatisfied claims and demands, for expences incurred during the late war in *Germany*, as appear to be due by the reports of the commissioners, appointed by his Majesty, for examining and stating such claims and demands - - 248259 8½ 4

 2. Upon account, out of the monies remaining to be applied of the exceedings of the several sums provided by parliament for sundry services, and of the monies that have been paid into the hands of the paymaster general, by contractors and others, to the 23d of *March* 1765, towards discharging such unsatisfied claims and demands - 251740 0 7

       3. For

3. For paying a bounty for 1765, of 2s. 6d. per day, to fifteen chaplains, and of 2s. per day, to fifteen more chaplains, who have served longest on board his Majesty's ships of war; provided it appears by the books of the said ships, that they have been actually borne and muftered thereon, for the space of four years, during the late war with *France* and *Spain*; and provided likewife, that fuch chaplains do not enjoy the benefit of some ecclefiaftical living, or preferment from the crown, or otherwife, of the prefent annual value of 50l. - - 1231 17 6

4. Upon account, towards enabling the governors and guardians of the Foundling Hofpital, to maintain and educate, or to place out as apprentices, fuch children as were received into the faid hofpital, on or before the 25th of *March* 1760, from the 31ft of *December* 1764, exclufive to the 31ft of December 1765, inclufive; and that the fame be iffued and applied, for the ufe of the faid hofpital, without fee or reward, or any deduction whatfoever - - - 38000 0 0

539231 17 6

April

A. 1765.   DEBATES.

April 20.

	l.	*s.*	*d.*
1. To be employed in maintaining and supporting the British forts and settlements upon the coast of Africa and putting the said forts into better repair - -	13000	0	0
2. For building a block-house at or near *Cape Appollonia*, on the coast of *Africa* -	7000	0	0
3. For defraying the charge of three independent companies of foot, to be raised for his Majesty's service, on the coast of *Africa*; and for provisions for the same; from the 25th of *December* 1764, to the 24th of *December* 1765, both days inclusive; being 365 days - -	6491	17	4 ½
4. Upon account, for defraying the charges of a civil establishment, upon that part of the coast of *Africa*, situate between the port of *Sallee*, in *South Barbary*, and *Cape Rouge*, for 1765 - - -	5500	0	0
	31991	17	4 ½

May 7.

1. To make good to his Majesty the like sum which has been issued by his Majesty's orders in pursuance of the addresses of this house - -	2400	0	0

2. To enable his Majesty to give a proper compensation to the government of the island of *Barbadoes*, for the assistance
given

given by them to his Majesty's forces, under Major General *Monckton*, in the expedition against *Martinico* — — 10000 0 0

12400 0 0

Sum total of the supplies granted in this session } 7763090 13 0

Resolutions of the committee of ways and means, agreed to by the House.

January 24.

That the annual malt duty be continued from the 23d of *June*, 1765, to the 24th of *June*, 1760, 750000 *l*.

January 29.

That the land tax of 4s. in the pound be continued for one year from the 25th of *March*, 1765, 203785 4*l*. 19s. 11*d*.

February 7.

No less than fifty-five resolutions of the committee were agreed to by the house, for laying nearly the same stamp duties upon the *British* colonies in *America*, as are payable in *England*; but as they were afterwards formed into a bill, and the bill passed into a law, it is not necessary to insert them here; therefore we shall only observe, that by the last it was resoved, that all the said duties be paid into the receipt of his Majesty's Exchequer; and there reserved, to be, from time to time, disposed of by parliament, towards further defraying the necessary expences of defending, protecting, and securing the said colonies and plantations[*].

Feb-

---

[*] As these resolutions were the foundation of the famous Stamp Act, it will not be improper to take notice of a particular circumstance relative to them; and of part of the argument, which was urged without doors (for very little was said within) *for* and *against*

February 16.

1. That for the better supply of our export trade to *Africa*, with such coarse printed calicoes and other

against that measure, as extracted from the papers and pamphlets published at the time.

"THE first and great principle of all government, and of all society, is, that *support is due in return for protection*; that every subject should contribute to the common defence, in which his own is included. *Nam neque quies gentium fine armis, neque arma fine stipendiis, neque stipendia fine tributis haberi queunt.* Tacit. Hist. lib. iv. It was necessary, and it was just, to recur to this principle at the close of the last war. It was found *necessary* to maintain upwards of 10,000 men for the defence of our *colonies*; an expence of between 3 and 400,000*l. per ann.* great part of which was entirely new, was, on that account, to be incurred, it was *just* that the *colonies* which had profited so much by the war, whose interests, commerce and security had been the first objects of *the peace*; and of whose ability to bear at least some proportion of that new expence there neither was nor is any reason to doubt, should contribute (not to support or to defend *Great Britain* but) *about a third part of the expence* necessary for their own defence and protection.

"Upon this general and acknowledged principle, and upon this application of it, which was just in itself, and which the situation of this country made necessary, and which it might have been expected, would appear neither unreasonable or unpleasing to an *English* ear, *the stamp act was planned*. In the beginning of the year 1764, the proposition of imposing, by a duty on stamps, *a tax on America*, in conformity to uninterrupted precedents for near 100 years, was made, and thrown into the form of *resolutions*. At that time the merits of this question were opened at large; those who have lately so loudly asserted the *privilege* and *exemptions* of *America* were then publickly called upon to deny, if they thought it fitting, the right of the legislature to impose any tax either internal or external upon that country: and not a single person ventured to controvert that right. A year's delay however was given, that any information might be received from *America*, with regard to the *expediency* of the particular tax proposed, not to permit the right of imposing it to be controverted. This distinction was fully opened at that time, and afterwards explained to *the agents* of the *provinces*.

"This delay was however abused by some of the *Americans*; and when, in the beginning of the year 1765, the plan was carried into execution by a bill, several *petitions* from *America* which *denied their right of imposing taxes on the colonies*, were presented to the *Parliament*, and were therefore *rejected without a division*; *no one person* having been then found, in either house, who would declare it to be his opinion that *America* was not, in this instance, subject to *Great Britain*. And yet it has been asserted that this opposition would have been made, if some intelligence relating to this matter had not been suppressed at that time; as this was

other goods, being the product or manufacture of the *East Indies*, or of other places beyond the *Cape of*

publickly said, the public is to be informed of the fact, which was this.

"On the 11th of December, 1764, the board of trade reported to the king, that the assemblies of *Massachuset*'s bay and *New-York* had, *in their resolutions and proceedings* (copies of which they transmitted with the report) *treated the acts and resolutions of the legislature of* Great Britain *with the most indecent disrespect*. The privy council advised the king, *to give directions that the same may be laid before Parliament, at such time and in such manner as his Majesty should be pleased to direct and appoint.*

"This postponed the laying it before Parliament, as it was meant to do; but it deprived the Parliament of no information, for the assemblies had instructed their agents here to prepare petitions in the same words; and particularly Mr. *Mauduit*, the agent for *Massachuset*'s bay, was directed to draw his principles and arguments from Mr. *Otis*'s book of The Rights of the colonies (which had been reprinted here.) The colonies were obeyed. Petitions were presented, asserting the right of freedom from taxes imposed by *Great-Britain*, on the very grounds of the resolutions and proceedings which the board of trade had transmitted to the king; these were rejected by Parliament, not from ignorance of their contents, but because their contents were known; because they denied the power of *Great-Britain*. No information was with-held therefore by this delay, the cause of which was tenderness to the colonies. For had the king called the attention of Parliament to proceedings in which their acts were treated with the most *indecent disrespect*; their own dignity must have drawn from them votes of censure and severity towards the offenders: and therefore the ministry, who were taking the proper methods to form and enforce the act, which would have sufficiently repressed the claims of the *Americans*, and effectually asserted the dignity and authority of *Great-Britain*, with-held a paper which would have given no information but what was given in a manner less calculated to irritate mens minds."

"It was urged in favour of the colonies, that those who first planted them, were not only driven out of the mother country by persecution, but had left it at their own risk and expence; that being thus forsaken, or rather worse treated, by her, all ties, except those common to mankind, were dissolved between them; they absolved from all duty of obedience to her, as she dispensed herself from all duty of protection to them; that, if they accepted of any royal charters on the occasion, it was done through mere necessity; and that, as this necessity was not of their own making, these charters could not be binding upon them; that, even allowing these charters to be binding, they were only bound thereby to that allegiance, which the supreme head of the realm might claim indiscriminately from all its subjects.

"That

of *Good Hope*, as are prohibited to be worn in *Great Britain*, the *East India* company be permitted

" That it was extremely abfurd, that they should be still thought to owe any fubmiffion to the legiflative power of *Great-Britain*, which had not authority enough to shield them against the violences of the executive; and more abfurd still, that the people of *Great-Britain* should pretend to exercife over them rights, which that very people affirm they might juftly oppofe, if claimed over themselves by others.

" That it cannot be imagined, that, when the fame people of *Great-Britain* contended with the crown, it could be with a view of gaining thefe rights, which the crown might have ufurped over others, and not merely recovering thofe, which the fame crown arbitrarily claimed over themfelves; that, therefore, allowing their original charters to be binding, as they had been deprived of them in an arbitary and tyrannical manner, fuch as the people of *Great-Britain* would not now by any means fuffer, they should be confidered as still entitled to the full benefit of them; that their being bound by thefe charters to make no laws, but fuch as, allowing for the difference of circumftances, should not clash with thofe of *England*, no more fubjected them to the Parliament of *England*, than their having been laid under the fame reftraint with regard to the laws of *Scotland* or any other country, would have fubjected them to the parliament of *Scotland*, or the fupreme authority of any other country; that, by thefe charters, they had a right to tax themfelves for their own fupport and defence.

" That it was their birth-right, even as the defcendents of *Englishmen*, not to be taxed by any but their own reprefentatives; that, fo far from being actually reprefented in the Parliament of *Great-Britain*, they were not even virtually reprefented there, as the meaneft inhabitants of *Great-Britain* are, in confequence of their intimate connection with thofe who are actually reprefented; that, if laws made by the *British* Parliament to bind all except its own members, or even all except fuch members and thofe actually reprefented by them, would be deemed, as moft certainly they would, to the higheft degree oppreffive and unconftitutional, and refifted accordingly, by the reft of the inhabitants, though virtually reprefented; how much more oppreffive and unconftitutional muft not fuch laws appear to thofe, who could not be faid to be either actually or virtually reprefented?

" That the people of *Ireland* were much more virtually reprefented in the Parliament of *Great-Britain*, than it was even pretended the people of the colonies could be, in confequence of the great number of *Englishmen* poffeffed of eftates and places of truft and profit in *Ireland*, and their immediate defcendents fettled in that country, and of the great number of *Irish* noblemen and gentlemen in both houfes of the *British* Parliament, and the greater number still conftantly refiding in *Great-Britain*; and that, notwithftanding, the *British* Parliament never claimed any right to tax the people of *Ireland*, in virtue of their being thus virtually reprefented amongft them.

" That,

ted to import the same from any part of *Europe* not within his Majesty's dominions, under proper limitations and restrictions.

2. That

"That, whatever assistance the people of *Great-Britain* might have given to the people of the colonies, it must have been given either from motives of humanity and fraternal affection, or with a view of being one day repaid for it, and not as the price of their liberty and independence; at least the colonies could never be presumed to have accepted it in that light; that, if given from motives of humanity and fraternal affection, as the people of the colonies had never given the mother country any room to complain of their want of gratitude, so they never should; if given with a view of being one day repaid for it, they were willing to come to a fair account, which, allowing for the assistance they themselves had often given the mother country, for what they must have lost, and the mother country must have got, by preventing their selling to others at higher prices than they could sell to her, and their buying from others at lower prices than they could buy from her, would, they apprehended, not turn out to her advantage so much as she imagined.

"That their having heretofore submitted to laws made by the *British* Parliament, for their internal government, could no more be brought as a precedent against them, than against the *English* themselves their tameness under the dictates of an *Henry*, or the rod of a star-chamber; the tyranny of many being as grievous to human nature as that of a few, and the tyranny of a few as grievous as that of a single person.

"That, if liberty was the due of those who had sense enough to know the value of it, and courage enough to expose themselves to every danger and fatigue to acquire it, they were better entitled to it than even their brethren of *Great-Britain*, since, besides facing, in the wilds of *America*, much more dreadful enemies, than the friends of liberty they left behind them could expect to meet in the fields of *Great-Britain*, they had renounced not only their native soil, the love of which is so congenial with the human mind, and all those tender charities inseparable from it, but exposed themselves to all the risks and hardships unavoidable in a long voyage; and, after escaping the danger of being swallowed up by the waves, to the still more cruel danger of perishing ashore by a slow famine.

"That, if in the first years of their existence one of them was guilty of some intemperate sallies, and all exposed to enemies which required the interposition and assistance of an *English* Parliament, they were now most of them arrived at such a degree of maturity in point of polity and strength, as in a great measure took away the necessity of such interposition and assistance for the future. At least, that interposition and assistance would not be the less effectual for the colonies being represented in the *British* Parliament, which was all the indulgence those colonies contended for.

"That,

2. That upon failure of the said company's keeping the said export trade supplied, with a sufficient quantity of such calicoes and other goods, other persons be permitted to import the same into this kingdom, from any such part of *Europe*, under proper limitations, and restrictions.

3. That the said calicoes and other goods, which shall be so imported, be liable to pay the same duties as if the same were imported by the said company from the *East Indies*, or any other place beyond the *Cape* of *Good Hope*, and no other.

4. That the bounty allowed by law, to be paid on the exportation of corn, grain, malt, meal, and flour, from *Great Britain* to the *Isle* of *Man*, be discontinued.

5. That a stamp duty of 10s. be charged upon every piece of vellum or parchment, or sheet or piece of paper, on which every licence for making and selling measures of capacity shall be ingrossed, written, or printed.

6. That a stamp duty of 10*l.* be charged upon every piece of vellum or parchment, or sheet or piece of paper, on which every licence for making

" That, allowing the *British* Parliament's right to make laws for the colonies, and even tax them without their concurrence, there lay many objections against all the duties lately imposed on the colonies, and more still and weightier against that of the stamps now proposed to be laid upon them; that whereas those stamp-duties were laid gradually on the people of *Great-Britain*, they were to be saddled all at once, with all their increased weight, on those of the colonies; that, if those duties were thought so grievous in *England*, on account of the great variety of occasions in which they were payable, and the great number of heavy penalties to which the best meaning persons were liable for not paying them, or not strictly conforming to all the numerous penal clauses in them, they must be to the last degree oppressive in the colonies, where the people in general could not be supposed so conversant in matters of this kind, and numbers did not understand even the language of these intricate laws, so much out of the course of what common sense alone might suggest to them as their duty, and common honesty engage them to practise, the almost only rule of action, and motive to it, compatible with that encouragement, which it is proper to give every new settler in every country, especially foreigners, in such a country as *America*."

and

and selling of weights, shall be ingrossed, written, or printed.

March 11.

That the annuities granted by two acts of parliament, the one passed in the thirty-third year of the reign of his late Majesty, and the other passed in the second year of the reign of his present Majesty in respect of certain capital stocks thereby established, amounting together to the sum of 20,240,000l. at the rate of 4l. *per centum, per annum*, for certain terms of years and then to be reduced to 3l. *per centum, per annum*, which annuities were by the said acts, made payable half yearly on the 5th day of *July* and on the 5th day of *January* in every year, and were, by the last mentioned act, consolidated and made one joint stock, shall, from and after the 5th day of *July* next ensuing, with the consent of the proprietors thereof, be payable in the manner following, that is to say; that one quarterly payment of the said annuities shall be payable on the 10th day of *October* next; and that the said annuities, from and after the said 10th day of *October*, shall be payable half yearly, on the 5th day of *April* and the 10th day of *October* in every year; and that such of the proprietors of the said annuities who shall not signify their dissent on or before the 1st day of *June* next, in books to be opened at the bank of *England* for that purpose, shall be deemed and taken to consent thereto.

March 12.

There were fifteen resolutions of the said committee agreed to by the house, relating to the postage of letters; but as they were afterwards formed into a bill, and the bill passed into a law, we shall not insert them.

March 14.

1. That all persons interested in, or intitled unto, any bills, or bill, payable in the course of

the navy or victualling offices, or for transports, which were made out on or before the 30th day of *June* 1764, who shall, on or before the 26th day of this instant *March*, carry the same (after having the interest computed thereupon to the 6th day of *April* next, and marked upon the said bills at the navy or victualling office respectively) to the office of the treasurer of his Majesty's navy, shall have in exchange for the same, from such treasurer or his pay-master or cashier, a certificate, to the governor and company of the bank of *England*, for every entire sum of one or more hundred pounds, of which such bill or bills, together with the interest so marked, shall consist, until the several intire sums of one or more hundred pounds, for which such certificates are to be made forth, shall amount together to one million five hundred thousand pounds, and also one other certificate for the fractional part of one hundred pounds, being the remainder of such bill or bills; and the persons who shall be possessed of such first-mentioned certificates, of the intire sum of one or more hundred pounds, shall, upon delivery thereof to the said governor and company, be entitled with respect of the same, to the annuities hereafter mentioned: that is to say; for two fifth parts of the sums therein mentioned, to an annuity, after the rate of three pounds, per cent. redeemable by parliament, and transferrable and paid at the bank of *England*: for two other fifth parts thereof, to a proportional number of tickets of the value of ten pounds, in a lottery, to consist of 60,000 tickets, every blank to be of the value of six pounds, the blanks and prizes to be attended with the like three per cent. annuities; and, for the remaining one fifth part, to a like annuity, after the rate of three pounds per cent. with liberty to convert the same into an annuity for life, after the same rate, with benefit of survivorship, in manner following;

following: that is to say; that every person who shall become possessed, in right of one hundred pound capital stock, of an annuity of three pounds in such last mentioned annuities, and shall produce, on or before the 5th day of *April* 1766, a certificate thereof, attested by the cashier of the bank of *England*, to the auditor of the receipt of his Majesty's Exchequer, shall in lieu thereof, be intitled, from the said 5th day of *April*, 1766, during the life of the nominee whom he shall appoint, to a life annuity of three pounds payable at the Exchequer, out of the sinking fund; and the several nominees, to be appointed in respect to such life annuities, to be divided into classes, the whole annuity belonging to each class not to be less than one thousand five hundred pounds, if life annuities to that amount shall be so subscribed; and, upon the death of every nominee, the annuity, so fallen in, to be distributed among the survivors of the same class: and the annuities, in respect of the said first two fifth parts, shall be immediately added to, and made a part of, the joint stock of annuities, reduced from four to three *per cent.* and consolidated, pursuant to certain acts of parliament, made in the 25th and 26th years of his late Majesty; and the annuities attending the said lottery, together with such of the annuities in respect of the said one fifth part as shall not be exchanged for annuities on lives, with the benefit of survivorship, in manner above mentioned, shall also be added to, and made a part of such joint stock, from the 5th day of *April* 1766; and all the said annuities, transferrable and paid at the bank, shall commence, from the said 5th day of *April* 1765, and be payable half-yearly, on the 10th day of *October*, and the 5th day of *April* in every year, out of the sinking fund: but, in case the several intire sums of one or more hundred pounds, for which certificates are to be granted

by

by the treasurer of his Majesty's navy, or his paymaster, or cashier, in respect of such bills so to be delivered in, on or before the 26th day of this instant *March*, and of the interest marked thereon, shall not then amount in the whole to the sum of one million five hundred thousand pounds, all persons possessed of the abovementioned certificates for the fractional parts of one hundred pounds, or of navy, victualling, or transport bills, which were made out on or before the 30th day of *June*, 1764, and do not amount, together with the interest thereupon computed to the 6th day of *April* next, to one hundred pounds, may, on or before the 5th of *April* next, after having had the interest upon such bills marked in such manner as is before mentioned, bring the same to the office of the treasurer of his Majesty's navy, and shall have, in exchange for the same, from such treasurer, or his pay-master or cashier, a certificate to the said governor and company of the bank of *England*, for the sums contained in such certificates, and for the amount of the principal and interest of which such bills shall consist; and, upon delivery thereof, and payment of so much money to the said governor and company as shall, with the sum so certified, amount to one hundred pounds, shall be entitled to the annuities and advantages before mentioned: and if any such certificates for fractional parts shall not be delivered in, and subscribed as aforesaid, on or before the said 5th day of *April* next, they shall be paid according to the course of the navy, in such order as the bills in part of which they were granted were payable; and such of them, as were granted in part of bills bearing interest, shall from the said 5th day of *April* next, carry the like interest to which such bills were intitled.

2. That there be granted to his Majesty, an additional duty of four shillings, for every chauldron

dron of coals, *Newcastle* measure, which shall be shipped for exportation to any part beyond the seas, except to *Ireland*, the *Isle* of *Man*, or the *British* dominions in *America*; and at the same rate for any greater lesser quantity.

3. That there be granted to his Majesty, upon all wrought silk, Bengals, and stuffs, mixed with silk or herba, of the manufacture of *Persia*, *China*, or *East India*, and upon all callicoes, printed, dyed, painted or stained there, which shall be exported from this kingdom, except to *Africa* or the *British* dominions in *America*, a subsidy of poundage, after the rate of twelve pence for every twenty shillings of the value of such goods, according to the gross price at which they were sold at the public sales thereof.

4. That upon the exportation from this kingdom of any sort of white callicoes or muslins, except to *Africa* or the *British* dominions in *America*, there be retained, besides the one half of the rate or duty commonly called the Old Subsidy, which now remains, and is not drawn back for the same, the further sum of two pounds for every hundred pounds of the true and real value of such goods, according to the gross price at which they were sold at the sale of the united company of merchants trading to the *East Indies*; but that such callicoes, which shall first have been printed, stained, painted, or dyed, in *Great Britain*, shall not be subject to the said duty of two pounds, to be retained as aforesaid.

5. That there be granted to his Majesty, a stamp duty of two pence, for every skin or piece of vellum or parchment, or sheet or piece of paper, on which shall be ingrossed, written, or printed, any policy of assurance, which shall be made or entered into, within the cities of *London* or *Westminster*, or elsewhere within the limits of the weekly bills of mortality, over and above all other duties.

6. That

6. That there be granted to his Majesty, a stamp duty of two shillings and six pence, for every skin, or piece of vellum or parchment, or sheet or piece of paper, on which shall be ingrossed, written, or printed, any policy of assurance, which shall be made or entered into *Great-Britain*, over and above all other duties.

7. That the said duties be carried to, and made part of, the sinking fund, towards making good the payment of the said annuities.

8. That a stamp duty of six pence, imposed by an act made in the twelfth year of the reign of Queen *Anne*, and the additional stamp duty of one shilling imposed by an act made in the 30th year of the reign of his late Majesty King *George* the IId, upon vellum, parchment, and paper, containing any indenture, lease, bond, or other deed, be declared to extend to every skin or piece of vellum or parchment, or sheet or piece of paper, on which shall be ingrossed, written, or printed, in *Great Britain*, any policy of assurance or charter-party.

March 25.

That authority be given to permit the importation into this kingdom from the *Isle* of *Man*, under proper limitations and restrictions, of any coarse printed callicoes and other goods of the product or manufacture of the *East Indies*, or or other places beyond the *Cape* of *Good Hope*, which are prohibited to be worn and used in this kingdom, and which were brought into the said isle before the first of *March*, 1765, upon payment of one half of the old subsidy only for such goods.

March 28.

1. That the monies remaining in the Exchequer on the 10th of *October*, 1764, for the disposition of parliament, which had then arisen of surplusses, excesses or overplus monies, and other revenues of the fund, commonly called the sinking fund,

be

be issued and applied, amounting to the sum of 135,213*l*, 5*s*. 0*d*. ¼.

2. That out of such monies as shall or may arise of the surplusses, excesses, or overplus monies and other revenues composing the said fund, there be issued and applied the sum of 2,100,000*l*.

April 4.

1. That, in case the monies, for which certificates have been or shall be granted, in pursuance of a resolution of this house, of the 14th day of *March* last, by the treasurer of his Majesty's navy, or his pay-master or cashier, to the governor and company of the bank of *England*, for and in respect of navy victualling, and transport bills, made out on or before the 30th day of *June* 1764, and for and in respect of such fractional parts of the said bills, as remained above the entire sums of one or more hundred pounds, together with the sums paid and payable at the bank of *England*, with the certificates for such fractional parts, and for such of the said bills, as, together with the interest computed thereupon, do not amount to one hundred pounds, shall not, on the 5th day of this instant *April*, make up the full sum of 1500,000*l*. the monies which shall be so wanting to complete the said sum of 1,500,000*l*. to be raised by contributions, to be received at the bank of *England*. in entire sums of one or more hundred pounds, to be paid to the cashier or cashiers of the said governor and company, on or before the 28th day of this instant *April*, and that the contributors be intitled for the monies so by them respectively advanced, to such annuities, benefits, and advantages, as are mentioned in the said resolution, to be allowed to the proprietors of certificates, granted in exchange for such navy, victualling, and transport bills, as shall have been delivered on or before the respective days therein limited.

2. That

A. 1763.   DEBATES.   33

2. That the money remaining in the exchequer, which was granted in the last session, upon account, for defraying the charge of the pay and cloathing of the militia for one year, beginning the 25th of *March*, 1764, be issued and applied towards raising the supplies granted this session, amounting to the sum of 80,000*l*.

April 20.

1. That there be raised by loans or exchequer bills, to be charged upon the first aids to be granted in the next session; and such exchequer bills, if not discharged with interest thereupon, on or before the 5th day of *April*, 1766, to be exchanged and received in payment, in such manner as exchequer bills have usually been exchanged and received in payment, 800,000*l*.

2. That, of the monies arisen or to arise, out of such of the duties granted or continued, by an act of last sessions as were thereby reserved to be disposed of by parliament, towards defraying the necessary expence of defending, protecting, and securing the *British* colonies and plantations in *America*, there be applied towards making good the supply granted for maintaining his Majesty's forces and garrisons in the plantations; and for provisions for the forces in *North America*, *Nova Scotia*, *Newfoundland*, and the ceded islands for 1765; 60,000*l*.

3. That a duty of six pence be laid upon every hundred weight of gum Senega, or gum Arabick, imported into this kingdom, over and above all duties now payable thereupon.

4. That a duty of 30*s*. be laid upon every hundred weight of gum Senega, or gum Arabick, exported out of this kingdom, over and above all duties now payable thereupon.

April 25.

That the monies which have been, or shall be paid at the bank, in pursuance of the resolutions of this house, of the 14th of *March* last and 4th instant, be applied towards discharging bills payable in the course of the navy or victualling offices, or for transports, which were made out, on or before the 30th of *June*, 1764.

April 30.

1. That the bounties and drawbacks, now paid upon the exportation, from this kingdom, of refined sugars and ground sugar, be discontinued.

2. That, upon the exportation from this kingdom of refined sugar in the loaf, compleat and whole, being nett, that is to say, of one uniform whiteness throughout, and which has gone through the operation of three clays at the least, and been properly and thoroughly dried in the stove, according to the present practice of refining, a bounty be allowed after the rate of 14*s.* 6*d.* for every hundred weight thereof.

3. That upon the exportation from this kingdom of refined sugar called bastard, and of ground and powdered refined sugar, and of refined loaf sugar broke in pieces (the said sugar having been twice clayed, and properly dried in the stove) a bounty or drawback be allowed, after the rate of 6*s.* 4*d.* for every hundred weight thereof.

4. That liberty be granted for a limited time, to carry rice from the province of *North Carolina*, directly to any other part of *America*, southward of *South Carolina* and *Georgia*, subject to such duty as is now payable upon rice, carried from *South Carolina* and *Georgia*, to any part of *America*, to the southward thereof.

5. That the duties, which shall arise in respect of rice, so carried from *North Carolina*, and the duties which shall arise in pursuance of an act made in the last session of parliament, intituled, *An act for granting, for a limited time, a liberty to carry rice from, &c.* be paid into the receipt of his Majesty's exchequer, and there reserved to be from time to time, disposed of by parliament, towards further

further defraying the neceſſary expences of defending, protecting, and ſecuring the *Britiſh* dominions in *America*.

6. That bounties be granted upon the importation of deals, planks, boards, and timber, into this kingdom, from the *Britiſh* dominions in *North America*, for the term of nine years, in manner following; that is to ſay, during the firſt three years, for every hundred, containing ſix ſcore of ſound merchantable deals, planks, and boards, not leſs than ten feet long, ten inches broad, and one inch and one quarter of an inch thick 20*s*. and ſo in proportion for any greater length, and for any greater thickneſs, not exceeding four inches, and for every load containing forty cubic feet, of ſound merchantable ſquared timber of all kinds (the timber not to be leſs than ten inches ſquare) 12*s*. and during the next three years, for every hundred of ſuch deals, planks, and boards, 15*s*. and for every load of ſuch timber, 8*s*. and during the laſt three years, for every hundred of ſuch deals, planks, and boards, 10*s*. and for every load of ſuch timber, 5*s*.

7. That the additional inland duty of 1*s*. granted by an act made in the thirty-ſecond of his late Majeſty upon every pound weight avoirdupois of coffee, ſold in *Great Britain*, do ceaſe and determine.

8. That there be granted to his Majeſty, an additional inland duty of 6*d*. upon every pound weight avoirdupois of coffee, not being of the growth and product of the *Britiſh* plantations in *America*, which ſhall be ſold in *Great Britain*.

9. That the ſaid additional inland duty be appropriated to the uſes, to which the ſaid duty of 1*s*. *per* pound weight was made applicable.

10. That the allowances directed by law, to be made in reſpect of hard ſoap, which ſhall be refreſhed or made new, be diſcontinued.

11. That

11. That in lieu thereof, the duties upon one pound, in every ten pounds weight of such soap, be allowed to the makers thereof.

12. That all linen cloth and diaper of *Russia*, which are not at present particularly rated in any act of parliament, or book of rates, be, upon the importation thereof into this kingdom, rated in manner following; that is to say, all such cloth and diaper, being in breadth more than 22 ½ and not exceeding 31 ½ inches at 4*l.* and being in breadth more than 31 ½ inches, and not exceeding 45 inches, at 6*l.* and exceeding 45 inches in breadth, at 10*l.* for every 120 *English* ells thereof respectively, and so in proportion for any greater or lesser quantity; and that the full amount of the several duties now required by law to be paid, for every 20*s.* of the value of the said goods, be raised and collected according to the said respective rates.

13. That no drawback or bounty be allowed upon the exportation of any goods, from this kingdom, to any of the islands of *Faro*.

May 6.

1. That every instrument, letter, entry, minutes, memorandum, or other writing whereby any officer is admitted, in any court whatsoever, to serve or to hold such office, as is charged with any stamp duty within the meaning of the acts 5. W. and M. 9 W. III. and 12 A. whereby the several duties of 40*s.* are imposed upon every piece of vellum, parchment, or paper, on which any admittance of such officer is ingrossed or written, shall be deemed and taken to be an admittance of such officer.

2. That the present stamp duty upon the admission into any corporation or company be repealed.

3. That instead thereof a stamp duty of 2*s.* be charged upon the entry, minute, or memorandum,

made

made of such admittance, in their court book, roll, or record.

4. That the present allowance for prompt payment at the stamp office be repealed.

5. That instead thereof an allowance at the rate of 4*l. per cent. per ann.* be for the future made.

6. That an additional stamp duty of 20*s.* be charged upon every policy of assurance, in which the properties of more than one person, in any ship cargo, or both, or more than a particular number of persons in partnership, or more than one body politic, to a greater amount in the whole than 100*l.* shall be assured.

7. That of the monies agreed to be paid by a convention, between his Majesty and the *French* King, concluded and signed at *London*, the 27th of *February* last, for the maintenance of the late *French* prisoners of war there be applied a sum not exceeding 308000*l.*

May 7.

1. That out of the monies which shall arise from the produce of the duties laid in this session, upon the importation and exportation of Senega and gum Arabick, there be issued and applied a sum not exceeding 12000*l.*

2. That the 2*s.* stamp duty to be imposed by the third resolution of yesterday, be applied to the uses, to which the stamp duty repealed by the second resolution of yesterday was applicable.

3. That the additional stamp duty of 20*s.* imposed by the sixth resolution of yesterday be applied to the like uses to which the duties upon policies of assurance are at present applicable.

4. That the same bounties be allowed upon all linens to be made in the *Isle* of *Man*, and imported into *Great Britain*, which shall be exported from thence, as are now allowed on the exportation of *British* or *Irish* linens, and under the same restrictions and limitations.

5. That

5. That the inhabitants of the *Isle* of *Man* may import into any lawful port of *Great Britain* or *Ireland*, the bestials, or any other goods, wares, and merchandizes, of the growth, produce, and manufacture, of the said *Isle*, except woollen manufacture, beer and ale, without paying any custom, subsidies, or duties, for and in respect thereof (except such excise or other duty, as is now, or shall hereafter for the time being, be due and payable for the like goods, wares, or merchandize, of the growth, produce, and manufacture of *Great Britain*) liable to certain limitations and restrictions.

May 9.

1. That towards making good and securing the payment of the sums of money directed by an act of 32 *Geo.* II. to be applied in augmentation of the salaries of the judges and justices therein mentioned, in *England* and *Wales*, there be granted an additional stamp duty of 4*l.* upon every piece of vellum or parchment, or sheet or piece of paper, upon which any admission into any of the four inns of court shall be ingrossed or written; and an additional stamp duty of 6*l.* upon every such piece, on which shall be ingrossed or written, any register, entry, testimonial, or certificate, of the degree of utter barrister, taken in any of the four inns of court.

2. That out of any of the surplusses which shall arise upon the funds established for payment of the said augmentation, and upon the said additional stamp duty, after the payments charged thereupon, are, from time to time, satisfied, a sum not exceeding 3625*l.* be applied in augmentation of the salaries of the said judges, and justices, from the 5th of *January* to the 5th of *July*, 1759, according to the proportions appointed by the said act, with respect to the augmentation therein mentioned.

3. That out of any of the duties and revenues in *Scotland*, which by an act of 10 *Anne* were charged, or made chargeable, with payment of the fees, salaries, and other charges allowed, or to be allowed, by her Majesty, her heirs, or successors, for keeping up the courts of session and justiciary, and exchequer court in *Scotland*, a sum not exceeding 2100*l*. be applied in augmentation of the salaries of the judges in the courts of session and exchequer there, from the 5th of *January* to the 5th of *July*, 1759, according to the proportions appointed by the said act of 32 *Geo*. II. with respect to the augmentation thereby granted of the salaries of the said judges.

Total of the liquidated sums provided for by the committee of ways and means -	7783068 4 11
Excess provided by the said committee more than granted by the committee of supply, omitting the fractions as they are very near equal -	119977 11 11
To this we ought to add the sum provided as well as granted by the second resolution of *April* second of the committee of supply, being	251740 2 7 $\frac{3}{4}$
Total excess - -	271787 14 6 $\frac{3}{4}$

On the 4th of *March Nicholson Calvert*, Esq; moved that part of an act, made in the 16th year of the reign of King *Charles* I, intitled, *An act for regulating the Privy-council, and for taking away the Court, commonly called the Star-Chamber*, might be read: and the same being read accordingly, he again moved, that leave be given to bring in a bill for relief of his Majesty's subjects, touching informations in the court of King's-bench, by and in the name of his Majesty's Attorney general. He was seconded by Mr. Serjeant *Hewitt* (afterwards Lord Chancellor of *Ireland*) but it passed in the negative.

On the 6th of *March*, it was resolved, that, for the further and more effectually preventing the mischiefs arising to the revenue and commerce of *Great Britain* and *Ireland*, from the illicit and clandestine trade to and from the *Isle* of *Man*, it is expedient to vest in the Crown, upon a proper compensation to be paid to the proprietors of the said island, the *Isle, Castle*, and *Peele* of *Man*, and all rights, jurisdictions, and interests, in and over the said island, and all its dependencies, holden by the said proprietors, under the several grants thereof, or under any other title whatsoever, excepting only their landed property, with all their rights in and over the soil, as Lords of the manor, with all courts baron, rents, services, and other incidents, to such courts belonging; their wastes, commons, and other lands, inland waters, fisheries, and mills, and all mines, minerals, and quarries, according to their present rights therein, felons goods, deodands, waifs, estrays, and wrecks at sea, together with the patronage of the bishopric, and of the other ecclesiastical benefices in the said island, to which they are now intitled. And

That the sum of 70,000*l*. may be proper to be paid, as a full compensation to the said proprietors, according to the proposal contained in the letter from the said proprietors, dated the 27th day of *February*, 1765, to the commissioners of the treasury.

An abstract of the clear revenue of the island was laid before parliament, of which the following is a copy.

ABSTRACT

ABSTRACT of the clear Revenue of the Isle of MAN for Ten Years, from the Year 1754 to the year 1763, both inclusive.

Years.	Land revenue clear amount.			Clear revenue of the customs for imports.			Clear revenue of the customs for herrings.			Felons goods, waifs, and strays, forfeitures, &c.			Clear revenue of the impropriated tythes.			Clear rev. of the abbey temporalities.		The income of lands in the lord's hands.			Total		
1754	£.1376	9	9 ½	5944	7	2 ¾	153	14	2	28	6	2 ¼	179	18	8	121	15	101	6	6 ¼	7905	17	7
1755	1380	13	2	4968	1	5 ¾	167	1	8	46	7		185	17	9	121	15	98	2	2	6967	18	2 ¾
1756	1445	16		4746	1	10	147	9	2	75	9	3	187	14	6	121	15	97	18	8	6785	4	10 ½
1757	1424	19	9 ¾	5233	17	½	136	4	8	103	3	5	1·7	5		121	15	102	15	11	7270		
1758	1395	16	4	5180	2	3 ¼	141	15	10	44	13	1 ¾	180	17	2	121	15	99	6	8	7170	6	5
1759	1396	7		8082	18		125	19	2	68	19	1	18·	15		121	15	107	19	1	10091	12	4
1760	1439	17	¾	7093	12	2 ½	121	19	2	406	17	9 ¼	287	13	1	121	15	135	4	2	9606	18	5 ¾
1761	1376	0	11 ¼	9544	2	11 ¾	92	4	2	37	16	9	318	1	6 ¾	121	15	106	8	9	11596	10	1 [illegible]
1762	1375	6	5	6291	6	01	90	19	2	81	7	9 ¾	317	15	4	121	15	107	8	9	8486	9	3 [illegible]
1763	1409	17	6 ¾	7029	10	7 ¼	81	1	8	142	2	10 ¾	306	2	4	121	15	107	8	9	9204	8	9 [illegible]
	£.13081	4	1	64127		5 ¾	1258	8	10	1042	3	3 ¾	2305		4 ¾	1217	13	1063	19	5 ¼	85085	6	6 ¾

The whole revenue of the Isle for ten Years, is £. 85085 6 6 ¼ Manks. £. 7 Manks make £. 6 British. So the revenue for ten Years is, in British money, £. 72930 5 7 which, at a medium, is £. 7293 0 6 ¾ *per annum*.

His Majesty having been indisposed in the month of *April*, 1765, the idea of a regency was suggested: Accordingly as soon as his recovery was effected, he went to the House of Lords on the 24th of *April*, and made the following speech to both Houses of Parliament.

My Lords and Gentlemen,

THE tender concern, which I feel for my faithful subjects, makes me anxious to provide for every possible event, which may affect their future happiness or security.

My late indisposition, though not attended with danger, has led me to consider the situation, in which my kingdoms, and my family, might be left, if it should please God to put a period to my life, whilst my successor is of tender years.

The high importance of this subject to the public safety, good order, and tranquillity; the paternal affection, which I bear to my children, and to all my people; and my earnest desire, that every precaution should be taken, which may tend to preserve the constitution of *Great Britain* undisturbed, and the dignity and lustre of its crown unimpaired; have determined me to lay this weighty business before my parliament: and as my health, by the blessing of God, is now restored, I take the earliest opportunity of meeting you here, and of recommending to your most serious deliberation the making such provision, as would be necessary, in case any of my children should succeed to the throne, before they shall respectively attain the age of eighteen years.

To this end, I propose to your consideration, whether, under the present circumstances, it will not be expedient to vest in me the power of appointing, from time to time, by instruments in writing, under my sign manual, either the queen, or any other person of my royal family usually residing in *Great Britain*, to be the guardian of the

the person of such successor, and the regent of these kingdoms, until such successor shall attain the age of eighteen years; subject to the like restrictions and regulations, as are specified and contained in an act, passed upon a similar occasion, in the 24th year of the reign of the late King, my royal grandfather: the regent so appointed to be assisted by a council, composed of several persons, who, by reason of their dignities, and offices, are constituted members of the council established by that act, together with those whom you may think proper to leave to my nomination.

As soon as the commons had returned to the house, this speech was, as usual, read to the house by Mr. Speaker, and presently after it was read, they received a message from the Lords, to desire that they would continue sitting for some time; which they agreed to do; and in the mean time went upon some other business then depending before the house, until they received another message from their Lordships by the Lord Chief Justice *Pratt* and the Lord Chief Baron *Parker*, to acquaint them that the Lords had agreed upon an address to be presented to his Majesty, to which their Lordships desired the concurrence of that house, which, after reading the address, was agreed to, and the blank therein being filled up with the words " and Commons," Mr. Chancellor of the Exchequer was ordered to carry the said address to the Lords, and acquaint them, that the house had agreed to the same, which he accordingly did, and reported, that he had left the address with their Lordships.

The next day they received a message from the Lords, to acquaint them, that his Majesty had appointed to be attended with the address of both houses, that day at one of the clock, at his palace of St. *James*, and their Lordships intended to be there at that time: upon this the House of Commons

mons about twelve o'clock adjourned their house till two o'clock that afternoon, and at one o'clock his Majesty was accordingly attended by both houses with their said address, which was as follows:

Most gracious Sovereign,

We, your Majesty's most dutiful and loyal subjects, the Lords spiritual and temporal, and Commons, in parliament assembled, presume to approach your sacred person, with our warmest acknowledgments of the peculiar goodness expressed in your most gracious speech from the throne.

We humbly intreat your Majesty's acceptance of our heartiest congratulations upon your recovery from your late indisposition. Your Majesty's return to your parliament has dissipated all those anxious sensations, which the occasion of your absence had excited: and as the re-establishment of your invaluable health is an object to your faithful people of the sincerest joy and exultation, your Majesty has shewn a most affectionate regard to their satisfaction, in condescending to take the earliest opportunity of giving them so pleasing a proof of it.

This great mark of your Majesty's attention must demand our most sincere and dutiful thanks: but we have before us a still more engaging instance of your watchful sollicitude for our future security and happiness.

The constant tenor of your just and constitutional government, distinguished and endeared to your kingdoms by an unwearied application to the advancement of their interest and prosperity, had already filled our minds with a most cordial sense of gratitude. The new proof, which your Majesty is now pleased to give us, of your truly paternal tenderness, by extending your concern for the stability, dignity, and lustre of your crown, with all the happy effects of your love to your royal

royal children, and to your faithful subjects, beyond the period of your own continuance among them, must inspire us with still higher degrees, if possible, of reverence and affection.

Whilst we contemplate, with admiration, that magnanimity which enables your Majesty to look forward, with a cool composure of thought, to an event, which, whenever it should please God to permit it, must overwhelm your loyal subjects with the bitterest distraction of grief; we cannot but be deeply affected with that compassionate sentiment of your royal heart, which suggests a provision for their comfort under so severe an affliction.

May it please the divine providence to exempt us from the fatal necessity of such a consolation! your Majesty has shewn, from the first day of your auspicious reign, so conscientious a regard to the laws and liberties, the religious and civil rights, of your kingdoms, that we should be insensible and unworthy the happiness we ourselves enjoy, if we did not ardently wish to transmit it under the same gracious care and protection to our children.

Yet, feeling, as we do, the infinite importance of every measure that may tend to the perpetuating, in all events, our happy constitution; in deference to your Majesty's recommendation, and under a full conviction of that consummate prudence, and beneficent intention, which were the motives of it, we will not fail to apply ourselves to the immediate discussion of the high and momentous object, which your Majesty has been pleased to propose to our consideration.

Our deliberations concerning it will be animated by the hopes of securing to our posterity, under the blessing of almighty God, and in concurrence with your Majesty's salutary designs, the inestimable blessing of a legal protestant succession to
the

the crown of these realms in your royal family; and will be influenced by a just confidence in your princely wisdom, and paternal concern for your people.

We shall go into this consultation with a sensible anxiety, arising from the subject of it; but we humbly assure your Majesty, that we will conclude it with all the dispatch compatible with its singular importance; repeating at the same time our earnest supplications, that, through the mercy of God upon this protestant church and nation, a precaution so expedient in prospect, may become useless in the event, by your Majesty's living to form under your own instruction, a successor, worthy to inherit the allegiance and affections of a free people, by a long and mature attention to the example of your royal virtues.

To this address his Majesty answered,

My Lords and Gentlemen,

Your affectionate congratulations upon my recovery, and the sense which you express of your happiness under my government, give me the greatest satisfaction.

Be assured, I have not a more sincere concern, or a more earnest desire, than to secure to myself and faithful people, both now and hereafter the religious and civil blessings of our invaluable constitution.

As the Lords had, in pursuance of his Majesty's speech, ordered a bill to be brought in, *to provide for the administration of government, in case the crown should descend to any of the children of his Majesty, being under the age of eighteen years, and for the care and guardianship of their persons*; nothing was done in the House of Commons, after the report of his Majesty's said answer to the joint address of the two houses, until the 6th of *May*, when the House received a message from the Lords, by the Lord Chief Justice *Pratt* and the Lord Chief Baron *Parker*, that their Lordships had passed a bill, intitled, as above-mentioned, to which

which they desired the concurrence of that house, and the bill having been carried up to the table, as soon as the messengers were withdrawn, it was read a first time and ordered to be read a second time the next morning; but before that order was next day read, a motion was made, that an humble address be presented to his Majesty, humbly to acknowledge his Majesty's great goodness, in proposing to secure the future quiet and peace of these kingdoms, by making a settled provision for a regency and for the guardianship of his children, in case (which God avert) these kingdoms should be deprived of the blessing of his Majesty's most invaluable life, before his royal successor shall have attained the age of eighteen years; and humbly to intreat his Majesty, out of his tender and paternal regard for his people, that he would be graciously pleased to name the person, or persons, whom in his royal wisdom, he shall think fit to propose to the consideration of parliament, for the execution of those high trusts; this house apprehending it not warranted by precedent, nor agreeable to the principles of this free constitution, to vest in any person, or persons, not particularly named and approved of in parliament, the important offices of regent of these kingdoms and guardian of the royal offspring, heirs to the crown. It passed in the negative. And then the bill being read a second time, it was committed to a committee of the whole house for the 9th, after which a motion was made, for having the bill printed; which was likewise carried in the negative.

Upon the 9th as soon as this order of the day was read, his Majesty's speech to both houses of parliament, on the 24th of *April*, was ordered to be referred to the said committee; and the house then having resolved itself into the same;

Mr.

PARLIAMENTARY A. 1765.

Mr. *Morton* moved, by way of amendment, to insert in the bill, after the Queen, *her royal highness Augusta Princess Dowager of Wales* *.

The

* This extraordinary motion requires a little explanation. It came from the Earl of *Bute*. The following short narrative, extracted from a well-known book, will render it more intelligible. The King having in his speech which introduced this business particularly asked, Whether it would not be expedient to vest in his Majesty, the power of appointing the Queen, *or any other person of the Royal Family*, usually residing in *Great Britain*, to be Regent of these kingdoms, and guardian of his successor, until he should be eighteen? The bill was brought in, giving such power; but a doubt arising concerning the extent of the explanation of the words, *or any other of the Royal Family*, it was affirmed, that the present Royal Family were only descended from the late King. The royal construction of those words was asked; and it was understood from authority, and the best public authority of the time, that that construction and the previous affirmation were the same. The bill passed the upper House, declaring the Royal Family to be only the descendents of the late King: which excluded the P. D. who was of another Family. The administration, to whom the bill was never supposed to be agreeable, are spoken of as considering this a kind of victory over the Favourite, whose particular views were thought to be destroyed by this exclusion, which was accomplished without a manifest opposition to the bill. But when it came into the Commons, a motion was made and supported by the friends of the favourite, to insert her Royal Highness's name; to which the House agreed. And with this amendment it went back to the Lords, where it met with no second opposition. But the following speech was said to have been intended to be spoken upon this occasion.

A speech intended to have been spoken when the Commons returned the Regency Bill, with an amendment respecting the Princess Dowager.

My Lords,

'I hope your Lordships will find no difficulty in disagreeing with the House of Commons in regard to this extraordinary amendment. I call it extraordinary, my Lords, because the resolution, which your Lordships came to upon this clause in the bill, was founded upon an implied, and (as your Lordships considered it) an authentick request from the Crown, delivered to this House by one of the first ministers of his Majesty; to which your Lordships did accordingly give an immediate and serious attention, and a most unanimous approbation.

'I take it for granted, that the persons who moved for this alteration in the other House, were men of undoubted loyalty, and therefore I will not inquire into the date or complexion of their loyalty. But I cannot comprehend, my Lords, what unintelligible and unostensible influence could turn the hearts of

The report of the committee was ordered to be made next morning. Upon this amendment the house divided, 167 were for it, and 37 against it. With this amendment the bill was sent to the Lords who agreed to it.

'that great assembly as the heart of one man, and call upon them to reject an article of the bill, so properly founded upon a declaration of his Majesty's inclinations, and so unanimously assented to by your Lordships. Was it because they were better acquainted and more impressed with the virtues of the Royal person, who is the object of this amendment? Your Lordships, I suppose, will not give way to the House of Commons, in doing all the justice to the character of this great Princess; most certainly, my Lords, the King himself will not be behind hand with the body of his subjects, in shewing every *proper* mark of affection to his royal mother.——And yet, my Lords, both the King and your Lordships saw very wise reasons for what you did; your Lordships treated the matter so circumstanced, with a steadiness, which became you; with the utmost delicacy, and without any improper explanations upon so nice a subject.

'I think there was no undutiful intimation contained in this method of proceeding. But it seems the House of Commons were determined to uncover the veil.—If they did it to shew their superior regard to his Majesty, they are contradicted by the only public evidence of his royal inclinations.—If they did it to shew their contempt of such of his Majesty's ministers, as sit in this house, they acted (at least, as I think) not a very wise part, because not a reconciling part; but yet such a one, as the freedom of that great and respectable assembly has ever entitled, and I hope in God will ever entitle them to. But in the midst of this strange and unaccountable fluctuation of things, what will the wise and the honest part of the world without doors think of this unfortunate country? What can they think, my Lords, but that we have really and truly no Ministers at all? And that every thing is done and undone (even in the highest and most important concerns of this kingdom) by the hint or the whisper of some idol in a corner?—If such a one there be, my Lords, I hope he will be found out in due time, and be treated, I will not say as he deserves, but consigned to some inoffensive situation, where he may be at liberty to contemplate the folly and vanity of his ambition, as it may affect his own person, and the danger and wickedness of it, as it may affect the true and lasting interest of his royal gracious master.

'In the mean time, my Lords, I think we cannot better shew our duty to the King, and our regard to the dignity of this House, than by disagreeing with the Commons in this amendment.'

It is proper to observe that the ostensible Ministers of the day, were not entrusted with the management of this *family business*.

LIST of the ACTS passed this Session.

AN Act, *to permit the importation of salted provisions from* Ireland, *for a limited time.*
An Act, *For a land tax at 4s.*
An Act, *For a duty on malt.*
An Act, *To punish mutiny and desertion.*
An Act, *To allow a further time for the importation of goods from the ceded islands.*
An Act, *To indemnify persons who have omitted qualifying themselves for offices.*
An Act, *For the better regulation of his Majesty's marine forces.*
An Act, *For the recovery of small debts at* Blackheath, Bromley, *&c.*
An Act, *For the recovery of small debts in the hundred of* Chippenham, *&c. in Wilts.*
An Act, *For permitting the free importation of cattle from* Ireland.
An Act, *For providing a public reward for persons who shall discover the longitude.*
An Act, *For laying a stamp duty in the* British colonies in America.
An Act, *For lighting, cleansing, and paving the streets, &c. in* Westminster, *and for collecting certain tolls on* Sundays.
An Act, *For rebuilding the parish church of* Allhallows, London Wall.
An Act, *To enlarge the times limited for executing certain acts of this sessions.*
An Act, *to encourage the growth of madder.*
An Act, *For preserving fish in ponds, and rabbets &c. in warrens.*
An Act, *To rebuild the parish church of* Tetbury.
An Act, *To provide for the administration of government in case of the demise of the King.*
An Act, *For raising the revenue in* America *by certain stamp duties.*

A. 1765.   DEBATES.

An act, *To vest the Isle of Man in the crown.*
An act, *To encourage the growth and cultivation of madder in* England.
An act, *For the harbour of* Ramsgate, *and haven of* Sandwich.
An act, *For vesting the glebe lands of the rectory of St.* Christopher, London, *in the* Bank *of* England, &c.
An act, *For regulating the postage of letters, &c.*

[By this act, the following regulations take place in *America*.

A single letter from *England* to *America*, and from *America* to *England* is to pay one shilling, a double letter two shillings, a treble letter three shillings, an ounce four shillings, and packets, heavier than an ounce, more in the same proportion.

A single letter by sea, from any one port in *America*, to any other, is to pay four pence, a double one eight-pence, a treble one a shilling, an ounce, one shilling and four-pence, &c.

A single letter, by land, through the interior part of the country, for any distance not more than sixty miles, four pence, a double one eight-pence; and so on, as above.

For any distance more than sixty and not exceeding one hundred miles, 6 pence, &c.

For any distance more than one hundred miles, and less than two, 8 pence, &c.

For every hundred miles above two hundred, each single letter is to pay two-pence, every double one four-pence, &c.

In *Ireland* and *Scotland*.] A single letter for the first post stage, from the office where it is put in, is to pay one penny, a double one two-pence, a treble one three-pence, and an ounce four-pence. The postage of letters beyond the first stage to be paid as before.

In

In *England*.] A single letter from the first post stage to the office where it is to be put in, is to pay one penny, a double one two-pence, and so on, as above. A single letter for the two first post stages is to pay two-pence, a double one four-pence, and so on.

The postage of letters beyond the second stage to be paid as before.

This act does not alter or affect the penny-post already established, but it empowers the post-master-general to establish penny post-offices in any city or town where it shall be thought necessary or convenient.]

An act, *For repealing the duties on raw silk.*

An act, *For repairing roads from* Ratcliff Highway *thro'* Cannon-street, &c.

An act, *For rendering more effectual in* America, *the act for punishing mutiny and desertion.*

An act, *For appointing additional commissioners of land-tax.*

An act, *For providing a public reward for discovering the longitude.*

An act, *For obliging agents to account for unclaimed monies.*

An act, *For encouraging the herring fishery.*

An act, *For laying additional duties on the importation of silks and velvets, &c.*

An act, *For granting duties on the exportation of coals, &c.*

An act, *For supplying the export trade to* Africa, *with coarse callicoes, &c.*

An act, *For encouraging the importation of bugles.*

An act, *For granting annuities, and a lottery out of the Sinking Fund.*

An act, *For augmenting the income of masters in Chancery, &c.*

An act, *For repealing the laws relating to width and length of woollen-cloth, &c.*

A. 1765.   DEBATES.   53

An act, *For granting a certain sum out of the Sinking Fund, for the service of the present year.*

An act, *To amend the laws relating to the militia.*

An act, *To prohibit the importation of foreign manufactured silk stockings, gloves, and mitts.*

An act, *To prevent the inconveniences arising from the present method of issuing notes and bills in* Scotland.

[By this act no bank or banker can issue notes after the 15th of *May*, 1766, containing optional clauses, but such optional notes as are then in the circle may freely pass from hand to hand during any after-period, and are as good, and intitled to as ready payment as if they were payable on demand.

That all notes after the passing of this act are liable to the same diligence, if not either paid or marked immediately on presenting, as if they were bills of exchange; and that one single protest narrating the numbers, dates, and sums of each note, with a copy of one note, is sufficient to raise a horning or diligence, for the whole sum.

That no bank or banker can issue notes under 20s. after the first of *June* next. But such of these as are then on the circle may freely pass from hand to hand, until the first of *June* 1766, and are intitled to as ready payment as if they were for larger sums, during any time thereafter.

Hence, those who consider any small notes as of service to themselves or benefit to the country, will circulate them so as they do not return upon the issuer; because they can never afterwards be sent back to the circle.]

An act, *To alter the duties on gum Senega and gum Arabick, to confine the import to* Great-Britain, *and to lay a duty on the exportation thereof.*

An act, *For better preserving the public roads throughout the kingdom.*

An act, *To amend the acts for paving the city and liberties of* Westminster.

An act, *For regulating the woollen manufactory in* Yorkshire.

An act, *For relief of insolvent debtors.*

[From the ending of the former act, to the commencement of this, there is an interval of no more than one year, three quarters, and six days; the shortest period between the passing two insolvent acts ever known in this kingdom.]

An act, *To enable his majesty with a consent of the privy council, to prohibit the exportation of corn, during the recess of parliament.*

An act, *To allow the free importation of corn, and to discontinue the bounty on corn exported.*

An act, *To redeem one fourth part of certain annuities.*

An act, *To enlarge the fund for paying the judges salaries.*

On the 25th of *May* his majesty put an end to the session with the following speech.

My Lords and Gentlemen,

'THE dispatch which you have given with
' so much zeal and wisdom to the public
' business, enables me now to put a period to this
' session of parliament.

' No alteration in the state of foreign affairs has
' happened since your meeting to disturb the
' general peace; and it is with pleasure that I
' inform you, that the present dispositions of the
' several powers of *Europe* promise the continuance
' of this blessing.

' I have seen with the most perfect approbation,
' that you have employed this season of tranquil-
' lity in promoting those objects, which I had
' recommended to your attention, and in framing
' such regulations as may best inforce the just
' authority

' authority of the legiflature, and, at the fame
' time, fecure and extend the commerce, and
' unite the interefts of every part of my dominions.

Gentlemen of the Houfe of Commons,

' The chearfulnefs and prudence which you
' have fhewn in providing for the neceffary ex-
' pences of the prefent year, deferve my parti-
' cular acknowledgments. The many bills
' which you have formed for the improvement
' and augmentation of the revenue in its feve-
' ral branches, and the early care which you
' have taken to difcharge a part of the national
' debt, are the moft effectual methods to efta-
' blifh the public credit upon the fureft founda-
' tions, and to alleviate by degrees, the burthens
' of my people.

My Lords and Gentlemen,

' The provifions which have been made for
' the adminiftration of the government, in cafe
' the crown fhould defcend to any of my chil-
' dren under the age of eighteen years, whilft
' they add ftrength and fecurity to our prefent
' eftablifhment, give me the kindeft and moft
' convincing proof of your confidence: the
' fenfe which I have of the important truft re-
' pofed in me, and my defire to repay this mark
' of your affection, by difcharging my part a-
' greeably to your intentions in the manner moft
' beneficial to my people, have concurred to
' make me execute, without delay, the powers
' with which you have entrufted me. This is
' already done; and you may be affured, that as
' far as it depends upon me, thofe falutary provi-
' fions fhall never be ineffectual. It is my ardent
' wifh, and fhall be my conftant endeavour, on

' this, and every other occasion, to perpetuate
' the happiness of my subjects, and to transmit
' to posterity the blessings of our invaluable con-
' stitution.'

During the recess of parliament the king changed his ministers. The *marquis* of *Rockingham* was placed at the head of the Treasury. *Mr. Dowdeswell* was made chancellor of the exchequer. *Gen. Conway* and the *Duke of Grafton*, secretary of state, &c. &c.

The FIFTH SESSION

OF THE

Twelfth Parliament of *Great-Britain*.

This Session was opened at Westminster, *on the seventeenth day of* December, 1765, *by the King, with the following speech from the Throne.*

My Lords and Gentlemen,

'THE present general state of tranquillity in Europe gave me hopes, that it would not have been necessary to assemble my parliament sooner than is usual in times of peace.

' But as matters of importance have lately occurred in some of my colonies in *America*, which will demand the most serious attention of parliament; and as further informations are daily expected from differents parts of that country, of which I shall order the fullest accounts to be prepared for your consideration; I have thought fit to call you now together, in order that opportunity may thereby be given, to issue the necessary writs on the many vacancies that have happened in the House of Commons, since the last session; so that the parliament may be full, to proceed, immediately after the usual recess, on the consideration of such weighty matters as will then come before you.'

The Commons agreed to the following address:

Most gracious Sovereign,

'We your Majesty's most dutiful and loyal subjects, the Commons of *Great Britain* in parliament assembled, beg leave to return your Majesty the thanks of this house, for your most gracious speech from the throne: and to assure your Majesty, that we will not fail, when this house shall be supplied with its members, to apply ourselves with the utmost diligence and attention to those important occurrences in *America*, which your Majesty recommends to our consideration, and to exert our most zealous endeavours, for the honour of your Majesty's government, and the true interest of your people in all parts of your extended empire.

'Permit us at the same time to congratulate your Majesty on the late encrease of your royal family, by the birth of a Prince. Your Majesty's happiness and that of your people are one; and every encrease of your Majesty's illustrious family is considered by your faithful Commons, as a further security to that religion, and those liberties we enjoy under your Majesty's most auspicious government.

'We also beg leave to offer to your Majesty, our sincere condolance on the great loss, which your Majesty and this kingdom have sustained by the death of his late Royal Highness the Duke of *Cumberland*; whose private and public virtues, whose duty and affection to your Majesty, and whose distinguished merits, and services to this country, as they made his person dear to this nation while he lived, so they cannot fail to render his memory sacred to the latest posterity.'

To which address the King returned the following answer:

Gentlemen,

I return you thanks for this loyal and dutiful address. The satisfaction you express in the increase of my family, and the affectionate share you take in the great loss I have sustained by the death of the Duke of Cumberland, are fresh proofs of your zeal and loyalty.

Your resolution at the same time to support the honour of my government, and to provide for the true interest of all my people, cannot but be most acceptable to me. My conduct shall always shew, that I consider their interest as inseparable from my own.

The writs being issued, the Parliament adjourned to the 14th of *January*, 1766.

On that day the Parliament met again, and the King being come to the House of Lords, made the following speech to both Houses:

My Lords and Gentlemen,

'WHEN I met you last, I acquainted you, that matters of importance had happened in *America*, which would demand the most serious attention of parliament.

' That no information, which could serve to direct your deliberations in so interesting a concern, might be wanting, I have ordered all the papers, that give any light into the origin, the progress, or the tendency of the disturbances which have of late prevailed in some of the northern colonies, to be immediately laid before you.

' No time has been lost, on the first advice of these disturbances, to issue orders to the governors of my provinces, and to the commanders of my forces in *America*, for the exertion of all
' the

' the powers of government in the suppression of
' riots and tumult, and in the effectual support of
' lawful authority.

' Whatever remains to be done on this occasion,
' I commit to your wisdom; not doubting, but
' your zeal for the honour of my crown, your at-
' tention to the just rights and authority of the
' *British* legislature, and your affection and con-
' cern for the welfare and prosperity of all my
' people, will guide you to such sound and pru-
' dent resolutions, as may tend at once to preserve
' those constitutional rights over the colonies, and
' to restore to them that harmony and tranquillity,
' which have lately been interrupted by riots and
' disorders of the most dangerous nature.

' If any alterations should be wanting in the
' commercial œconomy of the plantations, which
' may tend to enlarge and secure the mutual and
' beneficial intercourse of my kingdoms and colo-
' nies, they will deserve your most serious con-
' sideration. In effectuating purposes so worthy
' of your wisdom and public spirit, you may de-
' pend upon my most hearty concurrence and
' support. The present happy tranquillity, now
' subsisting in *Europe*, will enable you to pursue
' such objects of our interiour policy with a more
' uninterrupted attention.

Gentlemen of the House of Commons,

' I have ordered the proper estimates for the
' current service of the year to be laid before you:
' such supplies as you may grant shall be duly ap-
' plied with the utmost fidelity, and shall be dis-
' pensed with the strictest œconomy.

My Lords and Gentlemen,

' I earnestly recommend to you, to proceed in
' your deliberations with temper and unanimity.
' The

'The time requires, and I doubt not but your
'own inclination will lead you to those salutary
'dispositions. I have nothing at heart, but the
'assertion of legal authority, the preservation of
'the liberties of all my subjects, the equity and
'good order of my government, and the concord
'and prosperity of all parts of my dominions.'

An address, as usual, was moved, upon which a long debate ensued.

The gentlemen in support of the motion spoke very tenderly of the disturbances raised in *America*, in opposition to the stamp act, terming them only *occurrences*; which gave great offence to the friends of the late Minister, by whom that act had been projected.

Mr. *Nugent*, now Lord *Clare*, insisted, 'That
'the honour and dignity of the kingdom, obliged
'us to compel the execution of the stamp act,
'except the right was acknowledged, and the re-
'peal sollicited as a favour. He computed the ex-
'pence of the troops now employed in *America*
'for their defence, as he called it, to amount to
'nine pence in the pound of our land tax; while
'the produce of the Stamp-act would not raise a
'shilling a head on the inhabitants of *America*;
'but that a pepper-corn, in acknowledgment of
'the right, was of more value, than millions with-
'out. He expatiated on the extreme ingratitude
'of the colonies; and concluded, with charging
'the ministry with encouraging petitions to Parlia-
'ment, and instructions to members from trading
'and manufacturing towns, against the act.'

Mr. *Pitt* (now Lord *Chatham*) spoke next. As he always begins very low, and as every body was in agitation at his first rising, his introduction was not heard, 'till he said, 'I came to town but
'to-day; I was a stranger to the tenor of his Ma-
'jesty's

'jesty's speech, and the proposed address, 'till I
'heard them read in this house. Unconnected
'and unconsulted, I have not the means of infor-
'mation; I am fearful of offending through mis-
'take, and therefore beg to be indulged with a
'second reading of the proposed address.' The
address being read, Mr. *Pitt* went on:—' He
'commended the King's speech, approved of the
'address in answer, as it decided nothing, every
'gentleman being left at perfect liberty to take
'such a part concerning *America*, as he might
'afterwards see fit. One word only he could not
'approve of, an *early*, is a word that does not
'belong to the notice the Ministry have given to
'Parliament of the troubles in *America*. In a
'matter of such importance, the communication
'ought to have been immediate: I speak not
'with respect to parties; I stand up in this place
'single and unconnected. As to the late Ministry,
'(turning himself to Mr. *Grenville*, who sat within
'one of him) every capital measure they have
'taken, has been entirely wrong!

'As to the present gentlemen, to those at least
'whom I have in my eye (looking at the bench
'where Mr. *Conway* sat, with the Lords of the
'Treasury) I have no objection; I have never
'been made a sacrifice by any of them. Their
'characters are fair; and I am always glad when
'men of fair character engage in his Majesty's
'service. Some of them have done me the honour
'to ask my poor opinion, before they would
'engage. These will do me the justice to own,
'I advised them to engage; but notwithstanding
'—I love to be explicit—I cannot give them my
'confidence; pardon me, gentlemen, (bowing
'to the Ministry) confidence is a plant of slow
'growth in an aged bosom: youth is the season of
'credulity; by comparing events with each other,
'reasoning from effects to causes, methinks, I
'plainly

'plainly difcover the traces of an over-ruling in-
'fluence.

'There is a claufe in the act of fettlement, to
'oblige every Minifter to fign his name to the
'advice which he gives his Sovereign. Would
'it were obferved!—I have had the honour to
'ferve the Crown, and if I could have fubmitted
'to influence, I might have ftill continued to
'ferve; but I would not be refponfible for
'others.——I have no local attachments: it is
'indifferent to me, whether a man was rocked
'in his cradle on this fide or that fide of the *Tweed*.
'—I fought for merit wherever it was to be
'found.—It is my boaft, that I was the firft Mi-
'nifter who looked for it, and I found it in the
'mountains of the north. I called it forth, and
'drew it into your fervice, an hardy and intrepid
'race of men! men, who, when left by your
'jealoufy, became a prey to the artifices of your
'enemies, and had gone nigh to have overturned
'the ftate, in the war before the laft. Thefe
'men, in the laft war, were brought to combat
'on your fide: they ferved with fidelity, as they
'fought with valour, and conquered for you in
'every part of the world: detefted be the national
'reflections againft them!——they are unjuft,
'groundlefs, illiberal, unmanly. When I ceafed
'to ferve his Majefty as a Minifter, it was not the
'*country* of the man by which I was moved—
'but *the man* of that country wanted *wifdom*, and
'held principles incompatible with *freedom*.

'It is a long time, Mr. *Speaker*, fince I have
'attended in Parliament. When the refolution
'was taken in the houfe to tax *America*, I was ill
'in bed. If I could have endured to have been
'carried in my bed, fo great was the agitation
'of my mind for the confequences! I would have
'follicited fome kind hand to have laid me down
'on this floor, to have borne my teftimony againft
'it.

' it. It is now an act that had passed—I would
' speak with decency of every act of this House,
' but I must beg the indulgence of the House
' to speak of it with freedom.

' I hope a day may be soon appointed to con-
' sider the state of the nation with respect to
' *America*.—I hope, gentlemen will come to this
' debate with all the temper and impartiality that
' his majesty recommends, and the importance of
' the subject requires. A subject of greater im-
' portance than ever engaged the attention of this
' House! that subject only excepted, when, near
' a century ago, it was the question, whether you
' yourselves were to be bound, or free. In the
' mean time, as I cannot depend upon health
' for any future day, such is the nature of my
' infirmities, I will beg to say a few words at
' present, leaving the justice, the equity, the
' policy, the expediency of the act, to another
' time. I will only speak to one point, a point
' which seems not to have been generally under-
' stood—I mean to the right. Some gentlemen
' (alluding to Mr. *Nugent*) seem to have consi-
' dered it as a point of *honor*. If gentlemen
' consider it in that light, they leave all measures
' of right and wrong, to follow a delusion that
' may lead to destruction. It is my opinion that
' this kingdom has no right to lay a tax upon the
' colonies. At the same time, I assert the au-
' thority of this kingdom over the colonies, to be
' sovereign and supreme, in every circumstance
' of government and legislation whatsoever.——
' They are the subjects of this kingdom, equally
' entitled with yourselves to all the natural rights
' of mankind and the peculiar privileges of *Eng-
' lishmen*. Equally bound by its laws, and equally
' participating of the constitution of this free
' country. The *Americans* are the sons, not the
' bastards, of *England*. Taxation is no part of
' the

'the governing or legislative power.—The taxes
'are a voluntary gift and grant of the Commons
'alone. In legislation the three estates of the
'realm are alike concerned, but the concurrence
'of the Peers and the Crown to a tax, is only
'necessary to close with the form of a law. The
'gift and grant is of the Commons alone. In
'antient days, the Crown, the Barons, and
'the Clergy possessed the lands. In those days,
'the Barons and the Clergy gave and granted to
'the Crown. They gave and granted what was
'their own. At present, since the discovery of
'*America*, and other circumstances permitting,
'the Commons are become the proprietors of
'the land. The Crown has divested itself of its
'great estates. The Church (God bless it) has
'but a pittance. The property of the Lords,
'compared with that of the Commons, is as a
'drop of water in the ocean: and this House
'represents those Commons, the proprietors of
'the lands; and those proprietors virtually re-
'present the rest of the inhabitants. When,
'therefore, in this House we give and grant, we
'give and grant what is our own. But in an
'*American* tax, what do we do? We, your Ma-
'jesty's Commons of *Great-Britain*, give and
'grant to your Majesty, what? Our own pro-
'perty?——No. We give and grant to your
'Majesty, the property of your Majesty's Com-
'mons of *America*.—It is an absurdity in terms.—

'The distinction between legislation and taxa-
'tion is essentially necessary to liberty. The
'Crown, the Peers, are equally legislative powers
'with the Commons. If taxation be a part of
'simple legislation, the Crown, the Peers have
'rights in taxation as well as yourselves: rights
'which they will claim, which they will exercise,
'whenever the principle can be supported by
'*power*.

'There is an idea in some, that the colonies are virtually represented in this House. I would fain know by whom an *American* is represented here? Is he represented by any Knight of the shire, in any county in this kingdom? *Would to God that respectable representation was augmented to a greater number!* Or will you tell him that he is represented by any representative of a borough—a borough, which perhaps no man ever saw—This is what is called, *the rotten part of the constitution.*——It cannot continue the century—If it does not drop, it must be amputated.—The idea of a virtual representation of *America* in this House, is the most contemptible idea that ever entered into the head of a man—It does not deserve a serious refutation.

'The Commons of *America*, represented in their several assemblies, have ever been in possession of the exercise of this, their constitutional right, of giving and granting their own money. They would have been slaves if they had not enjoyed it. At the same time, this kingdom, as the supreme governing and legislative power, has always bound the colonies by her laws, by her regulations, and restrictions in trade, in navigation, in manufactures—in every thing, except that of taking their money out of their pockets without their consent.

'Here I would draw the line,

'*Quam ultra citraque nequit consistere rectum.*'

He concluded with a familiar voice and tone, but so low that it was not easy to distinguish what he said. A considerable pause ensued after Mr. *Pitt* had done speaking.

Mr. *Conway* at length got up. He said, 'he had been waiting to see whether any answer would

Mr. Conway.

' would be given to what had been advanced by
' the right honourable gentleman, referving him-
' felf for the reply: but as none had been given,
' he had only to declare, that his own fentiments
' were entirely conformable to thofe of the right
' honourable gentleman---That they are fo con-
' formable, he faid, is a circumftance that affects
' me with moft fenfible pleafure, and does me
' the greateft honour. But two things fell from
' that gentleman, which give me pain, as, what-
' ever falls from that gentleman, falls from fo
' great a height as to make a deep impreffion.---
' I muft endeavour to remove it.---It was objected,
' that the notice given to Parliament of the
' troubles in *America* was not early. I can affure
' the Houfe, the firft accounts were too vague
' and imperfect to be worth the notice of Parlia-
' ment. It is only of late that they have been
' precife and full. An over-ruling influence has
' alfo been hinted at. I fee nothing of it---I feel
' nothing of it---I difclaim it for myfelf, and (as
' far as my difcernment can reach) for all the
' reft of his Majefty's Minifters.'

Mr. *Pitt* said in anfwer to Mr. *Conway*, ' The
' excufe is a valid one, if it is a juft one. That
' muft appear from the papers now before the
' Houfe.' Mr. *Grenville* next ftood up. He
began with cenfuring the Miniftry very fevere-
ly, for delaying to give earlier notice to Parliament of the difturbances in *America*. He
faid, ' They began in *July*, and now we are in
' the middle of *January*; lately they were only
' occurrences, they are now grown to difturbances,
' to tumults and riots. I doubt they border on
' open rebellion; and if the doctrine I have heard
' this day be confirmed, I fear they will lofe that
' name to take that of revolution. The govern-
' ment over them being diffolved, a revolution
' will take place in *America*. I cannot underftand

'the difference between external and internal
'taxes. They are the same in effect, and only
'differ in name. That this kingdom has the
'sovereign, the supreme legislative power over
'*America*, is granted. It cannot be denied; and
'taxation is a part of that sovereign power. It
'is one branch of the legislation. It is, it has
'been exercised, over those who are not, who
'were never represented. It is exercised over the
'*India* company, the merchants of *London*, the
'proprietors of the stocks, and over many great
'manufacturing towns. It was exercised over the
'palatinate of *Chester*, and the bishoprick of
'*Durham*, before they sent any representatives
'to Parliament. I appeal for proof to the pre-
'ambles of the Acts which gave them repre-
'sentatives: the one in the reign of *Henry* VIII.
'the other in that of *Charles* II.' Mr. *Grenville*
then quoted the Acts, and desired that they might
be read; which being done, he said: 'When I
'proposed to tax *America*, I asked the House, if
'any gentleman would object to the right; I
'repeatedly asked it, and no man would attempt
'to deny it. Protection and obedience are reci-
'procal. *Great-Britain* protects *America*; *America*
'is bound to yield obedience. If not, tell me
'where the *Americans* were emancipated? When
'they want the protection of this kingdom, they
'are always very ready to ask it. That protection
'has always been afforded them in the most full
'and ample manner. The nation has run itself
'into an immense debt to give them their protec-
'tion; and now they are called upon to contri-
'bute a small share towards the public expence,
'an expence arising from themselves, they re-
'nounce your authority, insult your officers, and
'break out, I might almost say, into open rebel-
'lion. The seditious spirit of the colonies owes
'its birth to the factions in this House. Gentle-
'men

'men are careless of the consequences of what
'they say, provided it answers the purposes of
'opposition. We were told we trod on tender
'ground; we were bid to expect disobedience.
'What was this, but telling the *Americans* to
'stand out against the law, to encourage their
'obstinacy with the expectation of support from
'hence? Let us only hold out a little, they
'would say, our friends will soon be in power.
'Ungrateful people of *America!* Bounties have
'been extended to them. When I had the honour
'of serving the Crown, while you yourselves were
'loaded with an enormous debt, you have given
'bounties on their lumber, on their iron, their
'hemp, and many other articles. You have re-
'laxed, in their favour, the act of navigation,
'that palladium of the *British* commerce; and
'yet I have been abused in all the public papers
'as an enemy to the trade of *America*. I have
'been particularly charged with giving orders
'and instructions to prevent the *Spanish* trade,
'and thereby stopping the channel, by which
'alone *North America* used to be supplied with
'cash for remittances to this country. I defy
'any man to produce any such orders or instruc-
'tions. I discouraged no trade but what was
'illicit, what was prohibited by act of Parliament.
'I desire a *West-India* merchant, well known in
'the city (Mr. *Long*) a gentleman of character,
'may be examined. He will tell you, that I
'offered to do every thing in my power to ad-
'vance the trade of *America*. I was above giving
'an answer to anonymous calumnies; but in this
'place, it becomes one to wipe off the asper-
'sion.'

Here Mr. *Grenville* ceased. Several members Mr. Pitt. got up to speak, but Mr. *Pitt* seeming to rise, the House was so clamorous for Mr. *Pitt*, Mr. *Pitt*, that the Speaker was obliged to call to order.

After obtaining a little quiet, he said, 'Mr. Pitt was up;' who began with informing the House, 'That he did not mean to have gone any further upon the subject that day; that he had only designed to have thrown out a few hints, which, gentlemen who were so confident of the right of this kingdom to send taxes to *America*, might consider; might, perhaps, reflect, in a cooler moment, that the right was at least equivocal. But since the gentleman, who spoke last, had not stopped on that ground, but had gone into the whole; into the justice, the equity, the policy, the expediency of the Stamp-Act, as well as into the right, he would follow him through the whole field, and combat his arguments on every point.'

Ld Strange. He was going on, when Lord *Strange* got up, and called both the gentlemen, Mr. *Pitt*, and Mr. *Grenville*, to order. He said, 'they had both departed from the matter before the House, which was the King's speech; and that Mr. *Pitt* was going to speak twice on the same debate, although the House was not in a committee.'

Mr. Onslow. Mr. *George Onslow* answered, 'That they were both in order, as nothing had been said, but what was fairly deducible from the King's speech;' and appealed to the Speaker. The Speaker decided in Mr. *Onslow*'s favour.

Mr. Pitt. Mr. *Pitt* said, 'I do not apprehend I am speaking twice: I did expressly reserve a part of my subject, in order to save the time of this House, but I am compelled to proceed in it. I do not speak twice; I only finished what I designedly left imperfect. But if the House is of a different opinion, far be it from me to indulge a wish of transgression, against order. I am content, if it be your pleasure, to be silent.'---

Here he paused----The House resounding with, 'Go on, go on;' he proceeded:

'Gentlemen, Sir, (to the Speaker) I have been charged with giving birth to sedition in *America*. They have spoken their sentiments with freedom, against this unhappy act, and that freedom has become their crime. Sorry I am to hear the liberty of speech in this House, imputed as a crime. But the imputation shall not discourage me. It is a liberty I mean to exercise. No gentleman ought to be afraid to exercise it. It is a liberty by which the gentleman who calumniates it might have profited. He ought to have profited. He ought to have desisted from his project. The gentleman tells us, *America* is obstinate; *America* is almost in open rebellion. I rejoice that *America* has resisted. Three millions of people, so dead to all the feelings of liberty, as voluntarily to submit to be slaves, would have been fit instruments to make slaves of the rest. I come not here armed at all points, with law cases and acts of parliament, with the statute book doubled down in dogs-ears, to defend the cause of liberty: if I had, I myself would have cited the two cases of *Chester* and *Durham*. I would have cited them, to have shewn, that, even under any arbitrary reigns, Parliaments were ashamed of taxing a people without their consent, and allowed them representatives. Why did the gentleman confine himself to *Chester* and *Durham?* He might have taken a higher example in *Wales*; *Wales*, that never was taxed by Parliament, 'till it was incorporated. I would not debate a particular point of law with the gentleman: I know his abilities. I have been obliged to his diligent researches. But, for the defence of liberty upon a general principle, upon a constitutional principle, it is a ground on which I stand firm; on

'which

'which I dare meet any man. The gentleman
'tells us of many who are taxed, and are not
'represented---The *India* company, merchants,
'stock-holders, manufacturers. Surely many of
'these are represented in other capacities, as
'owners of land, or as freemen of boroughs.
'It is a misfortune that more are not actually
'represented. But they are all inhabitants, and,
'as such, are virtually represented. Many have
'it in their option to be actually represented.
'They have connexions with those that elect,
'and they have influence over them. The gen-
'tleman mentioned the stock-holders: I hope he
'does not reckon the debts of the nation as a
'part of the national estate. Since the accession
'of King *William*, many ministers, some of
'great, others of more moderate abilities, have
'taken the lead of government.'

He then went through the list of them, bringing it down 'till he came to himself, giving a short
sketch of the characters of each of them. 'None
'of these, he said, thought, or ever dreamed,
'of robbing the colonies of their constitutional
'rights. That was reserved to mark the æra of
'the late administration: not that there were
'wanting some, when I had the honour to serve
'his Majesty, to propose to me to burn my
'fingers with an *American* Stamp-Act. With
'the enemy at their back, with our bayonets at
'their breasts, in the day of their distress, per-
'haps the *Americans* would have submitted to
'the imposition; but it would have been taking
'an ungenerous, and unjust advantage. The
'gentleman boasts of his bounties to *America!*
'Are not those bounties intended finally for the
'benefit of this kingdom? If they are not, he
'has misapplied the national treasures. I am no
'courtier of *America*, I stand up for this king-
'dom. I maintain, that the Parliament has a
'right

'right to bind, to restrain *America*. Our legisla-
'tive power over the colonies, is sovereign and
'supreme. When it ceases to be sovereign and
'supreme, I would advise every gentleman to sell
'his lands, if he can, and embark for that
'country. When two countries are connected
'together, like *England* and her colonies, without
'being incorporated, the one must necessarily
'govern; the greater must rule the less; but so
'rule it, as not to contradict the fundamental
'principles that are common to both.

'If the gentleman does not understand the
'difference between internal and external taxes,
'I cannot help it; but there is a plain distinction
'between taxes levied for the purposes of raising
'a revenue, and duties imposed for the regula-
'tion of trade, for the accommodation of the
'subject; although, in the consequences, some
'revenue might incidentally arise from the latter.

'The gentleman asks, when were the colonies
'emancipated? But I desire to know, when they
'were made slaves? But I dwell not upon words.
'When I had the honour of serving his Majesty,
'I availed myself of the means of information,
'which I derived from my office: I speak there-
'fore from knowledge. My materials were good.
'I was at pains to collect, to digest, to consider
'them; and I will be bold to affirm, that the
'profits to *Great Britain* from the trade of the
'colonies, through all its branches, is two mil-
'lions a year. This is the fund that carried you
'triumphantly through the last war. The estates
'that were rented at two thousand pounds a year,
'threescore years ago, are at three thousand
'pounds at present. Those estates sold then from
'fifteen to eighteen years purchase; the same
'may be now sold for thirty. You owe this to
'*America*. This is the price that *America* pays
'you for her protection. And shall a miserable
'financier

'financier come with a boast, that he can fetch a pepper-corn into the Exchequer, to the loss of millions to the nation! I dare not say, how much higher these profits may be augmented. Omitting the immense increase of people, by natural population, in the northern colonies, and the migration from every part of *Europe*, I am convinced the whole commercial system of *America* may be altered to advantage. You have prohibited, where you ought to have encouraged; and you have encouraged where you ought to have prohibited. Improper restraints have been laid on the continent, in favour of the islands. You have but two nations to trade with in *America*. Would you had twenty! Let acts of parliament in consequence of treaties remain, but let not an *English* minister become a custom-house officer for *Spain*, or for any foreign power. Much is wrong, much may be amended for the general good of the whole.

'Does the gentleman complain he has been misrepresented in the public prints? It is a common misfortune. In the *Spanish* affair of the last war, I was abused in all the newspapers, for having advised his Majesty to violate the law of nations with regard to *Spain*. The abuse was industriously circulated even in handbills. If administration did not propagate the abuse, *administration never contradicted it*. I will not say what advice I did give to the King. My advice is in writing, signed by myself, in the possession of the Crown. But I will say, what advice I did not give to the King: I did not advise him to violate any of the laws of nations.

'As to the report of the gentleman's preventing in some way the trade for bullion with the *Spaniards*, it was spoken of so confidently,
'that

'that I own I am one of those who did believe it
'to be true,

'The gentleman must not wonder he was not
'contradicted, when, as the minister, he asserted
'the right of parliament to tax *America*. I know
'not how it is, but there is a modesty in this
'House which does not chuse to contradict a
'minister. I wish gentlemen would get the
'better of this modesty. If they do not, per-
'haps, the collective body may begin to abate
'of its respect for the representative. Lord *Bacon*
'had told me, that a great question would not
'fail of being agitated at one time or another. I
'was willing to agitate that at the proper season,
'the *German* war: my *German* war, they called
'it. Every sessions I called out, has any body
'any objections to the *German* war? No body
'would object to it, one gentleman only excepted,
'since removed to the upper House, by succes-
'sion to an ancient barony,' (meaning Lord
le Despencer, formerly Sir *Francis Dashwood*;)
'he told me, "he did not like a *German* war." I
'honoured the man for it, and was sorry when he
'was turned out of his post.

'A great deal has been said without doors, of
'the power, of the strength of *America*. It is a
'topic that ought to be cautiously meddled with.
'In a good cause, on a sound bottom, the force
'of this country can crush *America* to atoms. I
'know the valour of your troops. I know the
'skill of your officers. There is not a company
'of foot that has served in *America*, out of which
'you may not pick a man of sufficient knowledge
'and experience, to make a governor of a
'colony there. But on this ground, on the
'Stamp-Act, when so many here will think it a
'crying injustice, I am one who will lift up my
'hands against it.

'In

'In such a cause, your success would be hazardous.—*America*, if she fell, would fall like the strong man. She would embrace the pillars of the state, and pull down the constitution along with her. Is this your boasted peace? Not to sheath the sword in its scabbard, but to sheath it in the bowels of your countrymen? Will you quarrel with yourselves, now the whole House of *Bourbon* is united against you? While *France* disturbs your fisheries in *Newfoundland*, embarrasses your slave trade to *Africa*, and withholds from your subjects in *Canada*, their property stipulated by treaty; while the ransom for Manillas is denied by *Spain*, and its gallant conqueror basely traduced into a mean plunderer, a gentleman, (Colonel *Draper*) whose noble and generous spirit would do honour to the proudest grandee of the country. The *Americans* have not acted in all things with prudence and temper. They have been wronged. They have been driven to madness by injustice. Will you punish them for the madness you have occasioned? Rather let prudence and temper come first from this side. I will undertake for *America*, that she will follow the example. There are two lines in a ballad of *Prior*'s, of a man's behaviour to his wife, so applicable to you and your colonies, that I cannot help repeating them:

'*Be to her faults a little blind;*
'*Be to her virtues very kind.*

'Upon the whole, I will beg leave to tell the House what is really my opinion. It is, that the Stamp-Act be *repealed absolutely, totally,* and *immediately*. That the reason for the repeal be assigned, because it was founded on an erroneous principle. At the same time, let the sovereign authority of this country over the colonies,

' colonies, be asserted in as strong terms as can
' be devised, and be made to extend to every
' point of legislation whatsoever. That we may
' bind their *trade*, confine their *manufactures*, and
' exercise every *power* whatsoever, except that of
' taking their money out of their pockets without
' their consent !'---

The address was agreed to without a division; as follows:

Most gracious Sovereign,

' WE your Majesty's most dutiful and loyal
' subjects, the Commons of *Great Britain*,
' in Parliament assembled, return your Majesty
' our most humble thanks for your most gracious
' speech from the Throne.
 ' It is with the highest sense of your Majesty's
' goodness we acknowledge that care for the
' welfare of your people, and that confidence in
' the loyalty and affection of your faithful Com-
' mons, which your Majesty shews in the early
' communication, your Majesty has been pleased
' to order, of the necessary informations relative
' to the disturbances in *America*. Your reliance
' on the wisdom and duty of your Parliament in
' a matter of so great importance, and the atten-
' tion shewn by your Majesty, in reserving to our
' deliberation and advice, the joint concern of
' your Majesty's royal authority, the rights of
' your Parliament, and the happiness of your
' subjects, are at once objects of our highest
' admiration and gratitude.
 ' It is our duty, as it shall be our care, to
' imitate that temper and equanimity which ap-
' pears in your Majesty's conduct, by mixing
' with our zeal for the honour of your Majesty's
' government, and with our just regard for the
' dignity

'dignity and authority of Parliament, the utmost
'attention to the important objects of the trade
'and navigation of these kingdoms, and the
'tenderest concern for the united interest of all
'your Majesty's people.

'It is with inexpressible grief we are again
'called upon to condole with your Majesty, on
'the death of another Prince of your royal
'family, whose amiable disposition, and whose
'early virtues in the first dawn of life, while
'they shew him worthy of the illustrious race
'he sprung from, must now double our regret
'for his untimely loss.

'The general state of peace and tranquillity, so
'happily reigning in all parts of *Europe*, must
'give the greatest satisfaction, to every one, who
'has any concern for the true interest of this
'country, or who feels for the general happiness
'of mankind.

'Our assistance shall not be wanting to aid
'your Majesty with our advice, and to strengthen
'your authority, for the continuation of that
'harmony, so happily preserved by the wisdom
'of your Majesty's councils, and the influence of
'your mild auspicious government.

'We assure your Majesty that we shall, with
'the greatest chearfulness, grant your Majesty
'the supplies necessary for the current service
'of the year, having the firmest reliance on the
'promise your Majesty is graciously pleased to
'make, of seeing them duly applied, with that
'œconomy which your own wisdom will direct,
'and which the circumstances of this country so
'strongly demand.

'The unanimity and dispatch, which your
'Majesty is pleased to recommend, we shall from
'motives both of duty and inclination, endea-
'vour to make the rule of our proceedings;
'being sensible that nothing can more imme-
'diately

'diately tend to add weight to the deliberations of Parliament, or efficacy to their resolutions.

'And as the constant tenor of your Majesty's conduct, shews that the happiness and prosperity of your people, are the sole objects of your concern, we should be equally wanting in duty to our Sovereign, and care of our own honour, did we a moment neglect our part, in promoting all such wise and salutary measures as may tend to reflect dignity on your Majesty's government, and fix the welfare of your people on the most solid foundations.'

Copies of some of the most material letters and papers relative to the disturbances in America, *which Mr. Secretary* Conway, *by his Majesty's command, this day laid before the House.*

Copy of a Letter from Mr. Secretary Conway, *to Lieut. Gov.* Faquier.

Sept. 14. 1765.

SIR,

It is with the greatest pleasure I received his Majesty's commands to declare to you his most gracious approbation of your conduct. His Majesty and his servants are satisfied, that the precipitate resolutions you sent home did not take their rise from any remissness or inattention in you; nor is his Majesty at all inclined to suppose, that any instance of diffidence or dissatisfaction could be founded in the general inclination of his antient and loyal colony of *Virginia*; the nature of the thing and your representations induce a persuasion, that those ill-advised resolutions owed their birth to the violence of some individuals, who taking the advantage of a thin assembly, so far prevailed, as to publish their own unformed opinions to the world as the sentiments of the colony. But his Majesty, Sir, will not, by the prevalence of a few men, at a certain moment, be persuaded to change the opinion, or lessen the confidence, he has always entertained of the colony of *Virginia*; which has always experienced the protection of the crown. His Majesty's servants, therefore, with entire reliance on your prudence,

and

and on the virtue and wisdom of the colony entrusted to your care, persuade themselves, that when a full assembly shall calmly and maturely deliberate upon those resolutions, they will see, and be themselves alarmed at, the dangerous tendency and mischievous consequences which they might be productive of, both to the mother country and the colonies, which are the equal objects of his Majesty's parental care; and whose mutual happiness and prosperity certainly require a confidential reliance of the colonies upon the mother country.

Upon these principles, Sir, and upon your prudent management, and a proper representation to the wise and sober part of the people, how earnest his Majesty is to extend the happy influence of his fatherly care over every part of his dominions, it is expected that a full assembly will form very different resolutions, such as may cement that union, which alone can establish the safety and prosperity of the colonies, and the mother country.

As there is no intention in the crown to attempt, nor in the King's servants to advise, any incroachments on the real rights and liberties of any part of his Majesty's subjects; so neither will his Majesty undoubtedly submit, or servants advise, under any circumstances, that the respect which is due to parliament, and which is necessary for the general good of the whole *British* empire, should any where be made a sacrifice to local and dangerous prejudices.

As this important matter is, however, now before his Majesty's privy council, as well as the other consideration of the dangerous riot and mutinous behaviour of the people on the frontiers, *I shall not pretend to give any advice or instructions on these subjects*; not doubting, but you will soon have the fullest from the wisdom of that board, in all those things, in which, by your last accounts, the most essential interests of the colony are so deeply concerned.

You will therefore, in the mean time, be very attentive, by every prudent measure in your power, at once to maintain the just rights of the *British* government, and to preserve the peace and tranquillity of the provinces committed to your care.

But as these appear to me matters of government fit for his Majesty's more immediate notice and information, I must beg you will not fail to transmit to me such occurrences,

ences, from time to time, on these heads, as you may deem of importance in the light I mention.

I am, &c.

H. S. CONWAY.

Extract of a Letter from Mr. Secretary Conway, *to Major General* Gage.

October 24, 1765.

SIR,

It is with the greatest concern, that his Majesty learns the disturbances which have arisen in some of the *North American* colonies: these events will probably create application to you, in which the utmost exertion of your prudence may be necessary; so as justly to temper your conduct between that caution and coolness, which the delicacy of such a situation may demand on the one hand, and the vigour necessary to suppress outrage and violence on the other. It is impossible, at this distance, to assist you by any particular or positive instruction, because you will find yourself necessarily obliged to take your resolution as particular circumstances and emergencies may require.

It is hoped, and expected, that this want of confidence in the justice and tenderness of the mother country, and this open resistance to its authority, can only have found place among the lower and more ignorant of the people. The better and wiser part of the colonies will know, that decency and submission may prevail, not only to redress grievances, but to obtain grace and favour, while the outrage of a public violence can expect nothing but severity and chastisement. You, and all his Majesty's servants, from a sense of your duty to, and love of, your country, will endeavour to excite and encourage these sentiments.

If, *by lenient and persuasive methods*, you can contribute to restore that peace and tranquillity to the provinces, on which their welfare and happiness depend, you will do a most acceptable and essential service to your country: but *having taken every step which the utmost prudence and lenity can dictate*, in compassion to the folly and ignorance of some misguided people, you will not, on the other hand, where your assistance may be wanted to strengthen the hands of government, fail to concur in every proper measure for its support, by such a timely exertion of force, as may be necessary to repel acts of outrage and violence,

violence, and to provide for the maintenance of peace and good order in the provinces.

Copy of a Letter from Mr. Secretary Conway, *to Governor* Bernard.

October 24, 1765.

SIR,

Your letters of the 15th, 16th, 22d, and 31st of *August*, have been received; the three former not till yesterday.

It is with the greatest concern his Majesty learns the disturbances which have lately arisen in your province, the general confusion that seems to reign there, and the total languor and want of energy, in your government, to exert itself with any dignity or efficacy, for the suppression of tumults, which seem to strike at the very being of all authority and subordination among you. His Majesty cannot but, with the greatest surprize, hear of the refusal of your council to call for the aid of any regular force to the support of the civil magistracy, at a time when, it seems, you had reason to think, there was no other power capable of providing for the peace and quiet of the province.

Nothing can, certainly, exceed the ill-advised and intemperate conduct held by a party in your province, which can in no way contribute to the removal of any real grievance they might labour under, but may tend to obstruct and impede the exertion of his Majesty's benevolent attention to the ease and comfort, as well as the welfare, of all his people.

It is hoped, and expected, that this want of confidence in the justice and tenderness of the mother country, and this open resistance to its authority, can only have found place among the lower and more ignorant of the people; the better and more wise part of the colonies will know, that decency and submission may prevail, not only to redress grievances, but to obtain grace and favour, while the outrage of a public violence can expect nothing but severity and chastisement. These sentiments, you, and all his Majesty's servants, from a sense of your duty to, and love of, your country, will endeavour to excite and encourage: you will all, in a particular manner, call upon them not to render their case desperate; you will, in the strongest colours, represent to them the dreadful consequences that must inevitably attend the forcible and

violent

violent resistance to acts of the *British* Parliament, and the scene of misery and distraction to both countries, inseparable from such a conduct.

If, by lenient and persuasive methods, you can contribute to restore that peace and tranquillity to the provinces, on which their welfare and happiness depend, you will do a most acceptable and essential service to your country; but having taken every step which the utmost prudence and lenity can dictate, in compassion to the folly and ignorance of some misguided people, you will not, on the other hand, fail to use your utmost power for repelling all acts of outrage and violence, and to provide for the maintenance of peace and good order in the province, by such a timely exertion of force, as the occasion may require; for which purpose, you will make the proper applications to General *Gage*, or Lord *Colvil*, commanders of his Majesty's land and naval forces in *America*: for however unwillingly his Majesty may consent to the exertion of such powers as may endanger the safety of a single subject, yet can he not permit his own dignity, and the authority of the *British* legislature, to be trampled on by force and violence, and in avowed contempt of all order, duty and decorum.

If the subject is aggrieved, he knows in what manner legally and constitutionally to apply for relief: but it is not suitable, either to the safety or dignity of the *British* empire, that any individuals, under the pretence of redressing grievances, should presume to violate the public peace.

I am, &c.
H. S. CONWAY.

P. S. The sloop which carries this will carry orders to Lord *Colvil*, and to the Governor of *Nova Scotia*, to send to your assistance any force which may be thought necessary from thence, and which that province can supply.

Copy of Mr. Secretary Conway's *Circular Letter to the Governors in* North America.

October 24, 1765.

SIR,

It is with the greatest concern, that his Majesty learns the disturbances which have arisen in some of the *North American* colonies: if this evil should spread to the government of ———, where you preside, the utmost exertion of your prudence will be necessary, so as justly to temper your conduct between that caution and coolness which the delicacy of such a situation may demand, on the one hand, and the vigour necessary to suppress outrage and violence, on the other. It is impossible, at this distance, to assist you, by any particular or positive instruction; because you will find yourself necessarily obliged to take your resolution, as particular circumstances and emergencies may require.

His Majesty, and the servants he honours with his confidence, cannot but lament the ill-advised intemperance shewn already in some of the provinces, by taking up a conduct, which can in no way contribute to the removal of any real grievance they might labour under, but may tend to obstruct and impede the exertion of his Majesty's benevolence and attention to the ease and comfort, as well as the welfare, of all his people.

It is hoped and expected, that this want of confidence in the justice and tenderness of the mother country, and this open resistance to its authority, can only have found place among the lower and more ignorant of the people. The better and wiser part of the colonies will know, that decency and submission may prevail, not only to redress grievances, but to obtain grace and favour, while the outrage of a public violence can expect nothing but severity and chastisement. These sentiments you, and all his Majesty's servants, from a sense of your duty to, and love of, your country, will endeavour to excite and encourage.

You will all, in a particular manner, call upon them not to render their case desperate. You will, in the strongest colours, represent to them the dreadful consequences that must inevitably attend the forcible and violent resistance to acts of the *British* Parliament, and the scene of misery and calamity to themselves, and of mutual weakness and distraction to both countries, inseparable from such a conduct.

If, by lenient and persuasive methods, you can contribute to restore that peace and tranquillity to the provinces, on which depend their welfare and happiness, you will do a most acceptable and essential service to your country: but having taken every step which the utmost prudence and lenity can dictate, in compassion to the folly and ignorance of some misguided people, you will not,

on

on the other hand, fail to use your utmost power, for repelling all acts of outrage and violence, and to provide for the maintenance of peace and good order in the province, by such a timely exertion of force as the occasion may require; for which purpose, you will make the proper applications to General *Gage*, or Lord *Colvil*, commanders of his Majesty's land and naval forces in *America*. For however unwillingly his Majesty may consent to the exertion of such powers as may endanger the safety of a single subject; yet can he not permit his own dignity, and the authority of the *British* legislature, to be trampled on by force and violence, and in avowed contempt of all order, duty and decorum.

If the subject is aggrieved, he knows in what manner legally and constitutionally to apply for relief; but it is not suitable, either to the safety or dignity of the *British* empire, that any individuals, under the pretence of redressing grievances, should presume to violate the public peace.

I am, &c.

H. S. CONWAY.

P. S. *To Governor* WILMOT.

You will probably receive application from Governor *Bernard*, to send him part of the force which may be within your government. Lord *Colvil* has command to transport them; and you will be very attentive, that the public service should suffer no impediment from any delay in you, when such application is made.

Extract of a Letter from Mr. Secretary Conway, *to Major General* Gage.

December 15, 1765.

SIR,

I had the favour of your letters of the 4th, 8th, and 9th of *November* last, by which I learn, with the utmost concern, the disordered state of the Province where you reside, and the very riotous and outrageous behaviour of too many of the inhabitants.

I did not fail to lay your dispatches, together with those of Lieutenant Governor *Colden*, before his Majesty, who, though highly provoked by such an insult offered to his Governor there, is however pleased to hear, that matters were not pushed to such extremity, as might have cost the lives of many of his subjects, and perhaps have
tended

tended, as you seem apprehensive, to the great detriment, if not ruin, of the town of *New-York*; particularly if the fort had fired on that insolent and infatuated mob which so provokingly approached. The temper shewn, as well by Lieutenant Governor *Colden*, as by the officers there, is highly to be commended. His Majesty is willing to suppose, that both yourself and Governor *Colden* have acted on principles of duty to his service, in the advice and resolution formed to put the stampt paper into the hands of the magistrates of *New-York*; which, however, unless the necessity for it appeared very pressing, must certainly be looked upon as a step greatly humiliating and derogating to his Majesty's government.

If the post was not tenable, or the papers insecure there, it should seem much preferable to have put them on board the man of war, as was proposed: nor does there appear any good reason, why Captain *Kennedy* refused to take them. It is difficult, at this distance, to judge with the same propriety of the conduct, to be held on occasions of such difficulty and importance, as on the spot. Had the personal safety of those in the fort alone been considered, I am persuaded, there would not have been a moment's hesitation about the defence of it, against any attack that might rashly have been attempted: nor can his Majesty suppose any want of resolution for his service, in those who have, in their different stations, given so many proofs of their regard to it. It should otherwise seem, that the reality of the mobs being armed and prepared for an actual attack, should have been well ascertained before the papers were given up.

The step you have thought fit to take, in drawing together such forces as their situation allowed, was certainly prudent, and could not be too soon determined, on any positive grounds, to suspect an insurrection; and especially in regard to the securing his Majesty's stores, a circumstance which will still demand your greatest attention; and particularly those arms, which may be seized by the mob for their own mutinous purposes.

Your situation is certainly delicate and difficult; it requires both prudence and firmness in the conduct of all employed in his Majesty's service there; especially, considering what you say of the difficulty, or rather impossibility, of drawing any considerable number of men together, and of the impracticability of attempting any
thing

thing by force, in the present disposition of the people, without a respectable body of troops.

You seem to think there are still hopes, that as the spirits of those unhappy people have time to cool, there will be more submission shewn; you will not fail, I am persuaded, in your station, to avail yourself of every favourable symptom for the improvement of such favourable dispositions, any more than to exert yourself, where the necessity of the case may require, in support of the honour of government, and for suppressing any riotous or rebellious resistance offered to the laws, or those magistrates who have the execution of them.

I hope my former letters are come safe, as they will have conveyed to you his Majesty's sentiments and commands for your conduct, on the first notice of these disturbances.

Copy of a Letter from Mr. Secretary Conway, *to Lieutenant Governor* Colden.

December 15, 1765.

SIR,

I have received your letter of the 5th of *November* by Major *James*, and that of the 9th of the same month by the pacquet, with the minutes of the council of *New-York*, from the 31st of *October* to the 6th of *November*, &c.—From your last letter, I have hopes that time will produce a recollection, which may lead these unhappy people back to a sense of their duty; and that, in the mean time, every proper and practicable measure will be taken to awe that licentious spirit, which has hurried them to those acts of outrage and violence, equally dangerous to the sober and well-disposed part of the people, the ease and quiet of the city, and subversive of all order and authority among them.

Sir *Henry Moore* will certainly be arrived before this reaches you; it is expected, therefore, Sir, from your knowledge of the country and people, that you should inform the new governor of every thing necessary for his knowledge, as well respecting the state of things, as the characters and dispositions of men in that country. He will see that, by his instructions, he is empowered to suspend members of the council, and officers of the law, who shall appear to desire it; being, in that case, only obliged to send home immediately the reasons and causes of such suspension. It is not improbable, that such times as these may require the exercise of that power: as it is not doubted the governor will use it with discretion, so it is expected he should not want firmness to use it boldly, whenever it may seem useful to the King's service and the publice peace.

Copy of the Resolutions of the House of Burgesses in Virginia, in consequence of a motion made (May 29, 1765,) to take into consideration the late act for levying a duty upon stamps.

Resolved, That the first adventurers and settlers of his Majesty's colony and dominion of *Virginia* brought with them, and transmitted to their posterity, and all other his Majesty's subjects since inhabiting in this his Majesty's said colony, all the liberties, privileges, franchises and immunities, that have at any time been held and enjoyed, and possessed by the people of *Great-Britain*.

Resolved, That, by two royal charters granted by King *James* I. the colonies aforesaid are declared entitled to all liberties, privileges and immunities of denizens and natural subjects, to all intents and purposes, as if they had been abiding and born within the realm of *England*.

Resolved, That the taxation of the people, by themselves, or by persons chosen by themselves to represent them, who can only know what taxes the people are able to bear, or the easiest method of raising them, and must themselves be affected by every tax laid on the people, is the only security against a burthensome taxation, and the distinguishing characteristic of *British* freedom, without which the antient constitution cannot exist.

Resolved, That his Majesty's liege people of this his most antient and loyal colony have, without interruption, enjoyed the inestimable right of being governed by such laws, respecting their internal polity and taxation, as are derived from their own consent, with the approbation of their sovereign, or his substitutes, and that the same hath been constantly recognized by the King and people of *Great Britain*.

Oct. 1, 1765.

Copy of a representation of the Lords Commissioners for Trade and Plantations, touching the proceedings and resolutions of the House of Representatives of Massachuset's Bay, with respect to the act for levying a duty upon stamps in America, and to other acts of the Parliament of Great Britain.

To the KING's Most Excellent Majesty.

May it please your Majesty,

The House of representatives of your Majesty's province of *Massachuset's Bay* having, last year, printed and published, in the journals of their proceedings, a letter from a committee of that house to their agent here; in which letter the acts and resolutions of the Parliament of *Great Britain* were treated with the most indecent disrespect, and principles tending to a denial of the right of parliament to levy taxes upon your Majesty's subjects in the colonies, were openly avowed; our predecessors in office thought it their duty to transmit this transaction to your Majesty's consideration, to the end that such directions might be given, as the nature and importance of the matter should appear to require.

Since this, and since the passing the act of Parliament for levying a stamp duty in *America*, the grounds of which act gave rise to the reflexions contained in the above-mentioned letter, the same spirit that dictated the sentiments it expresses, has appeared throughout the whole proceedings of the said house of representatives.

Upon the election of counsellors, who, by the constitution of this colony, are annually chosen by the house of representatives, the strongest endeavours were used to preclude your Majesty's secretary of state, who has always been a member of the council, from his seat at that board; and this, as your Majesty's governor represents, merely on account of his having received an appointment (unsolicited) to be a distributor of the stamps: and the motion made in that house, to discontinue the annual salary allowed for the support of your Majesty's governor, upon which proceeding we have this day made a separate representation to your Majesty, seems to have arisen from the same motives.

These, however, being only attempts of individuals in the community, would not either have required or deserved your Majesty's attention, in the light in which we view them; but it further appears, from the journals of the house of representatives in their last session, that *this assembly*,

PARLIAMENTARY A, 1766.

assembly, having thought fit to make the propriety and expediency of the stamp-act, and of other acts of Parliament, a subject of open question and discussion, came to several resolutions and proceedings thereupon, which they kept secret till the last day of their session, when they published them in their printed journals.—Then follow the resolutions—Then the board of trade proceeds thus: the object of the resolutions and proceedings of *the house of representatives of* Massachuset's *bay*, is to recommend to, and induce, the rest of your Majesty's colonies in *America*, to join in *a general congress of committees from the several assemblies, independent of the other branches of the legislature, and without any previous application to your Majesty, to consider and deliberate upon the acts of the Parliament of this kingdom.* As this appears to us to be the first instance of a general congress, appointed by the assemblies of the colonies without the authority of the crown; a measure which we conceive of dangerous tendency in itself, and more especially so, when taken for the purposes expressed in the above-mentioned resolution, and connected with the spirit that has appeared throughout the whole conduct of this particular assembly; we therefore think it our indispensible duty to submit this matter to your Majesty's consideration, for such directions as your Majesty, with the advice of your council, may think proper and expedient to give thereupon.

All which is most humbly submitted, &c.

Whitehall, Oct. 1. 1765.

Copy of a representation from the Board of Trade, relative to the outrageous behaviour of the people at the town of Boston, *in opposition to the stamp-duty act.* Dated Oct 10, 1765.

To the KING's *Most Excellent Majesty.*

May it please your Majesty,

Since our humble representation to your Majesty of the first instant, in consequence of some alarming proceedings of the house of representatives, in the province of *Massachuset's* bay, we have received letters from———*, giving an account of a riot of a most dangerous tendency, which

---

* Some blanks have been left to prevent an improper discovery of persons. It is hoped this will be excused when the reason is given in the words of one of the writers of intelligence to the ministry, upon this subject. He says, " I shall communicate things as they happen, although at the risk of " my life; for the party, by their tools, frequently give out, that if they " knew the man that would so far assist Great-Britain, as to inform " against any man, in this or any other province, he should not live many " hours."

which had arisen in the town of *Boston*, and which, directing its fury against the houses and persons of the Lieutenant-governor, and other principal officers of government, continued with repeated acts of extraordinary violence, from the 15th of *August* to the 26th of the same month; at which period the tumult seemed suspended, rather than allayed.

In whatever light these disturbances may be viewed, whether in respect of the avowed object, which the perpetrators and abettors of them declare to be a general resolution, to oppose and prevent the execution of an act of the Parliament of *Great-Britain*, or in respect of the state of government and magistracy there, which —— represents to be utterly incapable of resisting or suppressing these tumults and disorders, they seem to us of such high importance, that we lose no time in laying the letters and papers relating thereunto before your Majesty, that your Majesty may direct such measures to be pursued, as your Majesty, with the advice of your council, shall think most prudent and effectual.

Which is most humbly submitted, &c.

Extract of a letter from ——, *to Mr. Secretary* Conway.
New-York, Sept. 23, 1765.

The resolves of the assembly of *Virginia*, which you will have seen, gave the signal for a general out-cry over the continent; and though I do not find, that the assembly of any other province has yet come to resolutions of the same tendency, they have been applauded as the protectors and assertors of *American* liberty; and all persons excited and encouraged by writings in the public papers, and speeches, without any reserve, to oppose the execution of the act: the general scheme concerted throughout seems to have been, first, by menace or force, to oblige the stamp-officers to resign their employments, in which they have generally succeeded; and next, to destroy the stampt papers upon their arrival; that, having no stamps, necessity might be an excuse for the dispatch of business without them; and that, before they could be replaced, the clamour and outcry of the people, with addresses and remonstrances from the assemblies, might procure a repeal of the act. The populace of *Boston* took the lead in the riots, and by an assault upon the house of the stamp officer, forced him to a resignation. The little turbulent colony of *Rhode-Island* raised their mob likewise; who were not content only to force a promise from the person appointed to distribute the stamps, that he would not act in that employment, but also assaulted and destroyed the houses and furniture of Mess. *Howard* and *Moffatt*, and obliged them to fly for safety on board a ship of war: the first, a lawyer of reputation, *had wrote in defence of the rights of the Parliament of* Great-Britain *to lay taxes upon the colonies*; the other a physician, who had supported the same in his conversations. The neighbouring provinces seemed inclined to follow these examples, but were prevented by the almost general resignation of the stamp officers. The *Boston* mob, raised first by the instigation of many of the principal inhabitants, allured by plunder, rose shortly after of their own accord; attacked, robbed, and destroyed several houses, and amongst others, that of the Lieutenant-governor, and only spared the Governor's, because his effects had been removed. People then began to be terrified at the spirit they had raised; to perceive that popular fury was not to be guided, and each individual feared he might be the next victim to their rapacity. The same fears spread through the other provinces, *and there has been as much pains taken since, to prevent insurrections of the people, as before to excite them.*

Extract of a state of the province, contained in a letter to Mr. Conway, *dated*, Dec. 13, 1765.

The gentlemen of the law make the second class, in which are properly included both the bench and the bar; both of them act on the same principles, and are of the most distinguished families in the policy of the province.

The merchants make the third class; *many of them have suddenly rose from the lowest rank of the people to considerable fortunes, and chiefly in the last war, by illicit trade; they abhor every limitation of trade and duties, and therefore gladly go into every measure, whereby they hope to have trade free.*

The gentlemen of the law, both the judges, and the principal practitioners at the bar, are either owners, or strongly connected in family interest with the proprietors in general.—The gentlemen of the law, some years since, entered into an association, with intention among other things, to assume the direction of government upon them, by the influence they had in the assembly; gained by their family connection, and by the profession of the law,

whereby

whereby they are unavoidably in the secrets of many families. Many court their friendship, and all dread their hatred; by these means, though few of them are members, they rule the house of the assembly, in all matters of importance; the greatest number of the assembly being common farmers, who know little of men and things, and are easily deluded and seduced.

By this association, united in interest and family connections with the proprietors of the great tracks, a domination of lawyers was formed in this province, which, for some years past, has been too strong for the executive powers of government.—Besides what is before related, it is necessary to observe, that, for several years past, the assembly grants the support of power only from year to year; they increase and lessen the salaries of all the officers at their pleasure; and the bill passed in the house of assembly (the author means the House of Commons) in the last sessions of Parliament, laying internal taxes on the colony, and paying all the officers of government, as it is suggested they may intend to do, will destroy the great and undue influence, which the assembly has gained over the administration, to the great prejudice of his Majesty's prerogative in the colonies; *and it is chiefly for this reason that the popular leaders so violently oppose the act for laying a stamp duty.*

Extract of a letter to the Lords of Trade, dated August 15, 1766.

Yesterday morning, at break of day, was discovered hanging upon a tree, in a street in the town, an effigy, with inscriptions, shewing, that it was intended to represent Mr. *Oliver* the secretary, who had lately accepted the office of stamp distributor. Some of the neighbours offered to take it down, but they were given to know, that would not be permitted. Many gentlemen, especially some of the council, treated it as a boyish sport, that did not deserve the notice of the governor and council. However, the Lieutenant-governor, as chief justice, directed the Sheriff to order his officers to take down the effigy; and a council was appointed to meet in the afternoon, to consider what should be done, if the Sheriff's officers were obstructed in removing the effigy.

Before the council met, the Sheriff reported, that his officers had endeavoured to take down the effigy, but
could

could not do it without imminent danger of their lives. The council met, reprefented this tranfaction as the beginning of much greater commotions, and defired their advice what fhould be done upon this occafion. A majority of the council fpoke in form againft doing any thing; but upon very different principles: fome faid it was a trifling bufinefs, which, if let alone, would fubfide of itfelf; but if taken notice of, would become a ferious affair. Others faid, it was a ferious affair already: that it was a preconcerted bufinefs, in which the greateft part of the town was engaged: that there was no force to oppofe it, and making an oppofition to it, without a power to fupport the oppofition, would only enflame the people, and be a means of extending the mifchief to perfons not at prefent the objects of it.—The Sheriff was ordered to affemble the peace-officers, and preferve the peace; a matter of form, rather than real fignificance.

It now grew dark; when the mob, which had been gathering all the afternoon, came down to the town-houfe, bringing the effigy with them; and, knowing that they were fitting in the council-chamber, they gave three huzzas, by way of defiance, and paffed on. From thence they went to a new building, lately erected by Mr. *Oliver* to let out for fhops, and not quite finifhed: this they called the ftamp-office, and pulled it down to the ground in five minutes. From thence they went to Mr. *Oliver*'s houfe, before which they beheaded the effigy, and broke all the windows next the ftreet. Then they carried the effigy to *Fort Hill*, near Mr. *Oliver*'s houfe, where they burnt the effigy in a bonfire, made of the timber they had pulled down from the building. Mr. *Oliver* had removed his family from his houfe, and remained himfelf with a few friends, when the mob returned to attack the houfe.

Mr. *Oliver* was prevailed upon to retire, and his friends kept poffeffion of the houfe: the mob finding the door barricaded, broke down the whole fence of the garden towards *Fort Hill*; and coming on, beat all the doors and windows of the garden front, and entered the houfe, the gentlemen there retiring. As foon as they had got poffeffion, they fearched about for Mr. *Oliver*, declaring they would kill him. Finding that he had left the houfe, a party fet out to fearch two neighbouring houfes, in one of of which Mr. *Oliver* was; but, happily, they were diverted from this pursuit by a gentleman telling them, that Mr. *Oliver* was gone with the Governor to the castle; otherwise he would certainly have been murdered. After eleven o'clock, the mob seeming to grow quiet, the Lieutenant-governor, Chief Justice, and the Sheriff, ventured to go to Mr. *Oliver*'s house, to endeavour to persuade them to disperse: as soon as they began to speak, a ringleader cried out, "The Governor and the Sheriff!---to your arms, my boys;" presently after, a volley of stones followed, and the two gentlemen narrowly escaped, through favour of the night, not without some bruises. I should have mentioned before, that a written order was sent to the Colonel of the regiment of militia, to beat an alarm: he answered, that it would signify nothing, for, as soon as the drum was heard, the drummer would be knocked down, and the drum broke: he added, that probably all the drummers of the regiment were in the mob. Nothing more being to be done, the mob were left to disperse at their own time, which they did about twelve o'clock.---Whilst I am writing, I saw a bonfire burning on *Fort Hill*, by which I understand the mob is up, and probably doing mischief; I shall therefore discontinue this letter till I can receive information of what is done this night.

August 16.

In the afternoon of yesterday, several gentlemen applied to Mr. *Oliver*, to advise him to make a public declaration, that he would resign the office, and never act in it; without which they said his house would be immediately destroyed, and his life in continual danger: upon which he was obliged to authorize some gentlemen to declare in public, that he would immediately apply for leave to resign, and would not act in the office (as indeed it was impossible for him to do) until he received further orders.

August 22.

I come now to pursue the subject of my letter, dated the 15th and 16th instant.---It is difficult to conceive the fury, which at present possesses the people of *Boston*, of all orders and degrees of men: if a gentleman, in common conversation, signifies his disapprobation of this insurrection, his person is immediately in danger. A gentleman having said, that, notwithstanding what was passed,

passed, he would accept of the stamp-office, a day was fixed for pulling down his house; it was prevented not without difficulty. Another gentleman having mentioned his expectation, that some regular forces would be sent into town, was obliged to make intercession to prevent his being mobbed. A Minister of the church of *England* having, in his sermon, obliquely condemned these proceedings, has been threatened with the resentment of the people. On the other hand, a Minister of one of the principal meetings told Mr. *Oliver*, that though he was sorry this mischief had fell upon him, yet it was a very proper and necessary proceeding, and he quite approved of it. Another congregational Minister, well known by his late polemical writings, has, as I have been told by several persons, justified this proceeding in his sermon, and prayed for its success: but there are congregational Ministers, I doubt not, (and I know some) who condemn it, but they dare not speak out, which is the case of every one who does not approve of it.---I would not willingly aggravate matters, but I really fear much worse to come than is passed: the Sheriff of this county, a prudent and resolute man, has told me, that he was applied to by some friends, who would have persuaded him to resign his office, for it would soon become dangerous for a civil officer to appear; and that both his deputies at *Boston* had applied to resign. The first of *November* is appointed for a grand jubilee; when, I suppose, there will be much mischief done, and vengeance wrecked upon those who remain friends to government.

August 31, 1765.

It is with the utmost concern, that I am obliged to continue the subject of my last letters of the 15th and 16th, and of the 22d inst. the disorders of the town having been carried to much greater lengths than what I have informed your Lordships of.

After the demolition of Mr. *Oliver*'s house was found so practicable and easy, and that the government was obliged to look on, without being able to take any one step to prevent it, and the principal people of the town publickly avowed and justified the act, the mob, both great and small, became highly elated, and all kinds of ill-humours were set on foot: every thing that, for years past, had been the cause of any unpopular discontent

tent, was revived; and private resentments against persons in office worked themselves in, and endeavoured to exert themselves under the mask of the public cause.

On *Monday, August* 26, there was some small rumour, that mischief would be done that night; but it was in general disregarded. Towards evening, some boys began to light a bonfire before the town-house, which is an usual signal for a mob. Before it was quite dark, a great company of people gathered together, crying, *Liberty and Property*; which is their usual notice of their intention to plunder and pull down an house. They went first to Mr. *Paxton*'s house, who is marshal of the court of admiralty, and surveyor of the port; and finding before it the owner of the house (Mr. *Paxton* being only a tenant) he assured them, that Mr. *Paxton* had quitted the house with his best effects, and that the house was his; that he had never injured them, and finally, invited them to go to the tavern and drink a barrel of punch: the offer was accepted, and so that house was saved. As soon as they had drank the punch, they went to the house of Mr. *Storey*, register-deputy of the admiralty, broke into it, and broke it all to pieces, and took out all the books and papers, among which were all the records of the court of admiralty, and carried them to the bonfire, and there burnt them: they also looked about for him with an intention to kill him. From thence they went to Mr. *Hollowell*'s, comptroller of the customs, broke into his house, and destroyed and carried off every thing of value, with about thirty pounds, sterling, in cash. This house was lately built by himself, and fitted and furnished with great elegance. But the grand mischief of all was to come.

The Lieutenant-governor had been apprized, that there was an evil spirit gone forth against him; but, being conscious that he had not in the least deserved to be made a party, in regard to the stamp act or the custom-house, he rested in full security that the mob would not attack him; and he was at supper with his family when he received advice that the mob was coming to him. He immediately sent away his children, and determined to stay in the house himself: but, happily, his eldest daughter returned, and declared she would not stir from the house, unless he went with her; by which means she got him away, which was undoubtedly the occasion of saving his life. For, as soon as the mob had got into the house, with a most irresistible fury, they immediately looked about for him, to murder him, and even made diligent enquiry whither he was gone. They went to work with a rage scarce to be exemplified by the most savage people. Every thing moveable was destroyed in the most minute manner, except such things of value as were worth carrying off; among which were near 1000*l.* sterling, in specie, besides a great quantity of family plate, &c. But the loss to be most lamented is, that there was in one room, kept for that purpose, a large and valuable collection of manuscripts and original papers, which he had been gathering all his life-time, and to which all persons, who had been in possession of valuable papers of a public kind, had been contributing, as to a public museum. As these related to the history and policy of the country, from the time of its settlement to the present time, and was the only collection of its kind, the loss to the public is great and irretrievable, as it is to himself, the loss of the papers of a family, which had made a figure in this province for a hundred and thirty years. As for the house, which, from its structure and inside finishing, seemed to be from a design of *Inigo Jones*, or his successor, it appears, that they were a long while resolved to level it to the ground: they worked three hours at the cupola before they could get it down, and they uncovered part of the roof; but I suppose, that the thickness of the walls, which were of very fine brick-work, adorned with ionic pilasters worked into the wall, prevented their compleating their purpose, though they worked at it till day-light. The next day, the streets were found scattered with money, plate, gold rings, &c. which had been dropt in carrying off. The whole loss in this house is reckoned at 3000*l.* sterling.---It was now becoming a war of plunder, of general levelling, and taking away the distinction of rich and poor: so that those gentlemen, who had promoted and approved the cruel treatment of Mr. *Oliver*, became now as fearful for themselves as the most loyal person in the town could be.---When first the town took this new turn, I was in hopes that they would have disavowed all the riotous proceedings; that of the first night, as well as the last. But it is no such thing; great pains are taken to separate the two riots: what was done against Mr. *Oliver*

Oliver is still approved of, as a necessary declaration of their resolution not to submit to the stamp-act; and even the cruel treatment of him and his family is justified by its consequences, the frightening him into a resignation: and it has been publickly hinted, that if a line is not drawn between the first riot and the last, the civil power will not be supported by the principal people of the town, as it is assured it shall be now.---So that the present authority of the government is only exercised upon condition, and with prescribed limitations.

Philadelphia. In Assembly, Sept. 21. 1765, A. M.

The house taking into consideration, that an act of Parliament has lately passed in *England*, for imposing certain stamp-duties, and other duties, on his Majesty's subjects in *America*, whereby they conceive some of their most essential and valuable rights as *British* subjects to be deeply affected, think it a duty they owe to themselves and their posterity, to come to the following resolutions, *viz.*

Resolved, *nem. con.* That the assemblies of this province have, from time to time, *whenever requisitions have been made by his Majesty for carrying on military operations for the defence of America*, most chearfully and liberally contributed their full proportion of men and money for those services.

Resolved, *nem. con.* That whenever his Majesty's service shall, for the future, require the aids of the inhabitants of this province, and *they shall be called upon for that purpose in a constitutional way*, it will be their indispensible duty, most chearfully and liberally to grant to his Majesty their proportion of men and money, for the defence, security, and other public services of the *British American* colonies.

Resolved, *nem. con.* That the inhabitants of this province are entitled to all the liberties, rights, and privileges of his Majesty's subjects in *Great-Britain* or elsewhere; and that the constitution of government in this province is founded on the natural rights of mankind, and the noble principles of *English* liberty, and therefore is, or ought to be, perfectly free.

Resolved, *nem. con.* That it is the interest, birthright, and indubitable privilege of every *British* subject, to be taxed only by his own consent, or that of his legal representatives,

presentatives, in conjunction with his Majesty, or his substitutes.

Resolved, *nem. con.* That *the only legal representatives of the inhabitants of this province are the persons they annually elect, to serve as members of assembly.*

Resolved therefore, *nem. con.* That *the taxation of the people of this province, by any other persons whatsoever than such their representatives in assembly, is unconstitutional, and subversive of their most valuable rights.*

Resolved, *nem. con.* That the laying taxes upon the inhabitants of this province in any other manner, *being manifestly subversive of public liberty*, must, of necessary consequence, be utterly destructive of public happiness.

Resolved, *nem. con.* That the resting an authority, in the courts of admiralty, to decide, in suits relating to the stamp duties, and other matters, foreign to their proper jurisdiction, is highly dangerous to the liberties of his Majesty's *American* subjects, contrary to Magna Charta; the great charter and fountain of *English* liberty, and destructive of one of their most darling and acknowledged rights, that of trials by juries.

Resolved, *nem. con.* That it is the opinion of this house, that the restraints, imposed by several late acts of parliament, on the trade of this province, at a time when the people labour under an enormous debt, must, of necessity, be attended with the most fatal consequences; not only to this province, but to the trade of our mother country.

Resolved, *nem. con.* That this house think it their duty thus firmly to assert, *with modesty and decency*, their inherent rights, that their posterity may learn and know that it was not with their consent and acquiescence, that *any taxes should be levied on them by any person, but their own representatives*; and are desirous, that these their resolves should remain on their minutes, as a testimony of the zeal and ardent desire of the present house of assembly, to preserve their inestimable rights, which, as *Englishmen*, they have possessed ever since this province was settled, and to transmit them to their latest posterity.

On the 17th of *January*, 1766, was presented to the House and read a petition of the merchants of *London*, trading to *North America*, setting forth, " that the petitioners had been long concerned in carrying

carrying on the trade between this country and the *British* colonies on the continent of *North America*; and that they had annually exported very large quantities of *British* manufactures, confisting of woollen goods of all kinds, cottons, linens, hardware, shoes, houshold furniture, and almost without exception, of every other species of goods manufactured in these kingdoms, beside other articles imported from abroad, chiefly purchased with our manufactures and with the produce of our colonies; by all which, many thousand manufacturers, seamen and labourers, had been employed, to the very great and increasing benefit of this nation; and that, in return for these exports, the petitioners had received from the colonies, rice, indico, tobacco, naval stores, oil, whale fins, furrs, and lately potash, with other commodities, beside remittances by bills of exchange and bullion obtained by the colonists in payment for articles of their produce, not required for the *British* market, and therefore exported to other places; and that from the nature of this trade, confisting of *British* manufactures exported, and of the import of raw materials from *America*, many of them used in our manufactures, and all of them tending to lessen our dependence on neighbouring states, it must be deemed of the highest importance in the commercial system of this nation; and that this commerce so beneficial to the state, and so necessary for the support of multitudes, then lay under such difficulties and discouragements, that nothing less than its utter ruin was apprehended, without the immediate interposition of Parliament; and that, in consequence of the trade between the colonies and the mother country, as established and as permitted for many years, and of the experience which the petitioners had long had of the readiness of the *Americans* to make their just remittances, to the utmost of their real ability, they had been induced to make and venture such large exportations of *British* manufactures, as to leave the colonies indebted to the merchants of *Great Britain* in the sum of several millions sterling; and that now the colonists, when pressed for payment, appeal to past experience, in proof of their willingness; but declare it is not in their power, at present, to make good their engagements, alledging that the taxes and restrictions laid upon them, and the extension of the jurisdiction of vice-admiralty courts established by some late acts of parliament, particularly by an act passed in the 4th year of his present Majesty, for granting certain duties in the *British* colonies and plantations in *America*, and by an act passed in the 5th year of his present Majesty, for granting and applying certain stamp duties, and other duties in the *British* colonies and plantations in *America*, with several regulations and restraints, which if founded in acts of Parliament for defined purposes, they represent to have been extended in such a manner as to disturb legal commerce and harrass the fair trader, and to have so far interrupted the usual and former most fruitful branches of their commerce, restrained the sale of their produce, thrown the state of the several provinces into confusion, and brought on so great a number of actual bankruptcies, that the former opportunities and means of remittances and payments were utterly lost and taken from them; and that the petitioners were by these unhappy events, reduced to the necessity of applying to the house, in order to secure themselves and their families from impending ruin; to prevent a multitude of manufacturers from becoming a burthen to the community, or else seeking their bread in other countries, to the irretrievable loss of this kingdom; and to preserve the strength of this nation intire, its commerce flourishing, the revenues increasing, our navigation, the bulwark

of

of the kingdom, in a state of growth and extension, and the colonies, from inclination, duty and interest, firmly attached to the mother country; and therefore praying the consideration of the premises, and intreating such relief as to the house should seem expedient."

This petition was referred to a committee of the whole house, as were also the following petitions, *viz.* Of the master, wardens, and commonalty, of the society of merchants venturers of the city of *Bristol*, under their common seal; of the merchants, tradesmen and manufacturers of the same city; of the merchants of *Liverpoole*, trading to and from *America* and the coast of *Africa*; of the merchants, tradesmen and manufacturers of the town and parish of *Halifax*; of the merchants and inhabitants of the borough of *Leeds*, trading to the several colonies of *North America*, and of the manufacturers of broad woollen cloth, and sundry other assortments of woollen goods, manufactured for supplying the *North American* markets; of the merchants of *Lancaster* trading to and from *North America*; of the merchants, manufacturers, and traders of the town of *Manchester*, and neighbourhood thereof; of the manufacturers of the town and county of *Leicester*; and of the clothiers and manufacturers of superfine broad cloth, in the town of *Bradford* in *Wiltshire*; all complaining of a great decay in the trade to the *North American* colonies, owing to the late obstructions and embarrassments laid thereon, and praying relief.

And afterwards there were presented to the House and read, and referred to the same committee, the following petitions, *viz.* of the principal inhabitants of the town of *Frome*; of the merchants, factors, and manufacturers of *Birmingham*; of the mayor, bailiffs, and commonalty, of the city of *Coventry*, and the principal tradesmen and manufacturers of silk ribbands and worsted goods, in and near the said city, whose common seal and names are thereunto respectively affixed, in behalf of themselves and others concerned in the said manufactures; of the merchants and dealers in the silk, mohair, and button manufactures, residing in the town of *Macclesfield*; of the merchants, traders, and manufacturers of *Wolverhampton*; of the merchants, traders, and manufacturers of *Stourbridge*; of the merchants and manufacturers of *Dudley*; of the tradesmen, manufacturers, &c. of the borough of *Minehead*; of the mayor, aldermen, burgesses, principal inhabitants, and traders in the woollen manufactory in *Taunton*; of the master, wardens, and commonalty of blanket weavers in *Witney*; of the mayor, recorder, aldermen, sheriff, and commonalty of the town and county of the town of *Newcastle upon Tyne*; of the merchants of *Glasgow* trading to *North America*; of the bailiff and burgesses of *Chippenham*; and of the principal tradesmen, manufacturers, and inhabitants of the town of *Nottingham*; all containing much the same complaint as in the former petitions, and concluding with the same prayer.

In giving this list of petitions we have been the more particular, as it not only shews how much the people even of this kingdom were interested in this affair, but also it shews how diligent the merchants and factors of *London* had been in procuring petitions upon this occasion from all parts of the kingdom; which shews how cautious ministers should be of adopting any scheme or measure which may affect the immediate interest of a great number of particular men.

On the 28th of *January*, 1766, the House resolved itself into a committee of the whole House, to consider of the petitions and papers; and on that day, the 29th, and 31st of *January*, and on the

the 3d, 5th, 7th, 10th, 11th, 12th, 13th, 17th, 18th, and 21ft, of *February*, on some of which days the committee continued sitting till after one o'clock in the morning. During this time great numbers of other petitions, letters and papers were laid before the house; particularly a petition of *Stephen Fuller*, Esq; agent of the island of *Jamaica* setting forth that in the year 1760, there broke out two rebellions in the said island, which threatened not only the destruction of the inhabitants, but the loss of that valuable colony to *Great Britain*; and that after the said rebellions, the assembly of the said island thought proper, in order to defray the expence that increased on account thereof, to lay a tax by way of stamps, which tax was laid in the year 1760, and continued till *December* 1763, when that law was suffered to expire, on account, as the petitioner is informed, and believes, of its being unequal and burthensome, as it certainly was in a high degree; and that the petitioner most humbly conceiving, that the act for imposing certain stamp duties, in the *British* colonies and plantations in *America*, will be attended with the same inconveniences, if not greater (on account that the forfeitures and penalties incurred may be sued for and recovered in any court of record, or in court of admiralty or vice admiralty in the island, at the election of the informer or prosecutor) prayed such relief in the premises, as to the house should seem meet.

There had also on the 21ft of *January* been presented and read a petition of *Edward Montagu*, agent for the colony of *Virginia*, and a petition of *William Knox*, agent for the province of *Georgia*, representing the inability of these provinces to pay the stamp duty; which three petitions were the only petitions presented this session in the name of any of the colonies.

The

The House, in committee, not only examined the petitions and papers laid before them, but also several persons whom they ordered to attend; and among them was Doctor *Benjamin Franklin*; whose examination being curious and interesting, it is here inserted from an accurate copy.

Q. What is your name, and place of abode?
A. *Franklin*, of *Philadelphia*.

Q. Do the *Americans* pay any considerable taxes among themselves?
A. Certainly many, and very heavy taxes.

Q. What are the present taxes in *Pennsylvania*, laid by the laws of the colony?
A. There are taxes on all estates real and personal, a poll-tax, a tax on all offices, professions, trades and businesses, according to their profits; an excise on all wine, rum, and other spirits; and a duty of ten pounds per head on all negroes imported, with some other duties.

Q. For what purposes are those taxes laid?
A. For the support of the civil and military establishments of the country, and to discharge the heavy debt contracted in the last war.

Q. How long are those taxes to continue?
A. Those for discharging the debt are to continue till 1772, and longer, if the debt should not be then all discharged. The others must always continue.

Q. Was it not expected that the debt would have been sooner discharged?
A. It was, when the peace was made with *France* and *Spain*---But a fresh war breaking out with the *Indians*, a fresh load of debt was incurred, and the taxes, of course, continued longer by a new law.

Q. Are not all the people very able to pay those taxes?
A. No.

A. No. The frontier counties, all along the continent, having been frequently ravaged by the enemy, and greatly impoverished, are able to pay very little tax. And therefore, in consideration of their distresses, our late tax laws do expresly favour those counties, excusing the sufferers; and I suppose the same is done in other governments.

Q. Are not you concerned in the management of the post-office in *America?*

A. Yes; I am Deputy Post-Master General of *North-America.*

Q. Don't you think the distribution of stamps, by post, to all the inhabitants, very practicable, if there was no opposition?

A. The posts only go along the sea-coasts; they do not, except in a few instances, go back into the country; and if they did, sending for stamps by post would occasion an expence of postage, amounting, in many cases, to much more than that of the stamps themselves.

Q. Are you acquainted with *Newfoundland?*

A. I never was there.

Q. Do you know whether there are any post-roads on that island?

A. I have heard that there are no roads at all; but that the communication between one settlement and another is by sea only.

Q. Can you disperse the stamps by post in *Canada?*

A. There is only a post between *Montreal* and *Quebec.* The inhabitants live so scattered and remote from each other, in that vast country, that posts cannot be supported among them, and therefore they cannot get stamps per post. The *English* colonies too, along the frontiers, are very thinly settled.

Q. From the thinness of the back settlements,
would

would not the stamp-act be extremely inconvenient to the inhabitants if executed?

A. To be sure it would; as many of the inhabitants could not get stamps when they had occasion for them, without taking long journeys, and spending perhaps, three or four pounds, that the Crown might get six pence.

Q. Are not the colonies, from their circumstances, vere able to pay the stamp duty?

A. In my opinion, there is not gold and silver enough in the colonies to pay the stamp duty for one year.

Q. Don't you know that the money arising from the stamps was all to be laid out in *America*?

A. I know it is appropriated by the act to the *American* service; but it will be spent in the conquered colonies, where the soldiers are, not in the colonies that pay it.

Q. Is there not a balance of trade due from the colonies where the troops are posted, that will bring back the money to the old colonies?

A. I think not. I believe very little would come back. I know of no trade likely to bring it back. I think it would come from the colonies where it was spent directly to *England*; for I have always observed, that in every colony the more plenty of means of remittance to *England*, the more goods are sent for, and the more trade with *England* carried on.

Q. What number of white inhabitants do you think there are in *Pennsylvania*?

A. I suppose there may be about 160,000.

Q. What number of them are Quakers?

A. Perhaps a third.

Q. What number of *Germans*?

A. Perhaps another third; but I cannot speak with certainty.

Q. Have

A. 1766. DEBATES.

Q. Have any number of the *Germans* seen service, as soldiers, in *Europe*?

A. Yes,---many of them, both in *Europe* and *America*.

Q. Are they as much dissatisfied with the stamp-duty as the *English*?

A. Yes, and more; and with reason, as their stamps are, in many cases, to be double.

Q. How many white men do you suppose there are in *North-America*?

A. About 300,000, from sixteen to sixty years of age.

Q. What may be the amount of one year's imports into *Pennsylvania* from *Britain*?

A. I have been informed that our merchants compute the imports from *Britain* to be above 500,000 pounds.

Q. What may be the amount of the produce of your province exported to *Britain*?

A. It must be small, as we produce little that is wanted in *Britain*. I suppose it cannot exceed 40,000 pounds.

Q. How then do you pay the balance?

A. The balance is paid by our produce carried to the *West-Indies*, and sold in our own islands, or to the *French*, *Spaniards*, *Danes* and *Dutch*; by the same carried to other colonies in *North-America*, as to *New-England*, *Nova-Scotia*, *New-foundland*, *Carolina* and *Georgia*; by the same carried to different parts of *Europe*, as *Spain*, *Portugal* and *Italy*. In all which places we receive either money, bills of exchange, or commodities that suit for remittance to *Britain*; which, together with all the profits on the industry of our merchants and mariners, arising in those circuitous voyages, and the freights made by their ships, center finally in *Britain* to discharge the balance, and pay for *British* manufactures continually used in the province, or sold to foreigners by our traders.

Q. Have

Q. Have you heard of any difficulties lately laid on the *Spanish* trade?

A. Yes, I have heard that it has been greatly obstructed by some new regulations, and by the *English* men of war and cutters stationed all along the coast in *America*.

Q. Do you think it right, that *America* should be protected by this country, and pay no part of the expence?

A. That is not the case. The colonies raised, cloathed and paid, during the last war, near 25,000 men, and spent many millions.

Q. Were you not reimbursed by parliament?

A. We were only reimbursed what, in your opinion, we had advanced beyond our proportion, or beyond what might reasonably be expected from us; and it was a very small part of what we spent. *Pennsylvania*, in particular, disbursed about 500,000 pounds, and the reimbursements, in the whole, did not exceed 60,000 pounds.

Q. You have said that you pay heavy taxes in *Pennsylvania*; what do they amount to in the pound?

A. The tax on all estates, real and personal, is eighteen pence in the pound, fully rated; and the tax on the profits of trades and professions, with other taxes, do, I suppose, make full half a crown in the pound.

Q. Do you know any thing of the rate of exchange in *Pennsylvania*, and whether it has fallen lately?

A. It is commonly from 170 to 175. I have heard that it has fallen lately from 175 to 162 and a half, owing, I suppose, to their lessening their orders for goods; and when their debts to this country are paid, I think the exchange will probably be at par.

Q. Do not you think the people of *America* would submit to pay the stamp-duty, if it was moderated? A. No,

A. No, never, unless compelled by force of arms.

Q. Are not the taxes in *Pennsylvania* laid on unequally, in order to burden the *English* trade, particularly the tax on professions and business?

A. It is not more burthensome in proportion than the tax on lands. It is intended, and supposed to take an equal proportion of profits.

Q. How is the assembly composed? Of what kinds of people are the members, landholders or traders?

A. It is composed of landholders, merchants and artificers.

Q. Are not the majority landholders?

A. I believe they are.

Q. Do not they, as much as possible, shift the tax off from the land, to ease that, and lay the burthen heavier on trade?

A. I have never understood it so. I never heard such a thing suggested. And indeed an attempt of that kind could answer no purpose. The merchant or trader is always skilled in figures, and ready with his pen and ink. If unequal burthens are laid on his trade, he puts an additional price on his goods; and the consumers, who are chiefly landholders, finally pay the greatest part, if not the whole.

Q. What was the temper of *America* towards *Great-Britain* before the year 1763?

A. The best in the world. They submitted willingly to the government of the Crown, and paid, in all their courts, obedience to acts of Parliament. Numerous as the people are in the several old provinces, they cost you nothing in forts, citadels, garrisons or armies, to keep them in subjection. They were governed by this country at the expence only of a little pen, ink and paper. They were led by a thread. They had not only a respect, but an affection for *Great-Britain,*

Britain, for its laws, its customs and manners, and even a fondness for its fashions, that greatly increased the commerce. Natives of *Britain* were always treated with particular regard; to be an *Old-England-man* was, of itself, a character of some respect, and gave a kind of rank among us.

Q. And what is their temper now?

A. O, very much altered.

Q. Did you ever hear the authority of Parliament to make laws for *America* questioned till lately?

A. The authority of Parliament was allowed to be valid in all laws, except such as should lay internal taxes. It was never disputed in laying duties to regulate commerce.

Q. In what proportion hath population increased in *America*?

A. I think the inhabitants of all the provinces together, taken at a medium, double in about 25 years. But their demand for *British* manufactures increases much faster, as the consumption is not merely in proportion to their numbers, but grows with the growing abilities of the same numbers to pay for them. In 1723, the whole importation from *Britain* to *Pennsylvania*, was but about 15,000 pounds sterling; it is now near half a million.

Q. In what light did the people of *America* use to consider the Parliament of *Great-Britain*?

A. They considered the Parliament as the great bulwark and security of their liberties and privileges, and always spoke of it with the utmost respect and veneration. Arbitrary ministers, they thought, might possibly, at times, attempt to oppress them; but they relied on it, that the Parliament, on application, would always give redress. They remembered, with gratitude, a strong instance of this, when a bill was brought into Parliament, with a clause, to make royal instructions

instructions laws in the colonies, which the House of Commons would not pass, and it was thrown out.

Q. And have they not still the same respect for Parliament?

A. No; it is greatly lessened.

Q. To what causes is that owing?

A. To a concurrence of causes; the restraints lately laid on their trade, by which the bringing of foreign gold and silver into the colonies was prevented; the prohibition of making paper money among themselves; and then demanding a new and heavy tax by stamps; taking away at the same time, trials by juries, and refusing to receive and hear their humble petitions.

Q. Don't you think they would submit to the stamp-act, if it was modified, the obnoxious parts taken out, and the duty reduced to some particulars, of small moment?

A. No; they will never submit to it.

Q. What do you think is the reason that the people of *America* increase faster than in *England*?

A. Because they marry younger, and more generally.

Q. Why so?

A. Because any young couple that are industrious, may easily obtain land of their own, on which they can raise a family.

Q. Are not the lower rank of people more at their ease in *America* than in *England*?

A. They may be so, if they are sober and diligent, as they are better paid for their labour.

Q. What is your opinion of a future tax, imposed on the same principle with that of the stamp-act; how would the *Americans* receive it?

A. Just as they do this. They would not pay it.

Q. Have not you heard of the resolutions of this House, and of the House of Lords, asserting the right of Parliament relating to *America*, including a power to tax the people there?

A. Yes, I have heard of such resolutions.

Q. What will be the opinion of the *Americans* on those resolutions?

A. They will think them unconstitutional and unjust.

Q. Was it an opinion in *America* before 1763, that the Parliament had no right to lay taxes and duties there?

A. I never heard any objection to the right of laying duties to regulate commerce; but a right to lay internal taxes was never supposed to be in Parliament, as we are not represented there.

Q. On what do you found your opinion, that the people in *America* made any such distinction?

A. I know that whenever the subject has occurred in conversation where I have been present, it has appeared to be the opinion of every one, that we could not be taxed in a Parliament where we were not represented. But the payment of duties laid by act of Parliament, as regulations of commerce, was never disputed.

Q. But can you name any act of assembly, or publick act of any of your governments, that made such distinction?

A. I do not know that there was any; I think there was never an occasion to make any such act, till now that you have attempted to tax us; that has occasioned resolutions of assembly, declaring the distinction, in which I think every assembly on the continent, and every member in every assembly, have been unanimous.

Q. What then could occasion conversations on that subject before that time?

A. There was in 1754, a proposition made (I think it came from hence) that in case of a war, which was then apprehended, the governors of of the colonies should meet, and order the levying of troops, building of forts, and taking every other necessary measure for the general defence; and should draw on the treasury here, for the sums expended, which were afterwards to be raised in the colonies by a general tax, to be laid on them by act of Parliament. This occasioned a good deal of conversation on the subject, and the general opinion was, that the Parliament neither would, nor could lay any tax on us, till we were duly represented in Parliament, because it was not just, nor agreeable to the nature of an *English* constitution.

Q. Don't you know there was a time in *New-York*, when it was under consideration to make an application to Parliament to lay taxes on that colony, upon a deficiency arising from the assembly's refusing or neglecting to raise the necessary supplies for the support of the civil government?

A. I never heard of it.

Q. There was such an application under consideration in *New-York*; and do you apprehend they could suppose the right of Parliament to lay a tax in *America* was only local, and confined to the case of a deficiency in a particular colony, by a refusal of its assembly to raise the necessary supplies?

A. They could not suppose such a case, as that the assembly would not raise the necessary supplies to support its own government. An assembly that would refuse it, must want common sense, which cannot be supposed. I think there was never any such case at *New-York*, and that it must be a misrepresentation, or the fact must be misunderstood. I know there have been some attempts, by ministerial instructions from hence, to oblige the assemblies to settle permanent salaries on governors, which they wisely refused to do; but I believe no assembly of *New-York*, or any other colony, ever refused duly to support government by proper allowances, from time to time, to public officers.

Q. But in case a governor, acting by instruction, should call on an assembly to raise the necessary supplies, and the assembly should refuse to do it, do you not think it would then be for the good of the people of the colony, as well as necessary to government, that the Parliament should tax them?

A. I do not think it would be necessary. If an assembly could possibly be so absurd as to refuse raising the supplies requisite for the maintenance of government among them, they could not long remain in such a situation; the disorders and confusion occasioned by it, must soon bring them to reason.

Q. If it should not, ought not the right to be in *Great-Britain* of applying a remedy?

A. A right only to be used in such a case, I should have no objection to, supposing it to be used merely for the good of the people of the colony.

Q. But who is to judge of that, *Britain* or the colony?

A. Those that feel can best judge.

Q. You say the colonies have always submitted to external taxes, and object to the right of Parliament only in laying internal taxes; now can you shew that there is any kind of difference between the two taxes to the colony on which they may be laid?

A. I think the difference is very great. An external tax is a duty laid on commodities imported; that duty is added to the first cost, and other charges on the commodity, and when it is offered to sale, makes a part of the price. If the people do not like it at that price, they refuse it; they are not obliged to pay it. But an internal

internal tax is forced from the people without their confent, if not laid by their own reprefentatives. The ftamp-act fays, we fhall have no commerce, make no exchange of property with each other, neither purchafe nor grant, nor recover debts; we fhall neither marry nor make our wills, unlefs we pay fuch fums, and thus it is intended to extort our money from us, or ruin us by the confequences of refufing to pay it.

Q. But fuppofing the internal tax or duty to be laid on the neceffaries of life imported into your colony, will not that be the fame thing in its effects as an internal tax?

A. I do not know a fingle article imported into the northern colonies, but what they can either do without, or make themfelves.

Q. Don't you think cloth from *England* abfolutely neceffary to them?

A. No, by no means abfolutely neceffary; with induftry and good management, they may very well fupply themfelves with all they want.

Q. Will it not take a long time to eftablifh that manufacture among them; and muft they not in the mean while fuffer greatly?

A. I think not. They have made a furprifing progrefs already. And I am of opinion, that before their old clothes are worn out, they will have new ones of their own making.

Q. Can they poffibly find wool enough in *North-America?*

A. They have taken fteps to increafe the wool. They entered into general combinations to eat no more lamb, and very few lambs were killed laft year. This courfe perfifted in, will foon make a prodigious difference in the quantity of wool. And the eftablifhing of great manufactories, like thofe in the clothing towns here, is not neceffary, as it is where the bufinefs is to be carried on for the purpofes of trade. The people will all spin, and work for themselves, in their own houses.

Q. Can there be wool and manufacture enough in one or two years?

A. In three years, I think, there may.

Q. Does not the severity of the winter, in the northern colonies, occasion the wool to be of bad quality?

A. No; the wool is very fine and good.

Q. In the more southern colonies, as in Virginia, don't you know that the wool is coarse, and only a kind of hair?

A. I don't know it. I never heard it. Yet I have been sometimes in *Virginia*. I cannot say I ever took particular notice of the wool there, but I believe it is good, though I cannot speak positively of it; but *Virginia*, and the colonies south of it, have less occasion for wool; their winters are short, and not very severe, and they can very well clothe themselves with linen and cotton of their own raising for the rest of the year.

Q. Are not the people in the more northern colonies obliged to fodder their sheep all the winter?

A. In some of the most northern colonies they may be obliged to do it some part of the winter.

Q. Considering the resolutions of Parliament, as the right, do you think, if the stamp-act is repealed, that the *North-Americans* will be satisfied?

A. I believe they will.

Q. Why do you think so?

A. I think the resolutions of right will give them very little concern, if they are never attempted to be carried into practice. The colonies will probably consider themselves in the same situation, in that respect, with *Ireland*; they know you claim the same right with regard to
Ireland,

Ireland, but you never exercise it. And they may believe you never will exercise it in the colonies, any more than in *Ireland*, unless on some very extraordinary occasion.

Q. But who are to be the judges of that extraordinary occasion? Is not the Parliament?

A. Though the Parliament may judge of the occasion, the people will think it can never exercise such right, till representatives from the colonies are admitted into Parliament, and that whenever the occasion arises, representatives will be ordered.

Q. Did you never hear that *Maryland*, during the last war, had refused to furnish a quota towards the common defence?

A. *Maryland* has been much misrepresented in that matter. *Maryland*, to my knowledge, never refused to contribute, or grant aids to the crown. The assemblies every year, during the war, voted considerable sums, and formed bills to raise them. The bills were, according to the constitution of that province, sent up to the council, or upper house, for concurrence, that they might be presented to the governor, in order to be enacted into laws. Unhappy disputes between the two houses, arising from the defects of that constitution principally, rendered all the bills but one or two, abortive. The proprietary's council rejected them. It is true, *Maryland* did not contribute its proportion, but it was, in my opinion, the fault of the government, not of the people.

Q. Was it not talked of in the other provinces as a proper measure to apply to Parliament to compel them?

A. I have heard such discourse; but as it was well known, that the people were not to blame, no such application was ever made, nor any step taken towards it.

Q. Was it not propofed at a public meeting?
A. Not that I know of.

Q. Do you remember the abolifhing of the paper currency in *New-England*, by act of affembly?
A. I do remember its being abolifhed, in the *Maffachufett's Bay*.

Q. Was not Lieutenant-Governor *Hutchinfon* principally concerned in that tranfaction?
A. I have heard fo.

Q. Was it not at that time a very unpopular law?
A. I believe it might, though I can fay little about it, as I lived at a diftance from that province.

Q. Was not the fcarcity of gold and filver an argument ufed againft abolifhing the paper?
A. I fuppofe it was.

Q. What is the prefent opinion there of that law? Is it as unpopular as it was at firft?
A. I think it is not.

Q. Have not inftructions from hence been fometimes fent over to governors, highly oppreffive and unpolitical?
A. Yes.

Q. Have not fome governors difpenfed with them for that reafon?
A. Yes; I have heard fo.

Q. Did the *Americans* ever difpute the controuling power of parliament to regulate the commerce?
A. No.

Q. Can any thing lefs than a military force carry the ftamp-act into execution?
A. I do not fee how a military force can be applied to that purpofe.

Q. Why may it not?
A. Suppofe a military force fent into *America*,
they

they will find nobody in arms; what are they then to do? They cannot force a man to take stamps who chuses to do without them. They will not find a rebellion; they may indeed make one.

Q. If the act is not repealed, what do you think will be the consequences?

A. A total loss of the respect and affection the people of *America* bear to this country, and of all the commerce that depends on that respect and affection.

Q. How can the commerce be affected?

A. You will find, that if the act is not repealed, they will take very little of your manufactures in a short time.

Q. Is it in their power to do without them?

A. I think they may very well do without them.

Q. Is it their interest not to take them?

A. The goods they take from *Britain* are either necessaries, mere conveniences, or superfluities. The first, as cloth, &c. with a little industry they can make at home; the second they can do without, till they are able to provide them among themselves; and the last, which are much the greatest part, they will strike off immediately. They are mere articles of fashion, purchased and consumed, because the fashion in a respected country, but will now be detested and rejected. The people have already struck off, by general agreement, the use of all goods fashionable in mournings, and many thousand pounds worth are sent back as unsaleable.

Q. Is it their interest to make cloth at home?

A. I think they may at present get it cheaper from Britain, I mean of the same fineness and neatness of workmanship; but when one considers other circumstances, the restraints on their trade, and the difficulty of making remittances, it is their interest to make every thing.

Q. Sup-

Q. Suppose an act of internal regulations connected with a tax, how would they receive it?

A. I think it would be objected to.

Q. Then no regulation with a tax would be submitted to?

A. Their opinion is, that when aids to the crown are wanted, they are to be asked of the several assemblies, according to the old established usage, who will, as they always have done, grant them freely. And that their money ought not to be given away, without their consent, by persons at a distance, unacquainted with their circumstances and abilities. The granting aids to the crown, is the only means they have of recommending themselves to their sovereign, and they think it extremely hard and unjust, that a body of men, in which they have representatives, should make a merit to itself of giving and granting what is not its own, but theirs, and deprive them of a right they esteem of the utmost value and importance, as it is the security of all their other rights.

Q. But is not the post-office, which they have long received, a tax as well as a regulation?

A. No; the money paid for the postage of a letter is not of the nature of a tax; it is merely a *quantum meruit* for a service done; no person is compellable to pay the money, if he does not chuse to receive the service. A man may still, as before the act, send his letter by a servant, a special messenger, or a friend, if he thinks it cheaper and safer.

Q. But do they not consider the regulations of the post-office, by the act of last year, as a tax?

A. By the regulations of last year the rate of postage was generally abated near thirty per cent. through all *America*; they certainly cannot consider such abatement as a tax.

Q. If an excise was laid by parliament, which they

they might likewise avoid paying, by not consuming the articles excised, would they then not object to it?

A. They would certainly object to it, as an excise is unconnected with any service done, and is merely an aid which they think ought to be asked of them, and granted by them, if they are to pay it, and can be granted for them, by no others whatsoever, whom they have not impowered for that purpose.

Q. You say they do not object to the right of parliament, in laying duties on goods to be paid on their importation; now, is there any kind of difference between a duty on the importation of goods, and an excise on their consumption?

A. Yes; a very material one; an excise, for the reasons I have just mentioned, they think you can have no right to lay within their country. But the sea is yours; you maintain, by your fleets, the safety of navigation in it, and keep it clear of pirates; you may have therefore a natural and equitable right to some toll or duty on merchandizes carried through that part of your dominions, towards defraying the expence you are at in ships to maintain the safety of that carriage.

Q. Does this reasoning hold in the case of a duty laid on the produce of their lands exported? And would they not then object to such a duty?

A. If it tended to make the produce so much dearer abroad as to lessen the demand for it, to be sure they would object to such a duty; not to your right of laying it, but they would complain of it as a burthen, and petition you to lighten it.

Q. Is not the duty paid on the tobacco exported a duty of that kind?

A. That, I think, is only on tobacco carried coast-

coastwise from one colony to another, and appropriated as a fund for supporting the college at *Williamsburgh*, in *Virginia*.

Q. Have not the assemblies in the *West-Indies* the same natural rights with those in *North-America*?

A. Undoubtedly.

Q. And is there not a tax laid there on their sugars exported?

A. I am not much acquainted with the *West-Indies*, but the duty of four and a half per cent. on sugars exported, was, I believe, granted by their own assemblies.

Q. How much is the poll-tax in your province laid on unmarried men?

A. It is, I think, fifteen shillings, to be paid by every single freeman, upwards of twenty-one years old.

Q. What is the annual amount of all the taxes in *Pennsylvania*?

A. I suppose about 20,000 pounds sterling.

Q. Supposing the stamp-act continued, and enforced, do you imagine that ill-humour will induce the *Americans* to give as much for worse manufactures of their own, and use them, preferably to better of ours?

A. Yes, I think so. People will pay as freely to gratify one passion as another, their resentment as their pride.

Q. Would the people at *Boston* discontinue their trade?

A. The merchants are a very small number, compared with the body of the people, and must discontinue their trade, if nobody will buy their goods.

Q. What are the body of the people in the colonies?

A. They are farmers, husbandmen or planters.

Q. Would

Q. Would they suffer the produce of their lands to rot?

A. No; but they would not raise so much. They would manufacture more, and plough less.

Q. Would they live without the administration of justice in civil matters, and suffer all the inconveniences of such a situation for any considerable time, rather than take the stamps, supposing the stamps were protected by a sufficient force, where every one might have them?

A. I think the supposition impracticable, that the stamps should be so protected as that every one might have them. The act requires sub-distributors to be appointed in every county town, district and village, and they would be necessary. But the principal distributors, who were to have had a considerable profit on the whole, have not thought it worth while to continue in the office, and I think it impossible to find sub-distributors fit to be trusted, who, for the trifling profit that must come to their share, would incur the odium, and run the hazard that would attend it; and if they could be found, I think it impracticable to protect the stamps in so many distant and remote places.

Q. But in places where they could be protected, would not the people use them rather than remain in such a situation, unable to obtain any right, or recover, by law, any debt?

A. It is hard to say what they would do. I can only judge what other people will think, and how they will act, by what I feel within myself. I have a great many debts due to me in *America*, and I had rather they should remain unrecoverable by any law, than submit to the stamp-act. They will be debts of honour. It is my opinion the people will either continue in that situation, or find some way to extricate themselves, perhaps by generally

nerally agreeing to proceed in the courts without stamps.

Q. What do you think a sufficient military force to protect the distribution of the stamps in every part of *America*?

A. A very great force; I can't say what, if the disposition of *America* is for a general resistance.

Q. What is the number of men in *America* able to bear arms, or of disciplined militia?

A. There are, I suppose, at least——

[*Question objected to. He withdrew. Called in again.*]

Q. Is the *American* stamp-act an equal tax on that country?

A. I think not.

Q. Why so?

A. The greatest part of the money must arise from law-suits for the recovery of debts, and be paid by the lower sort of people, who were too poor easily to pay their debts. It is therefore a heavy tax on the poor, and a tax upon them for being poor.

Q. But will not this increase of expence be a means of lessening the number of law-suits?

A. I think not; for as the costs all fall upon the debtor, and are to be paid by him, they would be no discouragement to the creditor to bring his action.

Q. Would it not have the effect of excessive usury?

A. Yes, as an oppression of the debtor.

Q. How many ships are there laden annually in *North-America* with flax-seed for *Ireland*?

A. I cannot speak to the number of ships, but I know that in 1752, 10,000 hogsheads of flax-seed, each containing 7 bushels, were exported from *Philadelphia* to *Ireland*. I suppose the quantity

tity is greatly increased since that time; and it is understood that the exportation from *New-York* is equal to that from *Philadelphia*.

Q. What becomes of the flax that grows with that flax-seed?

A. They manufacture some into coarse, and some into a middling kind of linen.

Q. Are there any slitting-mills in *America*?

A. I think there are three, but I believe only one at present employed. I suppose they will all be set to work, if the interruption of the trade continues.

Q. Are there any fulling mills there?

A. A great many.

Q. Did you never hear that a great quantity of stockings were contracted for, for the army, during the war, and manufactured in *Philadelphia*?

A. I have heard so.

Q. If the stamp-act should be repealed, would not the *Americans* think they could oblige the parliament to repeal every external tax-law now in force?

A. It is hard to answer questions what people at such a distance will think.

Q. But what do you imagine they will think were the motives of repealing the act?

A. I suppose they will think that it was repealed from a conviction of its inexpediency; and they will rely upon it, that while the same inexpediency subsists, you will never attempt to make such another.

Q. What do you mean by its inexpediency?

A. I mean its inexpediency on several accounts; the poverty and inability of those who were to pay the tax; the general discontent it has occasioned; and the impracticability of enforcing it.

Q. If the act should be repealed, and the legislature

flature should shew its resentment to the opposers of the stamp-act, would the colonies acquiesce in the authority of the legislature? What is your opinion they would do?

A. I don't doubt at all, that if the legislature repeal the stamp-act, the colonies will acquiesce in the authority.

Q. But if the legislature should think fit to ascertain its right to lay taxes, by any act laying a small tax, contrary to their opinion, would they submit to pay the tax?

A. The proceedings of the people in *America* have been considered too much together. The proceedings of the assemblies have been very different from those of the mobs, and should be distinguished, as having no connection with each other.——The assemblies have only peaceably resolved what they take to be their rights; they have not built a fort, raised a man, or provided a grain of ammunition, in order to such opposition.—— The ringleaders of riot they think ought to be punished; they would punish them themselves, if they could. Every sober, sensible man would wish to see rioters punished, as otherwise peaceable people have no security of person or estate. But as to an internal tax, how small soever, laid by the legislature here on the people there, while they have no representatives in this legislature, I think it will never be submitted to.—They will oppose it to the last.—They do not consider it as at all necessary for you to raise money on them by your taxes, because they are, and always have been, ready to raise money by taxes among themselves, and to grant large sums, equal to their abilities, upon requisition from the crown.———— They have not only granted equal to their abilities, but, during all the last war, they granted far beyond their abilities, and beyond their proportion with this country, you yourselves being

judges,

judges, to the amount of many hundred thousand pounds, and this they did freely and readily, only on a sort of promise from the secretary of state, that it should be recommended to parliament to make them compensation. It was accordingly recommended to parliament, in the most honourable manner, for them. *America* has been greatly misrepresented and abused here, in papers, and pamphlets, and speeches, as ungrateful, and unreasonable, and unjust, in having put this nation to immense expence for their defence, and refusing to bear any part of that expence. The colonies raised, paid, and clothed, near 25000 men during the last war, a number equal to those sent from *Britain*, and far beyond their proportion; they went deeply into debt in doing this, and all their taxes and estates are mortgaged, for many years to come, for discharging that debt. Government here was at that time very sensible of this. The colonies were recommended to parliament. Every year the king sent down to the house a written message to this purpose, that his majesty, being highly sensible of the zeal and vigour with which his faithful subjects in *North-America* had exerted themselves, in defence of his majesty's just rights and possessions, recommended it to the house to take the same into consideration, and enable him to give them a proper compensation. You will find those messages on your own journals every year of the war to the very last, and you did accordingly give 200,000 pounds annually to the crown, to be distributed in such compensation to the colonies. This is the strongest of all proofs that the colonies, far from being unwilling to bear a share of the burthen, did exceed their proportion; for if they had done less, or had only equalled their proportion, there would have been no room or reason for compensation.—Indeed the sums reimbursed them, were by no means adequate to the expence they incurred beyond their proportion; but they never murmured at that; they esteemed their sovereign's approbation of their zeal and fidelity, and the approbation of this house, far beyond any other kind of compensation; therefore there was no occasion for this act, to force money from a willing people; they had not refused giving money for the purposes of the act; no requisition had been made; they were always willing and ready to do what could reasonably be expected from them, and in this light they wish to be considered.

Q. But suppose *Great-Britain* should be engaged in a war in *Europe*, would *North-America* contribute to the support of it?

A. I do think they would, as far as their circumstances would permit. They consider themselves as a part of the *British* empire, and as having one common interest with it; they may be looked on here as foreigners, but they do not consider themselves as such. They are zealous for the honour and prosperity of this nation, and, while they are well used, will always be ready to support it, as far as their little power goes. In 1739 they were called upon to assist in the expedition against *Carthagena*, and they sent 3000 men to join your army. It is true *Carthagena* is in *America*, but as remote from the northern colonies as if it had been in *Europe*. They make no distinction of wars, as to their duty of assisting in them. I know the last war is commonly spoke of here as entered into for the defence, or for the sake of the people of *America*. I think it is quite misunderstood. It began about the limits between *Canada* and *Nova-Scotia*, about territories to which the crown indeed laid claim, but were not claimed by any *British* colony; none of the lands had been granted to any colonist; we had therefore no particular concern or interest in that dispute

pute. As to the *Ohio*, the contest there began about your right of trading in the *Indian* country, a right you had by the treaty of *Utrecht*, which the *French* infringed; they seized the traders and their goods, which were your manufactures; they took a fort which a company of your merchants, and their factors and correspondents, had erected there, to secure that trade. *Braddock* was sent with an army to re-take that fort (which was looked on here as another incroachment on the king's territory) and to protect your trade. It was not till after his defeat that the colonies were attacked. They were before in perfect peace with both *French* and *Indians*; the troops were not therefore sent for their defence. The trade with the *Indians*, though carried on in *America*, is not an *American* interest. The people of *America* are chiefly farmers and planters; scarce any thing that they raise or produce is an article of commerce with the *Indians*. The *Indian* trade is a *British* interest; it is carried on with *British* manufactures, for the profit of *British* merchants and manufacturers; therefore the war, as it commenced for the defence of territories of the crown, the property of no *American*, and for the defence of a trade purely *British*, was really a *British* war—and yet the people of *America* made no scruple of contributing their utmost towards carrying it on, and bringing it to a happy conclusion.

Q. Do you think then that the taking possession of the king's territorial rights, and strengthening the frontiers, is not an *American* interest?

A. Not particularly, but conjointly a *British* and an *American* interest.

Q. You will not deny that the preceding war, the war with *Spain*, was entered into for the sake of *America*; was it not occasioned by captures made in the *American* seas?

A. Yes; captures of ships carrying on the

British trade there, with *British* manufactures.

Q. Was not the late war with the *Indians*, since the peace with *France*, a war for *America* only?

A. Yes; it was more particularly for *America* than the former, but it was rather a consequence or remains of the former war, the *Indians* not having been thoroughly pacified, and the *Americans* bore by much the greatest share of the expence. It was put an end to by the army under general *Bouquet*; there were not above 300 regulars in that army, and above 1000 *Pennsylvanians*.

Q. Is it not necessary to send troops to *America*, to defend the *Americans* against the *Indians*?

A. No, by no means; it never was necessary. They defended themselves when they were but an handful, and the *Indians* much more numerous. They continually gained ground, and have driven the *Indians* over the mountains, without any troops sent to their assistance from this country. And can it be thought necessary now to send troops for their defence from those diminished *Indian* tribes, when the colonies are become so populous, and so strong? There is not the least occasion for it; they are very able to defend themselves.

Q. Do you say there were no more than 300 regular troops employed in the late *Indian* war?

A. Not on the *Ohio*, or the frontiers of *Pennsylvania*, which was the chief part of the war that affected the colonies. There were garrisons at *Niagara*, *Fort Detroit*, and those remote posts kept for the sake of your trade; I did not reckon them, but I believe that on the whole the number of *Americans*, or Provincial troops, employed in the

the war, was greater than that of the regulars. I am not certain, but I think so.

Q. Do you think the assemblies have a right to levy money on the subject there, to grant to the crown?

A. I certainly think so; they have always done it.

Q. Are they acquainted with the declaration of rights? And do they know that by that statute, money is not to be raised on the subject but by consent of parliament?

A. They are very well acquainted with it.

Q. How then can they think they have a right to levy money for the crown, or for any other than local purposes?

A. They understand that clause to relate to subjects only within the realm; that no money can be levied on them for the crown, but by consent of parliament. The colonies are not supposed to be within the realm; they have assemblies of their own, which are their parliaments, and they are, in that respect, in the same situation with *Ireland*. When money is to be raised for the crown upon the subject in *Ireland*, or in the colonies, the consent is given in the parliament of *Ireland*, or in the assemblies of the colonies. They think the parliament of *Great-Britain* cannot properly give that consent till it has representatives from *America*; for the petition of right expressly says, it is to be by common consent in parliament, and the people of *America* have no representatives in parliament, to make a part of that common consent.

Q. If the stamp-act should be repealed, and an act should pass, ordering the assemblies of the colonies to indemnify the sufferers by the riots, would they obey it?

A. That is a question I cannot answer.

Q. Suppose the king should require the colonies

nies to grant a revenue, and the parliament should be against their doing it, do they think they can grant a revenue to the king, without the consent of the parliament of *Great-Britain?*

A. That is a deep question.———As to my own opinion, I should think myself at liberty to do it, and should do it, if I liked the occasion.

Q. When money has been raised in the colonies, upon requisitions, has it not been granted to the king?

A. Yes, always; but the requisitions have generally been for some service expressed, as to raise, clothe and pay troops, and not for money only.

Q. If the act should pass, requiring the *American* assemblies to make compensation to the sufferers, and they should disobey it, and then the parliament should, by another act, lay an internal tax, would they then obey it?

A. The people will pay no internal tax; and I think an act to oblige the assemblies to make compensation is unnecessary, for I am of opinion, that as soon as the present heats are abated, they will take the matter into consideration, and if it is right to be done, they will do it of themselves.

Q. Do not letters often come into the post-offices in *America*, directed to some inland town where no post goes?

A. Yes.

Q. Can any private person take up those letters, and carry them as directed?

A. Yes; any friend of the person may do it, paying the postage that has accrued.

Q. But must not he pay an additional postage for the distance to such an inland town?

A. No.

Q. Can the post-master answer delivering the

the letter, without being paid such additional postage?

A. Certainly he can demand nothing, where he does no service.

Q. Suppose a person, being far from home, finds a letter in a post-office directed to him, and he lives in a place to which the post generally goes, and the letter is directed to that place, will the post-master deliver him the letter, without his paying the postage receivable at the place to which the letter is directed?

A. Yes; the office cannot demand postage for a letter it that does not carry, or farther than it does carry it.

Q. Are not ferrymen in *America* obliged, by act of parliament, to carry over the posts without pay?

A. Yes.

Q. Is not this a tax on the ferrymen?

A. They do not consider it as such, as they have an advantage from persons travelling with the post.

Q. If the stamp-act should be repealed and the crown should make a requisition to the colonies for a sum of money, would they grant it?

A. I believe they would.

Q. Why do you think so?

A. I can speak for the colony I live in; I had it in instruction from the assembly to assure the ministry, that as they always had done, so they should always think it their duty to grant such aids to the crown as were suitable to their circumstances and abilities, whenever called upon for the purpose, in the usual constitutional manner; and I had the honour of communicating this instruction to that honourable gentleman then minister.

Q. Would they do this for a *British* concern; as

suppose a war in some part of *Europe*, that did not affect them?

A. Yes, for any thing that concerned the general interest. They consider themselves as a part of the whole.

Q. What is the usual constitutional manner of calling on the colonies for aids?

A. A letter from the secretary of state.

Q. Is this all you mean, a letter from the secretary of state?

A. I mean the usual way of requisition, in a circular letter from the secretary of state, by his majesty's command, reciting the occasion, and recommending it to the colonies, to grant such aids as became their loyalty, and were suitable to their abilities.

Q. Did the secretary of state ever write for money for the crown?

A. The requisitions have been to raise, clothe and pay men, which cannot be done without money.

Q. Would they grant money alone, if called on?

A. In my opinion they would, money as well as men, when they have money, or can make it.

Q. If the parliament should repeal the stamp-act, will the assembly of *Pennsylvania* rescind their resolutions?

A. I think not.

Q Before there was any thought of the stamp-act, did they wish for a representation in parliament?

A. No.

Q. Don't you know that there is, in the *Pennsylvania* charter, an express reservation of the right of parliament to lay taxes there?

A. I know there is a clause in the charter, by which the king grants that he will
levy

levy no taxes on the inhabitants, unless it be with the consent of the assembly, or by an act of parliament.

Q. How then could the assembly of *Pennsylvania* assert, that laying a tax on them by the stamp-act was an infringement of their rights?

A. They understand it thus; by the same charter, and otherwise, they are intitled to all the privileges and liberties of *Englishmen*; they find in the great charters, and the petition and declaration of rights, that one of the privileges of *English* subjects is, that they are not to be taxed but by their common consent; they have therefore relied upon it, from the first settlement of the province, that the parliament never would, nor could, by colour of that clause in the charter, assume a right of taxing them, till it had qualified itself to exercise such right, by admitting representatives from the people to be taxed, who ought to make a part of that common consent.

Q. Are there any words in the charter that justify that construction?

A. The common rights of *Englishmen*, as declared by *Magna Charta*, and the petition of right, all justify it.

Q. Does the distinction between internal and external taxes exist in the words of the charter?

A. No, I believe not.

Q. Then may they not, by the same interpretation, object to the parliament's right of external taxation?

A. They never have hitherto. Many arguments have been lately used here to shew them that there is no difference, and that if you have no right to tax them internally, you have none to tax them externally, or make any other law to bind them. At present they do not reason so, but in time they

they may possibly be convinced by these arguments.

Q. Do not the resolutions of the *Pennsylvannia* assemblies say All taxes?

A. If they do, they mean only internal taxes; the same words have not always the same meaning here and in the colonies. By taxes they mean internal taxes; by duties they mean customs; these are their ideas of the language.

Q. Have you not seen the resolutions of the *Massachuset's Bay* assembly?

A. I have.

Q. Do they not say, that neither external nor internal taxes can be laid on them by parliament?

A. I don't know that they do; I believe not.

Q. If the same colony should say neither tax nor imposition could be laid, does not that province hold the power of parliament can lay neither?

A. I suppose that by the word imposition, they do not intend to express duties to be laid on goods imported, as regulations of commerce.

Q. What can the colonies mean then by imposition as distinct from taxes?

A. They may mean many things, as impressing of men, or of carriages, quartering troops on private houses, and the like; there may be great impositions that are not properly taxes.

Q. Is not the post-office rate an internal tax laid by act of parliament?

A. I have answered that.

Q. Are all parts of the colonies equally able to pay taxes?

A. No, certainly; the frontier parts, which have been ravaged by the enemy, are greatly disabled by that means, and therefore, in such cases, are usually favoured in our tax-laws.

Q. Can we, at this distance, be competent judges of what favours are necessary?

A. The parliament have supposed it, by claiming a right to make tax-laws for *America?* I think it impossible.

Q. Would the repeal of the stamp-act be any discouragement of your manufactures? Will the people that have begun to manufacture decline it?

A. Yes, I think they will; especially if, at the same time, the trade is opened again, so that remittances can be easily made. I have known several instances that make it probable. In the war before last, tobacco being low, and making little remittance, the people of *Virginia* went generally into family manufactures. Afterwards, when tobacco bore a better price, they returned to the use of *British* manufactures. So fulling-mills were very much disused in the last war in *Pennsylvania*, because bills were then plenty, and remittances could easily be made to *Britain* for *English* cloth and other goods.

Q. If the stamp-act should be repealed, would it induce the assemblies of *America* to acknowledge the right of parliament to tax them, and would they erase their resolutions?

A. No, never.

Q. Is there no means of obliging them to erase those resolutions?

A. None that I know of; they will never do it, unless compelled by force of arms.

Q. Is there a power on earth that can force them to erase them?

A. No power, how great soever, can force men to change their opinions.

Q. Do they consider the post-office as a tax, or as a regulation?

A. Not as a tax, but as a regulation and conveniency; every assembly encouraged it, and supported

ported it in its infancy, by grants of money, which they would not otherwise have done; and the people have always paid the postage.

Q. When did you receive the instructions you mentioned?

A. I brought them with me, when I came to *England*, about 15 months since.

Q. When did you communicate that instruction to the minister?

A. Soon after my arrival, while the stamping of *America* was under consideration, and before the bill was brought in.

Q. Would it be most for the interest of *Great-Britain*, to employ the hands of *Virginia* in tobacco, or in manufactures?

A. In tobacco, to be sure.

Q. What used to be the pride of the *Americans?*

A. To indulge in the fashions and manufactures of *Great-Britain*.

Q. What is now their pride?

A. To wear their old cloaths over again, till they can make new ones.

withdrew.

The committee of the whole house, having in a great measure finished their examination of persons and papers, it was at length moved, on the 21st of *January*, 1766.

That it is the opinion of this Committee, that the House be moved, that leave be given to bring in a bill to REPEAL an act passed in the last session of parliament, entituled, *An Act for granting and applying certain stamp-duties, and other duties in the* British *colonies and plantations in* America, *towards further defraying the expences of defending, protecting, and securing the same, and for amending such parts of the several acts of Parliament relating to the trade and revenues of the said*

A. 1766.   DEBATES.   141

said colonies and plantations, as direct the manner of determining and recovering the penalties and forfeitures therein-mentioned.

It was afterwards proposed, to leave out the word *repeal*, and insert *explain and amend*.

Upon which there ensued a debate.

The question was put, whether the word *repeal* should stand?

Ayes —— 275
Noes —— 167

Then the question was put and agreed to.

A LIST *of the* MINORITY, *who voted against the* REPEAL *of the* American *stamp-act.*

J. Abercrombie, Esq; *a major-general, and colonel of the* 44*th regiment of foot,* — Clackmannanshire
Edward Bacon, Esq; ———— Norwich
William Baggott, Esq; ———— Staffordshire
Sir Richard Warwick Bamfylde, Bart. Devonshire
Lord Barrington, *secretary at war* — Plymouth
Lord Bateman, *mast. of the buckhounds* Woodstock
Lord Robert Bertie, *a lord of the King's bedchamber, a lieutenant-general, governor of Cork, and colonel of the 7th regiment of foot* Boston
Lord Brownlow Bertie ———— Lincolnshire
Peregrine Bertie, Esq; ———— Westbury
William Blackstone, Esq; *solicitor-general to the Queen,* ———— Hindon
Sir Walter Blackett, Bart.   Newcastle upon Tyne
Richard Wilbraham Bootle, Esq; ---- Chester
Thomas Brand, Esq; ———— Gatton
William Bromley, Esq; ———— Warwickshire
Hon. Robert Brudenel, Esq; *a groom of the bed-chamber to the duke of* York, *and colonel of the* 4*th regiment of foot, and, lately made, vice-chamberlain to the Queen,* ———— ———— Marlborough
Sir Thomas Charles Bunbury, Bart.   Suffolk
Sir Robert Burdett, Bart. —   Tamworth

Hon.

Hon. John Burgoyne, Esq; *colonel of the 16th regiment of dragoons* — Midhurst
William Matt. Burt, Esq; — Marlow
Hon. Charles Sloane Cadogan, Esq; *surveyor of his Majesty's waters, and treasurer to the duke of York* — Cambridge town
Right Hon. Lord Frederick Campbell — Glasgow, Renfrew, &c.
James Campbell, Esq; *governor of Stirling castle* — Stirlingshire
Marquis of Carnarvon — Radnorshire
Lord Carysfort — Huntingdonshire
Timothy Caswell, Esq; — Hertford
Earl of Catherlough — Grimsby
Richard Clive, Esq; — Montgomery
James Edward Colleton, Esq; — Lestwithiel
Sir John Hynd Cotton — Cambridgeshire
James Coutts, Esq; — Edinburgh city
Tho. Coventry, Esq; *a director of the South-sea company* — Bridport
Patrick Crauford, Esq; — Renfrewshire
Asheton Cuzson, Esq; — Clitheroe
Sir Hugh Dalrymple, Bart. — Dunbar, &c.
Sir James Dashwood, Bart. — Oxfordshire
Sir John Hussey Delaval, Bart. — Berwick
John Dickson, Esq; — Peebleshire
Sir James Douglass, *adm. of the White* — Orkney, &c.
Archibald Douglass, Esq; *a lieutenant-general, and col. of the 13th regiment of dragoons* - - Dumfries-shire
William Drake, Esq; - - - Amersham
Thomas Erle Drax, Esq; - - Wareham
Sir Lawrence Dundass, Bart. Newcastle under line
Thomas Dundass, Esq; - - Richmond
Thomas De Grey, Esq; - - Norfolk
Jeremiah Dyson, Esq; *one of the lords of trade* - - - Yarmouth, Hants
John Eames, Esq; *one of the masters in Chancery* - - Yarmouth, Hants

Archibald

A. 1766.   DEBATES.

Archibald Edmonſtone, Eſq;   Dumbartonſhire
Right Hon. Gilbert Elliot, Eſq; *treaſurer of the chamber* - -   Roxburghſhire
Right Hon. Welbore Ellis - -   Ayleſbury
Simon Fanſhawe, Eſq; *a comptroller of the board of green cloth* - -   Grampound
Sir Charles Farnaby, Bart. - -   Eaſt Grinſtead
Earl of Farnham - - -   Taunton
Thomas Foley, Eſq; - -   Droitwich
Alexander Forreſter, Eſq; - -   Oakhampton
Colonel Fraſer, - -   Inverneſsſhire
Lord Garlies - - -   Morpeth
Bamber Gaſcoigne, Eſq; :   -   Midhurſt
Thomas Gilbert, Eſq; *comptroller of the King's wardrobe* - -   Newcaſtle under line
Sir John Glynne, Bart. - -   Flint town
Lord Adam Gordon, *colonel of the 66th regiment of foot* - -   Aberdeenſhire
The Marquis of Granby, *maſter of the ordnance, and colonel of the royal regiment of horſe-guards blue* -   Cambridgeſhire
Sir Alexander Grant, Bart. -   Fortroſe, &c.
Charles Gray, Eſq; - -   Colcheſter
David Græme, Eſq; *ſecretary to the Queen, a major-general, and colonel of the 49th regiment of foot* - -   Perthſhire
Rt. Hon. Geo. Grenville, Eſq;   Buckingham town
Thomas Groſvenor, Eſq; - -   Cheſter
Howell Gwynne, Eſq; - -   Old Sarum
John Hamilton, Eſq; *maſter of the King's works in* Scotland -   Wigtown, &c.
William Gerrard Hamilton, Eſq; *chancellor of the exchequer in* Ireland -   Pontefract
Hon. Thomas Harley, Eſq; - -   London
Sir Henry Harpur, Bart. -   Derbyſhire
James Harris, Eſq; - -   Chriſtchurch
Eliab Harvey, Eſq; *King's counſel* -   Dunwich
Edward Harvey, Eſq; *a major-general, colonel of the 3d regiment of light horſe, and adjutant-general in* North America   Gatton

George

George Hay, L. L. D. *dean of the arches court, and judge of the prerogative court of* Canterbury - - Sandwich
Edward Herbert, Esq; - - Ludlow
Lord Hinchinbrooke - - Brackley
Hon. George Hobart, Esq; - - Beeralston
Francis Holbourne, Esq; *vice-admiral of the red* - - - Dumferling, &c.
Rowland Holt, Esq; - - Suffolk
Jacob Houblon, Esq; - - Hertfordshire
Hon. Thomas Howard, Esq; - Castle Rising
Thomas Orby Hunter, Esq; - Winchelsea
Charles Jenkinson, Esq; *auditor of accompts to the Princess Dowager of* Wales - - Cockermouth
John Jolliffe, Esq; ——— Petersfield
Robert Jones, Esq; - - Huntingdon
Anthony James Keck, Esq; - Leicester
Edward Kynaston, Esq; Montgomeryshire
Peter Legh, Esq; ——— Ilchester
Marquis of Lorne, *a lieutenant-general, and colonel of the 1st regiment of foot* Dover
Richard Lowndes, Esq; - Buckinghamshire
Sir James Lowther, Bart. - Cumberland
Sir Herbert Lloyd, Bart. - - Cardigan town
Simon Luttrell, Esq; - - Wigan
William Lynch, Esq; - - Weobly
John Ross Mackye, Esq; *postmaster of the ordnance* - - Kircudbright
Alexander Mackay, Esq; *colonel of the 65th regiment of foot* - Sutherlandshire
Rt. Hon. James Stuart Mackenzie, Esq; Rossshire
Lord Robert Manners, *colonel of the 3d regiment of dragoons, and lieutenant-governor of* Hull - Kingston upon Hull
John Manners, Esq; *House-keeper at* Whitehall - - Newark
Samuel Martyn, Esq; *treasurer to the Princess Dowager of* Wales - Camelford

Paul

Paul Methuen, Esq; - - Warwick
Right Hon. Thomas Millar, Esq; *Lord Advocate for* Scotland - Anan, Sanquhair, &c.
Thomas Moore Molyneux, Esq; *a captain in the 3d regiment of foot-guards* Haslemere
Hon. Archibald Montgomery, Esq; *equerry to the Queen, governor of* Dumbarton *castle, and deputy-ranger of St. James's and* Hyde *parks* - Airshire
Sir John Mordaunt, *a general of his Majesty's forces, colonel of the 10th regiment of dragoons, and governor of* Sheerness - Cockermouth
Sir Charles Mordaunt, Bart. - Warwickshire
John Morton, Esq; *Chief Justice of* Chester - - Abingdon
John Mostyn, Esq; *groom of the bedchamber to the King, colonel of the 1st regiment of dragoon guards, and a lieutenant-general* - - Malton
Lord Mountstuart - - Bossiney
Richard Neville Neville, Esq; Tavistock
Sir Roger Newdigate, Bart. Oxford University
Lord North - - Banbury
Sir Fletcher Norton - - Wigan
Right Hon. Robert Nugent, Esq; Bristol
Edmund Nugent, Esq; *groom of the bedchamber to the King, and captain in the 1st regiment of foot-guards* - St. Maws
Robert Henley Ongley, Esq; - Bedfordshire
Lord Orwell - Ipswich
Right Hon. James Oswald, Esq; *joint vice-treasurer of* Ireland - - Kinghorn, &c.
Earl of Panmure, *a lieutenant-general, and colonel of the 21st regiment of foot* Forfarshire
Armstead Parker, Esq; - - Peterborough
Thomas Pitt, Esq; - - Old Sarum
Sir George Pococke, *admiral of the blue* Plymouth
George Prescott, Esq; - - Stockbridge

George Rice Esq; *a lord of trade* Carmarthenshire
John Robinson, Esq; - Westmoreland
John Lockhart Ross, *a captain of the royal navy* - - Peeblesshire
Lord George Sackville, *joint vice-treasurer of* Ireland - Hythe
Hon. Henry St. John, *groom of the bedchamber to the Duke of* York, *and a lieutenant-colonel* - - Wotton-Basset
Sir John Sebright, Bart. *a major-general, and colonel of the* 18*th regiment of foot* Bath
Henry Seymour, Esq; *groom of the bedchamber to the King* - - Totness
Fane William Sharpe, Esq; - Callington
Jennison Shaftoe, Esq; - Leominster
Henry Shiffner, Esq; - - Minehead
James Shuttleworth, Esq; - Lancashire
Coningsby Sibthorpe, Esq; - Lincoln
Lord Charles Spencer, *verdurer of* Whichwood *forest* - - Oxfordshire
Right Hon. Hans Stanley, Esq; *governor of the* Isle of Wight - Southampton
Sir Thomas Stapleton, Bart. Oxford city
John Stevenson, Esq; *a director of the* East-India *company* - St. Michael
Sir Simeon Stuart, Bart. *a chamberlain of the Exchequer* - - Hampshire
Lord Strange, *Chancellor of the dutchy of* Lancaster - - Lancashire
Lord George Sutton - - Grantham
Marquis of Tavistock - - Bedfordshire
Earl of Thomond - Minehead
Thomas Thoroton, Esq; *secretary to the master of the ordnance* - Newark
John Pugh Pryse, Esq; - Cardiganshire
Edward Thurlowe, Esq; *King's counsel* Tamworth
Hon. Henry Fred. Thynne - Weobly
Sir John Turner, Bart. - King's Lynn
Sir Charles Kemys Tynte - Somersetshire

Arthur Vanfittart, Efq;	Berkfhire
Richard Vernon, Efq;	Bedford
John Upton, Efq;	Weftmoreland
Charles Walcott, Efq;	Weymouth & Melcomb
Robert Waller, Efq;	Chipping Wycomb
John Rolle Walter, Efq;	Exeter
Henry Wauchope, Efq; *deputy privy-purfe to his Majefty*	Bute & Caithnefs
Hon. John Ward, Efq;	Worcefterfhire
Lord Warkworth, *aid de camp to the King*	Weftminfter
Philip Carteret Webb, Efq;	Haflemere
Alexander Wedderburn, *King's counfel*	Rothefay, &c.
Thomas Whately, Efq;	Luggerfhall
Hon. Thomas Willoughby, Efq;	Nottinghamfhire
Sir Armine Wodehoufe, Bart.	Norfolk
Robert Wood, Efq;	Brackley
167 Thomas Worfley, Efq; *furveyor of the board of works*	Orford
168 Right Hon. Richard Rigby, Efq; *teller*	Taviftock

The committee agreed to feveral other refolutions, which were ordered to be reported to the Houfe on the 24th of *February*.

On that day Mr. *Fuller*, chairman of the committee, reported, that they had come to the following refolutions.

1ft, That the King's Majefty, by and with the confent of the Lords fpiritual and temporal, and Commons of *Great-Britain*, in Parliament affembled, had, hath, and of right ought to have, full power and authority to make laws and ftatutes of fufficient force and validity to bind the colonies and people of *America*, fubjects of the crown of *Great-Britain*, in all cafes whatfoever.

2d, That tumults and infurrections of the moft dangerous nature have been raifed, and carried

carried on, in several of the *North-American* colonies, in open defiance of the powers and dignity of his Majesty's government, and in manifest violation of the laws and legislative authority of this kingdom.

3d, That the said tumults and insurrections have been greatly countenanced and inflamed by votes and resolutions, passed in several of the assemblies in the said provinces, highly injurious to the honour of his Majesty's government, and tending to destroy the legal and constitutional dependency of the said colonies on the Imperial crown and Parliament of *Great-Britain*.

4th, That such persons, who, on account of the desire which they have manifested to comply with, or to assist in carrying into execution, any acts of the legislature of *Great-Britain*, relating to the *British* colonies in *North-America*, have suffered any injury or damage, ought to have full and ample compensation made to them for the same, by the respective colonies in which such injuries or damages were sustained.

5th, That the House be moved to resolve and declare, that all his Majesty's subjects, residing in the said colonies, who have manifested their desire to comply with, or to assist in carrying into execution, any acts of the legislature of *Great-Britain*, relating to the *British* colonies in *North-America*, have acted as dutiful and loyal subjects, and are therefore intitled to, and will assuredly have, the protection of the House of Commons of *Great-Britain*.

6th, That all persons, who, by reason of the tumults and outrages in *North-America*, have not been able to procure stamped paper, since the passing of the act for laying certain duties of stamps in the colonies, ought to be indemnified from all penalties and forfeitures, which they may have incurred, by writing, ingrossing, or printing,

printing, on paper, vellum, or parchment, not duly stamped, as required by the said act, under proper restrictions.

7th, That the House be moved, that leave be given to bring in a bill to repeal an act passed in the last session of Parliament, entitled, *An act for granting and applying certain stamp-duties, and other duties, in the British colonies and plantations in America, towards further defraying the expences of defending, protecting, and securing the same; and for amending such parts of the several acts of Parliament, relating to the trade and revenues of the said colonies and plantations, as direct the manner of determining and recovering the penalties and forfeitures therein mentioned.*

The first of these resolutions being read a second time, a motion was made for its being postponed; but, after a debate, the question being put, it was carried in the negative, after which the resolution was agreed to; as were the 2d, 3d, and 4th, after being read a second time. without any opposition; and, after the 5th was read a second time, a motion being made accordingly, the house did resolve and declare in the terms thereby proposed; after which the 6th was read a second time, and agreed to: then the 7th and last, which had occasioned a debate in the committee, but was therein agreed to by 275 to 167; and now upon the report, as soon as it was read a second time, a motion was made for its being recommitted; whereupon some part of the act of the 5th of Queen Anne, chap. viii. for an union of the two kingdoms of England and Scotland, particularly the 18th article of that famous treaty, was, upon motion, read, and a debate ensued, but, upon the question's being put, it was carried in the negative; consequently a motion was in course made, pursuant to the said resolution, and it was ordered, that leave be given to bring in a bill to repeal an act passed in the last session, for granting and applying certain stamp-duties, &c.

A motion was made, that the persons appointed to bring in the bill do make effectual provision, in the said bill, for preserving the just rights and authority of the *British* legislature, by directing all votes and resolutions of the assemblies of any of the *American* colonies, repugnant to the said rights and authority, to be erased and expunged, before the said repeal shall take place in such respective colonies. This brought on a new debate; but, upon the question's being put, it was carried in the negative by 240 to 133, chiefly on account of the next motion; which was, that a bill or bills be brought in upon the first and sixth of the aforesaid resolutions. Then it was ordered that the 2d, 3d, 4th, and 5th, of the aforesaid resolutions be laid before his Majesty; and it was resolved to address his majesty, to desire, that he would be graciously pleased to give directions, that the said resolutions be transmitted to the governors of his Majesty's colonies and plantations in *America*, to be by them communicated to the assemblies of their respective governments.

The house having now continued sitting till after one o'clock in the morning of the 25th, they adjourned till next morning the 26th, on which day Mr. *Fuller* presented to the house according to order, a bill for the better securing the dependency of his majesty's dominions in *America*, upon the crown and parliament of *Great Britain*, which bill was then read a first time and ordered to be read a second time the next morning: and presently afterwards, Mr. Secretary *Conway* presented to the House, according to order, a bill to repeal an act made in the last session of parliament, entitled, *An act for granting and applying certain*

certain stamp-duties, and other, &c. which bill was then read a first time and ordered to be read a second time, also the next morning. Both bills passed.

On the 18th of *March*, after these two acts had received the royal assent, an instruction was ordered to the gentlemen who had been appointed to prepare and bring in a bill, pursuant to the said 6th resolution, that they do make provision in the said bill, for making valid in law all the writings, ingrossings, and printings, wrote, ingrossed, or printed, in *America* upon paper, vellum or parchment, not stamped according to law under proper restrictions; and a bill having been prepared in pursuance of the said resolution, and proper clauses added in pursuance of this instruction, Mr. *Fuller* presented the bill the next day to the House, being then entitled, *A bill to indemnify persons who have incurred, or may incur, penalties and forfeitures, by writing, ingrossing, or printing, in his majesty's dominions in* America, *upon unstamped paper, vellum, or parchment, contrary to an act passed last session of Parliament, for granting and applying certain stamp duties, and other duties, in the British colonies and plantations in* America; *and for making good and valid all writings, ingrossings, and printings, wrote, ingrossed, or printed, or which shall be wrote, ingrossed, or printed, upon unstamped paper, which by the said act would have been, or shall be, null and void* upon payment of certain sums of money. This was the title of the bill when it was presented to the House, and it was then read a first time and ordered to be read a second time, which it was on the 25th, and committed to a committee of the whole House for the 9th of *April*; but in the mean time an objection was raised to the bill as it then stood, that we had already by an act of that session repealed wholly, absolutely, and unconditionally, the stamp-duty act of the preceding session, whereas by the bill then depending before the House, we were to enact that the said act of the preceding session shall be repealed only in part and upon condition.

This objection had so much weight, that the order for committing the bill was from time to time put off until the 16th of *May*, on which day the House resolved itself into a committee of the whole House on the said bill, went through the same with several amendments, and ordered the report to be received on the 22d, when the amendments were agreed to, and the bill ordered to be ingrossed. On the 30th it was, according to order, read a third time, and a motion made to resolve, that the bill do pass, which after reading the above mentioned resolutions of the 24th of *February*, was agreed to, and as all restrictions and conditions for the payment of any money had been in the committee left out, it was resolved, that the title of the bill should be, *An act for indemnifying persons who have incurred certain penalties, inflicted by an act of the last session of Parliament, for granting certain stamp-duties, in the* British *colonies, and plantations in* America; *and for making valid all instruments executed or inrolled there, on unstamped paper, vellum or parchment.* And Mr. *Fuller* was then ordered to carry the bill to the Lords.

The committee, appointed to examine the affairs of the colonies, directed their chairman, Mr. *Fuller*, to report to the House the resolutions they had come to since the repeal of the Stamp-act. And on the 9th of *May*, 1766, the report was made.

Resolution 1st, That the duties imposed by an act or acts of Parliament, upon melasses, and syrups, of the growth, produce, or manufacture, of any foreign *American* colony or plantation, imported into any *British* colony or plantation in *America*, do cease and determine.

2d, That

2d, That a duty of one penny, sterling money, per gallon, be laid upon all melasses and syrups, which shall be imported into such *British* colony or plantation.

3d, That it is the opinion of this committee, that the duties imposed upon sugars, in the *British* colonies in *America*, by an act made in the 25th year of the reign of King Charles the second, for encouragement of the *Greenland* and *Eastland* trades, and better securing the plantation trade, do cease and determine.

4th, That the duty imposed in the *British* colonies and plantations in *America* by an act, made in the 4th year of the reign of his present Majesty, for granting certain duties in the said colonies and plantations, and for other purposes, upon wrought silks, Bengals, and stuffs mixt with silk, or herba, of the manufacture of *Persia*, *China*, or *East India*, imported from *Great Britain* do cease and determine.

5th, That the duty imposed in the said colonies and plantations, by the said act, made in the fourth year of his present Majesty's reign, upon callicoes, painted, dyed, printed, or stained, in *Persia*, *China*, or *East-India*, imported from *Great-Britain*, do cease and determine.

6th, That the duties imposed in the *British* colonies and plantations in *America*, by the said act, made in the fourth year of his present Majesty's reign, upon foreign linen cloth, called Cambrick, and upon *French* lawns, imported from *Great-Britain*, do cease and determine.

7th, That a duty be laid upon all such foreign linen cloth, called Cambrick, and upon *French* lawns, which shall be exported from this kingdom to the said colonies and plantations.

8th, That the duties imposed by the said act, made in the fourth year of his present Majesty's reign, upon coffee and piemento, of the growth and

and produce of any *British* colony or plantation in *America*, which should be shipped to be carried out from thence, do cease and determine.

9th, That a duty of seven shillings, sterling money, per hundred weight averdupois, be laid upon all such coffee as shall be imported into any such colony or plantation, except only such coffee as shall, upon the landing thereof, be immediately deposited and secured in warehouses, in order to be re-exported under proper restrictions.

10th, That a duty of one halfpenny, sterling money, per pound weight averdupois, be laid upon all such piemento which shall be imported into any such colony or plantation, except only such piemento as shall, upon the landing thereof, be immediately deposited and secured in warehouses, in order to be re-exported under proper restrictions.

11th, That no duties be paid upon such foreign sugars, coffee, or indico, as shall be imported into any *British* colony or plantation on the continent of *America*, and, upon the landing thereof, be immediately deposited and secured in warehouses, in order to be re-exported under proper restrictions.

12th, That foreign cotton, wool, and indico, be permitted to be imported by *British* ships, navigated according to law, into any *British* island, in that part of *America* commonly called the *West-Indies*, free from the payment of any duty or other imposition whatsoever.

13th, That the produce of such of the said duties, to be raised in the said colonies and plantations, be paid into the receipt of his Majesty's exchequer, and there reserved to be, from time to time, disposed of by Parliament, towards defraying the necessary expences of defending, protecting, and securing, the said colonies and plantations.

14th, That

14th, That it will be for the advantage of the trade, navigation, and manufactures, of this kingdom, to establish one or more port or ports in his Majesty's dominions in *America*, for the more free importation and exportation of certain goods and merchandizes under proper regulations and restrictions.

These resolutions were all agreed to by the House, and it was ordered, that the 4th, 5th, 6th, and 7th, should be referred to the committee of ways and means; and that a bill should be brought in pursuant to the rest.

The order of the day being then read, for the house to resolve itself into the committee of ways and means, it was severally ordered, that the said committee do consider of the duties payable upon the importation into this kingdom of sugars from the *British* colonies and plantations on the continent of *America*; of the proper methods for the encouragement of the importation of cotton-wool into this kingdom, and of the duties payable in this kingdom upon wrought silks, Bengals, or stuffs, mixed with silk or herba, of the manufacture of *Persia*, *China*, or *East-India*, and callicoes printed, dyed, painted, or stained there; the consequence of which instructions were the seven resolutions of the said committee agreed to on the 10th of *May*; and, as soon as they were agreed to, the said 4th, 5th, and 6th, resolutions of the *American* papers committee being upon motion read again, it was ordered, that it be an instruction to the gentlemen appointed to prepare and bring in a bill or bills pursuant to the other resolutions of that committee, that they do make provision in the said bill, or in one of the said bills, pursuant to the resolutions then again read, and also to the resolutions of the ways and means committee, that day reported and agreed to. And on the 14th of *May* it was ordered to be an instruction to the same gentlemen, that they do make provision in the said bill, or in one of the said bills, pursuant to the two last of the resolutions of the committee of ways and means, that day reported and agreed to.

In pursuance of this order and these instructions, Mr. Chancellor of the Exchequer, on the 15th presented to the House a bill for opening and establishing certain ports in the islands of *Jamaica* and *Dominica*, for the more free importation and exportation of certain goods and merchandizes; which bill was then read a first time, and ordered to be read a second time, as also to be printed. On the same day, after reading the order of the day for the House to resolve itself into the committee of ways and means, it was ordered, that it be an instruction to the said committee, that they consider (1st) of the proper method for raising money to defray the expences of carrying into execution, such provisions as may be made for opening certain ports in the islands of *Jamaica* and *Dominica*, for the more free importation and exportation of goods and merchandizes, and for maintaining, securing, and improving such ports; (2dly) of the duties to be paid upon the importation of goods into this kingdom, from such ports in the island of *Dominica*; and (3dly) of the duties to be paid upon the importation of goods into the island of *Dominica*. Accordingly the House then resolved itself into the said committee of ways and means, and came to those resolutions, which were reported and agreed to on the 16th of May.

But before these resolutions were on that day reported, the last mentioned bill was read a second time, and committed to a committee of the whole House for the 26th; and as soon as these resolutions were reported and agreed to, it was ordered,

ordered, that a bill should be brought in upon them, and that Mr. Paterson, Mr. Chancellor of the Exchequer, Mr. Attorney General, &c. should bring in the same. Presently after which, they were instructed to make provision in the said bill, for encouraging the importation of goods into this kingdom from the island of *Dominica*, to be re-exported. On the 22d they were further instructed to make provision in the said bill, for securing the duties payable in respect of goods imported into the *British* colonies in *America*, upon such goods as should be imported there from the island of *Dominica*; and on the same day Mr. Paterson, in pursuance of this order and these instructions, presented to the House a bill for granting duties to defray the expences of opening, maintaining, securing, and improving certain ports, in the islands of *Jamaica* and *Dominica*, for the more free importation and exportation of goods and merchandizes; for ascertaining the duties to be paid upon the importation of goods from the said island of *Dominica* into this kingdom; and for securing the duties upon goods imported from the said island into any other *British* colony; which bill was then read a first time, and ordered to be read a second time, as it accordingly was the next day, and committed to the committee of the whole House, to whom the said former bill had been committed.

On the 26th, these two bills were ordered to be made into one, which was accordingly done, and next day carried to the Lords.

February 26th, there were severally presented to the House, and read, petitions from the counties of *Hereford*, *Worcester*, *Gloucester*, *Devon*, *Somerset*, *Cornwall*, *Monmouth*, the city and county of *Exeter*, the city of *Hereford*, and from several of the boroughs in those counties, representing in general, that the petitioners were subject to many

Cyder-act repealed.

many grievances, by so much of two several acts passed in the 3d and 4th years of the reign of his present Majesty, which lays an additional duty on cyder and perry, both with respect to the tax itself, and to the mode of collecting it under the power of the excise-laws; and praying relief, by a repeal of the said acts, so far as the same relate to the laying a duty on the makers of cyder and perry, or in such other manner as the House shall think meet. These petitions were severally ordered to lie upon the table, and then several accounts relating to the late additional tax upon these liquors were ordered to be laid before the House, which, with an alteration as to one of them, were afterwards accordingly presented; and on the 5th of *March* there was presented to the House, and read, a petition to the same effect with the former from the borough of *Weobly*, in *Herefordshire*.

Though all these petitions against the two late cyder-acts were at first only ordered to lie upon the table, yet, on the 7th of *March*, as soon as the order of the day was read for the House to resolve itself into a committee of the whole House, to consider further of ways and means for raising the supply granted to his Majesty, after an instruction had been ordered to the said committee to consider of the laws relating to cyder and perry, all the said petitions, and also all the accounts relating to cyder and perry, that had been called for and presented in this session, were ordered to be referred to the same; in consequence of which, the committee came to the six resolutions which were on the 10th reported by Mr. Cornwall, and agreed to by the House*; whereupon it was ordered, that a bill be brought in upon the said resolutions, and that Mr. Cornwall,

---

* See the resolutions of the committee of ways and means this session, *March* 10.

wall, Mr. Chancellor of the Exchequer, Lord John Cavendish, Mr. Thomas Townshend, jun. Mr. Onslow, Mr. Attorney General, Mr. Sollicitor General, and Mr. Cooper, should prepare and bring in the same.

According to this order, Mr. Cornwall the next day presented to the House a bill for repealing the duties granted upon cyder and perry, by an act made in the third year of his present Majesty's reign, and for granting certain duties on cyder and perry in lieu thereof, and for the more effectual securing the duties on cyder and perry imposed by several former acts; when the bill was read a first time, and ordered to be read a second time, which it was the day following, and committed to a committee of the whole House for the next day. And so thoroughly had many gentlemen changed their sentiments with regard to this tax, or at least with regard to the mode of raising it, that this bill afterwards passed through both houses in common course, and received the royal assent on the 11th of *April*, without meeting with any considerable opposition in any part of its progress.

SUPPLIES *granted for the year* 1766.

January 27.   *l.   s.   d.*

1. That 16000 men be employed for the sea-service for 1766, including 4287 marines

2. That a sum not exceeding 4l. *per* man *per* month be allowed for maintaining them for thirteen months, including ordnance for sea-service - -   832000   0   0

February 15.

1. That a number of land-forces, including 2513 invalids, amounting to 17306 effective

men,

men, commission and non-commission officers included, be employed for the year 1766

2. That, for defraying the charge of this number for guards, garrisons, and other his Majesty's land-forces in *Great Britain, Guernsey,* and *Jersey,* 1766, *there be granted to his Majesty a sum not exceeding* - 605608 12 9

3. For the pay of the general and general staff officers in *Great-Britain* for 1766   11291 8 6 $\frac{1}{2}$

4. For maintaining his Majesty's forces and garrisons in the plantations and *Africa,* including those in garrison at *Minorca* and *Gibraltar,* and for provisions for the forces in *North-America, Nova-Scotia, Newfoundland, Gibraltar,* the ceded islands, and *Africa,* for 1766 - - -   392183 6 5 $\frac{1}{2}$

5. Towards the same service out of the monies, or savings, remaining of the grant by the third resolution of *April* 20th, in the preceding session   2321 13 10 $\frac{1}{3}$

6. For defraying the charge of the difference of pay between the *British* and *Irish* establishment of two corps of light dragoons, and of six regiments of foot, serving in the *Isle of Man,* at *Gibraltar, Minorca,* and the ceded islands, for 1766, - - -   7993 11 4

7. For

	l.	*s.*	*d.*

7. For paying the pensions to the widows of reduced land and marine officers, married to them before the 25th of *December*, 1716, for 1766.   -   -   1614   0   0

8. Upon account of the reduced land and marine officers, for 1766.   -   -   -   138674   0   0

9. For defraying the charge of full pay to officers reduced, with the tenth company of several battalions reduced from ten to nine companies, and who remained on half pay at the 24th of *December*, 1765, for 1766.   5718   6   8

10. Upon account towards defraying the charge of out pensioners of *Chelsea* hospital, for 1766.   -   -   -   109375   16   8

11. For the charge of the office of ordnance for land service, for 1766.   -   -   -   180445   19   3

12. For defraying the expence of services performed by the office of ordnance, for land service, and not provided for by parliament, in 1765.   -   35061   6   2

13. Towards enabling the trustees of the British Museum, to carry on the execution of the trust reposed in them by parliament   -   -   -   -   2000   0   0

	1492788	9	8¼

February 18.

1. For the ordinary of the navy, including half pay to sea and marine officers, for 1766,   412983   6   3

2. Towards

	l.	*s.*	*d.*

2. Towards the buildings, rebuildings, and repairs of his majesty's ships, docks, building ships, wharfs, and store houses, for 1766. - - -   277300   0   0

690283   6   3

March 13.
1. Towards defraying the extraordinary expence of his majesty's land forces, and other services incurred to the 24th of *January* 1766, and not provided for by parliament   -   404310   16   6¼

2. Out of the monies, or savings, arising from the pay of the land forces in the hands of the pay-master-general, towards defraying the extraordinary expences of his Majesty's land forces, and other services, incurred to the 24th of *January*, 1766, and not provided for by parliament. - - -   74777   14   0

3. For paying off and discharging the Exchequer bills, made out by virtue of the act 4 *Geo*. III. chap. 25. and charged upon the first aids to be granted by parliament for 1766,   - -   1000000   0   0

4. For paying off and discharging the Exchequer bills made out, by virtue of the act passed in the preceding session, chap. 19. and charged upon the first aids to be granted in this session,   -   -   -   800000   0   0

5. To

l. s. d.

5. To replace to the sinking fund the like sum paid out of the same, to make good the deficiency on the 5th of *July*, 1765, of the several rates and duties upon offices and pensions, &c. which were made a fund by the act 31 *Geo.* II. chap. 22. for paying annuities at the Bank, in respect of 5000000 borrowed for 1758,   45561 7 10½

6. To replace to ditto the like sum issued thereout, for paying annuities, after the rate of 4l. *per cent*, for the year ended the 26th of *September*, 1765, which were granted, in respect of certain, navy, victualling, and transport bills, and ordnance debentures, delivered in, and cancelled, pursuant to the act 3 *Geo.* III. chap. 9. -   139342 2 4

7. To replace to ditto, the like sum issued thereout, for paying the charges of management of the said annuities, for two years and one half, due 29th of *September* 1765   -   4898 14 9½

8. To replace to ditto, the like sum paid out of the same to make good the deficiency, on the 10th of *October* 1765, of the several additional duties upon wines imported, and certain duties on all cyder and perry, which were made a fund, by act 3. *Geo.* III. chap. 12, for paying annuities, in respect

	l.	s.	d.
of 350000 l. borrowed for 1763	29211	12	0
9. Upon account, for maintaining and supporting the civil establishment of *Nova Scotia* for 1766.	4866	3	5
10. Upon account, of sundry expences for the service of *Nova Scotia*, in 1750, 1751, 1752, 1762, 1763, not provided for by parliament	8008	12	7
11. Upon account, for defraying the charges of the civil establishment of *Georgia*, and other incidental expences attending the same, from the 24th of *June* 1765, to 24th of *June* 1766	3986	0	0
12. Upon account, for defraying the charges of the civil establishment of *East Florida*, for the same time	5250	0	0
13. Upon account, for defraying the charges of the civil establishment of *West Florida*, for the same time	5300	0	0
14. Upon account, for defraying the expence attending general surveys of his Majesty's dominions in *North America* for 1766	1784	4	0
15. Upon account, for defraying the charges of the civil establishment of *Senegambia*, for 1766	5550	0	0
	2,532,847	8	0¼

March

March 18.

1. To replace to the sinking fund the like sum, issued thereout, to discharge from the 29th of *September* 1765 to the 25th of *December* following, the annuities attending such part of the joint stock, established by act 3 *Geo.* III. chap. 9. in respect of several navy, victualling, and transport bills, and ordnance debentures as were redeemed in pursuance of the act of last session chap. 23.   8708 17 7¼

2. Upon account, for defraying the charge of the pay and cloathing of the militia, for one year, beginning the 25th of *March* 1766 - - -   150,000 0 0

                                   158708 17 7¼

March 24.

To be employed in maintaining and supporting the *British* forts and settlements on the coast of *Africa*, under the direction of the committee of merchants trading to *Africa* -   13000 0 0

March 27.

1. Upon account, to enable his Majesty to discharge such unsatisfied claims and demands for expences incurred during the late war in *Germany*, as appear to be due by the reports of the commissioners, appointed by his Majesty, for examining and stating such claims and demands - - - -   106043 13 8¼

2. Upon

2. Upon account, to enable his Majesty to compleat the payment of the money stipulated by treaty to be paid to the landgrave of *Hesse Cassel*, in extinction of all demands, under the title of reasonable succour, or otherwise - - -   50000   0   0

3. Upon account, towards enabling the *Foundling Hospital* to maintain and educate such children, as were received into the same, on or before the 25th of *March* 1760, from the 31st of *December* 1765 exclusive, to 31st 1766, inclusive, to be issued and paid for the said use, without fee or reward, or any deduction whatsoever -   32,725   0   0

4. And further for the said use and to be issued in the same manner upon account, the monies remaining unissued of those granted in the last session, for the use of the said hospital, amounting to - - -   1167   10   0

                         189,936   3   8¾

April 10.

1. Towards paying off and discharging the debt of the navy - - -   1,200,000   0   0

2. That one third part of the remaining capital stock of annuities, after the rate of 4l. *per cent per annum*, granted in respect of certain navy, victualling, and transport bills, and

	l.	*s.*	*d.*

ordnance debentures, delivered in and cancelled, pursuant to an act of *Geo.* III. chap. 9, be redeemed, and paid off, on the 25th of *December* next, after discharging the interest then payable in respect of the same.

3. To enable his Majesty to redeem, and pay off, one third part of the capital stock of the said annuities — — 870,888 5 5½

2,070,888 5 5½

April 14.
To make good the deficiency of the grants for the service of 1765 — — — 292,828 0 4¼

Sum total of the supplies granted in this session — 8,273,280 11 1⅝

Ways and means for 1766.

January 31.
That the usual temporary duties upon malt, &c. be continued from the 23d of *June* 1766, to the 24th of *June* 1767,—750,000l.

February 21.
1. That the usual land tax of 4s. in the pound be continued for one year, from the 25th of *March* 1766,—2,037,824l. 15s. 11d.

2. That provision be made, to remove all doubts concerning the ascertaining of the duties payable upon the importation of linen cloth of the manufacture of *Russia*, in pursuance of the act of last session chap. 43 and for supplying an omission in the said act, by declaring that all unrated linen cloth and diaper of *Russia*, being in breadth more

than twenty two inches and a half, and not thirty one and a half inches, were by the said act intended to be rated at 4l. for every 120 *English* ells thereof.

March 10.

1. That the duties granted upon cyder and perry by the act of Geo. III. chap. 12, shall from and after the 5th of *July* next ensuing cease, determine, and be no longer paid.

2. That, from and after the said 5th of *July*, an additional duty of 6s. *per* hogshead, be laid upon all cyder and perry, which shall be made within this kingdom, and sold by retail, to be paid by the retailer thereof.

3. That, from and after the said 5th of *July*, an additional duty of 3l. *per* ton, be laid upon all cyder and perry, which shall be imported into this kingdom.

4. That from and after the said 5th of *July*, a duty of 16s. 8d. *per* hogshead, be laid upon all cyder and perry, which shall be made within this kingdom, and sent or consigned to, and received by, any factor or agent, to be sold or disposed of, the said duty, to be paid by such factor or agent.

5. That, from and after the said 5th of *July*, a duty of 6s. *per* hogshead, be laid upon all cyder and perry, made for sale within this kingdom, by dealers in, or retailers of cyder, or perry, from fruit of their own growth, to be paid by such dealers and retailers.

6. That the said duties be appropriated unto such uses and purposes, as the duties granted by the said act, made in the third year of his present Majesty's reign, were thereby made applicable.

March 18.

That the sum of 1,800,000 l. be raised by loans, or Exchequer bills, to be charged upon the first aids to be granted in the next session of parliament, and such Exchequer bills, if not discharged, with
interest

interest thereupon, on or before the 5th of *April* 1767, to be exchanged and received in payment, in such manner as Exchequer bills have usually been exchanged and received in payment.

April 21.

1. That towards the supply granted to his Majesty, the sum of 1,500,000l. be raised in manner following: That is to say, the sum of 900,000l. by annuities, after the rate of 3l. *per centum*, to commence from the 5th of *January* last: and the sum of 600,000l. by a lottery, to consist of 60,000 tickets, every blank to be of the value of 6l. the blanks and prizes to be attended with the like 3 *per cent.* annuities, to commence from the 5th of *January* 767; and that all the said annuities be transferrable at the *Bank* of *England*, be paid half yearly, on the 5th of *July*, and the 5th of *January*, in every year, out of the sinking fund, and be added to, and made part of, the joint stock of 3l. *per cent.* annuities, which were consolidated at the *Bank* of *England*, by certain acts, made in the 25th and 28th years of the reign of his late Majesty, and several subsequent acts, subject to redemption by parliament. That every contributor towards the said sum of 900,000l. after his making the deposit herein after-mentioned, shall, in respect of every 60l. of his contribution to such sum, be entitled to receive four tickets in the said lottery, upon payment of 10l. for each ticket; and that every contributor, towards the said sum of 900,000l. shall, on or before the 8th of *May* next, make a deposit, with the cashiers of the *Bank* of *England*, of 15l. *per centum*, in part of the monies so to be contributed, as a security for making the future payments to the said cashiers, on or before the times herein after-limited; that is to say,

On

On the 900,000l.

10l. *per cent.* on or before the 8th of *June* next; 10l. *per cent.* on or before the 15th of *July* next; 15l. *per cent.* on or before the 15th of *August* next; 15l. *per cent.* on or before the 15th of *September* next; 15l *per cent.* on or before the 15th of *October* next; 20l *per cent.* on or before the 15th of *November* next:

And the monies to be contributed, in respect of the said lottery, shall be paid to the cashiers on or before the times herein after-limited: that is to say,

On the Lottery:

25l. *per cent.* on or before the 20th of *June* next; 35l. *per cent.* on or before the 15th of *July* next; 40l. *per cent.* on or before the 15th of *September*, 1766.

And that all the monies, received by the said cashiers, be paid into the receipt of his Majesty's Exchequer, to be applied, from time to time, to such services as shall then have been voted, by this house, in this session of parliament, and not otherwise; and that every contributor, who shall pay in the whole of his contribution, on account of his share in the annuities attending the said sum of 900,000l. at any time on, or before, the 13th of *October* next, or on account of his share in the said lottery, on or before the 14th of *July* next, shall be allowed an interest, by way of discount, after the rate of 3l. *per centum per annum.* on the sum so completing his contribution respectively, to be computed, from the day of completing the same to the 15th of *November* next, in regard of the sum paid on account of the first-mentioned annuities, and to the 15th of *September* next, in respect of the sum paid on account of the said lottery.

2. That the several rates and duties, now payable upon houses, in *Great Britain*, do cease and determine from and after the 10th of *October* 1766.

3. That

3. That from and after the 10th of *October*, 1766, there shall be paid for and upon every dwelling-house, inhabited, which now is or hereafter shall be erected, within that part of *Great Britain* called *England*, the yearly sum of three shillings.

4. That from and after the said 10th of *October*, 1766, there shall be paid, for and upon every dwelling house, inhabited, which now is or hereafter shall be erected, within that part of *Great Britain* called *Scotland*, the yearly sum of one shilling.

5. That the several rates and duties, now payable for windows or lights, in *Great Britain*, do cease and determine from and after the said 10th of *October*, 1766.

6. That from and after the said 10th of *October*, 1766, there shall be paid for every window, or light, in every dwelling house, inhabited, or to be inhabited, within the kingdom of *Great Britain*, which shall contain seven windows, or lights, and no more, the yearly sum of 2d. for each window, or light, in such house.

7. That from and after the said 10th of *October*, 1766, there shall be paid for every window, or light, in every dwelling house, which shall contain eight windows, or lights, and no more, the yearly sum of 6d. for each window, or light, in such house.

8. That from and after the said 10th of *October*, 1706, there shall be paid for every window, or light, in every such dwelling house, which shall contain nine windows, or lights, and no more, the yearly sum of 8d. for each window, or light, in such house.

9. That from and after the said 10th of *October*, 1766, there shall be paid for every window, or light, in every such dwelling house, which shall contain ten windows, or lights and no more, the yearly

yearly sum of 10d. for each window, or light in such house.

10. That from and after the said 10th of *October*, 1766, there shall be paid for every window, or light, in every such dwelling house, which shall contain eleven windows or lights and no more, the yearly sum of 1s. for each window or light in such house.

11. That from and after the said 10th of *October*, 1766, there shall be paid for every window or light, in such dwelling house, which shall contain twelve windows, or lights, and no more, the yearly sum of 1s. 2d. for each window or light in such house.

12. That from and after the said 10th of *October*, 1766, there shall be paid for every window, or light, in every such dwelling house, which shall contain thirteen windows, or lights, and no more, the yearly sum of 1s. 4d. for each window or light in such house.

13. That from and after the said 10th of *October*, 1766, there shall be paid for every window, or light, in every such dwelling house, which shall contain 14, 15, 16, 17, 18, or 19 windows, or lights, and no more, the yearly sum of 1s. 6d. for each window or light in such house.

14. That from and after the said 10th of *October*, 1766, there shall be paid for every window, or light, in every such dwelling house, which shall contain twenty windows, or lights, and no more, the yearly sum of 1s. 7d. for each window or light in such house.

15. That from and after the said 10th of *October*, 1766, there shall be paid for every window, or light, in every such dwelling house, which shall contain twenty one windows, or lights, and no more, the yearly sum of 1s. 8d. for each window or light in such house.

16. That

16. That from and after the said 10th of *October*, 1766, there shall be paid for every window, or light, in every such dwelling house, which shall contain twenty-two windows, or lights, and no more, the yearly sum of 1s. 9d. for each window or light in such house.

17. That from and after the said 10th of *October*, 1766, there shall be paid for every window, or light, in every such dwelling house, which shall contain twenty three windows, or lights, and no more, the yearly sum of 1s. 10d. for each window or light in such house.

18. That from and after the said 10th of *October*, 1766, there shall be paid for every window, or light, in every such dwelling house, which shall contain twenty four windows, or lights, and no more, the yearly sum of 1s. 11d. for each window or light in such house.

19. That from and after the said 10th of *October*, 1766, there shall be paid for every window, or light, in every such dwelling house, which shall contain twenty-five windows, or lights, or upwards, the yearly sum of 2s. for each window or light in such house.

20. That out of the said rates and duties there be set apart and applied to the general or aggregate fund, the yearly sum of 91,485l. 6d. three farthings, in lieu of the like sum, which, by an act made in the 20th year of the reign of his late Majesty, was directed to be set apart and applied to the said fund, out of the said rates and duties upon houses, and windows or lights thereby granted.

21. That there be also set apart out of the said rates and duties, the yearly sum of 93,217l. 10s. 1d. and one sixth part of a penny, which appears to have been the annual produce, upon a medium of six years last past, of certain rates and duties upon houses, and windows or lights, granted by an act made in the 31st year of his said late Majesty's

jesty's reign; and that such yearly sum be applied towards payment of the annuities, established by the said act.

22. That the residue of the produce of the said rates and duties be carried to the sinking fund, in lieu of such part of the said duties so to cease and determine, as were applicable to such fund, and also, for making good to the same, the payments to be made thereout, of the annuities attending the sum of 1,500,000l.

23. That towards raising the supply granted to his Majesty, there be issued and applied, the sum of 2,150000l. out of such monies as have arisen, and shall or may arise, of the surplus monies; and other revenues composing the fund, commonly called the Sinking fund.

April 29.

1. That the sum of 80000l. remaining in the receipt of the Exchequer, which was granted to his Majesty in the last session of parliament, upon account for defraying the charge of the pay and cloathing of the militia for one year, beginning the 25th of *March*, 1765, be issued and applied towards raising the supply granted in this session.

2. That a sum, not exceeding 181,000l. of the monies agreed to be paid by a convention between his Majesty and the *French* King, concluded and signed at *London*, the 27th of *February*, 1765, for the maintainance of the late *French* prisoners of war, be applied to ditto.

3. That such of the monies, remaining in the receipt of the Exchequer, for the disposition of parliament, and as shall be paid into the said receipt on or before the 5th of *April*, 1767, of the produce of the duties charged by an act made in the last session of parliament, upon the importation and exportation of gum senega and gum Arabick, be applied to ditto.

4. That

4. That a sum, not exceeding 60000l. of such monies remaining in the receipt of the Exchequer, for the disposition of Parliament, and as shall be paid into the said receipt on or before the 5th of *April*, 1767, of the duties granted or continued, by an act made in the 4th year of his Majesty's reign, as were thereby reserved to be disposed of by parliament, towards defraying the necessary expences, of defending, protecting, and securing the *British* colonies and plantations in *America*, be applied to ditto for maintaining his Majesty's forces and garrisons in the plantations, and for provisions for the forces in *North America*, *Nova-Scotia*, *Newfoundland* and the ceded islands, for the year 1766.

5. That provision be made, for declaring that the additional duties granted by an act made in the 3d year of his present Majesty's reign, upon wines imported, were by the said act, intended, and ought, to be paid without any discount or deduction inwards, or drawback on re-exportation.

May 5.

1. For continuing the 19th clause of act 9 and 10 *Will*. III. chap. 26, and the proviso in the 5th clause of the act 12 *Anne*, stat. 1. chap. 18.

2. For continuing the first twenty-four clauses of the act 8 *Geo*. I. chap. 15.

3. For continuing the act, 2 *Geo*. II. chap. 35, as amended by the act 25 *Geo*. II. chap. 35.

4. For continuing the act 5 *Geo*. II. chap. 24; except such part thereof as relates to the importation and exportation of foreign coffee into and from the *British* colonies in *America*.

5. For continuing the act 19 *Geo*. II. chap. 27.

6. That liberty be granted to export coals from *Great Britain* to the islands of *Guernsey*, *Jersey*, and *Alderney*, annually, free of the duty laid upon all coals exported, by the act of last session chap. 35. viz. to *Guernsey* any quantity of coals not exceeding

ing 1000 chaldrons, *Newcastle* measure, from the port of *Newcastle*, and 150 such chaldrons from *Swansey*; to *Jersey* 350 from *Newcastle*, and 150 from *Swansey*; and to *Alderney* 110 from *Newcastle*, and 10 from *Swansey*.

May 8.

1. That provision be made for declaring, that the power granted by the act, 2 *Geo.* III. chap. 5. to remove spirits made for exportation to warehouses for home consumption, should extend to such spirits only, as are made from corn, malt, or melasses.

2. That from and after the first of *August*, 1766, there be paid to his Majesty, upon every pound weight averdupois of *Italian* wrought silks, called crapes or financies, imported, a duty of 17s. 6d. to be paid by the importer, over and above all duties now payable thereon; and that the produce of the said duty be carried to the sinking fund.

3. That a quantity not exceeding thirty tons weight, in any one year, of gum senega and Arabic, be allowed to be exported, free of duty, under proper regulations and restrictions, to *Ireland*, for the use of the manufactures there.

4. That authority be given to permit, under proper limitations and restrictions, the importation into this kingdom, from the *Isle of Man*, of such bugles as were brought into the said isle before the first of *March*, 1765, on payment of one half of the old subsidy only.

May 10.

1. That all the duties now payable on the importation of cotton wool into this kingdom do cease and determine. 2. That a duty of 3s. per piece be laid upon all such foreign linen cloth, called cambrick, and upon *French* lawns, which shall be exported into this kingdom to the *British* colonies and plantations in *America*. 3. That the duties

duties imposed by an act made in the last session of parliament, upon the exportation from this kingdom, of wrought silks, *Bengals*, and stuffs mixed with silk or herba, of the manufacture of *Persia*, *China*, or *East-India*, and callicoes, printed, dyed, painted, or stained there, do cease and determine. (4.) That there be granted to his Majesty, on all such wrought silks, *Bengals*, and stuffs mixed with silk or herba, of the manufacture of *Persia*, *China*, or *East-India*, and callicoes, printed, dyed, painted, or stained there, as shall have been publickly sold in this kingdom, on or before a certain day, to be limited, a subsidy of poundage after the rate of 1s. for every 20s. of the value of such goods, according to the gross price at which the same were originally sold, at the public sales thereof, such subsidy to be paid by the proprietors of the said goods. (5.) That there be granted to his Majesty a like subsidy upon all such wrought silks, *Bengals*, stuffs, and callicoes, as shall be publickly sold, on or after such day to be limited, the said subsidy to be paid by the *East-India* company, for such of the said goods as shall be sold at their public sales, and by the buyer of the said goods, at any other public sale. (6.) That the monies arising by the said subsidies, be appropriated in like manner as the duties granted by the said act were thereby appropriated. (7.) That all sugars which shall be imported into this kingdom, from any *British* colony or plantation, on the continent of *America*, be made subject to the like duties as are now payable upon the importation of *French* sugars.

May 14.

1. That for every gallon of single brandy spirits or aqua vitæ imported into *Great Britain* from beyond the seas, not being the produce of the *British* colonies and plantations, there be paid by the importer,

porter, before landing, an additional duty of 6d.

2. That for every gallon of brandy spirits, or aqua vitæ, above proof, commonly called double brandy, imported into *Great Britain* from beyond the seas, not being the produce of the said colonies and plantations, there be paid by the importer, before landing, an additional duty of 1s.

3. That the said duties be applied to the same uses, as the duties laid on brandy spirits and aqua vitæ by the act 33 *Geo*. II. chap. 9. are now applicable.

4. That for encouraging the exportation of hempen cordage manufactured in *Great Britain*, from hemp imported from foreign parts, and also from hemp of the growth of *Great Britain*, there be allowed upon the exportation thereof, a bounty of 2s. 4d. ¼ for every hundred weight of such cordage so exported; the said bounty to be paid upon the exportation, out of the net duties which have been, or shall be, paid upon the importation of all foreign hemp into this kingdom.

5. That for encouraging the exportation of hempen cordage manufactured in *Great Britain*, the drawback of 2s. 10d. ½ now payable on all foreign hemp exported from *Great Britain* to foreign parts, do cease, determine, and be no longer paid.

6. That such part of the duties laid by a resolution of this house, of the 10th instant upon sugars imported into this kingdom, from any *British* colony or plantation on the continent of *America*, as shall arise over and above the duties now payable upon sugars so imported, be paid into the receipt of the Exchequer, and reserved for the disposition of parliament.

7. That the duty of 3s. laid by a resolution of this house, of the said day upon every piece of cambrick

cambrick and *French* lawns, exported from this kingdom to the *British* colonies and plantations in *America*, be also paid into the said receipt, and reserved for the disposition of parliament.

May 16.

1. That a duty of 1l. 10s. sterling be paid for every negro, which shall be exported in foreign vessels from the island of *Jamaica*. 2. That a duty of 1l. 10s. sterling be paid for every negro which shall be imported into the island of *Dominica*. 3. That a duty of 6d. sterling, be paid for every barrel of beef and pork, which shall be imported into the said island of *Dominica*. 4. That a duty of 6d. sterling, be paid for every firkin of butter, which shall be imported into the said island. 5. That a duty of 6d. sterling, be paid for every hundred weight avoirdupois of sugar, which shall be imported into the said island. 6. That a duty of 2s. sterling, be paid for every hundred weight avoirdupois of cocoa, which shall be imported into the said island. 7. That a duty of 6d. sterling, be paid for every hundred gallons of melasses, which shall be imported into the said island. 8. That a duty of 6d. sterling, be paid for every hundred weight avoirdupois of coffee, which shall be imported into the said island. 9. That the said duties shall be applied in defraying the expence of carrying into execution such directions and regulations, as may be given and made by any act in this session of parliament, for opening and establishing any ports in the said island, for the more free importation and exportation of goods and merchandize, and for maintaining, securing, and improving, such ports. 10. That no other duties be paid upon the importation of any foreign *American* goods, in any such port in the island of *Dominica*. 11. That all goods of *American* produce, which shall be imported into this kingdom, from

such ports as may be so opened, in the said island of *Dominica*, be deemed foreign, and be made subject to the same duties respectively, as are now payable upon the importation of the like goods, of the produce of the *French* plantations in *America*, except only certain quantities of sugars, coffee, cocoa, piemento, and ginger, the amount of the importation whereof shall be limited, under proper regulations and restrictions, in respect of the produce of the said goods, within the said island.

12. That the said duties be appropriated to such uses, as the duties upon such foreign goods are now applicable unto.

These are all the resolutions of the committee of ways and means, which, in this session, were agreed to by the house, but as the sums to be raised by many of them cannot be known, I shall therefore add a list of those that may, as follows:

By the resolutions of *January* 31	750000	0	0
— — — *February* 21	2037824	15	11
— — — *March* 18	1800000	0	0
By the 1st and 23d resolution of *April* 21	3650000	0	0
By the 1st, 2d and 4th resolutions of *April* 29	321000	0	0
Sum total of the ways and means provided by this session	8558824	15	11
Excess of the provisions — *	285544	4	9½

January

* Upon one of the days of account, a circumstance happened, rather singular than important, which deserves to be noted.

Mr. Dowdeswell, as chancellor of the Exchequer, having stated some public accounts, Debtor and Creditor; Mr. Nicholson Calvert, stood up, and, with infinite humour, said, "he too would state some public accounts. When the gentlemen, now in office were in opposition, they engaged to perform several things whenever they came into power. Let us turn to the account (pulling a paper out of his pocket) here it is.

" DEBTOR

January 15th, it was resolved, that the house would on the 17th resolve itself into a committee of the whole house, to consider of the price of corn, on which day there was presented to the house and read, a petition of the court of mayor and aldermen of the city of *London*: this petition says that the petitioners thought it a duty they owed to the publick, in the exercise of this great trust, humbly to represent to the house, that by such returns made upon oath as aforesaid, it appeared to them, that the price of wheat fit for bread, had been for three months past, from 39s. to 42s. *per* quarter; and that the petitioners had observed, that notwithstanding these high prices, a large quantity of wheat and wheat flour had, within the aforesaid time, been exported from *London*; and that it being evident, that the old stock of wheat was nearly exhausted when the new wheat came to market, and there being reason to believe that the consumption of the new wheat would be increased, in some parts of this kingdom by the almost general failure of the last crop of barley, the petitioners begged leave to express their fears, that, if the exportation should continue, this nation might be so drained of corn, as to be again reduced, as in the last summer, to the necessity of having foreign supplies; or, at least, that the price of bread corn

"Debtor and	Creditor.
General warrants, to condemn	not done
Seizure of papers, ditto	ditto
Canada bills, to procure the payment of	not paid
Manilla ransom, ditto,	ditto
Cyder tax to repeal	done in part; but balanced by a most black and impotent attempt on the militia.
Mr. Pitt, never to forsake	Mr. Pitt is kept out by his best friends; and advised to stay in the country for the good of his health.
The last ministers, to impeach	The last ministry all merry, and in no danger."

would

would greatly advance, to the distress of the poor, and to the prejudice of the manufactures of this city, and the kingdom in general; and that the petitioners apprehend that the prohibiting the exportation of wheat, and other grain and flour, for a time, might be a means of preventing this evil; and therefore praying the house to take the premises into consideration, and to grant such relief therein, as to the house should seem meet.

Other petitions of the like import came from *Sheffield*, *Norwich*, and *Scotland*.

On the 20th the house resolved itself into the said committee, whose resolutions, being the next day reported by Sir *Joseph Mawbey*, their chairman, were agreed to by the house, and were as followeth: 1st. That the exportation of corn and grain, malt, meal, flour, bread, biscuit, and starch, be prohibited for a limited time. 2d. That the importation of corn and grain from his Majesty's colonies in *America*, into this kingdom, be allowed duty free, for a limited time. Upon this it was ordered, that a bill, or bills, be brought in pursuant to these resolutions. And a resolution was afterwards agreed to, that liberty be given to import oats for a limited time, duty free. Upon these resolutions bills were brought in, and passed.

Leave was also given, to bring in a bill to enforce the laws against forestallers of cattle and provisions. The bill was brought in by Sir *George Yonge*, Bart. and read, but there were no further proceedings upon it.

General Warrants condemn'd.

Another bill was brought in which met with the same fate, relative to the great question of general warrants. On the 22d of *April*, the house was moved that the proceedings of that house of the 14th of *February*, 1764, in relation to the question proposed, that a general warrant for apprehending and seizing the authors, printers, and publishers, of a seditious libel, together with their papers,

papers, is not warranted by law; and also in relation to the discharge of the complaint against Robert Wood, Esq; Philip Carteret Webb, Esq; members of this house, John Money, Robert Blackmore, and James Watson, for a breach of privilege of this house, might be read, and the same being read accordingly, it was then moved, that the proceedings of the house of the 17th of the same month, when the house resumed the debate upon the first part of the preceding motion, might be read; and the same being read accordingly, a motion was made that the proceedings of the house on the 29th of *January*, 1765, in relation to the question then proposed, that a general warrant for apprehending authors, printers, and publishers, of a libel, together with their papers, is not warranted by law, and is an high violation of the liberty of the subject might be read, and the same being read accordingly, a motion was made, and the question proposed, that a general warrant to apprehend the author, printer, or publisher, of a libel is illegal; and if executed on the person of a member of this house, is also a breach of the privilege of this house. Upon this question, after a long debate, the previous question was at last put, which being carried in the affirmative, the main question was then put, and likewise carried in the affirmative, and accordingly resolved; after which the following resolution was moved for, and in the same manner agreed to, viz. That the seizing or taking away the papers of the author, printer, or publisher, of a libel, or the supposed author, printer, or publisher, of a libel, is illegal, and that such seizing, or taking away the papers of a member of this house, is a breach of the privilege of this house.

On the 25th, these resolutions being again read, an amendment was proposed, and in the same manner agreed to, whereupon the resolution then stood

stood as follows, viz. That a general warrant for seizing and apprehending any person or persons being illegal, except in cases provided for by act of parliament, is, if executed upon a member of this house, a breach of the privilege of this house. And on the 29th, it was moved and ordered, that leave be given to bring in a bill to restrain the issuing of any warrant, for seizing papers, except in the cases of treason or felony without benefit of clergy, under certain regulations; and that Mr. *Grenville*, Mr. *Wedderburn*, the Master of the Rolls, and Mr. *Pitt*, do prepare and bring in the same. Then after having had the resolution of the 25th again read, a motion was made for leave to bring in a bill, to declare all general warrants, for seizing and apprehending any person or persons, to be illegal, except in cases provided for by act of parliament, agreeably to the said resolution; but upon the question's being put, it was carried in the negative.

In pursuance of the said order of the 29th, Mr. *Grenville*, on the 2d of *May*, presented the bill to the house, when it was received, and, upon his motion, being then near four o'clock, it was read a first time, and ordered to be read a second time, and to be printed. On the 6th it was read a second time, and committed to a committee of the whole house for the 9th, on which day, after reading the order of the day, a motion was made for resolving, that the house would, on that day two months, resolve itself into a committee of the whole house, upon the said bill; but, upon the question's being put, it was carried in the negative: whereupon Mr. *Bacon* was ordered to take the chair of the said committee, into which the house then resolved itself, as it did again on the 12th; when Mr. *Bacon* reported from the committee, that they had gone through the bill, and made several amendments thereunto, which they
had

had directed him to report, when the house would please to receive the same; and the report being ordered to be received the next morning, the amendments were then all agreed to, one of which was almost a total alteration of the title; for the bill was now intitled, A bill to prevent the inconveniencies and dangers to the subject from searching for and seizing papers, by establishing proper regulations, in such cases where searching for and seizing papers is justifiable by law. This being now the title, the bill, with the amendments, was then ordered to be engrossed; and on the 14th it was read a third time and passed, and ordered to be carried to the lords; where it miscarried.

When the motion for leave to bring in this bill was first made, some of those who supported the motion had an intention to have prohibited, by express statute, the issuing of a general search warrant in any case whatsoever, but upon more mature consideration it was probably thought, that such a statute would give encouragement and protection to several sorts of real and dangerous crimes, and a new statute to prohibit the issuing of a general warrant by a secretary of state, to be executed by his messengers, against the authors, printers, and publishers of what he was pleased to call a seditious libel, there was no occasion for, because the issuing of such a warrant was then allowed to be illegal, and had then lately been not only declared to be so, but severely punished by our courts of common law. It may in general be said, that no general search warrant can legally be granted, unless some fact has been committed, which is already declared by law to be criminal, or an information upon oath of a well-grounded suspicion that such a fact has been, or is to be committed; but the writing, printing, or publishing a book, pamphlet, or paper, is not surely a fact as yet by our law declared to be criminal: It is its contents
that

that renders the writing of it criminal; and as the printer may print it, and the bookseller may publish it, without knowing any thing of its contents; therefore none of them can as such be with justice punished for printing or publishing it in the way of their trade, before it was declared to be criminal by due course of law, unless it can be proved that they knew of its being so, and had due notice thereof before it was by them printed and published.

A LIST *of the* ACTS *passed this* SESSION.

AN Act, *To prohibit the exportation of corn*, &c.
An act, *To allow the free importation of oats.*
An act, *To continue the free importation of* Irish *provisions.*
An act, *To make a navigable canal from* Little Gwendraeth *river* Caermarthenshire.
An act, *To repair the roads from* Tunbridge *in* Kent.
An act, *To inclose* Doddington *common, in* Northamptonshire. *And other private bills.*
An act, *To raise* 1,800,000l. *by loans on Exchequer-bills,* &c.
An act, *For repealing the duties on cyder, and granting other duties in lieu.*
An act, *For building a new bridge from* Chelsea *to* Battersea.
An act, *For the improvement of tillage.*
An act, *For prohibiting foreign mitts and gloves.*
An act, *For supporting the parish church of* Folkstone *in* Kent, &c.
An act, *For better regulating the poor of St.* Botolph Aldgate.
An act, *For continuing the duty of one farthing per chaldron on coals, for repairing the piers and harbour of* Whitby.

An

An act, *For punishing mutiny and desertion in the* American *colonies.*

An act, *For encouraging the leather manufactory.*

An act, *For the improvement of tillage.*

An act, *For better regulating and employing the poor of* Richmond *in* Surry.

An act, *For improving the navigation of the river* Stort.

An act, *For paving, lighting, cleansing, and adorning* Berkley-square.

An act, *For taking down certain houses adjoining to the Bank.*

An act, *For better regulating and employing the poor of St.* Mary, Whitechapel.

An act, *For redeeming certain annuities respecting the navy, victualling and transport bills.*

An act, *For employing the sum granted for the militia to the service of the present year.*

An act, *For making the river* Soar *navigable.*

An act, *For making a navigable cut from* Wilden Ferry *to the river* Mersey.

An act, *For making a navigable cut from the* Severn, *to communicate with a canal intended to be made between the rivers* Trent *and* Mersey.

An act, *For better paving, lighting, and cleansing the city of* London.

An act, *For opening certain new ways and streets in the city of* London.

An act, *For paving* Southwark.

An act, *To establish a proposal made by* Wm. Constable, *Esq; to the governors of the charity for poor widows and children, in relation to a piece of land, called* Cherry-Cubb Sand *in* Yorkshire.

An act, *For the preservation of fish in ponds, and conies in warrens, in* Lincolnshire.

An act, *To regulate loading ships with coals in the ports of* Sunderland *and* Newcastle.

An act, *To prohibit the importation of foreign wrought silks and velvets for a limited time.*

An act, *To prevent the fraudulent making of framework knitted stockings.*

An act, *For regulating apprentices and journeymen.*

An act, *For repealing the* American *stamp act.*

An act, *For securing the dependence of* America *on* Great Britain.

An act, *For preserving timber trees.*

An act, *For establishing free ports in the* West-Indies.

An act, *For prohibiting the importation of* Irish *Cattle.*

An act, *For granting his Majesty a certain sum out of the sinking fund.*

An act, *For raising* 1,500,000l, *by annuities and lottery.*

An act, *For extending the duties on houses, windows,* &c.

An act, *For establishing four free ports in the* West-India Islands.

An act, *For repealing certain duties on goods in the colonies, and also on* East-India *goods exported from* Great Britain, *and for granting other duties in lieu thereof.*

An act, *For laying additional duties on spirits.*

An act, *For indemnifying persons for using unstamped paper in the* American *colonies.*

An act, *For amending an act relating to wines imported, and for securing the stamp-duties for copies of court-rolls,* &c.

An act, *For laying an additional duty on the importation of silk, crapes, and taffaties, and for allowing the exportation of gums to* Ireland.

An act, *For making the river* Chelmer *navigable from* Malden *to* Chelmsford.

An act, *For allowing the exportation of salt from* Europe *to* Quebec.

An act, *For amending the act for regulating buildings, and preventing fires.*

An act, *For explaining the act to prevent frauds in the admeasurement of coals.*

An

An act, *For regulating the poor, cleansing and lighting the streets, &c. of St. Andrew's Holborn, above the Bars.*

On the 6th of *June*, 1766, the King put an end to this session with the following speech:

My Lords and Gentlemen,

'It is with the utmost satisfaction, that I have
'observed the wisdom and moderation which have
'uniformly guided you through the many im-
'portant deliberations, in which you have been
'engaged during the course of this long and in-
'teresting session of parliament. I persuade my-
'self, that the most salutary effects must be the
'natural result of deliberations conducted upon
'such principles.

Gentlemen of the House of Commons,

'I thank you for the supplies which you have
'so chearfully given for the several establishments,
'and for the support of public credit: And you
'may rest assured, that no œconomy will be want-
'ing to render them effectual for the purposes for
'which they were granted.

My Lords and Gentlemen,

'The present general disposition of all the pow-
'ers of *Europe* seems to indicate a continuance of
'peace: And it is my earnest desire to preserve the
'general tranquillity, by fulfilling on my part, all
'the engagements I am under by treaties. And
'on this foundation, I may reasonably hope and
'expect the same strict performance of those en-
'gagements, which other powers are under to my
'crown.
'The many regulations which you have made
'for extending and promoting the trade and ma-
'nufactures of *Great Britain*, and for settling the
'mutual

'mutual intercourse of my kingdoms and plantations, in such a manner, as to provide for the improvement of the colonies, on a plan of due subordination to the commercial interests of the mother country, are the strongest proofs of your equitable and comprehensive regard to the welfare of all my dominions; and objects truly worthy of a *British* parliament.

'It shall be my endeavour, that such care be taken, as may tend to secure and improve the advantages which may be expected from such wise and salutary provisions.

'I have nothing further to recommend to you, than that you will exert your best endeavours in your respective counties, to enforce the execution of the laws, and to promote good manners and good order among my people; whose true and lasting happiness shall be my constant care, and upon whose affections I shall always firmly rely.'

A few weeks after the close of this session, the King again changed his ministers: The Marquis of *Rockingham*, and his friends were removed; and Mr. *Pitt*, who was at this time created Earl of *Chatham*, was introduced with a new set of men in most of the great offices.

The SIXTH SESSION

OF THE

Twelfth Parliament of *Great-Britain*.

On the 11th of November, 1766, the King went to the House of Lords at Westminster, and opened this Session with the following Speech.

My Lords and Gentlemen,

'THE high price of wheat, and the defective
' produce of that grain last harvest, toge-
' ther with the extraordinary demands for the same
' from foreign parts, have principally determined
' Me to call you thus early together, that I might
' have the sense of parliament, as soon as conve-
' niently might be, on a matter, so important,
' and particularly affecting the poorer sort of my
' subjects.

' The urgency of the necessity called upon me,
' in the mean time, to exert my royal authority
' for the preservation of the public safety, against
' a growing calamity, which could not admit of
' delay. I have therefore, by and with the advice
' of my Privy Council, laid an embargo on wheat
' and wheat flour going out of the kingdom, un-
' til the advice of my Parliament could be taken
' thereupon.

' If further provisions of law be requisite or ex-
' pedient with regard to the dearness of corn, so
' necessary to the sustenance of the poorer sort,
' they

'they cannot escape the wisdom of Parliament, to which I recommend the due consideration thereof.

'At the same time I must with concern take notice, that, notwithstanding my cares for my people, a spirit of the most daring insurrection has in divers parts broke forth in violences of the most criminal nature.

'Necessary orders have been given for bringing such dangerous offenders to condign punishment, and speedy justice; nor shall vigilance and vigour on my part be wanting, to restore obedience and reverence to law and government.

'I have the satisfaction to inform you, that, since I last met you, I have concluded a treaty of commerce with my good sister the Empress of *Russia*, whereby that considerable branch of trade is fixed on a just and satisfactory footing.

'It is with pleasure that I also acquaint you, that the marriage between my good brother the King of *Denmark*, and my sister the Princess *Caroline Matilda* has been solemnized, and the natural alliance between the two crowns happily strengthened by an additional tye of so agreeable a nature.

Gentlemen of the House of Commons,

'I have ordered the proper estimates for the current service of the year to be laid before you. Such supplies as you may grant shall be duly applied with the utmost fidelity, and strictest regard to the objects for which they are granted.

My Lords and Gentlemen,

'The general posture of affairs in *Europe* affords no occasion to lay any thing new before you on that head. My purposes are constant and 'fixed,

'fixed, to maintain, on my part, the public tran-
'quillity inviolate, and to support the dignity of
'my crown, and the rights of my subjects. The
'justice and wisdom of the other great Powers of
'*Europe* leave no room to apprehend any intentions
'of a contrary nature.'

As soon as the Commons had returned to their house, and the speech had been read to them as usual, by Mr. Speaker, a motion was made, and the question proposed, That an humble address be presented to his Majesty, to return his Majesty the thanks of this house for his most gracious speech from the throne.

To express the grateful sense we entertain of the paternal care and tender regard his Majesty has shewn for the welfare of his people, by laying an embargo on wheat and wheat-flour going out of the kingdom, until his Majesty should have the advice of Parliament on that important subject.

To assure his Majesty, that his faithful Commons will not fail, agreeably to his Majesty's recommendation, to take this weighty matter into their most serious consideration, in order, by timely and effectual measures, to pursue the two great ends, which his Majesty's wisdom has pointed out, of providing against the many evils attending a dearness or scarcity of provisions, especially to the poorer sort of his Majesty's subjects; and, at the same time, of suppressing that daring and dangerous spirit of riot, which has of late too generally shewn itself in many parts of this kingdom.

To assure his Majesty of our unfeigned joy, on the safe and happy delivery of her Majesty, and on the birth of a princess; every increase of his Majesty's royal family being a fresh pledge of the future liberty and happiness of his people.

To congratulate his Majesty on the solemnization of the marriage of his Majesty's sister, the princess *Caroline Matilda*, with the King of Den-

mark; by which the union with that ancient and potent ally of his Majesty's crown is established, on a fixed and permanent foundation.

To return his Majesty our thanks, for his gracious communication, that a treaty of commerce has been lately concluded with the Empress of *Russia*, which, while it gives us hopes of seeing that important branch of our trade continued hereafter on a solid and advantageous footing, is a new proof of his Majesty's constant regard for the true interest of this commercial nation.

To assure his Majesty, that his faithful Commons will chearfully grant such supplies, as shall be necessary for the service of the year; having the utmost confidence in the assurance his Majesty is pleased to give, that they will be punctually applied to those purposes for which they shall be granted.

To express our highest satisfaction in the present happy establishment of the public tranquillity; and the well grounded hopes we entertain, from the wisdom of his Majesty's councils, and the influence of his example, that, while he wisely unites with the resolution to support the dignity of his crown and the rights of his people, a true zeal for the general peace and happiness of mankind, the same spirit of equity and moderation, which animates his Majesty's conduct, will direct the councils of the other great powers of *Europe* to the like pacific and salutary views.

Upon this the house was moved, that part of the act 15 *Charles* II. chap. 7. might be read, meaning, clause the second of that act; the house was then moved, that part of the act 22 *Charles* II. chap. 13. might be read, meaning, the first part of clause the first of that act; which being read accordingly, the house was then lastly moved, that part of the act 1 *Will.* and *Mary*, sess. 2. chap. 2. might be read, meaning the first article of the declaration

claration of our rights and liberties contained in the firſt clauſe, and alſo the ſixth clauſe of that act; and the ſame being read accordingly, a debate enſued upon the firſt two paragraphs of the addreſs.

Before we give the arguments made uſe of in the debate, it will be proper to mention a few facts which happened during the receſs of Parliament. The act paſſed laſt ſeſſion prohibiting the exportation of corn, expired on the 26th of *Auguſt*, this year, and this year's crop having failed in many parts; our merchants had large orders to ſend corn to *Spain*, *Portugal*, *Italy*, &c. the moment the prohibiting law ſhould expire: this alarmed the lower ſort of people, who became exceedingly riotous, and aſſembled in bodies, at different places to prevent this exportation. Corn roſe to a great price, and government ſeeing the matter likely to become ſerious, iſſued a proclamation on the 26th of *September*, laying an embargo on all outward bound ſhips laden with corn or flour. This was ſuſpending the law, under which the exportation was authorized by the power of the King *only*. That it was neceſſary to ſtop the exportation every man admitted, but many ſaid, Parliament ought to have been called, and to have been made the judges of the neceſſity; and if it was neceſſary to ſuſpend the law, it ought to be done by an act of the three eſtates, and not by the King alone. The miniſtry defended, and attempted to juſtify their conduct upon the principles of law and right. And Mr. Alderman *Beckford* aſſerted, " That " whenever the public is in danger, the King has a " diſpenſing power." His words being taken down, he was called upon for an explanation, which he gave, by ſaying, " Whenever the Salus Populi " requires it." The argument upon this great and intereſting queſtion was fully ſtated in a pamphlet, publiſhed ſoon after the Debates upon it, entitled,

A Speech against the suspending and dispensing Prerogative, &c. Though the pamphlet, as it was esteemed, is, no doubt, in the hands of several gentlemen, yet, it is presumed, it will not be improper to preserve it here.

A SPEECH, *against the suspending and dispensing* PREROGATIVE, &c.

"IT IS BUT FORTY DAYS TYRANNY AT THE OUTSIDE."
PER LEGEM TERRÆ.

Populus Romanus beneficii et injuriæ memor esse solet.
Nemo civis, qualis sit vir, potest latere.
—Quemdam, hominem nobilem, factiosum, novis rebus studere, advorsum quem—neque LEGES valerent.
Neque modestia, neque modus contentionis erat.—
Sed eos frequens Senatus judicavit contra REMPUBLICAM et salutem omnium *dixisse.*

SALL.

PERMIT me, late as it is, to express my thoughts upon one of the most momentous subjects, in my opinion, that I have ever heard agitated in ——t. I hardly know what more important matter could occupy your — attention, short of a question touching the actual dissolution of government. Sure I am, if what we have this day heard strikes your ———, as it does me, it must have brought fresh to your remembrance the fatal ground upon which that unhappy question was decided, with a vengeance, when it was debated in th— h—e, near fourscore years ago.

We are, as it were, surprized into a debate upon the *dispensing power*, and what astonishes me still more, we are got, at least some of us, into a vindication and defence of it ;—a thing I had long thought so odious in its very name, but so settled in the notions of it, and so exploded in theory as well as practice, that no body ever thought of it, but to hate it, and to thank God it was utterly exterminated out of the pure solar system of the English Government, and English Liberty.

One —— has told us he rose in this debate not as *a Patron of Liberty*, in the *modern phrase*, as he was pleased

sed to call it, but as a *Patron of Law*. Modern phrase did the ⸺ say? I hope it will never cease to be a modern phrase; though it is an ancient, and has in all countries been a glorious title. Our ancestors were Patrons of Liberty at the cost of their lives; but they secured our LIBERTY by protecting the LAW against a *dispensing power*, which they resisted unto blood. *Quid a majoribus defensum est aliud quam* LIBERTAS: *neu cui nisi* LEGIBUS *pareremus!* Shall we then be the *præclara proles, geniti ad ea, quæ majores virtute peperere, subvertunda?* We are yet free, and " The freedom of men " under Government is to have a standing rule to live " by, common to every one of the society, and made by " the Legislative Power created in it." So says Locke, *who is* appealed to as a great authority. What he says in these few words is equally in favour of LAW and LIBERTY. I shall be proud to shew myself the Patron of *both*.

⸺, The same ⸺ has been pleased to claim, if not the whole, yet the best knowledge of the Constitution on behalf of the profession which has raised his ⸺ to the stations he has enjoyed. But I have always looked upon lawyers, at the best, to be but the most skilful midwives to help forward the birth of the wisdom of Great Statesmen, sound, enlightened, and enlarged Politicians, to the energy and sagacity of whose genius, in all ages, and in every country, the best models of Government have been most indebted: of this the appeal made to-day, as well as on a late *notable* occasion, to the speculations of Mr. *Locke,* that great Philosopher, Legislator, and Senator, (as we have been told he was) is a strong proof.

This also I will be bold to say from the history of *England,* that our liberties owe most to great Noblemen who were not lawyers. Sure I am, lawyers have often appeared amongst us, to be the worst guardians of the Constitution, and too frequently the wickedest enemies to, and most treacherous betrayers of the liberties of their country. Of this truth, the preamble of the Bill of Rights, which the ⸺ has himself appealed to in the debate, as his chief, though I think, much mistaken, and much misrepresented authority, will be a perpetual monument, in these words: " Whereas K. J. II. by the as- " sistance of divers evil Counsellors, JUDGES, and *Mini-* " *sters,* employed by him, did endeavour to subvert and " extirpate the Protestant Religion, and the LAWS and " LIBER-

"LIBERTIES of this Kingdom." Certain it is, that no arbitrary prince, when meditating the subversion of the Constitution, ever was at a loss for Lawyers and Judges to second his designs; in spite of their learning, and in spite of the religion of the oaths that bound them to support and maintain the Constitution. And so *ship-money* and the *dispensing power* have, in former times, had the vile countenance, and, if it could be so called, the authority of the bench, and of the sages, or the *Fathers of the Law* (as Charles I. named his ship-money Judges) while a Hampden, and such-like Patriots, who were the greatest honour, and the greatest blessing of *England* in their day, stood forth the saviours of their country, by resisting the usurpations of the crown, supported by the perfidy of corrupt Judges.

Such a sort of monopoly as the --- --- suggests in favour of the long robe savours too much of what a Lord Keeper (who made many excellent *perogative speeches* for *Charles* the First) said in the conclusion of the speech he delivered, after publishing that shameful opinion of the judges on *ship-money*. The words I allude to are these: "If any contrary opinion should yet remain among "men, it must proceed from those who are sons of the "Law." Of the *latter*, I will say, "*Felices demum essent* "*artes, si de illis solum judicarent artifices.*" So that *Prerogative Lawyer* was for keeping the judgment of the Constitution to the art and mystery of the law. Y------ will not, from the occasion, be fond of adopting the example.

If the ------ has now got so high an opinon of the advantages of the long robe, I remember when he had it not. But this is not the only proof this day has furnished from his --- and from some others too, of the wonderful change in opinions, that difference of interests, as well as situation, brings with it. For I think the same --- has likewise told us to-day, that we are undone by divisions, though I can recollect the time when his --- regretted in th---h---e that we were ruined by an *intoxicated unanimity*, under an a---n of which one of his *new* friends constituted a most brilliant part. I congratulate the --- --- on this change of mind for the better, which is more than I can say of all the opinions his --- has given to day, though I believe they proceed also from a *new light*. I cannot however say, the --- and ----'s opinions are *modern*. They are *old*, and, what is more, they are

are *antiquated*. His ---- has but revived an old farce, not acted near these hundred years. It will therefore be fit, I think, to examine opinions that have slept so long, before they are *restored*, or licensed, so as to pass current.

But it is necessary, for preventing mistakes, to premise, that I heartily concur with all your — who have spoke in the debate, in expressing my approbation of the measure immediately under consideration, *when taken*, --- the embargo on wheat and wheat flour laid by order of Council *so late* as the 26th of *September*. The evil of an enhanced price of that grain, which had for so considerable a time before been prognosticated, and growing by a quick pace, was then come to so alarming a height, that it awakened even our a----n from the pleasing dream of pecuniary emolument, and extravagant compensations, most liberally doled about to one another, beyond the example of any former time. It awakened them to the cries and risings of the poor, and at last made them take notice that there was such an imminent danger of famine, that it became indispensibly necessary to put a stop to the exportation: And by a long prorogation of Parliament, which themselves had so culpably advised, that there was no other way left of doing it, but by an interposition of the *Royal Power*. I choose to use that word, though *authority* is the word used in the S---, from the T--, because I materially distinguish between the two expressions, for reasons I shall afterwards give.

--- ---, On the other hand, I most warmly deplore and lament the calamity produced by the want and dearness of provisions, mentioned likewise in the speech, I mean that spirit of insurrection, riot, and disorder, that has gone forth, and rages in all corners of the kingdom, big with fire and sword, to afflict a country, already groaning under a weight and pressure of evils, greater than she can bear. It would ill become this place to palliate or excuse, on any account whatever, such dangerous tumults and riots, much less to incite and encourage them, by saying as I have once heard it said within these walls, by one sworn to execute the laws, that the subjects, cruelly harrassed by burthens and other grievances, imposed upon them by the Legislature, are made desperate. This daring and lawless expression, I confess, related only to the justification of the *American subject*

subject in wanton rebellion. God forbid that I should adopt the detestable language, even in favour of the *English subject*, taxed till the power of taxing can no further go, famished, and starving. It must, however, grieve one to see the nerves of government so totally relaxed, and its proper energy and vigour almost wholly lost. The truth of the matter, and the root of the evil is, we have had no government for some years, or, which is much the same thing, we have had the *form* of it only, without any reality, energy, or spirit, descending ever from bad to worse.

Tota discors machina divulsi turbat fœdera mundi.

And the —— in the blue ribbon has too good reason to put us in mind of what he told your — last year, that you would import rebellion from America. Would to God he had not been so true a prophet! The indulgence shewn to *Americans* is not I fear! altogether free of the blood that must be sacrificed, in *England*, at the altars of justice, to restore and preserve peace and good order, maintain authority and secure property. Nor can I acquit the blunders of administration in this very corn business, of that charge. I am afraid, the unseasonable, and extraordinary long prorogation of Parliament, which excluded the prospect of relief from famine, by a *legal* prohibition of the exportation, had no small share in producing the riots and risings: And by a shameful blunder in the Proclamation against forestalling, misreciting the laws it promulgates, a pretence was given for the riotous people to seize the grain for their own use, under a mistaken notion that the *grain* itself was forfeited, as the Proclamation declares it to be, instead of a forfeiture, of the *value* of it, which is what the misrecited statute enacts.

I said I approved of the embargo as necessary, *when* laid on; but I do not approve, on the contrary I complain of the preceding conduct of administration, by which they brought themselves into that dilemma, which necessitated them to advise his M— to that measure, by what is called the Royal Authority. And as to the principles I have heard laid down to day, and the doctrine that has been advanced in justification of the legality of the embargo; so far am I from approving of them, or acquiescing in them, that I cannot even hear them with patience.

patience. I declare they make all the Whig-blood in me boil; for, to use an expression that has, I think, been miserably misapplied on the other side, these doctrines, if adopted, lay the ax to the root of the constitution. They can tend to nothing but an utter subversion of the power of Parliament, and of the most fundamental and essential rights and liberties of the subject. Upon my word, if I did not know I was awake, I should be apt to think I had been in a dream, and that some fairy midnight scene had carried my imagination back an hundred and thirty or forty years, in an illusory audience of some of the speeches of a James or Charles, or their Lord Chancellors and Lord Keepers; for with no other standard of the prerogative, that I know of, will such notions square; and *these* they will fit.

I shall hereafter endeavour to point out that assemblage of circumstances on which I found the complaint of blunder, inattention, and neglect in the administration: But your —— will allow me, in the first place, to consider the general *doctrine* that has been drawn into the debate, as by much the most important matter, and what indeed principally called me up: I say has been *drawn* into the debate, for sure I am it could never have come from the measure in question, if it had been allowed to rest upon its true bottom, with a claim to such a sanction as could be given it by *Law:* which sanction, by the way, I fancy your —— will find necessary, notwithstanding all that has been said in support of the embargo as a legal exercise of perogative.

The question debated is, whether the embargo on corn, the largest freedom of exportation of which is permitted by many Acts of Parliament, and encouraged by a statute bounty, is a prohibition according to law; a *legal* act of *government*, within the constitutional bounds of the prerogative of the crown; or is only a mere *act of power*, induced by an urgent necessity in the state, exceeding the true limits of the royal prerogative, but that ought, for its beneficial tendency and effect to be approved, and must be confirmed by the sanction of law, to give it legal force, and valid operation.

This question comes to a general point, and it has been brought to that in the debate. A general proposition must be maintained, and the general proposition has been maintained, that of *any*, and if of any, of *every* act of parliament, the King, with the advice of the Privy Concil,

Council, may *suspend* the execution and effect, whenever his Majesty, so advised, judges it necessary for the immediate safety of the people.

I limit it so to give the proposition fair play. I shall likewise, to be as candid as I can, add, because it has been added, *during the recess of parliament:* and if —— please, they shall have the other words too, *when parliament cannot be conveniently assembled.* Such precisely is the proposition that has been maintained in this debate. For God's sake! —— is this the doctrine of the Constitution? Is this doctrine that Englishmen will swallow? Can it go down! I do not say with your ——, will it with the most unread or unlearned in the Constitution? If this is Constitutional doctrine, I make bold to pronounce the Revolution, the Glorious Revolution! (as I have been taught to call, and to think it,) nothing but a successful rebellion, the most lawless and wicked invasion of the rights of the Crown, — and the Bill of Rights, that illustrious monument of English liberty, the Palladium and Bulwark of the Constitution, the most false and scandalous libel that ever was published; the most infamous imposition, both on prince and people, ever invented. James the Second neither abdicated, nor forfeited; he was robbed of his crown. His Majesty is an usurper, and his Royal Ancestors, of blessed memory, even our great and glorious deliverer himself, have all been usurpers; the act of settlement is a nullity, and your —— are a generation of Rebels, whose fathers revolted; many of you are not ——s of the —m. Pardon me if I am warm, I cannot help it.

The —— at the head of the C— B— who spoke early in this debate, is called a Whig, —— a zealous Whig he calls himself; but he has defended the legality of the embargo, by maintaining the very proposition I have rehearsed. I say he has defended the *legality*, for we are not now debating the *necessity*, and the argument goes to exclude the method pointed at in the — moved, of *legalizing* the measure, and validating it, by a bill of indemnity.

The —— has told us, he would prove his point from no less authorities, than the Bill of Rights, Acts of Parliament, and the usage of the Privy-Council.— Very respectable authorities indeed! who could desire better? I shall consider them all, as far as I am able to follow the —— on memory; and I was as attentive as possible.

Now,

Now, —— to the proposition; and I would first speak a word to the last part of it ---the *recess of Parliament*. This is either an old, or a new distinction. If it is an old one, the —— should shew us where it is to be found; if it is a new one, he should tell us what authority, warranted by the law of the land, has made it. But the truth is, it is the distinction of the day, and I suspect it will never grow older; it is an alleviation of the dispensing power, to sweeten it to your ———, because too nauseous in the full stinking potion.

There was no such distinction in the days, when the *Law-making*, and the *Law-breaking Prerogative* walked forth at noon-tide. The princes that were then endeavouring to establish the *dispensing* and *suspending* power, in their best moods, and when they were speaking soft words to parliament, told them, that though they *condescended* to call them together, it was not because they could not do without them; and that if Parliament refused what they deigned to ask, they would only be forced to use the other powers for attaining it, which God had given them. The concomitant, and the fatal principal of those days was, that the Rights of Parliament were so many concessions of the Crown, resumable at pleasure, and the calling them but a gracious compliment from the prince: and so the maxim of the *idolaters* of prerogative, as then understood, that is of *absolute* and *arbitrary Power*, was *a Deo Rex, a Rege Lex*.

I cannot conceive the ground of this distinction as to the recess of Parliament. By the Constitution as now modelled, Parliament must always be in being, ready to be called, so much so, that even an expired Parliament revives when necessary to be assembled, and another is not chosen. With regard to acts of Parliament, I know of no days, either *fausti* or *festi*, in which they sleep. They are not like jurisdictions that may be evaded by going into a sanctuary. They are of equal force, while in being, at all times, in all places, and over all persons; or, as Mr. Locke says, " Laws, though " made in a short time, have a constant and lasting force." Acts of the executive power are incident, temporary, and instantaneous; but Acts of Parliament are permanent, made as the general rule by which the subject is to live, and be governed.

Unless therefore it can be said that the moment Parliament breaks up the King stands in its place, and that

the

the continuance of Acts is confined into his hands; he cannot of right *suspend*, any more than he can *make* laws, both requiring the same power. *The Law is above the King*; and the Crown, as well as the subject, is bound by it, as much during the recess, as in the sessions of Parliament; because no point of time, nor emergent circumstance, can alter the Constitution, or create a right not antecedently inherent. These only draw forth into action the power that before existed, but was quiescent. There is no such prerogative in any hour or moment of time, as vests the semblance of a legislative power in the Crown.

If we next examine the foundation of *necessity*, it will appear to be equally destitute of authority, as the other distinction. But it would be to tire your patience unreasonably, because there is no use in it, to enter into this argument at large. For who has ever read the arguments on *ship-money*, and the *dispensing power* in former and bad reigns, that does not know, that a *supposed* necessity was the plea to justify the acts complained of? And the answer is ready in the mouth of every one, that if the crown is the judge of that necessity, the power is unlimited; because the discretion of the prince, and his council, may apply it to any instance whatever: and so discretion degenerates into despotism. Therefore the wisdom of the constitution has excluded every discretion in the crown over positive statute, and emancipated acts of parliament from the Royal Prerogative, leaving the power of *suspension*, which is but another word for a temporary repeal, to reside where the legislative is lodged, to which only it can belong; that is in King, Lords and Commons, who together constitute the only *supreme sovereign authority* of this government. Nor did Parliament ever allow of the *dispensing* power, or any thing of the kind, because it was exercised under the specious pretence of *the safety of the nation being concerned, and the whole kingdom in danger*, which was the usual jargon, and, if true, implied the most urgent necessity.

The —— and ———— on the cross bench, who like a true friend of Liberty, has given us so excellent a definition of the Constitution, *as a government by Law*, (which I must do his —— the justice to acknowledge has often come from his lips in this house) has very accurately stated the extent of the crown's discretion, in matters within the legal prerogative, H———— has truly said, that in

these

these the crown which is entrusted with the power, and has the right to act, must be judge of the necessity and season of acting, subject always to the controul of that constitutional advice, by which the crown must act in all cases. But these acts, as his —— justly observed, are legal, not because they are necessary and proper, but because they flow from the proper power; and they are legal and valid, though wrong in themselves, 'till corrected; as a legal power may be improperly exercised, for which the advisers are responsible. But I heartily agree with his —— that the constitution has entrusted the crown with no power to *suspend* any act of Parliament, under any circumstances whatever; and with his —— I also declare I never shall, nor can, consent to any such power, being intrusted *with the Crown*.

For my own part it is difficult for me to form an idea of the *necessity*, in any case, of *suspending* an act of Parliament by *Royal Authority*; as the Parliament may always be assembled in time to prevent an irremediable evil from any statute. Sword and famine seem to be the most alarming evils; but neither of these can possibly ever catch the nation in a case of unavoidable necessity, without culpable neglect. Invasion is not the work of an instant, and government must be totally asleep, the ministers, both at home and abroad, dozing strangely, if there is not intelligence in time to assemble parliament. Scarcity, it is impossible, can ever come at a moment's notice, so as to make famine stare us in the face; and even in the present case it is apparent, that the necessity which, at *the instant*, justified the embargo, was owing to an inattention that loads the authors of it, and reduces it to the case of *Esau*'s necessity, who sold his birthright for a mess of pottage, because he had not been prudent enough to provide in time for satisfying his hunger at a cheaper rate. The Marquis of Halifax has some words so applicable to this subject, that I cannot help quoting them. " By the advantage of our situ-
" ation, (says he) there can hardly any such sudden dis-
" ease come upon us, but the King may have time
" enough left to consult with his physicians in Parlia-
" ment. Pretences indeed may be made, but a real ne-
" cessity, so pressing that no delay is to be admitted, is
" hardly to be imagined; and it will be neither easy to
" give an instance of any such thing for the time past,
" or

" or reasonable to presume it will ever happen for the
" time to come. But if that strange thing should fall
" out, our constitution is not strait-laced as to let a
" nation die or be stifled, rather than it should be helped
" by any but the proper officers. The cases themselves
" will bring the remedies along with them." This doctrine I can subscribe to in all its parts. But still, I say, that if a clear case of undeniable necessity could be figured, the *legality* of the act done under that force would just stand where it did, upon the general principles of the Constitution, and not the particular exigency of the instance, and the Justification be effected by an *ex post facto* law, has not pointed at. For I apprehend it to be bad politicks, and I should imagine it worse law, that any special case can ever derogate from a general fixed rule, such as a fundamental law of the Constitution.

Let us therefore — — take what road we will, still we come back to the general question, Has or has not the crown a right to *suspend* an act of Parliament, in any case, or on any pretence whatever? And let the question be tried by the House's own authorities.

I begin with the lowest and last named—the usage of the Privy Council. The — — produced no instances of this usage of the Privy Council, in prohibiting the exportation of corn. The present is the first we have been informed of. It is clear the Queen's ministers would not venture upon it in 1709. On the contrary, when the Queen was advised to call Parliament on purpose to make provision for preventing famine, it is remarkable that she tells them in the Speech from the throne, that she had done all that she could *by law*; referring to the proclamations issued against forestalling, &c. The Queen was not advised even to use the device of laying on a general embargo, thereby to prevent the exportation of corn; tho' being in time of war, the Crown had an undoubted right to lay an embargo. As that would have been using the war-power of embargoes indirectly for another end than a war-purpose; such an evasion of the law was not judged wise or fit. In the same manner the example of the Queen's reign was followed in 1756; which was also a time of war. Lord Hardwick would not then advise an embargo: We see at all other times of the like exigency, from an apprehension of scarcity, parliament has been constantly resorted to: And from the bare recital of the several acts of parliament on the subject, as well the laws permitting the exportation, as those temporary acts prohibiting it in times of scarcity, it is plain that there is not, perhaps, another instance of a thing so well guarded against the fangs of prerogative in practice as well as by statute.

—— The only example of this usage mentioned by the —— was the prohibition of the exportation of gun-powder, which is frequently laid on by the King and Council. But to that there is a very short answer, *viz.* that there is an express provision in one of the acts that have been alluded to, the 12th of Charles the Second, allowing the King by Proclamation to prohibit the exportation of gun-powder, though by the same act the exportation of it is permitted; which is an authority in point against, instead of being one for, the ——'s argument. And this express statute provision, as to gun-powder, to avoid doubts upon prerogative powers, even in such a case as that of warlike stores, proves how jealous Parliament is of a *dispensing power*, and how scrupulous Government has been to rest any thing upon constructive arguments of *right*, or cases of *necessity*, to justify the Crown's interfering with acts of Parliament.

In regard to the authority of acts of Parliament, the only one mentioned by the ——, I think, was that converting the declaration of rights into a bill, and making it a statute. We may therefore take both together, the ——s argument being founded on a comparison of the declaration with the bill or statute, and what the —— is pleased to call a difference between them, as if the bill limited and restrained the words in the declaration.

They —— read from his *own copy* the first article of the declaration of rights, presented to the Prince and Princess of Orange, and *verbatim* recited in the bill, or act of parliament. The words of the article are, " whereas King James," &c. did so and so, " by assuming and exercising a power of *dispensing* with, and *suspending* laws, and the execution of laws without consent of parliament." And says the —— this to be sure is general, and would leave no latitude, but this is only the *claim* as put in by the subject, and therefore when parliament came to enact upon the article,

ticle, they restrained it, knowing that it was impossible but there might be a necessity for the Crown's *suspending* some particular acts of parliament, *during the recess of parliament*. I appeal to your —— if this was not the ——s reasoning precisely, and his very words, I marked them well, for I own they surprised me.

And the —— next reads on your —— the second article of the bill, in the enacting part, which stands thus (viz. declared by parliament) "that the pre-" tended power of dispensing with laws, or the exe-" cution of laws by legal authority, *as it has been af-" sumed and exercised of late*, is illegal." Hence says the ----- it is clear that Parliament, when they came to make the statute, would not deny every degree or kind of a *dispensing* power in the Crown, but only as *exercised of late*, that is by King James. I confess the reasoning astonished me, and I think it could not convince y----- or any man living, if the thing rested on the very words the ---- has read, to prove his distinction between the declaration and the enacting bill.

The history of these words *as exercised of late* is well known. They were an amendment made by the Lords to the bill to save some old charters and grants, with *non-obstantes*: And to secure against all dispensations whatever with statutes in time to come, there is a clause in the end of the act, declaring that no dispensation by *non-obstinante* of, or to any statute, should be thereafter allowed, except a dispensation be allowed in such statute. But what was the *dispensing* power exercised *of late* by King James? It was only dispensing with *penal* laws; that is, a remitting or *dispensing* with penalties inflicted by act of parliament in certain cases: And even that sort of dispensation, or exercise of the *dispensing* power by King James, is condemned by the Bill of Rights as illegal.

These words therefore upon which the —— has laid so much stress, furnish one particular remark, but it is most unfavourable to the purpose for which he has quoted them. Your --- will have prevented me in it, by recollecting what I had just now mentioned. For tho' King James undertook to shew, by the means of his corrupt judges, *that a power in the King to dispense with law was law*, the only acts of parliament upon which he made his essay of the *dispensing* and *suspending ng* power were the *penal* statutes against non-conformity: from which, for the sake of the Papists, he gave a general exemption, by the lump, to all his subjects. He took that method, because parliament had remonstrated against his *dispensing* with the Test-Act, in favour of the Roman Catholick officers he employed: And the language which the parliament held in that remonstrance deserves our most particular notice. They told the King " that the consequences of *dispensing* with " that law, *without an act of parliament* were of the " greatest concern to the *rights of the subject*, and to " *all the laws*." King James suspended no acts of parliament besides these penal laws; and to *penal* laws *only* did the judges he corrupted extend that shameful opinion for the *dispensing* power, which they gave judicially in a particular case; an opinion grounded upon such notable reasons as these, " that the laws of England were the King's laws, and therefore it was an incident, inseparable prerogative of the Kings of England, as of all other Sovereign Princes, to *dispense* with all *penal* laws; and that it was not a trust invested in, or granted to the King, but the antient remains of the sovereign power of the Kings of England, which never had been taken from them, nor could be." Yet for dispensing with and *suspending* these *penal laws* only, laws that in so far as they affected Protestant Dissenters were truly a grievance, and therefore were repealed after the Revolution, did the estates of this kingdom *dethrone* King James: And it was declared in the bill of Rights, that the pretended power of *dispensing* with laws, or the execution of laws by legal authority, as it had been *so* assumed and exercised *of late*, was illegal. What then must we think, in these times, of such a construction, as is now held out of the bill of rights, which attempts to invalidate and pervert the Great Charter of the Revolution, by setting up, as a Prerogative of the Crown, a right, in *all cases of necessity*, to *dispense* with *all* laws, touching our Liberty, and our Property?---a right to which in these instances K. James the IId, with his most corrupt judges, never dared to aspire.

But my wonder is not confined to the ---s construction or interpretation of these words. For I am utterly at a loss to understand how the --- got at the *second* article of the enacting bill, without reading the

first;

first; or how he took the second article *alone* of the bill for the *whole* echo of the first article of the declaration or claim of rights recited in it, as the preamble of the enacting part, when the half of the answer to the first article of the *Claim* or declaration is in the first article of the Bill. But however the --- may have past over that first article of the enacting part, I dare say it is not out of any of your --- memory. Hear the words of it. (Art. 1. of the enacting bill) " Declare that the pretended power of *suspending* of " laws, or the execution of laws, by *regal authority*, " *without consent of parliament*, *is illegal*:" the very precise letters and words of the first article of the declaration, or claim of rights, only leaving out the word *dispensing*, because that it is made an article by itself in the second of the enacting bill. After reading this first article of the enacting part of the bill, I certainly need not ask your ---, or the --- himself, where the limitation is, in *that article*, on which his --- has founded his whole argument? Nor will the --- deny that the first article is as much a part of the Act of Parliament as the second. Most undoubtedly there is not the least difference between the *Bill* and the *Claim* in this *general*, unlimited and unrestrained position, that the *pretended* power of *suspending* of laws, or the execution of laws, by regal authority, without consent of parliament, is illegal; every word of which is emphatical. And so parliament in the same bill enacts, " that all and singular the Rights " and Liberties *asserted* and *claimed* in the said *declara-* " *tion*, are the true, ANTIENT, and *indubitable* RIGHTS " and LIBERTIES of the people of this kingdom, and " shall be so esteemed, allowed, adjudged, deemed, " and taken to be; and that all and every the parti- " culars aforesaid shall be firmly and strictly holden " and observed, as they are expressed in the said *decla-* " *ration*; and all officers and *ministers* whatsoever shall " serve their Majesties and their successors according " to the same."

The ------ says it is a narrow and illiberal idea that the Crown has not, or ought not to have, a power, for the publick good, *to suspend* an act of parliament. I do not know what the ------s notions of liberality are, or how liberal his own ideas may be. Extraordinary liberality *received*, may beget extravagant *returns*. Profusion

fusion in giving may produce vast compliance in yielding; and to whom much is given, of them the more will be required. A great authority says, that gifts blind even the wise. For my part I confess, I have no opinion of that liberality of which the Constitution is the subject. Of the Constitution no man can be too sparing or abstemious. She has cost much, and she is worth all that she has cost, and without it, every thing else will be of little value. I hope nothing shall ever tempt Y--- to be liberal so much at the expence of your fellow-subjects. Slices of the Constitution, are the last thing I will give away, nor shall I consent to maim it, to gratify any man, or to justify any measure.

As to the ---s question, what would be the distress on many occasions, if there was in no case a power in the Crown, to *suspend* an act of parliament? After the words of the *Bill*, that is the *Statute* of *Rights*, which I have quoted, I will give no other answer than this, that they exclude totally, absolutely, and in the most general terms possible, any such power: And I am yet to learn what posterior statute has repealed one article of the Bill of Rights, or vested in the Crown, or the Privy Council such a sort of *Chancery* powers, to *suspend* laws and acts of Parliament, or suggestions of equity, or expediency, for the safety or relief of the subject: Nor do I see that such an alteration would be an amendment of the Constitution, I think it would destroy it, to the very foundation.

We have had a philosophical argument upon *Prerogative*, to prove that the prohibition in question was a *legal* exercise of *legal Prerogative:* and Mr. Locke's authority has been quoted, a page or two of whose chapter on Prerogative the --- in my eye has read.

Nobody has greater respect for Mr. Locke's writings than I have; yet if I found any thing in them that did not square with the settled fundamentals of the Constitution, I should not be moved by him. It is highly improper, I am afraid, to enter here into a general discussion of Mr. Locke's ideas, and nothing but the deference, I will add the justice, due to so venerable a name, would have made me go into this. But I believe Mr. Locke and I do not at all differ, and I think he is misunderstood, when brought as an authority on the other side. It is not doing him justice; for surely there was not a man in England a greater enemy to the *dispensing* power than himself.

Prerogative, is a word that has been the occasion of great wranglings, and certainly the princes of the house of Stuart understood by it arbitrary power, or something so very near it as not to be distinguishable. I have a very simple notion of it, and it is this, that *Prerogative* is that share of the government which, by the Constitution is vested in the King alone. Lord Coke, after giving the etymology of the word as denominated from the most excellent part, because the King must be first asked before any law is made, says, " the Prerogative comprehends all the powers, preeminences, and privileges which the Law giveth to the Crown. It is no distinct or separate inheritance in the Crown opposed to the interest of his people. It is a trust *ad communem totius populi salutem*, just as much as the powers of Parliament are. Now I can never conceive the prerogative to include a power of any sort to *suspend* or *dispense* with laws, for a reason so plain that it cannot be overlooked unless because it is plain; and that is, that the great branch of the prerogative is the *executive* power of Government, the duty of which is to see to the execution of the laws, which can never be done by *dispensing* with or *suspending* them.

When Mr. Locke speaks of the prerogative *as acting sometimes against law, or of the laws themselves yielding to the executive*, it is far from his meaning that the prerogative or executive can *dispense* with or *suspend* laws. His example makes it clear, *viz.* that of pardoning offenders where the law condemns, which is certainly undoubted prerogative. There the law yields, not in its force or subsistence, but only in its consequences, and in a particular instance: And though the King can pardon, he cannot beforehand, even in a particular instance, *dispense* with the law. The expression of acting *against law*, is perhaps not well chosen, but it is evident Mr. Locke intended to express no more than this, that the Crown can by pardon (for instance) prevent that execution which the law would effect. As for the other instance mentioned by Mr. Locke of the law *yielding*, *viz.* pulling down a house to stop a fire, it is a clear inaccuracy: for that has nothing in the world to do with prerogative, or even with magistracy, no more than the throwing goods overboard to keep a ship from sinking. It is an instantaneous act of self-defence, to authorize which no man waits

waits for, nor needs seek the order of a magistrate. The *fact* of danger which is *visible*, justifies it *in law*, just as the danger of a ship justifies *in law* the throwing goods overboard: and both acts are *legal*, and allowed by all the laws in the world. No body ever heard or read of a proclamation or edict from the sovereign to pull down a house in the midst of a conflagration. So that if Mr. Locke's whole definition of Prerogative is taken together and fairly expounded by what he himself says, it will be found he perfectly agrees with what other sound Constitutionalists have advanced, that " Prerogative is " a power in the person of the Sovereign, to command " or act in matters not repugnant to the law, or for which " the law has not provided, and certain acts of grace " and favour, which the King might exercise with re" gard to some particular persons, provided these acts " were not very prejudicial to the rest of the nation." Let Mr. Locke be but allowed to speak in his own words, and no error can be drawn from them. His reasoning in support of what he calls the law *yielding* to *prerogative* or the *executive* is this, " Since many accidents may hap" pen, wherein a strict and rigid *observation* (he should " have said *execution*) of the laws may do harm, and a " man may come sometimes within the reach of the " law, which makes no distinction of persons, by an " action that may deserve reward and pardon, 'tis fit the " ruler should have a power in many cases to mitigate " the severity of the law, and pardon some offenders."

And in the other places alluded to, where he speaks of prerogative *acting against law*, he reasons thus, " For " since in some governments the law-making power is " not always in being, and is usually too numerous, and " too slow for the dispatch requisite to execution; and " because it is also impossible to foresee, and so by laws " to provide for all accidents and necessities that may " concern the public, or to make such laws as will do " no harm, if they are executed with inflexible rigour on " all occasions, and upon all persons that may come in " their way, therefore there is a latitude left to the exe" cutive power, to do many things by choice, *which the* " *laws do not prescribe*." Mark the last words! *which the law does not prescribe*. He does not say of doing things to *make laws of no force*. Nor in any one place of the book does he speak of prerogative as having a power to *suspend* any law. On the contrary, he largely handles

the

the power of positive laws over the prerogative itself, to declare limitations of it; and shews the absurdity of calling such limitations encroachments upon the prerogative: And he is very clear and express " that the legislature " is the supreme power of the common wealth, and that " *no edict of any body else, in what form soever con-* " *ceived, or by what power soever backed*, can have the " *force and obligation* of a *law*, which has not its sanction " from that legislature which the public has chosen and " appointed, and that no obedience is due but ultimate- " ly to the *supreme* authority, which is the legislature."

Any author may be misunderstood by taking detached pieces of his writings, and that only can render Mr. Locke's sense of this matter dark or obscure; though I do not think he is always nicely correct in his expression.

For one instance, he says, in one place, that " the " supreme power cannot take from any man any part of " his property without his consent, because the end of " government is to secure property." Yet would not any man be justly laughed at to produce this sentence from Mr. Locke, to prove that parliament could not divest the owners of the property of the houses which the bank has thrown down in Threadneedle-street, upon giving them a compensation? Mr. Locke knew better than to doubt it; though that single sentence, if it stood by itself, might import a contrary opinion.

A great deal has been said on this occasion by the --- who has quoted Mr. Locke, upon a few other words of that great author, where he says, that " if " there comes to be a question between the executive " power and the people, about a thing claimed as a pre- " rogative, the *tendency of the exercise* of such a preroga- " tive to the good or hurt of the people will easily decide " that question." And the argument drawn from these words is to shew that the *tendency* of the embargo in question, to the *good*, and not to the *hurt* of the people, must decide for the legality of the measure, as an exercise of legal prerogative. But I must say there never was, in my poor apprehension, an argument founded in a greater mistake, or an author more unseasonably cited.

Mr. Locke is not here speaking of the tendency of a single act done in exercise of a right of prerogative, as a rule to decide the legality of that particular act: he speaks, (and his words are plain) of the tendency, that is, the *general* tendency of the exercise of a power or

thing

thing claimed as a prerogative, as a rule by which the question may be decided, whether that power or thing claimed as a prerogative, be really a legal prerogative, or only an usurpation. And most undoubtedly it may be a safe rule of decision. It is upon that very rule that I, and I trust every Englishman in his senses does, and for ever will decide, that a *suspending* power *is* not, *cannot* be a legal prerogative, in any circumstances, or under any pretence whatsoever, because the tendency of the exercise of such a prerogative is destructive to the Constitution. I say *the tendency of the exercise:* for it tends to render acts of parliament uncertain, and to bring positive law under the discretion, that is the pleasure of the Crown, and consequently to set the whole Rights and Liberties of the subject afloat, so that no man can for a moment be sure of the law, though it is his inheritance and *birth-right.* Then indeed it would be *vis mensura juris.*

Far therefore, am I from differing with Mr. Locke, in what he says in the words quoted. I find myself at full liberty to express my approbation of his reasoning. I adopt his rule of decision of that great question, whether a thing claimed as a prerogative, be, or ought to be one. And I also heartily concur with Mr. Locke's sentiments in the only other quotation that has been read from him, " that when that great question does arise, " (and it must be the greatest of misfortunes when it " does) between an executive and a legislative power, " constituted as ours are, there is no judge on earth to " decide it; and therefore the only remedy is the appeal " to Heaven, that is, to the sword." On that principle do I appove and justify the conduct of those great and brave men, who maintained our Liberties at the expence of their lives. They first contended for them, in parliament, by force of reason, and particularly against the *dispensing power* of the Crown; and when the obstinacy of unhappy princes, enslaved with the notions of arbitrary power, which they called Prerogative, left no other option but to submit to the usurpation of the Crown, or to fight, they drew their swords, and Heaven, to which they appealed, propitious to English Liberty, justified their cause, and crowned it with success. In that extremity it was their right, their undoubted right, upon the doctrine of legal resistance, which is incorporated in this Constitution, to take the field againſt the princes who were the enemies of their people, the oppreſſors of their Liberties. For as Mr. Locke truly ſays, in the forcible expreſſions that have been read by the ——, " The people have by a " law antecedent, and paramount to all poſitive laws of " men, reſerved that ultimate determination to them-" ſelves, which belongs to all mankind, when their lies " no appeal on earth, *viz.* to make their appeal to Hea-" ven: and this judgment they cannot part with." That, (to uſe the Marquis of Halifax's words, a little, and but a very little differently applied) " is the hidden power in " this Conſtitution, which would be loſt if it was defined; " a certain myſtery, by virtue of which a nation may " at ſome critical times, be (as ours has been) ſecured " from ruin: but then it muſt be kept as a myſtery: " it is rendered uſeleſs, when touched by unſkilful " hands; and no people ever had, or deſerved to have " that power, which was ſo unwary as to anticipate their " claim to it."

I think I might with great ſafety to the queſtion before us, leave the authority of Mr. Locke, without any apprehenſion of the leaſt impreſſion from it. But as the doctrine of *tendency* has been brought on the carpet, I cannot diſmiſs it without a few words more; becauſe I think it is of importance that it ſhould be ſtated upon its true grounds; and I ſhall endeavour to do it very ſhortly.

I admit, as in this very caſe before us, (*the neceſſity being allowed*) that a power which is not a legal prerogative, may be exerciſed for the good of the people: and ſo I will allow too, that the moſt legal prerogative that exiſts may be exerciſed to the hurt of the people. But as the hurtful exerciſe of a legal prerogative, in a particular inſtance, will not make the prerogative ſo hurtfully exerciſed, ceaſe to be a legal prerogative, or prove that the general tendency of ſuch a prerogative is to the hurt of the people, and therefore that it ought not to be a prerogative; ſo neither will a beneficial exerciſe, in a particular inſtance, of an illegal or uſurped Prerogative, change its nature and general tendency, ſo as to decide that it is or ought to be a legal prerogative.

I will explain myſelf, though I hardly think it neceſſary, by examples. It is the undoubted prerogative of the Crown, to declare war, make peace, and

treaties,

treaties, to create peers, and to pardon offenders. And the general tendency of the exercise of all these prerogatives is for the good, and not for the hurt of the people. The Constitution has therefore vested these powers in the Crown, and they are legal prerogative. But who will deny that any one of these prerogatives may be improperly and hurtfully exercised? If they are, the advisers of the Crown are responsible, though the power exercised is legal, and the acts valid. As the — and — on the cross bench truly said, when the King makes war, it is war to all its consequences, however improperly the Crown may have beeen advised in taking the measure; and so of the rest. On the other hand, if a *suspending* power were exercised in an instance never so beneficial, the power is not a legal prerogative, and is not to be endured, because of its dangerous tendency. Nevertheless, the particular act done, under colour or pretence of such a power, if in itself for the advantage of the people, will not cease to be so, however illegal the power to do the act may be. Let me only just ask, as it comes in my way, and may in some respects be particularly applicable to the case of the embargo under consideration—Could the Crown now legally create a foreigner a peer, because it is the general prerogative of the Crown to make peers, when the act of settlement has in that particular instance, restrained the general prerogative of the Crown? Certainly not. And for the same reason, even supposing it to have been at any time an inherent power in the Crown to prohibit the exportation of Corn, the Crown cannot now do it, as positive statute has clearly divested the Crown of the power.

What I have said is, I think, sufficient to shew, that Mr. Locke is very much misunderstood and misapplied, in the words last referred to, which have been much insisted upon, when they are produced as an authority to prove, that the *tendency* of the embargo to the good of the people, is the rule for deciding if it is an exercise of a legal Prerogative or not. I will even venture to say, Mr. Locke's words are a clear authority upon my side, to prove, as far as the reasoning and opinion of that great writer can do it, that the *dispensing* or *suspending* power, which is the only thing that can be named as a Prerogative, under or by virtue of which

the

the embargo is laid, is not, and cannot be a Prerogative.

I will however go yet a step farther, and I hope I shall satisfy y---, that the use made of this authority of Mr. Locke, taken as the ―― has stated and explained it, even upon his own argument, is as dangerous and unsatisfactory as any thing can be. For --- suppose for once, it was the tendency of a particular act that was to decide for or against the legality of that act, as an exercise of a legal Prerogative, I only ask, what would be a more uncertain or dangerous rule of decision, with regard to the suspension of an act of Parliament by the Crown, if the decision is to be with the Crown; and with the Crown it must be, when the suspension is to be the act of the Crown; and consequently, according to the argument, the legality of the act to depend upon the Crown's decision? I say, what more uncertain or dangerous rule of decision? I do not say but a case may be put, so strong, that there cannot among men be a doubt as to the tendency of a particular act of suspension, as in the very instance of prohibiting the exportation of corn, when famine is staring you in the face; and in such a case, the Crown would decide just as every other person would. At the same time, one may affirm, that even that case is not such an one as will always admit of an absolute mathematical certainty; for men may be, and they often are, divided in opinion as to the appearances of scarcity, whether real or not, and to what degree; and consequently whether it is fit to prohibit the exportation of corn or not. But supposing that to be one clear case, I ask, how many more clear ones can be mentioned? And I am intitled to ask the question, because if a power in the Crown to *dispense* with an act of Parliament, for the good of the people, is the foundation of prohibiting exportation, supposing exportation to be authorized by act of Parliament, the same *dispensing* power may be exercised as to other acts of Parliament, on the like ground of the good of the people; and so must extend to the whole statute book. Now ---, how many cases are there, in which all mankind would, to a man, be agreed, that it was for the good of the people to *suspend* any one particular act of Parliament? What act is it, that if a question of Repeal were in Parliament, ――― and t ――― o --- h ---- e might not

not be divided in opinion about? some thinking it of a tendency for the good of the people, others thinking the contrary, and the people without doors also divided in opinion. Would it then be a safe rule to make any one act of Parliament, *in the general view of things*, depend on the decision of the Crown, for a *suspension*, be it never so short, which is nothing else than a temporary repeal?— Or is that a rule, upon which to rest or trust the decision of the Legality of any particular act of a *suspending* power exercised by the Crown? I will not, I need not, lengthen the argument. It is clear nothing could be a more dangerous, uncertain, and arbitrary rule: nothing so naturally tending to found a despotic power in the Crown over acts of Parliament. And therefore nothing can be so fallacious or misapplied an argument, as that drawn from Mr. Locke, explaining his words in such a sense. His rule would not apply: it could not even to particular acts or exercises of any power or prerogative. He did not intend so to apply it. As a rule with regard to one or another general power claimed as a prerogative, it is a sound and safe one; and he applies it no otherwise himself: But, as I said, it is not only foreign to the purpose, as it has been applied in the argument, but it is clearly against the thing contended for by those who do apply, or rather misapply it in that manner.

One single remark I must be allowed to make, before I close my observations upon Mr. Locke's authority. The last s———n of P————t set out with the wildest doctrines, extracted *piecemeal* from the same Mr. Locke, in favour of Liberty; of Liberty run mad with notions extravagant, ridiculous, exploded, and thank God! by the whole legislature condemned. This s———n begins with doctrines again extracted also *piecemeal* by the same persons, from the same author, trumpeting forth a tone of tyranny, more hateful, and more dangerous, because more extensive, than any promulgated in the worst reign of the worst of the Stewarts. I hope, *these* will meet with the same contempt as the others did. Indignation is the due of *both*.

After all —— what is this old and stale argument now revived, as to the *tendency of the exercise of a prerogative for the good*, and not for the *hurt of the people*? What is it, I say, taking things on a general view, but the exploded argument of *necessity* repeated in other words? The wildest bigot to Prerogative, or ab-

solute

solute Power, (if I may imitate the enthusiasm of the ———— and ———— ————'s expression who spoke of the wildest zealots for Liberty) I say, the wildest bigot to Prerogative never pretended, that any Prerogative whatever, the *dispensing* power itself, could or ought to be exercised, but for the good of the people; the Prince indeed always being judge of that. Even *Manwaring* and *Sibthorp* themselves would not have said otherwise;—those monsters of men, who prostituted the pulpit, to preach the impious and nonsensical doctrines, " that if Princes
" commanded things against the laws of God or of na-
" ture, or impossible, yet subjects were bound to undergo
" the punishment, without resisting, railing, or reviling.
" ————And that the King is not bound to observe the
" laws of the realm concerning the subjects rights and
" liberties, but that his royal will, in imposing taxes
" without consent of Parliament, bound the subjects
" conscience, upon pain of eternal damnation:"————
Even these men, and their stupid doctrines, suppose that what was done by the Prince should be for the public good; and that what was not so, was in itself wrong; as certainly what is against the laws of God or of nature must be; and therefore, as they admit, could not in conscience be *actively* obeyed, for which reason they wickedly and senselessly say they ought to be obeyed *passively*, by suffering punishment. But did not every Prince who exercised the *dispensing* or *disabling* power, pretend that he did it for the good of the people, and that the particular acts by which it was exercised were for the best ends? Look at James the IId's declarations for liberty of conscience. What more specious pretences could be devised than are mentioned in those acts of the dispensing power?
" To unite the hearts and affections of his subjects to
" God in religion, to him in loyalty, and to their neigh-
" bours in christian love and charity." For these great
" and good purposes, " he thought fit, by his *sovereign*
" *authority, Prerogative royal and absolute power*, which
" all his subjects were to obey, without reserve, to grant
" his royal Toleration." And for that purpose, " with
" the consent of his privy council, by *his sovereign au-*
" *thority, Prerogative royal, and absolute power*, he *sus-*
" *pends, stops*, and *disables* all laws or acts of Parliament
" made or executed;" and so forth. These are the words used in one, and they are only a little softened, but
not

not substantially varied, in another of the Declarations of this sort.

Part of that same very illegal act of the *dispensing* power, the declaration in favour of liberty of conscience, unquestionably was, in its tendency, for the good of the people. The first part of it, artfully introduced to colour all the rest, is a toleration to protestant dissenters, exempting them from the absurd penalties of nonconformity. But did that tendency of the exercise make either the particular exercise, or the pretended Prerogative exercised, legal? No. It was equally an exercise of the *dispensing* power, and consequently equally *illegal* in favour of protestant dissenters as of papists, though the tendency was very different in regard to the two. And accordingly when government came to itself, and was upon a right foot, one of the first acts passed after the Revolution was, for exempting protestant dissenters from the penalties of those grievous laws that affected them. The preamble of the act adopts the very motives with which K. James gave a colour to his declaration; and the act itself is the best proof in the world, if the fact needed one, that the tendency of K. James's exercise of the illegally assumed power, was so far for the good of the people. Yet that very act of K. James was one of those that cost him his Crown, and, as I have said before, stands the very point condemned by the second article of the bill of rights, *as exercised of late*, without any distinction as to the tendency of any part of it; though the posterior act of exemption manifests the opinion of parliament that one part of it tended to the good of the people. The difference is this: the act of Parliament was the constitutional relief from the grievance; the act of K. James, let its tendency, in any part, be what it would, was, in the whole of it, the exercise of an unconstitutional and usurped power, against law, and in its tendency dangerous to the liberties of the people.

I will venture to say, that there is not any one notion more exploded, and more condemned by the statute book than that notion of the *tendency* of acts for the public good being sufficient to make them legal: and indeed it is one of the wildest notions that ever entered the mind of man; for it goes to cut up all government by the roots, and to make every man a judge and lawgiver for himself. I might have said, that it is condemned and exploded by all morality and sound divinity; avowed and

professed

professed only by Jesuits, and such diabolical casuists. But I say, look only to the statute book. What is the language of all your acts of indemnity, passed upon great occasions? I need not mention those in our own memory, passed after the rebellions 1745 and 1715, on purpose to indemnify those who had done acts for the public service against law, and that could not be justified by law, as the stile of these statutes runs. Let me only refer your ------ to one of the first acts passed after the Revolution, *the act for preventing vexatious suits against such as acted in order to bring in their majesties, or for their service.* What does it say? " Whereas about the time of his majesty's GLO-
" RIOUS enterprize for delivering this kingdom from
" popery and arbitrary power, and in aid and pursuance
" of the same, divers lords, gentlemen, and other good
" people, well affected to their country, did act, &c.
" in which proceedings, some force, &c. were unavoid-
" able, which in a time of common peace and safety,
" would not have been warrantable: and also since their
" Majesties happy accession to the crown, by reason of
" the wars and troubles raised and occasioned by the ene-
" mies of their majesties and this kingdom, divers like
" matters and things have been done; all which were
" *necessary* and *allowable*, in regard to the exigence of
" public affairs, and *ought* to be *justified*, and the parties
" concerned therein indemnified," &c.

Surely, — ———, if ever there were acts that tended to the good of the people, these mentioned in this act were :--------acts to rescue the kingdom, its religion and laws, from ruin and destruction ;---and done at a time, of all others, when no law could be said to be in force, but the law of nature, which stimulated and justified what was done, the government being totally dissolved; so that one might say there existed no law of the land to be transgressed, or that could be a ground of action or charge, as where there is no law there can be no transgression. Yet even for such acts done, acts *necessary and allowable*, as the statute speaks, and done under such circumstances of a suspension *in fact* of all the laws in the kingdom, did these saviours of their country take and pass to themselves an indemnity? They loved the constitution they had saved so much, that they would not suffer the very act of saving it to have the appearance of giving it a wound. And though these were the acts of subjects, it makes no manner of difference; for I do

maintain,

maintain, that in law, and legal and conſtitutional language, the Crown has no more right to *ſuſpend* acts of Parliament, or to act againſt them, than any ſubject; becauſe, as I ſaid before, the one is not more than the other the legiſlature. This however is a diſtinction totally immaterial, becauſe according to this Conſtitution, there can be no act of the Crown, but ſome ſubject is reſponſible for it as the adviſer: and in the matter before us, the lords of his Majeſty's Privy Council ſtate themſelves, juſtly, as anſwerable to Parliament for the act they adviſed. Over and above all which I might add, that the caſe I have referred to was the ſtrongeſt and moſt favourable that could be; for if it was not the Crown which did the acts indemnified, it was not *one* or a *few* ſubjects, but the whole people and Parliament itſelf that were the actors; and had not the caution for the ſafety of the conſtitution been great, in proportion to the zeal that had juſt redeemed it, men might have thought, with good reaſon, that the very act of Revolution, and the ſtatute that placed the Crown on William and Mary's heads, were ſufficient to juſtify every part of the work, as well as the beſt proof of the tendency of every thing done in aid and purſuance of it.

—— There were other acts in the reign of William and Mary, of the ſame tenor and effect with that I have quoted, particularly in 1690 and 1692, on occaſion of threatened invaſions. I only mention them becauſe the perſons firſt named as the actors in the things thereby juſtified and indemnified, are *the lords and others of the Privy Council*, and the chief act done againſt the law, was the cauſing the militia to be raiſed *otherwiſe than as authorized* by the acts of Charles the Second, which were not more ſacred than the acts of the ſame reign, permitting the exportation of corn. The Privy Counſellors, even of thoſe days, were not ſhy to acknowledge on the records of Parliament, that they had acted againſt law and againſt acts of Parliament, though the acts they had done were *neceſſary* and for the *public good*; nor did they deſpiſe and refuſe an indemnity, but accepted it to tranſmit it to poſterity as a ſafeguard of the conſtitution, that in future times no evil might come to it, from a precedent of the higheſt neceſſity, and moſt important ſervice to the country; becauſe they knew, as we do, *omnia mala exempla a bonis orta ſunt*. His preſent Majeſty's Miniſters are aſhamed or afraid to own that an act they adviſed

advised was not legal, though they say it was necessary, and all agree with them, that from various neglects and criminal blunders, it was *at the time* become so necessary as to be unavoidable. Rather than own a breach of the law, even a *necessary* one, that ought to be justified, they will defend the act done as strictly legal, at the expence of maintaining *a degree* of the *dispensing* power: I say *a degree*, for I will not make it worse than they do themselves—They are so much more delicate or infallible than King William's Ministers and Privy Counsellors, that they are affronted with the offer of an indemnity: and one —— —— says, *timeo Danaos et dona ferentes*. I believe it. All ministers, when they are in the wrong, are afraid, especially of those that are able to shew their error, and by offering a plaister discover the sore. I truly believe they are afraid, for the same reason as the Trojans dreaded their enemies, and suspected their gifts, that is, lest the *city should be surprized and taken*. But —— —— the fall of fifty ministers, or fifty successions of them, if the greatest that ever were, is not to be compared with one thrust at the Constitution, let the instrument be never so harmless or the intention never so innocent: for she may be wounded even *in the house of her friends*, and *alta sedent civilis vulnera dextræ*. If the —— is afraid of those who profer gifts, I will be jealous of those who refuse such as are now tendered, and refuse them on such grounds as I have heard this day, in my opinion, dangerous in the last degree to the Constitution; and only so much the more so that they are the arguments of her once most zealous friends, to whose past services I will consent to give any reward but that of wounding the Constitution further; one hair of the head of which I would not have hurt for all Ministers, or any *prime Minister* on earth.

The —— —— who founded so much upon the authority of Mr. Locke, in his second speech, has taken up some time to justify the argument of the —— —— who sits near him, from a misinterpretation which he thought some other —————— put upon it, as if the —————————— had argued for a *general* and unlimited *dispensing* power; whereas he only maintained it in cases of *necessity*, and till Parliament could meet: and says the —————— that is the circumstance which distinguishes the act in question from those exercises of the *dispensing* power complained of in former times ————————, that it was done only when Parliament could not meet, and till it assembled:

bled: and farther, says the ----- -----, it is singular for criminals to call their judges to condemn them; yet the King's servants have called the parliament to judge of the act they advised, and to condemn it if it is wrong.

--- --- if you have honoured me with any attention to what I have said, you will not think that I mistook or misstated the argument of the --- and ----- which the other ---- ---- has explained and enforced, as well as justified. I do not think any of your ----- did mistake it: but I did not like it as he gave it us, and I hope very few of your ----- were pleased with it. It is true, the ---- and ---- was but for giving us a taste of the *dispensing* power; I do not chuse to touch the cup: and therefore I reject the distinction, as to the recess of parliament, totally, and I have endeavoured to disprove the foundation of it. Whether I have succeeded, your ---- are to judge. I can make no distinction but one, and that I do make, between an act of *Power*, and an act of *Prerogative*. The Crown has the whole force of Government in its hands, all inferior Magistrates and Ministers of Government under its orders; and what the Crown commands they will obey, and in general I think they ought, as it must indeed be a very strong act against law, that they should dispute or disobey, as it would be dangerous to constitute them judges over the Crown. But Parliament will make the distinction between Power and Prerogative, and judge upon the act done accordingly. The act in question, I say is an act of mere power supposed to have been impelled by necessity, and tending to the safety of the people, and as such it is to be allowed and justified; but it is not to be taken as an act of Prerogative, because it is not a legal act, there being no such prerogative in the Crown, as a *dispensing* power for one moment, or in any one moment: and therefore it was, that I very soon told your ———— I objected to the words *Royal Authority*, as I hold *authority* to be *legal power*, whereas the embargo is, in my opinion, *power without law*, and *against law*, consequently is not authority in a just sense.

As to what the ———— ———— says of the Ministers calling Parliament *their judges* to judge of the act they advised, I see no weight in the observation at all, upon the footing of the doctrine advanced by himself, and by others whose arguments he has supported. Had the Ministers told us, that they had advised the Crown to an act of power which they were sensible was not agreeable to law, but was so necessary and salutary, that they were confident it would be approved, and that they had, in that confidence, called Parliament to submit their conduct to the judgment of Parliament — I say, had they held this language, I admit they might have said there was some modesty at least in calling their judges to sit upon them, and that it would have passed for a presumption of innocence as well as a proof of candour. But what are we told? Why that the Crown had a right to do what it has done; that it was the Prerogative of the Crown to do it; and all the modesty that can be pretended, is that the ministers did not give a longer line to the exercise of this Prerogative, but called Parliament a little more early than usual, though perhaps, if the whole truth were known, Parliament was really called (as it was at the time alledged) only for the India business. It is impossible it could be for the embargo, as the embargo was not laid when the Proclamation for calling the Parliament was issued, viz. 10th September. However, if the doctrine that has been advanced is just, Parliament has no judgment to give of the act done by the Crown; but only to judge what they themselves ought to do in the same affair. For now that Parliament is met, all that is told them is this:—"You may have thought, when at your country houses, that the embargo was not a legal act; but we let you know you are mistaken; for the embargo is the exercise of the ordinary and *undoubted Prerogative* of the Crown." I own I did not expect to hear such news, and if I believed them I should not think the Parliament was met upon a very foolish errand, but I would say it was upon a very unhappy occasion; and at the best I think there would have been as good reason, and not more modesty, in calling Parliament in the beginning of the winter, to acquaint them, that during the recess, his Majesty had thought fit to create some new Peers, and to change his Ministers, which are both the undoubted Prerogatives of the Crown, whether exercised properly or improperly.

The ----- and ---- ---- upon the ---- ----k, a new convert to Prerogative, has thrown his abilities, and the weight of his situation, gained by other doctrines, into the scale of the *dispensing* power; and in maintaining that degree of it contended for by the other ---- whom he has supported, his ---- has taken the ground of the law of nature, that first of all laws, *self-defence*, recurring again to to that *necessity* which is superior to all law, and calling up the great maxim, *Salus Populi Suprema Lex:* and his ---- tells us he goes to *common sense*, he wants no statute for that which is written in the breast of every man, that law of instinct, that inherent power which must be in every state as much as in a single person, to defend itself:---and that if he thought the law of England (which he had hitherto thought to be perfect) was so destitute of sense and reason, as not to have that great fundamental of all law and government, *Salus Populi*, &c. for a part of it, he would move for a Bill to enact it, and make it part of the law of the land.

The ----- ---- says he was one of those who a------d his ----- to the measure in question, and he thought he had done right. He thought his ------y deserved thanks for the care he had taken of his People, but he now finds there is to be blame even when he is *dispensing good* to the nation, and the view is to cast a slur upon the gracious act of the Crown, and to hold forth to the Publick that there has been a violation of the Constitution. And if it is so, says his ---, he ought to change his tone and *cry mercy*; and the first thing y---- ------ ought to have done was to call the offenders who gave this criminal advice to the bar --- but says his ---, I will not be so mean as to sculk under a pardon till I find I am condemned, and it is hoped y---- ---- will not condemn any unheard. The --- --- is ready to enter upon that ground with any man, and to maintain that it is not only the *Right* but the *Duty* of the Crown to *suspend* the execution of a law, for the safety of the people, as much as to keep them from starving;---that the Crown is bound in duty to protect the people from ruin, and the Prerogative (as another ------- ------ had expressed it) is nothing but a power to protect them; and, says the — and — — upon the —k, it is a strange thing if the act was wrong which every body says they would have advised—that it is a strange crime to be meritorious—a strange criminality to save a country from ruin—from famine. His —, however, challenges any one to shew that act of parliament, that excludes the Crown from the power of stopping the exportation of grain;—there is nothing, he says, in the whole statutes, from Magna Charta down, but this one simple thing, that the sea shall be open, *soit la mer ouverte* — that the Crown had done no more than to keep wheat in the country to prevent a famine at home, and that only for

forty

forty days, till the parliament should meet;—and, says the ——— in the warmth of his fancy, that is such *a power as he believes Lucius Junius Brutus would have entrusted Nero himself with*;—adding, as if that was not an expression strong enough — *it is but forty days tyranny at the outside.*

When I repeat these words, in which I am sure I am not mistaken, I cannot go farther without disburthening my own mind of its feelings. That ——— ——— is the last person from whom I should have expected to hear such words. But I own a great deal of what he has said shocks me;——— by nothing that he has offered am I convinced: And though it may be bold for one of those not entitled, and not expected to be so learned in the constitution, and with still less pretensions to be learned in the law; yet I cannot stir from my p——e till I have done some justice, unable as I am, to what presses upon my poor understanding.

Forty days tyranny!——— *Tyranny* is a harsh sound. I detest the very word, because I hate the thing. But are these words to come from a ——— ——— whose glory it might, and ought to have been, to have risen by steps that Liberty threw in his way, and to have been honoured, as his country has honoured --m, not for trampling her under foot, but for holding up her head? The ——— ——— in the b———r——— has said, as it became him to say, *forty hours, nay forty minutes tyranny* is more than Englishmen will bear. I have used my best endeavours to answer the argument which is the foundation of the distinction to which the forty days alludes, by argument founded in principles; I will now give the ——— ——— one answer more, and it shall be *argumentum ad hominem* ——— That ——— ——— has, I believe, said on other occasions, and he said well, that the price of *one hour's* English Liberty none could tell but an English Jury, and juries under the guidance of a *certain* ———, have estimated it very high, in the case of the meanest of the subjects, when oppressed only by the servants of the state. But forty days Tyranny over the nation, by the Crown! who can endure the thought?———, less than forty days tyranny, such as this country has felt in some times, would I believe bring your ——— together without a summons, *from your sick beds, riding even upon post horses, in hot weather, faster than our great Patriots themselves to get a place or a pension, or both*; and, for aught I know, make the

subject

subject of your consultations that *appeal to Heaven* which has been spoken of. Yet establish a *dispensing power*, and you cannot be sure of either liberty or law for forty minutes.

I have as great a regard for the principles of the law of nature as the —— —— can have. I love them. I know indeed the law of nature is not a law for men in their present state; it is too weak to bind them; and it will always with some danger be recurred to, as a rule of conduct, even in cases of the most extreme necessity. However —— —— I am ready enough to admit that every state, that is, all government, as well as every individual, has an inherent right to act, and must, for self-preservation, act upon that principle of the law of nature *self-defence*. But —— do not let us be led away with a name without proper ideas. Even that great principle of *self-defence*, sacred as it is, does not suspend or make void any positive law or constitution whatever: it only takes the case acted in *out of the law*, leaving the law in its full force. So a man who kills in self-defence is acquitted, not because there is no law against murder, but because his case is not within that law. I cannot help therefore thinking, it is but an incorrect use of the term *self-defence* to apply it to this case, by saying the embargo was self-defence against famine. The laws for exportation have not overlooked or omitted to provide for the case of self-defence against famine. Your —— will understand what I mean, when you recollect, that as the laws stand there are limits set to the liberty of exportation, to stop it when the prices come to a certain pitch, and that is the remedy which the legislature has saved against dearth; the *fact* then suspending the *law*. I do not say but such a necessity may occur as to make it necessary to draw another line, and so we have had, and now again, I presume, shall have a temporary law narrowing the line. But that is an extraordinary case, the cognizance of which, Parliament has reserved to itself, to apply an extraordinary remedy to it; and has not left it to the superior wisdom of the Crown and Privy Council to anticipate that extraordinary remedy by a *suspensation* of the laws, within the bounds prescribed by parliament, which will of themselves stop the exportation as soon as Parliament has thought, in a general view of things, it ought to be prevented.

— — I revere the principle of *salus populi suprema lex*. And I do not think we need an act of parliament to introduce such a fundamental into the law of England. But what does this principle teach? Why this, that in the *making* of laws, the safety of the people ought to be paramount to every other consideration, public or private: and in the *execution* of laws, or obedience to them, that it may for an instant transcend them all; so that if a case happens in which positive laws cannot be executed or obeyed, and at the same time that great principle pursued, positive laws are and ought to be disobeyed, or not executed at peril, the maxim followed, and the justice of government relied upon for the justification and indemnity: a hazard which under no wise and good Government, any man acting with an upright intention need be afraid of.

But the Principle, even upon the widest ground of the law of nature, does not import that all positive laws are by the force of it *ipso facto* suspended or repealed; in cases that concern the execution or obedience of them. It supposes the very contrary; and never could do otherwise, unless we were at once to say a thing so absurd as this, that not only the Executive Power of Government, but every subject is vested with a *dispensing* power; as the principle operates with equal force on single subjects, as on the Executive Power itself; and is upon every individual a binding duty, as far as there is an obligation upon any one to consult the safety of the Commonwealth. If therefore the debate were, upon the Act in question, whether to be justified or not upon this great principle, supposing it not justifiable upon any other, Government most surely is intitled to avail itself of the principle, so qualifying the act, as to bring it within it. But if Government maintains the Act to be the exercise of Legal Power, and consequently against no law, the principle of *Salus Populi*, &c. which always supposes the direct contrary, is totally out of the question: and indeed I cannot help taking notice of it as an inconsistency, that, in my apprehension, runs through the whole of the argument of the — and —, which I am now considering, that he resorts at all to extraordinary principles, and particularly to those of the law of nature; for if, as his — and other — have argued, the Act in question is a legal Act, and the exercise of a legal Prerogative, it needs no *Salus Populi suprema lex*, for a justification or excuse. It defends

defends itself, and is within the protection of the positive law of the land; and consequently the law of nature has no more to do with it than the law of any foreign State, that has no authority in this Country. For my part—the application I do, and shall, upon every such subject, and occasion, as the present, make of the maxim *Salus Populi*, is this, that as I think the safety of the People could not be secure one moment, if the Constitution were not preserved entire, and unhurt, the supreme law with me shall ever be to maintain unrelaxed and unenervated the fundamentals of the Constitution, and, as one of the principal of them, to exclude every, even the least degree of a *dispensing* or *suspending* Power in the Crown, the natural and necessary tendency of which is to destroy the Constitution, and of consequence to destroy the safety of the People.

And here ———— I would only ask by the way, if ever the principle of *Salus Populi* was made or pretended to be made, a ground for the Crown's assuming or exercising a power to *suspend* the *Habeas Corpus* act by order of Council, though nothing perhaps more directly concerns the safety of the State, on some occasions; and therefore it is the first thing Parliament does in emergencies of imminent danger? These *suspensions* are, I hope, the only species of *Dictatorial* power, that this Government is acquainted with. But, thank God, they are no part of the Constitution, nor do they depend on the pleasure, or even the discretion of the Crown. One Great — has indeed mentioned the *Dictatorial* power, in the debate, and endeavoured to assimilate this act of the Crown, of suspending the laws for the exportation of corn to it. But surely, after saying what I have just now said of the suspension of the *Habeas Corpus*, as totally beyond the power of the Crown, it is needless to give any other answer to this attempt to compare the Crown's *suspending* these laws with the *Dictatorial* power among the Romans. If the *suspending* or *dispensing* power of the Crown were any part of this Constitution, it would indeed be a *Dictatorial* power with a witness; and a perpetual one too. So that we should be so much worse than the Romans were, as their Constitution slept only during the existence of the *Dictatorial* power, which was but short, and expresly given by the Senate; whereas ours, without the intervention of our Senate; would at once and forever be destroyed totally.

The — and —— speaks of *meritorious criminality* as strange; and it would be so. But meritorious *illegality* is not so strange, or an action meritorious in itself and happy in its effects, though against law. The merit consists in running the risk of the law, for the publick good; as in the instance alluded to by the other — and — on the cross bench, of the Roman General who fought against orders, and was rewarded for saving his country. On the other hand, if an Act is authorized by law, there can be no such risk, nor consequently any other merit than that of doing one's duty.

I agree with the — who hold the --ls of S. of S. that he would be a poor Minister indeed, who would not run such a risk, when the safety of the State required. I will not take the ---'s instance of signing a General Warrant, as he *arbitrarily* said he would do, notwithstanding all the noise that has been about them; for a General Warrant is such a piece of nonsense as deserves not to be spoken of, being no warrant at all, and incapable of answering any one purpose, in any case whatever, that a legal warrant would not better attain. But this I will say, that without being a Minister, as an inferior Magistrate, or even as a private subject, I should not hesitate, upon good ground of public safety, to stop, if I could, any ship from sailing out of port, to the destruction of the State, although no embargo subsisted: and in this case, if Ministers had held to the justification of the particular Act, upon the circumstances, they had done well. But they have justified the Act, by maintaining a Power which I cannot acknowledge. I blame not the Crown, nor the advisers of the Crown for *dispensing good*, nor do I wish to hold out to the people a violation of the Constitution; but I will blame Ministers for asserting a Prerogative in the Crown, which, instead of dispensing good, would dispense much evil; and if they will hold out a power unconstitutional, and destructive of the vitals of the Constitution, they must excuse others for holding up the barrier against such a power, and defending the Constitution. I think Prerogative is a Power, and it is a duty also to protect the people; but I think a *dispensing* Power is no Part of the Prerogative, and equally against the duty of the Prerogative, and the safety and protection of the People; and to tell y— the truth, I am astonished how a H--- of L--- could have patience to sit and hear so much of it: The --- spoke as if he joked, and certainly was in

jest

jest when he talked of *crying mercy*, and *skulking under a pardon*, of calling to the bar and condemning. I will not enter into what the other --- and --- who spoke before him said of his not being a wise man who refuses God's pardon and the King's. But I have had occasion to mention instances of your --- ancestors, when they did things meritorious indeed, though not authorized by law. They did not cry out for the *mercy*, but they claimed the *justice* of their Country: and their Country protected as well as applauded them. Parliament past indemnities; nor did these brave men think it any meanness to cover themselves; I will not disgrace their heroism so far as to say they *skulked* under a pardon, tho' they sued for and accepted an indemnity *in their own persons* for the Constitution. Let me tell the --- who jokes at this rate, that the time has been, (and I almost wonder we have not seen it *very lately*) when a word in defence of any sort of *dispensing* power would have brought the greatest --- in the kingdom to the Bar: Sure I am it is wonderful forbearance that no one --- insisted upon some very alarming expressions being taken down. It is a kind of complaisance or acquiescence that I fear more than the --- needs fear the *dona ferentes*. Language of this sort, sat under quietly, --- Language so directly trenching on the Constitution, is, I am afraid, a disagreeable symptom of want of health in the Body Politic. We have heard, *it has been said*, in justification of the subjects resisting law, and rebelling, that the *original Compact* was broken by the Legislative Power, in one Act of Parliament, which was but a just and seasonable exertion of what stands the declared, asserted, and recognized power and right of Parliament: and now a jurisdiction is to be given to the Crown over the Legislature, by a *suspending* Power, by which every Act of parliament may be broken. Is it lest Parliament would again, as it was traiterously said last year, BREAK THE ORIGINAL COMPACT by some other Acts of Parliament? How two such opposite opinions are to be reconciled, I know not! or how they can *both* be made to quadrate with a zeal for Liberty, which has perhaps run wild; I leave that to those who hold and have given both opinions. But I think they are both dangerous opinions; and by much the more so that they are the opinions of the same persons, which puts their *principles* beyond the reach of my line. Thus much I will say, the *dispensing* Power, and the sacredness of Acts

of

of Parliament, are no jokes: they are not subjects, nor is it a season for levity, to sport with. Your — fathers thought them no jokes: and if such doctrine, as has this day been advanced, prevails or takes root in this ---e, I doubt the Constitution must seek for sanctuary elsewhere than within these walls, the very hangings of which ought to put us in mind of the glorious deliverances English Liberty and English Spirit have obtained.

--- The --- calls upon any one to shew the Act of Parliament that hinders the Crown from stopping the Exportation of Corn. I think many Acts have been pointed out; and I shall not now go back to them. But as to the idea that all the Statutes from *Magna Charta* down import no more than that the Sea shall be open, I confess I do not understand it: it must be owing to my dulness. I have no notion of an act of Parliament to make the sea open to our own subjects; there is not a single word to that purpose in *Magna Charta*, and I thought the Controversy, that has loaded the world with learning as to *mare clausum et apertum*, had only been between us and foreign nations. I hold it to be a fundamental law, that the sea is open to ourselves: and I wish the --- would point out a Statute opening the sea, to the subjects of England, where exportation had not been restrained by some antecedent law. But I can surely tell h--- of some laws relating to this very matter of the exportation of Corn, which do much more than make the sea open: for the Bounty Act makes the Treasury open too, and gives the exporter an indefeasible right, unless taken away by Act of Parliament, to a reward, in certain cases, for carrying his corn to the open sea. Whether it be true or not what a --- said of Corn having been made too much an article of Commerce, is not the present enquiry: but so the law stands: and it has proved a beneficial law to the nation, not only by promoting agriculture, and bringing money from abroad, but by preserving plenty of corn at home, more than ever was known before; and by saving the great expence to the nation occasioned by frequent scarcities that prevailed before these laws were made: and I do not think such a sudden instance of scarcity as the present, or the present benefit to the public, from the stopping of the exportation by the Royal Power, will appear to be a sufficient ground for vesting in the Crown a *dispensing* power, as a subsisting right, in order to *suspend* these laws when Parliament is

not

not sitting, or till it meet, even under the favourable colour, or for the necessary end of preventing famine.

The —— —— has indeed been pleased to say that *Brutus* would have entrusted *Nero* with such a power. A —— —— has already given this good answer, that though Brutus might have entrusted Nero with that power, Brutus would have been very sorry if Nero had exercised it when not entrusted to him. I will add to that answer, that however Brutus might have entrusted Nero safely with a single act which could do nothing but good, he certainly would not have chosen to entrust the best of the Cæsars that ever governed the Roman empire, with a power, under which, for one good act of a *Titus*, a *Nero* might have done as many bad as he pleased, and swallowed up Liberty entirely. Such and no other is the *suspending* power, under which the act in question is justified by the —— ——, as an act of legal Prerogative.

The ———— and ———— the better to accommodate the present case to the great principle of *Salus Populi*, and to prove the embargo to be within the inherent power of the Crown, upon that principle, has pointed at a similarity between the stopping of the exportation of corn, and the obliging to the performance of quarantine. And the —— —— asks, Where is the act of parliament that enables his Majesty to impose quarantine, all the statutes on the head being only to regulate it? Now for answer, I hope I may have leave to ask a question in my turn, to make the two cases parallel: and my question is, Where is the act of parliament that forbids his Majesty to impose quarantine; or that enacts, that all ships foreign and domestic, shall have free entrance into the ports of the kingdom without performing it? I know there is none, and such a law would be indeed absurd. But till such a law does exist, it is equally ridiculous to ask for one to impose quarantine, by repealing the other. For, most undoubtedly, it must be inherent in the executive power, to have a right to use means to protect the nation from the plague, not only upon the general principle, that the executive power may act in things for the good of the whole, where there is no prescription of law, but because self-preservation is a fundamental law interwoven in all government, as well as in the human frame: and the end of government is, to protect and defend the whole from all external evils, of which pestilence is among the worst. But not to rest on general principles, nobody can be so ignorant

rant surely as not to know, that the power to impose quarantine is the prerogative of the Crown, settled by prescription, and proved by immemorial usage, which gives it a legal beginning. The acts of Parliament on the subject do not create, but recognize this prerogative. However, if I could suppose so senseless, and perhaps I might say so intrinsically void an act of parliament, as one to exempt from quarantine, I believe I should not scruple to break the law if I could, in a proper case, and trust to the justice of my country: but I should neither justify the breach under an act of the *dispensing* power, nor be a bit more ready to run the risk for the having such an illegal protection. I should think the principle of *Salus Populi* applied to excuse the act, not to justify the power, a better shield. And at the same time, it is worth observation, that these very quarantine laws, confined as they are to regulations, prove how jealous parliament has been of leaving either the necessity or mode of it to depend upon the discretion of the Prerogative, though the thing itself be a fair instance of the original, inherent, and just prerogative of the Crown; these regulating laws being, as I understand them, of the nature of explanatory limitations of that part of the Prerogative.

Another thing has fallen from the — and —— —— on the —k, which I cannot help taking notice of. The —— — has been pleased to complain of the other —, and — — on the cross bench, for declining to give a decisive opinion upon the legality of the embargo, because (as the — on the —k expressed himself) of questions that may arise in *his* —t. And the — on the —k, says, He does not ask what may be pleaded on a demurrer in the *inferior courts?* he stands on *wider ground*, and asks in P—t, what is sufficient to justify the act in question? It is very true, the — and —— — on the cross bench did decline giving an opinion at present, as to the legality of the embargo, and the reason he gave was a very fair one, having been informed, as his — says he has been, of actions being brought, which may come before a certain judicature. But his — very candidly, and with great perspicuity, stated what the legality would turn upon, if judicially tried; and mentioned how fit it might be to prevent such questions on this occasion by a law for that purpose. This was all very consistent, I think, though it has been glanced at as inconsistent, with the clear and firm opinion given by the —— — upon the general point of the *dispensing penfing power*, which his —, without hefitation, and in the true fpirit of the Conftitution, condemned and fpurned. * As for the queftion of the — and — on the —k, I own both parts of it ftrike me with furprize, as well what the — — does not, as what he does afk: and I would have that ———, inftead of the queftion he ftates, afks what *can* juftify an act queftioned in any court of law, inferior or fuperior, but a legal defence? For certainly, if the embargo is not itfelf a legal act, within the known powers of the Prerogative, it can afford no legal defence againft any action brought in the courts of Weftminfter-hall. I am fure the —on the —k, can neither have forgot, nor can he differ from a very well founded opinion, which he *knows well* has been given in *one* of thefe courts, and not a great while ago, " That judges can de-" cide only *according to law*, and are upon their oaths " to pronounce what is law, and that they can regard " nothing but law, not even votes of Parliament." Why then afk even in P— or in the H— of L—, fitting in its political, not in a judicial capacity, hearing no caufe, nor having any caufe before them. What is fufficient to juftify any act, if a *legal* juftification is meant? Where the H— of L— hearing a caufe touching the embargo upon a writ of error, would any — in the H—, would the great —— who prefides in that H—j—e, give his opinion upon any other ground than the *known law* of the land, which no opinion, even of the H— of L— in its political capacity, can alter? Courts of law will receive the law from Parliament, and the expofitions of it from the H— of L—, as the judicature of the laft refort: but I hope they will always judge by the law, and by no other rule whatever. I truft never to fee the time come again, when judges will pronounce upon the Prerogative of the Crown, as dictated to them by a Prince or a Mi-

---

* The --- and --- --- on the crofs bench declined, for the reafon he mentioned, at *that time* giving any opinion on the *legality* of the embargo, on its own particular grounds of law; he has fince had occafion to declare his opinion, that the embargo, by *order of Council*, is a direct fufpenfion of an Act of Parliament, and therefore *illegal*. In delivering this opinion, the --- --- made a moft excellent fpeech, fupporting it by the deareft principles of the CONSTITUTION, and animated with the true fire of LIBERTY; which has met with univerfal applaufe, and for which his ---- had (upon the fpot) the *warmeft thanks* of the known and moft zealous friends of Liberty, and of the Conftitution.

nifter,

nifter, or even by a political opinion of either House of Parliament.

There is but one thing more I can at present remember, of what dropt from the — and — — on the —k. His —, aware of the great affinity between the *suspending* power, and that other usurpation of the Crown which usually attended it, the *raising money* without consent of Parliament, (as to which, and even the power of Parliament in the matter, perhaps his — entertains some peculiar notions) has thought fit to make a distinction between these two powers; and the one, I mean that of raising money, his —— totally condemns and explodes, though his argument of this day has been to support and maintain a degree of the other; that is, in cases of urgent necessity for the public good, and at least till Parliament conveniently can be assembled.

The — says, that the *purses* of the subject stand upon quite a different footing; that the matter of money has undergone many statutes, down from *Magna Charta* and the statute, *that no taillage shall be levied*, &c. and, in short, that it is clear law and constitution, that no money can be raised but in Parliament. And his — further adds, that as to money, there never can be a pretence of necessity for raising it during the recess of Parliament by an act of the Crown, not even in case of the most imminent danger of invasion; because every body knows the difficulty of assembling forces, and of bringing an army into the field, with all its appendages of artillery and baggage, which occasions so much delay, even where there is no want of money; and how long time it would take to levy any money from the subject by such means as could be used in the greatest haste: so that there never could be any difficulty in convening the Parliament before any thing could be done that way, and therefore no pretence to anticipate their meeting by such attempts.

I think the purse of the subject is very sacred, and that none have a right to put their hands in it but Parliament. I go in that doctrine as far as the Constitution carries me, and that is far enough for the security of the subjects property, though I have not any peculiar notions about the magical virtue of representation, and other dreams of that sort. The King and Common-Council of the kingdom are the known ancient, and acknowledged legislature, and I am not for loosening this pin of the Constitution as to money, more than any other thing.

But

But I must at the same time fairly tell your —, that if the opinion I have as to the *suspending* power, or the raising money, which are, I am sure, brother's children, stood upon any of the distinctions made by the ——— I should think it very poorly supported. Nor can I in any sort or kind distinguish between these two usurpations which always went together. I have one short logic for both: I have mentioned it before; namely, That the Crown is not the supreme sovereign legislative power of this constitution: and that as money must be raised by Parliament, whether the thing be taken on the more abstracted and radical principles of the original constitution, or on the statutes and usage respecting it, which I hold to be all but declaratory and explanatory, from the first to the last of them; so I think every other law, of whatever kind, must be both made and repealed, or suspended mediately or immediately, by the same legislative power that can alone raise money: and I know no greater degree of sacredness in those acts of Parliament that secure the purse of the subject, than in those that secure to him the possession of every benefit of law he is entitled to enjoy. I see no difference between an edict of the Crown to take money from the subject without authority of parliament, and one to keep money from him that he has a right by act of Parliament to receive; and therefore, I think the Crown has not, in any case, a right to suspend the bounty-act, by which the exporter of corn is entitled to receive so much money for every quarter he exports.

The princes who were put to shifts for raising money without consent of Parliament, because they quarrelled with their Parliaments for not tamely surrendering the constitution and all their rights and liberties to them, had no other way of doing it but by levying and forcing money from the subject by various ways and devices. But if that trade were ever to be resumed as the country is now situated, perhaps a fit state casuist might for once at least, or for a short while *during the recess of Parliament*, fall upon a method of raising more money, without calling for a penny from the subject directly, than was ever raised by ship-money, loans, &c. Suppose only the King was to be advised by the casuists of state necessity, to suspend all the appropriating acts, and stop the issues at the Exchequer to the public creditors,

ditors, it would turn to a better account than when Charles II. shut up his Exchequer, to save paying his own debts, that would not be raising money without consent of Parliament, but only *suspending* some acts of Parliament; yet I believe this country would hardly furnish a minister bold enough to advise the project, even if an enemy were burning our fleet again at Chatham; which has been mentioned by one great — as an instance of urgent necessity and immediate danger; though the — and — — on the —k does not seem to think even that or any other exigency would be a pretence for raising money without consent of Parliament.

To me the *dispensing and suspending* power, and the raising of money without consent of Parliament, are precisely alike, and stand upon the very same ground: They were born twins; they lived together, and together were, I hoped, buried in the same grave at the Revolution, past all power of resurrection; and as I think neither of them ever did belong to the Crown, I cannot admit of any doctrine that maintains the one or the other. If I were to make a difference between raising money and the *suspending* or *dispensing* power, I rather think the *suspending* and *dispensing* power the most dangerous of the two, as that which might do most universal mischief, and with the greatest speed, as it includes the whole. I must therefore enter my most solemn protest, and I do it with all my heart against the *suspending* and *dispensing* power in every degree, even to the smallest vestige of it.

But — —, I pledged myself to lay before you the grounds upon which I charge the servants of the Crown in this business: and I think they are chargeable with the act itself, which is a dangerous infraction of the constitution, made yet more dangerous by the attempt to justify it under the pretence of Prerogative; because, if they had done their duty, there would have been no occasion at all for such an act of power by the Crown; and their not doing their duty, to prevent it, is only to be accounted for by the doctrine we have heard to-day, from which we learn, that the Ministers had taken up the notion of a defensible *dispensing Prerogative*, and were resolved to venture upon the exercise of it, rather than to call for the aid of Parliament. So that the necessity which at last forced them to advise the Crown to interpose, was

not

not only of their own making, but of their *choice*, which caused them to prefer an exercise of power under the name of Prerogative to a relief by law, under the authority of Parliament. For had the Ministers been of another mind, they would have called Parliament, when they might and ought to have seen, nay, when the Proclamation they caused to be issued against forestalling, &c. testifies they did see, that the remedy was wanted: and if Parliament had been called even *then*, (as it ought to have been sooner,) a legal and more effectual remedy might still have been applied by the legislature, as early as the embargo by the Crown took place; instead of which, Parliament was not only not called, but was prorogued beyond the length of an ordinary prorogation; and still the remedy which then only could come from the Crown, was delayed till it was unreasonably late, and the evil much encreased by the injudicious procrastination. But even this is not all; for I shall also shew, that the conduct, or rather the misconduct, which produced the necessity for the Crown to interpose at last, if it had been attended with no such consequence as a violation of the Constitution, and an usurpation upon the rights of Parliament, was, in itself, the most culpable neglect of the public safety, too gross to be reconcileable with any notion of the duty of those who undertake the care of the state, or with any measure of fitness for that situation.

I will say in general, that he is not a moderate Minister, who will rashly decide in favour of Prerogative in a question where the rights of parliament are on the other side: and I am sure he is not a prudent Minister, who, even in a doubtful case, *commits* the Prerogative, by a wanton experiment, to what degree the people will bear the extent of it.

But —, rashly, and wilfully, to claim or exercise as Prerogative a power clearly against law, is too great boldness for this country: and of all things in the world, the *suspending or dispensing power*, that edged tool which has cut so deep, is the last that any man in his wits would handle in England:—that rock which the English history has warned against with such awful beacons:—an attempt that lost one prince his crown, and another both his crown and his head; and that at length expelled their family out of this land of liberty to the regions of tyranny, as the only climate that suited their temper and genius:

—a power, the exercise of which stands branded as the subversion of the constitution, in the front of that *truly* GREAT CHARTER of your liberties, the BILL OF RIGHTS. A Minister who is not afraid of that power, is neither fit for the sovereign nor the subject.

I love a bold Minister when he keeps in the true sphere. In times of distress and danger, boldness is a jewel: and with joy I have seen bold, even *wild* enterprizes succeed, though hardly within the die when undertaken.—But the enemies of our country are the proper subjects of our boldness,—not the constitution.

I must further observe, that if Parliament was either not called when it might have been called, or was prorogued, and prorogued to an unusual distance, when it ought to have been assembled, the power that has been exercised, as a pretended Prerogative competent to the Crown during the interval of Parliament, is, even upon the principles argued from the other side, as mere an usurpation, as if those who contend for it, in that way, admitted what I maintain, that the power has no being at all, in any case or under any circumstances whatever. For it is precisely the same thing, upon the argument, as as if the deputy or substitute, who has power to act only in the absence of a principal, should supersede the principal, merely by not calling for him, when there was occasion to act. And at the same time there cannot be a stronger demonstration of the exceeding great danger of this pretended Prerogative of a *suspending power*, even under the restrictions conceded, than this, that the occasion which creates it, depends upon the Crown itself, whose undoubted Prerogative it is to call Parliament, and fix the time of their meeting; so that there can at no time be any security against the exercise of this power, if there were a sinister view to be answered by exercising it.

This, ——, at least we may venture to affirm, that if there were really such a Prerogative, depending for its existence upon the recess of Parliament, there would need to be the greatest imaginable circumspection observed in calling it as soon as practicable, when there was occasion for the exercise of the power, that it might be as short-lived as possible, and as soon brought under the controul of Parliament as could be. On the other hand, if necessity is the sole foundation of this dangerous power, or Prerogative, which-ever it be, it behoves those who advise the
exercise

exercise of it, not only to see that the necessity is indeed *invincible*, but that it has not been occasioned by any fault of their own. For if it is not the one, the act is in no way justifiable; and if the other, that very necessity which is the excuse of the act, will be the accusation of those who occasion it; and in place of being justifiable in their conduct, they must be chargeable first with the blame of the necessity, and next with the danger of the violation of the law, as the drunken man who commits murder, justly bears the guilt both of inebriation and bloodshed.

But nothing can so well put the conduct of administration in the true light, which will shew it to be most indefensible, as a few facts, of which it will not cost many words to remind your ——. And let me first beg your —— attention to the defence made for administration by themselves, as it has been given by two of the M——rs. One —— in a great —— (the S—— of —e) has said, he was astonished when he found that in the act passed last session, there was no provision giving power to the King and Council to prolong the prohibition beyond the 26th of August, and that he could hardly believe it. Another —— in a h——e (my L—— P——l) says, he was amazed when he made the same discovery; and to distinguish his *greatness* by a superiority above the *trifles* of the end of last S——n, he informs the—that he went to B——h before P—— rose, and did not know so much as whether it broke up in May or June.—This is really an extraordinary tone of *hurlo-thrumbo* greatness, and it may, for aught I know, carry a great air with it; but I think it is very *strange* language. And fancy if your —— find any other reason to join in the amazement and astonishment of these two great ——, it must be that they were both so ignorant of what it was their indispensible and most urgent duty to be acquainted with, and what I should imagine very few besides themselves did not know. The surprize can only be sunk in another wonder, still greater, that so unaccountable ignorance should be avowed and offered as an apology for the most inexcusable neglect of a most necessary duty, upon an attention to which the safety of the kingdom depended.

But when was it that these *attentive* Ministers made this *amazing* discovery? So very early, we are told, as the last day of August or first of September, when the prohibition by the last year's act was expired. And what was it that brought so *immaterial* an object, as an alarming scarcity, a threatned famine, under the consideration of the Ministry? A letter which it seems was received from a *watchful Magistrate*, the late *Lord Mayor* of London, who is but an inferior Minister of government, though in an office of great state and dignity.

Thus, by the Ministers own account, from the middle of July, when his — called them into his service, to the beginning of September, they had not once bestowed a thought upon the prognostics or proofs of a general scarcity, though it was the subject of writing in all the daily news papers, the cause of disquiet in all quarters of the kingdom, and of conversation in every company, that of ministers, I suppose, only excepted:

*Sidera quis, mundumque velet spectare cadentem,
Expers ipse metus?*

The *patriotic* Ministers, however, did not themselves feel; and if we may judge of things that are not seen by those which do appear, they were engaged in the more important business of settling who should *cede* that another might *succeed*, what reversion or pension one should have, and what compensation or encrease of emolument another should have out of the over-flowing treasury of this *rich, opulent, and unincumbered* country. Had a single hour of the many days spent in adjusting the arrangement for one office, been employed in consulting about the means of preserving bread to the poor, miserable, hungry, and oppressed subject; the flints that struck each other in that jostle for place, might have cast as much light upon the *law* at least, as to have shewn what the contents were of *one*, not to say of *three* acts of Parliament to prevent scarcity and famine, passed but a few months before.

What were the circumstances of the country, when Administration was in this callous, torpid and benumbed state? If we compare them with the situation in which things were when Parliament took up the consideration of the corn last session, and passed the several acts for securing a national supply, we shall not be able to avoid seeing a remissness and inattention in government, on this occasion, that is really not to be conceived, even after the ministers have told us, that truly they had not so much as once looked into these laws of last session, so

late

late as the 30th of August, when the Lord Mayor wrote to them.

In the petition of the city of London presented to Parliament, which is dated the 17th of January last, it is set forth, that wheat for bread had for three months been from thirty-nine shillings to forty-two shillings. In that situation Parliament thought the matter worthy their attention, and that a remedy was necessary: And three bills were brought into the H. of C. which all passed into acts; one to prohibit the exportation of corn; another for liberty to import oats and oatmeal; and a third for liberty to import American corn. These bills passed the H. of C. about the seventh of February, after which they had their course through the H. of L. and received the royal assent some time after, and your — will please to attend to it, that even before these bills passed, wheat was come down to thirty-five shillings and six-pence; and in April the best corn was down at thirty-four shillings and six-pence, the worst at thirty-two shillings, owing to the remedy interposed by Parliament; which your — see was so quick and immediate in its operation, that the prices fell even before the law was passed: Of such importance and effect is the *proper* remedy, when applied by Parliament *seasonably* and *timely*. Yet under that fall, three or four shillings below the prices upon consideration of which the city of London petitioned and the Parliament proceeded to bring in bills, did the legislature judge fit to pass the several laws; and very wisely, because their not doing so would have had just the contrary effect, and have raised the prices above what they were, when the matter was taken up, for the same reason that the doing of it lowered them so greatly immediately.

The prohibition act was made to expire the 26th of August, and the two others for liberty of importation expired the 29th of September: And there was no power given by the act to the K. and C. to continue the prohibition.—So much for what past last session.

Now for what concerns the Ministry of this year, to shew their *attention*. By the weekly returns of the prices at Bear-key, it appears that upon the 28th of July (by which time I believe the administration had taken its form, for the Dictator was set to work about the 12th) wheat was at forty-four shillings, that is two shillings above the highest price when the city of London petitioned parliament in January, and no less than eight shillings and six-pence higher than when the bills of last session passed. August the 4th it was forty-five shillings, advanced a shilling; August 11th it was forty-three shillings; August 18th forty-four shillings; 25 at forty-five shillings; and by September 18th it was got up to forty-eight shillings and three-pence; and was at forty-nine shillings on the 15th and 22d of September.

The prices at Bear-key are the barometer for plenty and scarcity, which the law has pointed out to Magistrates, and to *Ministers* too, unless it be no part of the duty of Ministers to take care of the provision of the country, because they have not, like the Lord Mayor and Aldermen, the assize of bread to set weekly. The authentic and legal information is at hand, if they will but send to Bear-key or Guildhall for it: And one would think *that* ought not to be omitted at any time when the state of the country as to corn is but doubtful or suspicious. In a year when there had been a scarcity, and no less than three temporary acts of Parliament to provide against it, such an omission must be deemed strange inattention, an unaccountable neglect.

From the list of prices I have given your —, you see how much worse the state of the country was in the months of July and August, than when Parliament was applied to last sessions; still more so than when the acts of last session passed: And the state of the weather we all know was for a long time most threatening, especially coming after a year of scarcity. God knows what would have been the case, if the season had not taken a favourable turn towards the harvest, as in kind providence it did: Yet all this while, not the least mark of care in administration. The Ministers who had the watch, instead of looking out, seem to have been the only quiet and unconcerned persons in the kingdom: they did not so much as enquire whether government was armed with a power of prohibition.

This is really hard to be credited. If the Ministers had no friends to inform them of the expiring laws; surely their own reflection, had they used any, might have told them long before the 26th of August, that there was too great a probability some farther remedy would be necessary. And Parliament (if it had been worth while to give any attention to what they had done) had marked a line of direction for Administration, with the greatest exactness, by making the prohibition continue till the

26th of August, and no longer; because there could not sooner be any supply from the new crop, and it must before then be known what the harvest was, and how the crop turned out: So that if, by disappointment in crop, there were need for a fresh prohibition or other remedy, Parliament could be called in time to apply it. Parliament had thereby given at the same time, the most explicit testimony, not only that they understood it to be *their* province to give the remedy, but that they had now reserved the cognizance of the affair to themselves, not chusing to delegate it to the crown, even *during the recess*, as had been done frequently before. If Administration had chosen to follow the line given them by Parliament, they had a plain path to walk in; which was no other than this, To keep their eye upon the state of the country; and if there appeared to be the least hazard of the need of a further prohibition, to keep the prorogation of Parliament upon such a foot, as that it could be called in time, and with a reasonable notice too;—a method that the Journals shew has been often practised on like occasions. Instead of this, Administration took no thought, gave no attention to the matter at all; and of themselves neither did, nor shewed any intention to do any thing, notwithstanding the circumstances of the country, as events turned out, made the affair of such consequence.

But was the conduct of Administration a bit better, or wiser, or more like government, when they were waked out of their first sleep, and goaded on to their duty, by others to whom their country was more obliged? Not one whit: but if possible rather worse. Of this also there is the fullest evidence.

After waiting till the end of August, when the state of the country was beyond conjecture, the Lord Mayor of London, in the letter which he wrote to the three great Ministers*, told them the stock of grain on hand was very small; that the harvest had failed, and was unproductive; and that there were then (already) come commissions for buying up corn here, unlimited in price, and to an immense extent; that therefore it was indispensably necessary some measure should immediately be taken to stop the exportation, otherwise the kingdom would very soon be drained, and a want at home. This

* D. of G. E. of C. and E. of S.

was material information indeed, and it was as authentic as material; for your — will reflect from whom it came—Not only from the chief Magistrate of the metropolis, but that Magistrate himself the best informed that any one could be, from his private situation, being the greatest corn-factor in England, perhaps in Europe; a worthy and sensible gentleman, well known in both houses of Parliament, where he has often attended on occasions relating to corn, called upon as the ablest in the kingdom to give information in these matters. Such was the person who gave this information to government; and it was the more worthy of regard, and ought to be mentioned to his honour, that his duty as a citizen of the commonwealth, as well as a Magistrate, in the high office he then bore in the city of London, prevailed over his own private interest, as there was not another man in the kingdom so much interested in the profit to be had by the commissions from abroad. It were to be wished, though I am not enthusiastic enough to hope it, that such an example of *disinterested* patriotism and public virtue would *ascend*. But in late transactions, my Lord Mayor's vigilance in his office as a Magistrate, has not been more wofully contrasted by the Neglect of Ministers, than his noble contempt of gain in his private character as a man, by the *pensioned* avarice of his superiors;—An excellent foil to illustrate the splendor of his virtues!

What did this information produce? Just nothing; at least nothing for the relief of the country. My L— P— S— and the S— of S— went to statute-books before unopened, not *dog-eared*, and there made the *amazing astonishing* discovery, that the act of Parliament of last session gave no power to the King and Council to prolong the prohibition. There government rested: the kingdom was left to be *amazed* in their turn, and my Lord Mayor's letters added to the lumber of the public offices.

The consideration of some weighty and important affair thus forced upon Administration, was yet laid aside for some days; and your — will not forget, that at this time Parliament was *not* prorogued, though there had been no thought of calling it, as there should have been much sooner; and if it had been called when my Lord Mayor's letter came, which represented the indispensible necessity there was of taking some measures, and when the *wonderful* difcovery was made that no powers were left with the King and Council, it might have been affembled by the 20th of September, on twenty days notice, which even the — on the W—k has condefcended to agree would be *due notice*; or if fix days more had been given, ftill it might have met to apply the legal conftitutional relief as early as the time when the *difpenfing power* was exerted under pretence of the recefs of Parliament.

It would feem however, that after a week or ten days confideration, it was thought neceffary to put fome mark of refpect upon my Lord Mayor's letter: And it has been faid, that a Council was held about the 8th of September, when, by the Bear-key prices, wheat was *only* at forty-eight fhillings and three-pence. But that Council ordered no embargo; neither was it judged reafonable or neceffary to call Parliament. The council however *did* fomewhat, rather I think to amufe and fhew their ignorance than any thing elfe; though it is like the amufement in the fable of the frogs. Accordingly that wife and ufeful Proclamation againft foreftalling was brought forth, bearing date the 10th of September: And for quieting the minds of the poor ftarving people, and miniftring prefent and effectual relief to their diftrefs, it publifhes this comfortable news, that *the prices of corn are already* very *much encreafed, and the fame is likely to grow much dearer, to the great oppreffion of the poor.* The people cry for bread, and the Minifters gave them a Proclamation; nay left one fhould not be enough, they gave them two of the fame date, and in the fame Gazette; and the fecond much worfe than the firft. I cannot on this occafion drive from my mind thefe words of the Scripture, which fay, "If a fon afk bread from "any of you that is a father, will he give him a ftone? "Or if he afk a fifh, will he for a fifh give him a ferpent? Or if he fhall afk an egg, will he offer him a "fcorpion?" Perhaps two fuch Proclamations never were coupled together. The one proclaims a *growing* dearth, when the ports were by *law* open for the free exportation of every ounce of grain in the kingdom, with the higheft temptation to export, by an unlimited demand from abroad, to prevent which no remedy could be *legally* applied but by authority of Parliament: and under thefe circumftances does the other Proclamation prorogue the Parliament to the 11th of November, *sixty-one days.*

If it had been the purpose or deliberation of Government to aggravate rather than to alleviate the distress of the country, and by driving to despair, to promote insurrection and fire, what more effectual method could have been pursued? I speak to facts; and it is well they are proved, for I should not expect to be believed without evidence. What were the consequences? The question may well be asked; but I shall not answer it, for fear I should seem to justify what I condemn and regret.

But I will tell your ----- what happened after these Proclamations. Wheat that was at forty-eight shillings and three-pence on the 8th of September, was at forty-nine shillings on the 15th and 22d: and there were risings, riots and tumults, in all corners of the kingdom, and troops marched from county to county, to quell insurrections by military force: Famine and the sword met: Murders have been, and executions must be: the laws trampled upon and transgressed by the people: Acts of Parliament from a *careless necessity* broken, and suspended by power without right, Royal authority, that is, unfounded prerogative, (for royal authority and prerogative, (for royal authority and prerogative are synonimous convertible terms): Royal authority, I say, exerted against law. For *at last,* when no *legal* remedy was left for an insupportable evil, the embargo by order of Council, that *violent,* but *then* necessary, and also inadequate remedy, was issued the 26th of September. It was *forced* by the cries and risings of the people, and by petitions from the great cities, and particularly the petition presented to the King on the 23d, from the Lord Mayor and Court of Aldermen of London, who could no longer remain silent spectators of the distress and danger, which near a month before had been represented in such strong terms to the Ministry, by their worthy and vigilant chief Magistrate, in a more private capacity and form.

As to what has been said in the debate, that the facts laid before the Council on the 10th of September, which issued the Proclamations against forestalling, and for proroguing the Parliament, were not sufficient foundation for their proceeding to an embargo; that it was then only a *surmise* of scarcity; and that the circumstances were

were so much changed before the 26th, when the embargo was ordered, that it could be no longer delayed; I own I cannot understand what it means: for we see by the Bear-key returns, that (as already mentioned) wheat was at forty-eight shillings and three-pence, on the 8th of September, *that is*, above the bounty price; and it was but nine-pence higher, viz. forty-nine on the 22d of September. But the order for an embargo is really the Ministry's indictment drawn up by themselves: for it sets forth as its ground the very information that the Lord Mayor of London had given the Ministry twenty-six days before: and upon those *grounds of urgent necessity now impending*, that is, that they had been certified of as impending a month before, and *for the safety, benefit and sustenance* of his majesty's subjects, his majesty *then only, by the advice of his Privy-Council*, orders an embargo on wheat and wheat flour, and *nothing else*. And the *necessity* of laying it on by the *Royal Authority* is stated in these expressive words: " And whereas the Par-
" liament *standing prorogued* to the 11th of November
" next, his majesty has not *an opportunity* of taking the
" advice of his Parliament *speedily enough* upon the *pre-*
" *sent emergency* to stop the progress of a mischief daily
" encreasing, and which, if not immediately provided
" against, might be productive of *calamities past all possi-*
" *bility of remedy*:" A very just account of the situation of things that had been the *present emergency* for the two preceding months, and of the necessity of the *speedy* remedy that had been so unaccountably *delayed* to be applied in any way during that time, and that a voluntary act of Administration, in the prorogation of Parliament, when the emergency was come to the worst, had rendered impracticable in the legal and proper way. But the most curious part of the whole is, that the *want of an opportunity* of advising *speedily enough* with the Parliament, is spoken of as a common or unavoidable and unforeseen casualty, though the Ministry themselves were the cause that his Majesty could not *then* have, and had not even sooner had that opportunity.

But if the proclamation for the embargo is considered as a *remedy*, even this act of Power now justified as *prerogative*, was itself but the crowning blunder, by confining the embargo to wheat and wheat flour. The wisdom of Parliament extended their prohibition, under less pressing circumstances and lower prices, to all grain,

and

and every thing of corn kind, bread, biscuit, and starch. And one would have thought, that when the Crown was advised to suspend acts of Parliament for the public good, the *dispensing* power might also for the greater good of the public, have paid that compliment to the act of Parliament, to have followed it fully, and not in a part only, when the whole prohibition was far more necessary than at the time the law was made: not to say that the example of parliament was at least a sort of shelter for a *prerogative-usurpation* upon its power. But even without resorting to the wisdom of Parliament for instruction, such an error as the omission of prohibiting the exportation of all manner of grain in the Proclamation, could not have been fallen into, without either the greatest inattention, or most amazing unskilfulness; for hardly any body is so ignorant as not to know that a diminution of any one species of grain, not only raises the price of that particular species, but affects all the rest, because of the increase of consumption of these occasioned by the want of the other. And so the exportation of barley, which was not restrained by the embargo, has contributed to keep up the price of wheat, besides enhancing that of malt to an intolerable degree *.

If Parliament had been called in time, there might have been a more early, and there certainly would have been a more adequate and satisfactory remedy applied to the evil: and the very prospect of the meeting of Parliament would have kept the people quiet, as they will always have more confidence in parliament than in any administration, and will patiently wait for the relief for which they naturally look up to the Legislature. But in a Ministry that from the beginning had paid no attention to the calamity, either in its presages or effects,

---

* The Parliament lost no time in remedying, as fast as they could, the blunders of administration. They revived the *Prohibition act* in its *full extent*; renewed the two other acts before mentioned, which expired on the 29th of September; and have taken other wise and necessary precautions. But that there might be no public act with regard to this great concern, the prevention of famine, executed by administration, without some egregious blunder, and some glaring proof of ignorance and inattention, the Privy Council, though they had a power to prohibit distillation till *twenty* day after the meeting of Parliament, prohibited it only for *three*. In consequence of which, all the distillery might go on till the act passed to stop it.

and

and that cut off all hopes of Parliamentary relief by a prorogation, when they proclaimed the evil to be come to a great height, and still growing; in such a Ministry the people could take no confidence, nor could they indeed be expected to continue quiet under such circumstances. From Ministers capable of blundering so grosly in so plain and necessary a business as the care of provision for bread to the kingdom, what may not be expected of the blundering kind, in other matters of more difficulty, for of more importance there can hardly be any? With steersmen at the rudder so inexpert in our own ports, the ship is not to be trusted in the wide sea.

Some pretences have been made, I cannot call them excuses, for not calling the Parliament, which has been the *origo mali*. One —— speaks in a contemptuous stile; he says all the difference is, that the King has been advised by his *Little* instead of his *Great* Council.

This way of speaking is unconstitutional, and ridiculous. I hope Parliament will always maintain its own super-eminent distinction, and mark it so as it shall not be the by-word of any Minister, by shewing on this, and every other occasion, that the King's Privy Council, which the —— calls the *Little* Council, is indeed little in comparison of the great Council of the *Nation*, as well as of the *Crown*; and that this Little Council, or any *one Man*, who dictates to them, never shall be entrusted with the power of *suspending* or *dispensing* with the standing law of the land, on any pretence whatever. If that were allowed of, there is no law so fundamental but might be subverted, nor any government more absolute than that which might be introduced.

The —— says, "he does not enquire whether my Lord Mayor's letter was wrote a day sooner or a day later.— There is a *littleness*, says he, in minding dates of Proclamations,— the day of laying the embargo, of proroguing the Parliament, and the day fixed for its meeting —— These are *minutiæ*, beneath notice. Saving a country from ruin is a great object.— He goes to the great object of preventing famine.

—— Saving a country from famine *is* a great object; but it may depend on nothing so much as *minutiæ*, such as the —— would overlook. It did depend upon such *minutiæ* as dates in this instance; and the oversight promoted the famine, which attention might have prevented, sooner, and to much better effect.—But surely no instance can

ever

ever be more unfortunate, of contemptible *minutiæ*, than that of minding of days and dates, when the safety of a country is concerned. States have perished by the neglect of an hour, and moments have decided the fate of empires. The Prorogation of Parliament, in such a season of calamity and danger, was no *minute* blunder. Last year that —— said *he could not commend* the then administration for calling Parliament *early*, as they termed it, because he thought *their* speed was delay, in such a conjuncture as that was; though the ground of his complaint of delay was *not* that America had been suffered to continue in rebellion for months, *but* that so much time had been lost in giving these poor oppressed subjects relief from the grievances, which he thought justified their mutiny. Now when *one* greater and wiser than all other men is Minister, days and dates are *minutiæ*. It is *his* Prerogative to blunder and be blameless.

But, says the ——, Parliament could not have been *conveniently* assembled sooner.—— It may do for great —— who live at their fine palaces in the neighbourhood of the capital, to come up here at any time;—— and to be sure any man may get upon *the back of a post horse*, and ride as fast as he can:—— but it will not suit all the members of the two houses, that are to be brought from the East and the West, from the South and the North of this large kingdom, to call them from their houses and their domestic affairs, at an inconvenient season, and upon short notice.——This cannot be done without *notable inconvenience*.——And nothing is so dangerous as surreptitious meetings of Parliament.——The great security of our Liberties consists in calling Parliament upon full notice, to prevent all surprize.——And by surreptitious Conventions, *all countries that have been enslaved, have lost their liberties*, of which confident assertion, he however neither did nor can give one instance from any history.

Must we then, ——, for fear of a surreptitious surrender of our Liberties by Parliament, trust the Privy Council with a power that would subvert our liberties, and render our property precarious? But can the *lowest* number of Lords and Commoners that can make a Parliament, be less safe than the *Little* Council? The law of the land has taught me that Parliament assembled without any notice at all, is a better security for our Liberties than any Privy Council; and therefore, upon the critical emergency of a demise of the Crown, Parliament is by

statute

statute appointed to assemble *immediately*, however it may happen to stand prorogued at the time. So jealous is the constitution of a pretence left to the successor to the throne to govern with his Privy Council without Parliament. But ———, it is very extraordinay to bear the danger of a surreptitious assembling of Parliament, used as an argument against haste in a season of imminent danger, by those who argue for *necessity* as sufficient to *suspend* and *dispense* with laws and acts of Parliament? Is there more safety in making *necessity* a law-maker, or a *lex temporis*, than in making it only a hasty conveener of the true legislature of the kingdom? —— Ministers may not be fond of the meeting of Parliament, even when they do do not fear much harm from it to their power; because, though it does not immediately or certainly destroy, it puts them to mind, in the midst of their arrogance, that they are mortal, like the Slave in the Triumphal Car. For my part, I have no fear of Parliament, called any how: but I have great fear of a power in the Privy Council that would supersede Parliament. It was the Rump of a well-weeded Parliament that abolished the monarchy, but no proclamation can garble either a House of Lords or Commons: and before any number assembled surreptitiously could sit long enough to attempt a surrender of our liberties, the most distant member, who did not chuse to be a slave, would find his way to Westminster, if *the back of a post-horse* would carry him; and the traitors would very soon find that they had only forfeited their own heads, to confirm the Liberty of their incensed country. In the present case, however, there was no occasion for a hasty convocation of Parliament. Government needed not to have been run to the *minutiæ* of hours or days. Had Parliament been called, even when it was culpably prorogued, it might have had a longer notice than many sessions have sat upon. Nor can I see any *notable inconveniency* in calling it so soon, unless that the —— could not have staid so long at the Waters; as I presume it could not have safely met without his —— presence to *guide* it. As to forty days notice being necessary for calling Parliament, it is an assertion without all foundation, contradicted by usage, and by the very stile of the usual Proclamations which speak only of *due* and *convenient* notice; to effect which there is no charm either in the number forty, thirty, or any other. I was surprized to hear the —— and —— say, he held it to be the *law*

of

of Parliament, that forty days was neceſſary. There is no ſuch *mos Parliamentarius*. And the —— muſt have forgot himſelf: for in the very firſt year of this reign, Parliament was called and ſat for diſpatch of buſineſs on twelve days notice by proclamation. The —— knows *who* then adviſed his Majeſty, and was in the *firſt* office in the kingdom. But if it were neceſſary to go into them, numberleſs inſtances ſince the Union are ready to be pointed out, of Parliament being called and ſitting on twelve, ſixteen, twenty days, and other indifferent numbers: and the — and —— is unſupported in this opinion, which is, indeed, totally a miſtake; the other — and —— on the ——k having agreed that twenty days is due notice. There remains therefore no cloak for excuſe for the blunder of proroguing Parliament for *ſixty-one* inſtead even of *forty* days, at a time when it was ſo neceſſary to have aſſembled it upon the ſhorteſt notice for which there was any precedent; and when, if it had been called even upon twenty days from the date of the Proclamation proroguing it, it would have prevented the neceſſity for an embargo by the Crown againſt law, and hindered thoſe dangerous tumults and inſurrections that at laſt extorted an act of ſuch dangerous example from Adminiſtration.

—— The occaſion is my apology for having ſaid ſo much; yet it is but a ſmall part of what might have been ſaid on the ſubject, upon which I have taken the liberty to trouble you.

—— I am not afraid of the juſt *prerogative* of the crown. It is a part of the conſtitution, and it is ſalutary. "The people's liberties ſtrengthen the King's prerogative, and the King's prerogative defends the people's liberties." So ſaid the unfortunate Prince Charles the Firſt. But he ſaid it falſely and deceitfully, applying it to his own depraved principles of government, in which he was nurſed up to his ruin, by a father who never ſat in *that chair*, but he taught like a royal profeſſor the doctrines of arbitrary power to your —— anceſtors, who were but unapt ſcholars. What the ſelf-deluded, and ſelf-deſtroyed King ſaid deceitfully, I think ſincerely in the juſt ſenſe.

Neither, —— —, do I fear the *power* of the Crown, in the hands of the gracious Prince now reigning. He made it his early declaration from the throne, that our Liberty was as dear to him as his own prerogative: And I truſt

I trust a long line of illustrious descendents sprung from him, will inherit his zeal for the liberties of this country, the LAWS of which transferred the imperial diadem of these realms from those who were not worthy of it, to his Majesty's august house. The freedom of the subject is the brightest jewel in the crown. It is the super-eminent prerogative of the Kings of England, by which they excel in glory all the sovereigns on earth, that they rule over FREEMEN, not over *slaves*. The Brunswick line esteems it so. They have shewn it.

But, —— I dread principles, the scars of which this nation yet bears: —— Principles destructive to the people, dangerous to the prince: —— Principles that lie at the root of all the illegal prerogatives usurped, and all the arbitrary power exercised by a Charles or a James.—— These principles I will resist, adopt or countenance them who will. I will resist them not more from regard to Liberty, than from love to my Sovereign and his family. They are poisonous principles, and they are infectious. If it were possible to deceive even the *elect* family—to impose upon a prince of that house *chosen* to maintain our Liberties; it could only be done by principles found in the mouths of the professed friends of Liberty, who have got access to the royal ear by such professions. The safety of the crown, as well as the security of the subject, requires us to shut up every avenue that could lead to tyranny: And he who would unbar those gates which exclude it, is not, in his heart, far from the lust of it. I will suspect no man without a cause. But I will trust no man with what the constitution has not made a trust;—with any power that *must* do a general mischief; tho' in a particular emergency, it *might* have a *chance of* doing some good. Such a power I will not trust in the crown; no, not for a case of *necessity*. —— For as Lord Falkland, while he remained the advocate for Liberty, and before he listed in the service of King Charles's despotism, said, speaking of the ship-money judges, and their criminal opinion,
" When that *necessity* which they would have so absolute
" and certain, takes place, the law of the land ceases;
" and that of general reason and equity, by which par-
" ticular laws at first were framed, returns to the King's
" throne and government, where *Salus Populi* becomes
" not only *Suprema* but *Sola Lex*; at which, and to
" which

" which end, whosoever dispenses with the King, dis-
" penses with us, to make use of his and one another's."
—— Men are but men. Unwise and unsafe trusts, are the surest inlet of treacherous, and infamous breaches of trust. The History of England shews how quickly, and shamefully, heroes for liberty have become tools of despotism. But, to use words I *have heard* from a certain *noble Lord*, when such expressions served his turn,—If we see an *arbitrary and tyrannical disposition somewhere*, the call for watchfulness is loud. Danger knocks at the gate. A *tyrannical* subject wants but a tyrannical disposed master, to be a minister of arbitrary power. If such a minister finds not such a master, he will be the tyrant of his Prince, as much as of his fellow-servants and fellow-subjects. I should be sorry to see my Sovereign in chains, even if he were content to wear them; —to see him unfortunately in chains, from which perhaps he could with difficulty free himself, till the person who imposed them runs away; which every good subject would, in that case, heartily wish might happen, the sooner the better for all. We are a FREE PEOPLE; and I am for a FREE KING *.

There was no division upon the Address. On the first day of the session, an address was presented to the King, to continue the embargo on shipping; and a bill was on the same day brought in for prohibiting the exportation of corn, malt, meal, flour, bread, biscuit, and starch; and for prohibiting the extraction of spirits from wheat and wheat-flour, which was passed.

SUPPLIES *granted this Session.*

November 27.   *l.   s.   d.*

1. THAT 16000 men be employed for the sea service for 1767, including 4287 marines

2. That

* The parliament passed an act to permit the importation of foreign barley, barley flour, and pulse, to remedy, if possible, the mischiefs which have arisen from the embargo on wheat and wheat flour only; so that the public were obliged to buy, at an enormous price, the very grain which had been exported out of the kingdom, and which administration would not prevent, although the necessity was both obvious and pressing.

2. That a sum not exceeding 4l. *per* man *per* month, be allowed for maintaining them, including ordnance for sea service - - - 832000 0 0

January 27, 1767.

1. That a number of land forces, including 2461 invalids, amounting to 16754 effective men, commission and non-commission officers included, be employed for 1767

2. For defraying the charge of the said number of land forces for 1767 - - 593986 15 7

3. For the pay of the general and general staff officers in *Great Britain* for 1767 - 12203 18 6½

4. For maintaining his Majesty's forces and garrisons in the plantations and *Africa*, including those in garrison at *Minorca* and *Gibraltar*, and for provisions for the forces in *North America, Nova Scotia, Newfoundland, Gibraltar*, the ceded islands, and *Africa* for 1767   405607 2 11⅞

5. For defraying the charge of the difference of pay between the *British* and *Irish* establishment, of six regiments of foot serving in the *Isle* of *Man*, at *Gibraltar*, *Minorca*, and the ceded islands, for 1767 - 7201 14 7

6. For paying the pensions to the widows of such reduced officers of the land forces and marines, as died upon the establishment

lishment of half pay in *Great Britain*, and who were married to them before the 25th of *December* 1761, for 1767 — 1536 0 0

7. Upon account of the reduced officers of the land forces and marines, for 1767 — 135299 8 4

8. For defraying the charge for allowances, to the several officers and private gentlemen of the two troops of horse guards, and regiment of horse reduced, and to the superannuated gentlemen of the four troops of horse guards for 1767. 2103 11 3

9. For defraying the charge of full pay for 365 days, for 1767, to officers reduced with the 10th company of several battalions, reduced from ten to nine companies and who remained on half pay at the 24th of *December* 1765 — — 5633 3 4

10. For the charge of the office of ordnance for land service, for 1767 — — 169600 0 2

11. For defraying the expence of services performed, by the office of ordnance for land service and not provided for by parliament in 1766 — — 51190 6 6

1384362 1 8¼

January 29.

For the ordinary of the navy, including half pay to sea and marine officers, for 1767 — 409177 4 8

1. Towards the buildings, rebuilding

A. 1766.   DEBATES.

	l.	s.	d.

rebuildings, and repairs of ships of war, in his Majesty's yards, and other extra-works, over and above what are proposed to be done upon the heads of wear and tear and ordinary, for 1767 — 298144　0　0

2. For purchasing a quantity of hemp, to replenish his Majesty's magazines　-　-　30000　0　0

328144　0　0

February 12.

1. For paying off and discharging the Exchequer bills, made out by virtue of the act of last session chap. 15, and charged upon the first aids, to be granted in this session　-　1800000　0　0

2. To make good to his Majesty, the like sum issued by his orders, in pursuance of the addresses of this house　-　-　12951　2　2

1812951　0　0

February 19.

1. Towards defraying the extraordinary expences of his Majesty's land forces and other services, incurred to the 3d of *February* 1767, and not provided for by parliament　-　315917　16　5

2. Upon account, towards defraying the charges of out pensioners of *Chelsea* hospital, for 1767.　-　-　-　106083　2　6

421000　18　11

S 3   *March* 5.

March 5.

That provision be made for the pay and cloathing of the militia, and for their subsistence during the time they shall be absent from home, on account of the annual exercise, for 1767.

March 19.

	l.	*s.*	*d.*
1. Upon account, for maintaining and supporting the civil establishment of *Nova Scotia*, for 1767	4866	3	5
2. Upon account of sundry expences for the service of *Nova Scotia*, for 1760 not provided for by parliament	691	8	0
3. Upon account for defraying the charges of the civil establishment of *Georgia*, and other incidental expences attending the same, from *June* 24, 1766, to *June* 24, 1767	3986	0	0
4. Upon account, for defraying the charge of the civil establishment of *East Florida*, and other incidental expences attending the same from *June* 24, 1766, to *June* 24 1767	4750	0	0
5. Upon account, for defraying the charges of the civil establishment of *West Florida*, and other incidental expences attending the same, from *June* 24 1766, to *June* 24 1767	4800	0	0
6. Upon account, for defraying the expence attending general surveys of his Majesty's dominions in *North America*, for 1767	1601	14	0

	l.	s.	d.

7. Upon account, for defraying the charges of the civil establishment of *Senegambia*, for 1767 — — — —   5550 0 0

26245 5 5

March 24.
For the marriage portion of the Queen of *Denmark* —   40000 0 0

March 31.
1. Towards carrying on an additional building for a more commodious passage to the House of Commons, from St. *Margaret's Lane*, and *Old Palace Yard* — — —   2000 0 0

2. To be employed in maintaining and supporting the *British* forts and settlements on the coast of *Africa*, under the direction of the committee of merchants trading to *Africa* —   13000 0 0

15000 0 0

April 9.
1. To replace to the sinking fund, the like sum issued thereout, to discharge for the year ended the 29th of *September*, 1766, the annuities after the rate of 4l. *per cent.* attending such part of the joint stock, established by an act of the third of his present Majesty, in respect of certain navy, victualling, and transport bills, and ordnance debentures, as remained unredeemed on the

said 29th of *September* - 104506 11 10

2. To replace to ditto, the like sum issued thereout for paying the charges of management of the annuities attending the said joint stock, for one year, the 29th of *September* 1766   1592 1 9¾

3. To replace to ditto, the like sum issued thereout to discharge, from the 29th of *September*, 1766, to the 25th of *December* following, the annuities attending such part of the said joint stock, as was redeemed in pursuance of an act made in the last session of parliament   8708 17 7¼

4. To replace to ditto, the like sum paid out of the same, to make good the deficiency on the 5th of *July*, 1766, of the several rates and duties upon offices and pensions, and upon houses, and upon windows or lights, which were made a fund, by an act of the 31st of his late Majesty, for paying annuities in respect of five millions borrowed towards the supply granted for the service of 1758 - 49660 9 3½

5. To replace to ditto, the like sum paid out of the same, to make good the deficiency on the 10th of *October* 1766, of several additional duties on wines imported, and certain duties on cyder and perry, which were made a fund for paying annui-

	l.	s.	d.

ties in respect of 3500000l. borrowed towards the supply granted for the service of 1763 — 12758 13 2

6. To make compensation to Dr. *Peter Swinton*, for the damage done to his estate in the city of *Chester* at the time of the late Rebellion, by order of the officer commanding the garrison of the said city — — — 700 0 0

177926 14 1

April 13.

1. That the remainder of the capital stock of annuities, after the rate of 4l. *per cent.* granted in respect of certain navy, victualling, and transport bills, and ordnance debentures, delivered in, and cancelled, pursuant to an act made in the third year of his Majesty's reign, be redeemed, and paid off on the 25th of *December* next, after discharging the interest then payable in respect of the same.

2. To enable his Majesty to redeem and pay off the said remainder — — — 1741776 10 11

3. That one fourth part of the capital stock of annuities, after the rate of 4l. *per cent.* established by the act 3. *Geo.* III. chap. 12. be redeemed, and paid off, on the 5th of *January* next, after discharging the interest then payable in respect of the same

4. To

4. To enable his Majesty to redeem, and pay off, the said one fourth part - - 875000 0 0

5. Towards paying off and discharging the debt of the navy 300000 0 0

6. To make good the deficiency of the grants for the service of 1766 - - - 129144 2 8

3045920 13 7

May 5.

1. Upon account, for enabling the Foundling Hospital to maintain and educate such children as were received into the same, on or before the 25th of *March* 1760, from the 31st of *December* 1766 exclusive, to the 31st of *December* 1767 inclusive, and that the said sum be issued and paid as on former occasions - - - 28000 0 0

2. Upon account, for enabling the said hospital to put out apprentice the said children, so as the said hospital do not give with any one child more than 7l. 1500 0 0

29500 0 0

May 19.

That the half pay of the lieutenants of his Majesty's navy is unequal to the rank their commission bear, and the time they have been in his Majesty's service.

June 15.

1. Upon account towards satisfying

tisfying the expences incurred by the committee of the company of merchants trading to *Africa*, on account of the establishment at *Senegal*, and its dependencies, after the 29th of *October* 1765 - - - 3500 0 0

2. For further enabling his Majesty to defray the contingent expences of the forces serving in *North America*. - - 2000 0 0

                                          5500 0 0

Total of the supplies granted in this session - - 8527728 0 6¼

Ways and Means this SESSION.

November 26, 1766.

That the usual temporary malt tax be continued from the 23d of *June*, 1767, to the 23d of *June* 1768, 700,000l.

March 2, 1767.

That the sum of 3s. in the pound, and no more, be raised within the space of one year, from the 25th of *March* 1767, upon lands, tenements, hereditaments, pensions, offices, and personal estates, in that part of *Great Britain* called *England*, *Wales*, and the town of *Berwick* upon *Tweed*; and that a proportionable cess, according to the 9th article of the treaty of Union, be laid upon that part of *Great Britain* called *Scotland* 1,528,568l. 11s. 11d. ¼.

March 9.

1. That the charge of the pay and cloathing of the militia, in that part of *Great Britain* called *England*, for one year, beginning the 25th of *March*, 1767,

1767, be defrayed out of the monies arising by the land tax, granted for the service of 1767.

2. That the sum of 1,800,000l. be raised by loans on Exchequer bills, if not discharged with interest thereupon, on or before the 5th of *April*, 1768, to be exchanged and received in payment, in such manner as Exchequer bills have usually been exchanged and received in payment.

April 2.

1. That an additional duty of 6 s. be laid upon every dozen of bast, or straw, chip, cane, and horse-hair hats, and bonnets, which from and after the second of *April*, 1767, shall be entered inward at any port, or place, in this kingdom.

2. That an additional duty of 6s. be laid upon every pound weight avoirdupoise of platting, or other manufacture of bast, or straw, chip, cane, or horse-hair, to be used in, or proper for, making of hats or bonnets, which from and after the said 2d of *April*, shall be entered inward at any port, or place in this kingdom.

April 16.

1. That towards the supply granted to his Majesty, the sum of 1,500,000l. be raised in the manner following, that is to say, the sum of 900,000l. by annuities, after the rate of 3l. *per cent.* to commence from the 5th of *January* last, and the sum of 600,000l. by a lottery to consist of 60,000 tickets, the whole of such sum to be divided into prizes, which are to be attended with the like 3l. *per cent.* annuities, to commence from the 5th of *January*, 1768; and that all the said annuities be transferrable at the Bank of *England*, paid half yearly on the 5th of *July*, and the 5th of *January*, in every year out of the Sinking Fund, and added to, and made part of, the joint stock of 3l. *per cent.* annuities, which were consolidated at the Bank of *England*, by certain acts made in the 25th and 28th years of the reign of

his

his late Majesty, and several subsequent acts, and subject to redemption by parliament; that every contributor towards the said sum of 900,000l. shall in respect of every 60l. agreed by him to be contributed for raising such sum, be intitled to receive four tickets in the said lottery, upon payment of 10l. for each ticket; and that every contributor shall, on or before the 29th of *April* next, make a deposit with the cashiers of the Bank of *England*, of 20l. *per cent.* in part of the monies so to be contributed towards the said sum of 900,000l. and also a deposit of 5l. *per cent.* in part of the monies so to be contributed in respect of the said lottery, as a security for making the respective future payments to the said cashiers, on or before the times herein after limited; that is to say, on the 900,000l. 10l. *per cent.* on or before the 27th of *March* next; 10l. *per cent.* on or before the 26th of *June* next; 15l. *per cent.* on or before the 27th of *August* next; 15l. *per cent.* on or before the 25th of *September* next; 15l. *per cent.* on or before the 30th of *October* next; 15l. *per cent.* on or before the 17th of *November* next. On the Lottery for 600,000l. 25l. *per cent.* on or before the 16th of *June* next; 30l. *per cent.* on or before the 28th of *July* next; 40l. *per cent.* on or before the 11th of *September* next. And that all the monies so received by the said cashiers be paid into the receipt of his Majesty's Exchequer, to be applied, from time to time, to such services as shall then have been voted by this house in this session of parliament; and that every contributor who shall pay in the whole of his contribution towards the said sum of 900,000l. at any time on or before the 27th of *October* next, or towards the said lottery on or before the 24th of *July* next, shall be allowed an interest by way of discount, after the rate of 3l. *per cent. per annum*, on the sums so compleating his contribution respectively, to be computed from the

the day of compleating the same, to the 17th of *November* next, in respect of the sum paid on account of the said 900,000l. and to the 11th of *September* next, in respect of the sum paid on account of the said lottery.

2. That an additional duty of 3d. *per* ell be laid upon all linen cloth, or sheeting, above one yard English in width, which shall be imported into this kingdom, except from *Holland* and *Flanders*.

3. That an additional duty of 3d. *per* ell be laid upon all canvas drilling, which shall be imported into this kingdom.

4. That the said duties be carried to the Sinking Fund, towards making good to the same the payments to be made thereout of the annuities attending the said sum of 1,500,000l.

5. That the additional duties upon bast, or straw, chip, cane, and horse-hair hats and bonnets, and upon platting, or other manufacture of bast, or straw, chip, cane, or horse-hair, to be used in, or proper for, making of hats or bonnets, imported into any port, or place, in this kingdom, granted to his Majesty in this session, be also carried to the said fund, towards making good the said payments.

6. That towards making good the said supply, there be applied the sum of 469,147l. 14s. 3d. ¼ remaining in the receipt of the Exchequer, on the 5th of *April*, 1767, for the disposition of parliament, of the monies which had then arisen of the surplusses, excesses, or overplus monies, and other revenues, composing the fund commonly called the Sinking Fund.

7. That, towards raising the said supply, there be applied the sum of 2,010,121l. 10s. 3d. ½ out of such monies as shall or may arise of the surplusses, excesses, or overplus monies, and other revenues, composing the said fund, commonly called the Sinking Fund.

8. That,

8. That, towards making good the said supply, there be applied the sum of 35,202l. 9s. 2d. also remaining in the receipt of the Exchequer, for the disposition of Parliament.

9. That a sum not exceeding 261,517l. 13s. 3d. ¼. out of the savings arising upon grants for the payments of several regiments upon respited pay, by off-reckonings, and by stoppages made for provisions delivered to the forces in *North America*, the *West Indies*, and at *Minorca*, to the 24th of *December*, 1764, and received of *William* Earl of *Chatham*, formerly paymaster general of his Majesty's forces, for the balance remaining over and above the monies found necessary to be applied for defraying the expences of the forces in former years; and also out of the sum of one million granted in the second year of his Majesty's reign, on account to enable him to defray extraordinary expences of the war, for the service of 1762, and to assist the kingdom of *Portugal*, and for other purposes, be applied towards making good the supply granted, towards defraying the extraordinary expences of his Majesty's land forces, and other services, incurred to the 3d of *February*, 1767, and not provided for by parliament.

10. That out of such monies remaining in the hands of *Edward Sainthill*, Esq; as were issued to him for the relief and maintenance of the widows of officers of the land forces and marines, who died in the service, the sum of 7844l. 17s. 9d. be paid into the hands of the paymaster general of his Majesty's forces, and be also applied towards making good the same supply granted, towards defraying the extraordinary expences of his Majesty's land forces, and other services, incurred to the 3d of *February*, 1767, and not provided for by parliament.

11. That a sum, not exceeding 110,000l. out of such monies as shall be paid into the receipt of the

the Exchequer, after the 5th of *April*, 1767, and on or before the 5th of *April*, 1768, of the produce of all or any of the duties and revenues, which, by any act or acts of parliament, have been directed to be reserved for the disposition of parliament, towards defraying the necessary expences of defending, protecting, and securing, the *British* colonies and plantations in *America*, be applied towards making good such part of the supply as hath been granted to his Majesty, for maintaining his Majesty's forces and garrisons in the plantations, and for provisions for the forces in *North America*, *Nova Scotia*, *Newfoundland*, and the Ceded Islands, for the year 1767.

12. That such of the monies as shall be paid into the receipt of the Exchequer, after the 5th of *April*, 1767, and on or before the 5th of *April*, 1768, of the produce of the duties charged by an act of parliament, made in the 5th year of his present Majesty's reign, upon the importation and exportation of Gum Senega, and Gum Arabic, be applied towards making good the supply granted to his Majesty.

13. That the sum of 150,000l. remaining in the receipt of the Exchequer, which was granted to his Majesty, in the last session of parliament, upon account, for defraying the charge of the pay and cloathing of the militia for one year, beginning the 25th of *March*, 1766, be applied towards raising the said supply.

14. That a sum not exceeding 181,000l. of the monies agreed to be paid by a convention between his Majesty and the *French* King, concluded and signed at *London*, the 27th of *February*, 1765, for the maintenance of the late *French* prisoners of war, be applied towards making good the said supply.

15. That the sum of 84,604l. 3s. 3d. remaining in the receipt of the Exchequer on the 5th of *April*,

April, 1767, of the Two Sevenths Excise, granted by an act of 5 and 6 W. and M. after satisfying the several charges and incumbrances thereupon, for the half year then ended, be carrried to and made part of, the aggregate fund, and that the said fund be made a security for the discharge of such annuities, and other demands, payable out of the said sum, as the growing produce of the said Two Sevenths Excise shall not be sufficient to answer.

May 5.

1. That an additional duty of 3d. *per* ell, be laid upon all linen cloth, or sheeting, above one yard *English* in width, which shall be imported into this kingdom, from *Holland* and *Flanders*, except cloth of the manufacture of those countries.

2. That an additional duty of 3d. *per* ell, be laid upon all drilling, other than canvas drilling, which shall be imported into this kingdom.

3. That the said duties be carried to the Sinking Fund, towards making good to the same, the payment, to be made thereout, of the annuities to be established in respect of the sum of 1,500,000l. to be raised in pursuance of a resolution of this house, on the 16th of *April* last.

4. That an act made in the 7th of *Geo.* II. chap. 18. which was to continue in force from the 24th of *June*, 1734, for seven years, and from thence to the end of the then next session of Parliament, and which, by several subsequent acts passed in the 14th, 20th, 27th, and 33d of his said late Majesty, was further continued, from the expiration thereof, until the 29th of *September*, 1767, and from thence to the end of the then next session, is near expiring, and fit to be continued.

May 7.

1. That there be laid an additional duty of one halfpenny *per* ell, upon all foreign canvas, packing spruse, Elbing, or Quinsborough, imported into this kingdom.

2. That there be laid an additional duty of 1d. *per* ell, on all foreign canvas, *Dutch* barrass, or *Hessens*, imported into this kingdom.

3. That all foreign lawns imported into this kingdom, be rated as *Silesia* lawns, and pay accordingly.

4. That over and above the said duty an additional duty of 3d. *per* yard be laid upon all foreign lawns.

5. That a sum, not exceeding 15,000l. *per annum* arising from the said duties, do remain in the receipt of the Exchequer, as a fund for the encouragement of raising and dressing hemp and flax in this kingdom, in such way and manner as parliament shall hereafter direct, and that the remainder of the said duties be reserved in the Exchequer for the future disposition of parliament.

May 19.

1. That there be granted to his Majesty, upon the postage and conveyance of letters and packets between *Great-Britain* and the *Isle of Man*, for every single letter 2d. for every double letter 4d. for every treble letter 6d. and for every ounce 8d. and so in proportion for every packet of deeds, writs, and other things.

2. For the postage and conveyance of letters and packets, within the said island, such rates, in proportion to the number of miles, or stages, as are now established for the island, port, or conveyance of letters and packets in *England*.

3. That the monies arising by the said rates be appropriated to such uses as the present rates of postage are now made applicable.

June 2.

1. That the duties upon logwood, exported from this kingdom, be discontinued.

2. That, the properties of any number of persons whatsoever, in any ship or cargo, or both, be allowed to be assured, to the amount of any sum, not exceeding 1000l. by a policy stamped with one

one 5s. stamp; and to the amount of any larger sum, by a policy stamped with two such stamps.

3. That the allowance authorized to be made by an act passed in the 29th of his late Majesty, upon prompt payment of the stamp duties on licences for retailing beer, ale, and other exciseable liquors, be reduced to the same rate as the allowances for prompt payment of other stamp duties.

4. That upon the exportation from this kingdom of coffee and cocoa nuts, of the growth or produce of the *British* colonies, or plantations in *America*, as merchandize, a drawback be allowed, of the duties of customs, payable upon the importation thereof.

5. That grey or scrow salt, salt scale, sand scale, crustings, or other foul salt, be allowed to be taken from the salt-works in *England*, *Wales*, or *Berwick* upon *Tweed*, to be used as manure, upon payment of a duty of 1d. *per* bushel only.

6. That provision be made, for declaring that ribbands and silks, printed, stained, or painted, in this kingdom, though less than half a yard in breadth, are within the meaning of certain acts made in the 10th and 12th of Queen *Anne*, and liable to the duties therein mentioned.

7. That the duties payable upon Succus Liquoritiæ, imported into this kingdom, be repealed.

8. That in lieu thereof, a duty of 30s. *per* hundred weight, be laid upon Succus Liquoritiæ, imported into this kingdom.

9. That the said duty be appropriated to such uses, as the duty so to be repealed was made applicable.

10. That a subsidy of 6d. in the pound, according to the value specified in the book of rates, referred to by an act made in the 12th of King *Charles* II. be laid upon the exportation from this kingdom, of such rice as shall have been imported duty free, by virtue of an act made in this session of parliament.

11. That the said duty on rice be reserved in the Exchequer, for the disposition of parliament.

12. That the drawbacks payable on China earthen ware, exported to *America*, be discontinued.

13. That a duty of 4s. 8d. *per* hundred weight, avoirdupois, be laid upon all crown, plate, flint, and white glass, imported into the *British* colonies and plantations in *America*.

14. That a duty of 1s. 2d. *per* hundred weight, avoirdupois, be laid upon all green glass, imported into the said colonies and plantations.

15. That such duties as shall be equal to a moiety of the duties granted by two acts of parliament, made in the 10th and 12th of her Majesty Queen *Anne*, and now payable in pursuance thereof, or of any subsequent act of parliament, upon paper pasteboards, millboards, and scaleboards, respectively, be laid upon paper pasteboards, millboards and scaleboards imported into the said colonies and plantations.

16. That a duty of 2s. *per* hundred weight, avoirdupois, be laid upon all red and white lead, and painters colours, imported into the said colonies and plantations.

17. That a duty of 3d. *per* pound weight avoirdupois, be laid upon all tea, imported into the said colonies and plantations.

18. That the said duties, to be raised in the said colonies and plantations be applied, in making a more certain and adequate provision for the charge of the administration of justice, and the support of civil government, in such of the said colonies and plantations, where it shall be found necessary, and that the residue of such duties be paid into the receipt of his Majesty's Exchequer, and there reserved to be, from time to time, disposed of by parliament, towards defraying the necessary expences of defending, protecting, and securing, the said colonies and plantations.

19. That upon the exportation of teas to *Ireland*, and the *British* dominions in *America*, a drawback

back be allowed, for a time to be limited, of all the duties of customs, which shall have been paid thereupon; and that such indemnification be made, by the *East-India* Company, to the public, in respect of such drawback, as is mentioned in the petition of the said Company.

20. That the inland duty of 1s. *per* pound weight, upon all black and singlo teas consumed in *Great Britain* be taken off, for a time to be limited, and that such indemnification be made, by the said company, to the public, in respect of such duty, as is mentioned in the petition of the said company.

June 10.

There were twenty resolutions of the said committee reported and agreed to by the house: by the first of which, all duties then payable to his Majesty, upon goods imported into, or exported from the *Isle of Man*, were abolished; but by the eighteen next following resolutions, a great variety of new duties upon such goods were imposed, which I do not think it necessary to transcribe, as so very few people in this kingdom can now have any trade or correspondence with that island, and those that have must provide themselves with a copy of the act itself. And as to the 20th resolution of this day, it was as follows.

That such bounties as may hereafter become due and payable, under the several acts which have been made for the encouragement of the *British* white herring fishery, be paid by the receiver general of the customs, in that part of *Great Britain* called *Scotland*, out of any monies remaining in his hands.

These were all the resolutions of the committee of ways and means agreed to by the house: and with regard to the sums thereby provided for, and which can now be ascertained, they stand as follows:

	l.	*s.*	*d.*
By the resolution of *Nov.* 27 -	700000	0	0
By that of *March* 2 - -	1528368	11	11¼
By the second of *March* 9 -	1800000	0	0
By the first of *April* 16 - -	1500000	0	0
By the sixth of ditto - - -	469147	14	0
By the seventh of ditto - -	2010121	10	3½
By the eighth of ditto - - -	35202	9	2½
By the ninth of ditto - -	261571	13	3
By the tenth of ditto - - -	7844	17	9
By the eleventh of ditto - -	110000	0	0
By the thirteenth of ditto -	150000	0	0
By the fourteenth of ditto -	181000	0	0
Sum total of such provisions as can be now ascertained	8753256	16	6
Excess of the provisions - -	225528	15	11¼

A new kind of money bill was brought in this session, not founded upon any resolution of the committees of supply or ways and means. Early in the Session, that is on the 25th of *November*, a part of the act 9 and 10 *William* III. intitled, An act for raising a sum, not exceeding two millions, upon a fund for payment of annuities, after the rate of 8l. *per cent. per annum*, and for settling the trade to the *East Indies*; and also part of the act 7 *George* I. intitled, An act to enable the *South Sea* Company to ingraft part of their capital stock and fund, into the stock and fund of the Bank of *England*, and another part thereof into the stock and fund of the *East-India* Company, &c. were, upon motion, read to the house, and thereupon it was resolved, that a committee be appointed to enquire into the state and condition of the *East-India* Company; that the said committee be a committee of the whole house; and that the house would, on that day fortnight, resolve itself into the said committee.

This enquiry gave rise to this new money bill. After the house had several times resolved itself into this committee of enquiry, and had called for many papers and accounts relating to this affair, at last on the 20th of *May*, there was presented to the house, and read, a petition of the united company of merchants of *England*, trading to the *East-Indies*, setting forth, that the petitioners, being duly sensible of the great obligation they lie under to government, and that their interests are, and must ever be, inseparable from those of the state, are most earnestly desirous that the public, and the *East-India* Company should mutually reap the benefits arising from the acquisitions and revenues, lately obtained in *India*; and the petitioners conceiving, that in the present state of things, a temporary agreement, for the space of three years, may be conducive to the advantage of both, do submit to the consideration of parliament the following propositions, in order to the carrying such agreement into execution. First, they beg leave humbly to suggest, that it will be not only expedient but necessary to the extending their commerce, and enabling them to invest those revenues in *India* in the produce of the country, that this house will take under their consideration the inland duties upon teas, in order to prevent the pernicious practice of smuggling, and encourage the consumption of that commodity, by such an alteration in the duties as to the house shall seem fitting, and by granting a drawback on such teas as may be exported to *Ireland*, or to any of his Majesty's colonies, and also by such alterations, as may conduce to the same salutary purposes, in regard to the duties on callicoes, muslins, and raw silk. 2. That in order to render the advantages expectant from the revenues before-mentioned certain and permanent, the house will provide effectual methods, as well for recruiting the forces necessary in

India, as for regulating the Company's civil and military servants there, for preventing the exportation of military stores thither, except for the Company's service, and for preventing illicit trade. 3. That from the said revenues, there shall be deducted, the expences attending the collection thereof, together with the civil, military, and marine establishments, and also the charges incurred for fortifications, buildings, and repairs, the same to be adjudged by annual accounts, transmitted from, and properly authenticated by, the several precedencies, in which the same shall be incurred. 4. That an account of the commerce of the Company, including the residue of the said revenues, and the produce of their exports, shall be annually made up, and that out of the sums arising from the general sales, the sum of 400,000l. shall be deducted, in lieu of profits, which the petitioners have hitherto enjoyed. 5. That the net surplus shall be equally divided between the public and the Company. 6. That the Company's share of the said surplus shall be duly and solely appropriated to the payment of their present debts, until they shall be reduced to the sum due to the Company from the public. 7. That this agreement shall commence from the 1st of *February*, 1767, upon all goods to be imported from *India*, and shall continue for three years provided the Dewanhee of *Bengal*, Bahar, and Orixa, shall remain in the Company's hands. 8. But if it should be the opinion of the house, that it will be more beneficial for the public to enjoy a specific sum, instead of the proportion of the revenues and trade abovementioned, then the petitioners proposed to pay, in lieu thereof, 400,000l. *per annum* for three years, by half yearly payments; the first payment thereof to commence the 25th of *March* 1768; and they are also willing to indemnify the public in respect of such drawback on teas exported, as shall be be granted by parliament, taking the same in a medium of the duties on the quantity of teas exported for five years past; and that such indemnification shall also extend to the inland duty of one shilling in the pound on the quantities of all black and singlo teas, consumed in *Great Britain*, upon a like medium of five years, in case it shall also appear a fit measure to parliament to take off the said duty; and provided the duties on the increased consumption shall not be sufficient to replace or supply the aforesaid duty of one shilling in the pound: and the petitioners hope, that what is hereby proposed, either in the mode of participation, or by a certain yearly payment, will appear reasonable and equitable to the house, more especially considering that the public revenue, during this interval, must continually increase in the same proportion with the commerce of the company, and the petitioners intreat the house, to recollect the imminent dangers to which in many critical conjunctures, their properties have been often exposed, the very large sums they have expended since the commencement of the wars in *India*, in which they were never the aggressors, the low dividends, which notwithstanding their few losses at sea, they have received during a course of years; whilst the public remained in the uninterrupted perception of an annual revenue, arising from the company's trade, of the full value of one-third of their capital; circumstances, which, the proprietors flatter themselves, will procure them the favour and protection of this honourable house, and intitle them to that candour and justice, which have ever been the characteristics of the *British* senate.

This petition was referred to a committee, who came to the following resolutions, viz. That it is the opinion of this committee, 1. That it would be for the mutual benefit of the public, and the

East

East India company, that a temporal agreement be made, in regard to the territorial acquisitions and revenues lately obtained in *India*. 2. That it is expedient, for the purposes of the said agreement, that it should continue for a term, not exceeding three years, to commence from the first day of *February*, 1767. 3. That the said acquisitions and revenues do remain in the possession of the company, during the continuance of such agreement; and that the company do pay to the publick, annually, during the said term, the sum of four hundred thousand pounds, by half-yearly payments, each payment to be made within six months after the same shall have become due. 4. That it will be necessary and proper, for the better carrying on, and extending, the trade of the said company, that provision be made, for granting a drawback on teas exported to *Ireland*, and the *British* dominions in *America*; and for taking off the inland duty of one shilling *per* pound weight on black and singlo teas, consumed in *Great Britain*; upon such indemnification to be made by the Company to the publick, in respect to such duty and drawback, as is mentioned in the petition of the said Company.

The three first of these resolutions were agreed to by the house, *nem. con.* and a bill ordered to be brought in upon them. And the fourth resolution was referred to the committee of ways and means.

Charles Townshend. 23. When the land tax was proposed in the committee by the late right hon. *Charles Townshend*, it was for 4*s.* in the pound. He contended, that in order to take off some of that weight which pressed the public funds, and to give room for the most brilliant operation of finance, which this country ever saw, it was necessary that four shillings should have been paid for one year longer, to give us dignity abroad, stability at home, and to enable us to enter with advantage into any future war. The country gentlemen were surprised, that he should imagine even his eloquence capable of persuading them, that a debt of about five millions could be cancelled, public credit restored, our fleets and armies equipped and victualled, by the addition of five hundred thousand pounds for one year, which is the produce of one shilling in the pound land tax. But in taking this ground, he did not so much consult the propriety of his present argument as his general reputation, and was wisely unwilling to stand forth the avowed patron of a perpetual burthen. The new and less considerable supporters of administration had less hesitation and prudence; they endeavoured to support the opinion, by avowing principles which concluded for a perpetual land tax at four shillings at least. It is true by this, that they abandoned and betrayed the first speaker, and alienated the minds of many indifferent men by the roundness of their declarations; and actually lost the end they proposed. They contended that the land tax, instead of being considered as an annual supply for the service of the current year, ought to be a perpetual fund for the payment of the national debt, and that till this was reduced to about seventy millions, the land-tax could not, with propriety, be lessened.

All these sentiments were answered in the course of the debate: to those whose arguments concluded for the perpetuity of a four shilling land tax it was replied, that this tax was first proposed for other purposes, and submitted to in other confidence; a confidence, which for near fourscore years had never been abused; that to continue the imposition at its present height during the time of peace, in order to discharge the public debt, was the most direct breach of this faith, and in fact a new and unprecedented tax imposed for new purposes;

poses; and that this new imposition of a tax so unequally laid, doubled the injustice, by oppressing a set of men, whose patient acquiescence in the time of necessity, merited the earliest relief from the state. In answer to those who rested the success of the measures of the year, and the reduction of the public debt, upon continuing the larger sum this year, it was replied, that it was an imposition on the public understanding, to attempt to persuade men that the safety of this kingdom depended on an addition of 500,000*l.* to a supply already much too large for the peace establishment of this country, and more than adequate to the real necessities of the state, though nothing can be adequate to the profusion of its ministers: that this additional burthen was the more unnecessary, as the unfunded debt which had so long lain heavy upon the stocks was now provided for; but, that admitting the necessity of it, it would be more just and equally feasible to borrow the sum of 500,000*l.*

Mr. Grenville. And Mr. *Grenville* who spoke with more weight on the subject, undertook to point out more than one method by which the interest of that sum, amounting only at three and an half *per cent.* to 17,500*l.* might be raised, without laying any sensible burthen upon the subject. When the house divided, the numbers were, for 4*s.* 188, for 3*s.* 206. There was no debate, or division upon the report,

A List of the Majority upon this Question.

ABDY, Sir Anthony, Tho. *Knaresboro'*
Abercromby, James, *Clackmannanshire*
Acland, Sir Tho. Dyke, *Somersetshire*
A'Court, Gen. William, *Heytsbury*

Adams, Geo. *Saltash*
Amcotts, Charles, *Boston*
Anstruther, Sir J. *Anstruther*
Archer, Andrew, *Coventry*
Armytage, Sir George, *York-city*
Aufrere,

A. 1766. DEBATES.

Aufrere, Geo. *Stamford*
Bacon, Edward, *Norwich*
Bagot, Sir Walter, *Oxford-University*
Bagot, William, *Staffordshire*
Baker, Sir Wil. *Plimpton*
Baldwin, Charles, *Shropshire*
Bampfylde, Sir Rich. *Devonshire*
Barne, Miles, *Dunwich*
Barrow, Charles, *Gloucester*
Bertie, Peregrine, *Westbury*
Best, Tho. *Canterbury*
Blacket, Sir Walter, *Newcastle*
Bootle, Richard Wilbr. *Chester-city*
Brand, Thomas, *Gatton*
Bridges, Sir Brooke, *Kent*
Bullock, John, *Malden*
Burdett, Sir Rob. *Tamworth*
Burke, William, *Bedwin*
Burt, William Mat. *Great Marlow*
Byde, Thomas Plumer, *Hertfordshire*
Campbell, Dan. *Lanerkshire*
Carysfort, Lord, *Huntingtonshire*
Caswell, Timothy, *Hertford*
Cautherlough, Lord, *Grimsby*

Cave, Sir Tho. *Leicestershire*
Cavendish, Lord Geo. *Derbyshire*
Cavendish, Lord John, *Knaresborough*
Child, Robert, *Wells*
Cholmley, Nath. *Aldborough, Yorkshire*
Cholmondeley, Thomas, *Cheshire*
Clive, Richard *Montgomery*
Coke, Wenman, *Oakhampton*
Colebrooke, Sir George, *Arundel*
Colleton, Ja. Ed. *Lestwithiel*
Coleraine, Lord, *Bridgwater*
Cook, George, *Middlesex*
Cornewall, Velters, *Herefordshire*
Cotes, Admiral Thomas, *Bedwin*
Cotton, Sir John Hynde, *Cambridgeshire*
Coventry, Tho. *Bridgport*
Craven, Thomas, *Berks*
Curzon, Asheton, *Clitherow*
Dalrymple, Sir Hugh, *Haddington*
Darker, John, *Leicester*
Dashwood, Sir James, *Oxfordshire*
Douglas, Arch. *Dumfriesshire*

Douglas,

Douglas, Sir James, *Orkneyshire*
De Grey, Tho. *Norfolk*
Delaval, Geo. Shafto, *Northumberland*
Dempster, George, *Forfar*, &c.
Dickson, John, *Peeblesshire*
Dowdeswell, William, *Worcestershire*
Down, Ld. *Cirencester*
Drake, William, *Amersham, Bucks*
Duke, John, *Honiton*
Duncombe, Tho. *Morpeth*
Dundass, Sir Law. *Newcastle*
Dundass, Tho. *Richmond*
Egerton, Sam. *Cheshire*
Eyre, Sam. *New Sarum*
Ewer, William, *Dorchester*
Farnham, Ld. *Taunton*
Fetherstonhaugh, Sir Matth. *Portsmouth*
Fife, Lord, *Bamffshire*
Filmer, Sir John, *Steyning*
Forrester, Alexander, *Oakhampton*
Foley, Tho. *Droitwich*
Garth, Charles, *Devizes*
Gascoyne, Bamber, *Midhurst*
Gilbert, Thomas, *Newcastle*
Glynn, Sir Rich. *London*
Glynne, Sir John, *Flinttown*
Grenville, Right Hon. Geo. *Buckingham*
Grey, Ld. *Staffordshire*
Grosvenor, Rich. *Chester-city*
Hales, Sir Thomas Pym *Downton*
Hamilton, William Gerard, *Pontefract*
Hamilton, John, *Wigtown*
Hanbury, John, *Monmouthshire*
Harbord, Harbord, *Norwich*
Hardy, Sir Charles, *Rochester*
Harley, Hon. Thomas, *London*
Harley, Robt. *Droitwich*
Harris, James, *Christchurch*
Hay, Dr. Geo. *Sandwich*
Herbert, Edward, *Ludlow*
Herne, Francis, *Bedford*
Hewett, John, *Nottinghamshire*
Hinchinbroke, Lord *Brackley*
Hobart, Hon. Geo. *Beeralston*
Holt, Rowland, *Suffolk*
Houblon, Jacob, *Hertfordshire*
Howard, Tho. *Castlerising*

Hunter,

A. 1766. DEBATES. 287

Hunter, Thomas Orby, *Winchelsea*
Hussey, Wm. *St. Germain's*
Joliffe, John, *Petersfield*
Jones, Robert, *Huntingdon*
Isham, Sir Edmund, *Northamptonshire*
Keck, Anthony, *Woodstock*
Keck, Ant. James, *Leicester*
Keppel, Admiral Aug. *Windsor*
Keppel, Gen. Wil. *Chichester*
Knightley, Lucy, *Northampton*
Kynaston, Edw. *Montgomeryshire*
Lambton, Gen. J. *Durham*
Lascelles, Edwin, *Yorkshire*
Lascelles, Dan. *Northallerton*
Lascelles, Edward, *Ditto*
Legh, Peter, *Newton*
Legh, Peter, *Ivelchester*
Lenox, Lord George, *Sussex*
Lewis, Edward *New Radnor*
Lowndes, Rich. *Bucks*
Luttrel, Simon, *Wigan*
Lynch, William, *Weobly*
Mackworth, Herbert, *Cardiffe*
Mackay, A. *Sutherland, co.*
Mawbey, Sir Jos. *Southwark*
Meredith, Sir William, *Liverpool*
Milles, Richard, *Canterbury*
Molesworth, Sir J. *Cornwall*
Molyneux, T. M. *Haslemere*
Montagu, Edw. *Huntingdon*
Montagu, Fred. *Northampton*
Mordaunt, Sir Charles, *Warwickshire*
Morgan, Thomas, *Breconshire*
Morgan, Thomas, jun. *Monmouthshire*
Morgan, Sir J. *Herefordshire*
Morton, John, *Abingdon*
Mostyn, Sir Roger, *Flintshire*
Murray, James, *Wigtonshire*
Neville, Rich. Neville, *Tavistock.*
Newdigate, Sir Roger, *Oxford University*
Norton, Sir Fletcher, *Norton*
Ongley, Rob. Henley, *Bedfordshire*
Osbaldeston, Fountayne, *Scarborough*

Orwell,

Orwell, Lord, *Ipswich*
Owen, Sir Wil. *Pembroke Town*
Palmer, Sir John, *Leicestershire*
Panmure, Lord, *Forfarshire*
Parker, John, *Devonshire*
Pelham, Thomas (comptroller of the King's houshold) *Sussex*
Penington, Sir J. *Cumberland*
Philipps, Sir Richard, *Pembrokeshire*
Pitt, Thomas, *Old Sarum*
Plumer, William, *Lewes*
Proctor, Sir Wil. Beauchamp, *Middlesex*
Rashleigh, Philip, *Fowey*
Rice, Geo. *Carmarthenshire*
Rigby, Rich. *Tavistock*
Rushout, John, *Evesham*
Sackville, Lord George, *Hyth*
Sargent, John, *West Looe*
St. John, Henry, *Wotton Basset*
St. Aubyn, Sir J. *Cornwall*
Scawen, James, *St. Michael*
Scudamore, J. *Hereford city*
Sebright, Sir John, *Bath*
Seymour, Henry, *Totness*
Sharpe, Fane William, *Callington*
Shiffner, Henry, *Minehead*
Sibthorpe, Coningsby, *Lincoln*
Smith, Sir Jarrit, *Bristol*
Smith, John, *Bath*
Southwell, Edw. *Gloucestershire*
Stevens, Richard, *Callington*
Stevenson, J. *St. Mitchel*
Tavistock, Marquis of, *Bedfordshire*
Thomond, Ld. *Minehead*
Thurlo, Ed. *Tamworth*
Thyne, Hon. Hen. Frederick, *Weobly*
Tracy, Tho. *Gloucestersh.*
Tuckfield, John, *Exeter*
Tudway, Clement, *Wells*
Tynte, Sir Char. Kemys, *Somersetshire*
Vansittart, Arthur, *Berkshire*
Vaughan, William, *Merionethshire*
Verney, Ld. *Caermarthen*
Vernon, Hon. Geo. Venables, *Bramber*
Vincent, Sir Francis, *Surry*
Upton, John, *Westmoreland*
Waller, Robt. *Chippingwicomb*
Walter, John Rolle, *Exeter*
Ward, Hon. J. *Worcestershire*

Way,

Way, Benjamin *Bridport*
Weddel, William, *Kingston*.
Weymiss, James, *Fifeshire*
West, James, *St. Albans*
Whatley, Thomas, *Luggershall*
White, John, *Retford*
Willoughby, Thomas, *Nottinghamshire*
Winnington, Sir Ed. *Bewdly*
Winterton, Earl, *Bramber*
Wodehouse, Sir Arm. *Norfolk*
Yorke, Hon. Cha. *Ryegate*
Yorke, Hon. John, *Higham Ferrers*

A LIST *of the* Gentlemen, *who were for continuing the* LAND TAX *at* 4s. *in the Pound.*

Aislable, William, *one of the auditors of the imprest* ——— ——— Rippon
Allen viscount, *a captain in the first regiment of guards* ——— ——— Eye
Amherst, William, *aid de camp to the King* ——— Hythe
Ashburnham, William, *deputy keeper of the great Wardrobe* ——— Hastings
Bacon, Anthony ——— ——— Aylesbury
Barre, Isaac, *one of the joint vice-treasurers of* Ireland ——— Wycomb
Barrington, Sir John ——— Newtown
Bayntun, Sir Edward ——— Chippenham
Beauchamp, Lord, *(son to Lord* Hertford, *Lord Chamberlain)* ——— Lestwithel
Beckford, William ——— London
Bertie, Lord Robert, *a Lord of the bedchamber, colonel of the 7th regiment of foot, and governor of* Cork ——— Boston
Bertie, Lord Brownlow, *(brother to the Duke of* Ancaster, *master of the horse* ——— ——— ——— Lincolnshire
Bindley, John ——— Dover
Boscawen,

Boscawen, *lieutenant general* George, *governor of* Scilly *islands, and colonel of the 23d regiment* — Truro
Brett, Sir Piercy, *a lord of the admiralty* — Queenborough
Bridgeman, Sir Henry — Ludlow
Brudenell, Hon. Robert, *vice-chamberlain to the Queen, and colonel of the 4th regiment of Foot* — Marlborough
Brudenell, Hon. James, *master of the robes to the King* — Hastings
Brudenell, George Bridges, *a clerk of the board of green-cloth* — Stamford
Bull, Richard — Newport
Buller, John, *a lord of the admiralty* — Eastlooe
Burghersh, Lord — Lyme Regis
Burgoyne, John, *colonel of the 16th regiment* — Midhurst
Burrard, Henry, *ranger of* New forest — Lymington
Burrel, Sir Merrick — Grampound
Burrel, Peter — Launceston
Burton, Bartholomew — Camelford
Calcraft, John — Calne
Calcraft, Thomas, *a lieutenant-colonel in the army* — Poole
Calvert, Nicholson — Tewksbury
Campbell, Lord Frederick — Renfrew, &c.
Campbell, Robert — Arygleshire
Campbell, James, *governor of* Stirling *castle* — Stirlingshire
Champion, Anthony — Liskeard
Clare, Lord, *first lord of trade* — Bristol
Cleveland, John — Barnstaple
Conway, Right Hon. Henry Seymour, *secretary of state* — Thetford
Conway, Hon. Henry Seymour, *constable of* Dublin *castle* — Coventry
Cooper, Grey, *secretary to the treasury* — Rochester
Cotton,

Cotton, Sir Lynch Salusbury	Denbighshire
Coutts, James	Edinburgh city
Crauford, Patrick	Renfrew country
Cunliffe, Sir Ellis	Liverpool
Cust, Sir John	Grantham
Cust Peregrine	Bishops-castle
Deering, Sir Edward	New Romney
De Grey, William, *attorney-general*	Newport
Delaval, Sir John Hussey	Berwick
Dennis, Peter, *a captain in the navy*	Hedon
Dod, John	Reading
Drake, Sir Francis Henry, *a clerk of the board of green-cloth*	Beeralston
Drax, Thomas Erle	Wareham
Drummond, Adam	Lymington
Dyson, Jeremiah, *a lord of trade*	Yarmouth
Eames, John	Yarmouth
Earle, William Rawlinson, *clerk of the ordnance*	Newport
Edmonstone, Archibald	Dumbartonshire
Elliot, *captain in the navy*	Cockermouth
Elliot, Gilbert Sir, *treasurer of the chamber, and keeper of the signet in Scotland*	Roxburghshire
Ellis, Welbore	Aylesbury
Evelyn, Sir John, *a clerk of the board of green cloth*	Helston
Fane, Henry	Lyme
Fanshaw, Simon, *a clerk of the board of green cloth*	Grampound
Bisher, Brice	Boroughbridge
Fitzherbert, William, *a lord of trade*	Derby
Fitzmaurice, Hon. Thomas, *brother to Lord* Shelburn	Calne
Fitzroy, Hon. *colonel, brother to the Duke of* Grafton, *and colonel of a regiment of dragoons*	Bury
Fludyer, Sir Samuel	Chippenham
Fonnereau, Thomas	Sudbury

Fonnereau,

Fonnereau, Zachariah Philip - Aldborough
Frankland, *vice-admiral* - Thirsk
Frederick, Sir Charles, *surveyor of the ordnance, &c.* - - Queenborough
Fuller, Rose - - Maidstone
Fuller, Richard - - Steyning
Gage, Viscount, *pay-master of the pensions* Seaford
Galway, Viscount, *master of the stag-hounds* - - - Pontefract
Gibbons, Sir John - - Wallingford
Gilmour, Sir Alexander, *a clerk of the board of green cloth* - Edinburghshire
Grandby, Marquis, *commander in chief of the army* - - Cambridgeshire
Grant, Sir Alexander - Fortrose
Grenville, Right Hon. James, *one of the the vice treasurers of* Ireland - Buckingham
Grenville, James, *his son* - - Thirsk
Grey, Hon. John, *a clerk of the board of green cloth* - - Bridgnorth
Griffin, Sir John Griffin, *colonel of the 1st troop of horse grenadier guards* - Andover
Harris, John, *master of the houshold* - Ashburton
Harvey, Eliab, *one of the King's counsel* Dunwich
Harvey, Edward, *a major general, and colonel of the 3d regiment of light horse* Gatton
Hawke, Sir Edward, *first lord of the admiralty* - - Portsmouth
Hays, James, *a Welch Judge* - Downton
Henniker, John - - Sudbury
Herbert, Hon. Robert, *surveyor of the King's honours, &c.* ——— Wilton
Herbert, Hon. Nicholas, *secretary of Jamaica* - - - Ditto
Hervey, Hon. William, *brother to Lord Bristol* - - St. Edmundsbury
Holborne, *admiral* - Stirling borough, &c.
Hotham, Charles, *a groom of the King's bedchamber, and colonel of the 63d regiment* - - St. Ives

Howe,

A. 1766. DEBATES.

Howe, Viscount, *treasurer of the navy* Dartmouth
Jackson, Richard - Weymouth and M. R.
Jenkinson, Charles, *a lord of the admiralty* - - - Appleby
Jennings, George - Whitchurch
Jennings, Soame, *a Lord of trade* - Cambridge
Knight, Thomas - - Romney
Ladbroke, Sir Robert - London
Lamb, Sir Matthew - Peterborough
Lane, Hon. Robert, *son to Lord* Bingley *and son in-law to Lord* Northington York city
Lawrence, William, *son-in-law to Mr.* Aislabie - - Rippon
Lindesaye, Sir John, *a captain in the navy* - - - Aberdeen, &c.
Linwood, Nicholas - - Stockbridge
Mackenzie, James Stuart, *brother to Lord* Bute, *and privy seal of* Scotland Rossshire
Mackye, John Ross, *paymaster of the ordnance* - - Kircudbright
Manners, Lord Robert, *colonel of the 3d regiment of dragoons, and governor of* Hull - - - Kingston
Martin, Samuel, *treasurer to the Princess Dowager of* Wales - Camelford
Maynard, Sir William - Essex
Medlicot, T. Hutchings - Milborne
Mellish, Joseph - - Grimsby
Meyrick, Owen - - Anglesea
Milbank, Sir Ralph - - Richmond
Montgomery, Archibald, *governor of* Dumbarton, *deputy ranger of St. James's and Hyde-parks, equerry to the Q. &c.* Air county
Montgomery, J. *Lord advocate of* Scotland - - Annan, &c.
Morice, Humphry, *Lord Warden of the Stanneries, and steward of* Cornwall Launceston
Mountstuart, Lord, *son to Lord* Bute - Bossiney
Newnham, Lord, *son to Lord* Harcourt St. Albans
Nisbet, Arnold - - Cricklade

U 3   North

North, Lord, *paymaster of the army* - Banbury
Nugent, Edmund, *son to Lord* Clare, *a groom of the King's bedchamber, and captain in the 1st regiment of guards* St. Maws
Onslow, George, *a Lord of the treasury* Surry
Onslow, George - - Guildford
Oswald, James, *one of the vice-treasurers of* Ireland - Burntisland, &c.
Owen, Sir William - Pembroke town
Palmerston, Viscount, *a Lord of the admiralty* - - East-Looe
Pennant, Richard - - Petersfield
Penton, Henry, jun. *letter-carrier to the King* - - Winchester
Percy, Earl, *son-in-law to Lord* Bute, *and aid de camp to the King* - Westminster
Phillipson, Richard, *major of the 1st regiment of dragoons* - - Eye
Pigot, Lord - - Wallingford
Pilkington, Sir Lionel - - Horsham
Pitt, George, *a groom of the King's bedchamber, and minister to the court of* Turin - - Dorsetshire
Pitt, John - - Wareham
Powell, Harcourt - - Newton Hants,
Powlett, George, *groom-porter to the King, gentleman usher to the Princess Dowager of* Wales - Winchester
Pownal, Thomas - - Tregony
Praed, H. Mackworth - St. Ives
Pratt, Robert, *nephew to the lord Chancellor* - - Horsham
Prescott, George - Stockbridge
Price Chase - - Leominster
Pringle, James, *a lieutenant-colonel of the army* - - Berwickshire
Reynolds, Francis, *clerk of the crown for the county of* Lancaster, *and provost-marshal of* Barbadoes - Lancaster
Roberts, John, *a Lord of trade* - Harwich

A. 1766.   DEBATES.   295

Robinson, Thomas, *a Lord of trade*   Christchurch
Ryder, Nathaniel   -   -   Tiverton
Sandys, Edwin   -   -   Westminster
Scott, John, *colonel of the 6th regiment
    of foot*   -   -   -   Tain Digwoll, &c.
Scudamore, Cha. Fitz. R. *deputy-cofferer*,
    &c.   -   -   -   Hereford
Selwyn, George Aug. *surveyor of the
    mint, and paymaster of the board of
    works*, &c.   -   -   Gloucester city
Sewell, Right Hon. Sir Thomas, *master
    of the rolls*   -   -   -   Winchelsea
Shafto, Robert   -   -   Durham county
Shelley, John, *treasurer of the houshold,
    clerk of the pipe, keeper of the records*,
    &c. &c.   -   -   -   Retford
Stanley, Hans, *cofferer of the houshold*
    -       -   -   -   Southampton town
Staunton Thomas,   -   -   Ipswich
Stephens, Philip, *secretary to the admi-
    ralty*   -   -   -   Leskard
Strange, Lord, *chancellor of the dutchy
    of Lancaster*   -   -   -   Lancashire
Sturt, Humphry   -   -   Dorsetshire
Sulivan, Lawrence   -   -   Taunton
Tempest, John   -   -   -   Durham
Thoroton, Thomas, *page of honour under
    the master of the horse, and secretary to
    the master of the ordnance*   -   Newark
Thrale, Henry   -   -   Southwark
Touchet, Samuel   -   -   Shaftsbury
Townshend, Hon. Tho. *a teller of the ex-
    chequer*   -   -   Camb. University
Townshend, Right Hon. Ch. *chancellor
    of the Exchequer*   -   -   Harwich
Townshend, Thomas, jun. *a Lord of the
    Treasury*   -   -   -   Whitchurch
Townshend, Charles, *a lord of the admi-
    ralty*   -   -   Great Yarmouth

U 4   Townshend,

Townshend, Chauncy - - Westbury
Tucker, John - Weymouth, and M. R.
Tuffnel, George Foster - Beverley
Vane, Frederick Hon. - - Durham
Villiers, Viscount, *vice-chamberlain to the King* - - - Aldborough
Walcott, Cha. *nephew to Lord Despencer* - - - Weymouth and M. R.
Walpole, Hon. Horace, *comptroller of the pipe, usher of the exchequer,* &c. King's Lynn
Walpole, Hon. Thomas - Ashburton
Warren, Sir George - - Lancaster
Whitshed, James - - Cirencester
Whitworth, Charles, *late governor of Tilbury fort* - - Blechingley
Worsley, Thomas, *surveyor of the board of works* - - - Orford
Wyndham, William - Helston
Wynne, Thomas, *auditor of Wales* Carnarvonshire
Yonge, Sir George, *a Lord of the admiralty* Honiton

A Petition of the Lieutenants of his Majesty's Navy being presented to the House, setting forth, among other things, that great numbers of the petitioners, being now reduced to Half-pay, the Amount whereof is so far from being adequate to their Situation as Officers, that it will not supply them, even singly, with the common necessaries of life; and many of them being charged with Families, are particularly labouring under the most mortifying distresses; and therefore beseeching the House to take the same into consideration, and grant them such relief as to the House shall seem meet; the Hon. Capt. Hervey stood up and said,

Capt. Hervey.

'THE paper which I shall ask leave to present to this House, is on a subject, that, 'in my opinion, should have been one of our ear-
'liest

'liest cares; and which, if I had not received re-
'peated assurances of its coming before you in a
'very different manner, with all that weight, dig-
'nity and authority, I must wish to see it accom-
'panied with, I should have much earlier desired
'to have laid before you; but as I have lost all
'hopes of that sort now, I cannot help imploring
'the serious attention of this house, for a few mo-
'ments, to what I think myself obliged, from e-
'very sense of feeling, for my King, my country,
'and the service I have the honour to belong to,
'to recommend to your compassion as well as to
'your justice.

'I am sorry, Sir, this has not an abler conductor;
'I flatter myself it will not want abler supporters:
'But as the cause I am now engaged in neither re-
'quires art to represent its situation, nor eloquence
'to enforce its equity, I shall be the less anxious
'on that head. I know it carries with it the good
'wishes of every man that I ever conversed with
'upon the subject without doors. I had reason to
'hope it carried with it the good wishes of most,
'if not all his Majesty's ministers; and I have the
'satisfaction of knowing it had the good wishes of
'that great and brave admiral, whom his Majesty
'has placed at the head of that service which is so
'much interested in the success of the petition, I
'beg leave to open to you, and lay before you.

'Sir, in the success of this motion, in my poor
'opinion, is comprehended the very existence of
'as useful a body of men as any this country has;
'in whom, in war-time, is lodged the honour and
'safety of these kingdoms: by whom the honour
'and safety of these kingdoms have been often pre-
'served; and without whom, neither the bene-
'ficial services, nor the great glory this country
'has reaped, could have been obtained.

'After this description, I should scarce think it
'necessary to tell gentlemen, that I mean the *Lieu-
'tenants of his Majesty's royal navy*, without whose
'watchful

' watchful care, constant labour, and intrepid con-
' duct, the fleet could not have proved itself, as it
' has done, the true defence and support of this
' country; and yet this very body of men, on
' whom alone our fleet must depend, without whom
' we could have no fleet, at least no active fleet,
' are now starving (or the major part of them,
' those that are on half pay) for want of subsistence,
' hiding themselves, in the remotest corners of the
' country; some for fear of jails, which their ne-
' cessities and their misfortunes, not their extrava-
' gancies nor their faults, have reduced them to be
' afraid of; others to hide their wants from the
' world, being ashamed to appear where they can-
' not support that character, which their long
' services, great merits, and delicate sense of
' honour, had justly entitled them to.---These, Sir,
' in a few years, must be all lost to this country;
' already but too many of them have been obliged
' to seek, with their families, a settlement in *Ame-*
' *rica*. Many are reduced to go even as second
' mates, in merchant ships, to the most distant
' countries, where the merits of an English officer
' are too well known for them not to meet with
' every allurement and seducement for their re-
' maining, and consequently for their leaving this
' country. Others have fixed themselves in trades,
' to endeavour to maintain their numerous fami-
' lies; and these must also be all lost to the service,
' on any emergency or sudden call for them.

' I have no occasion to remind gentlemen when
' this half-pay was first established, nor has the
' House time, at present, to let me enter into a
' comparison of that with the present time.---The
, high price of every necessary of life will sufficiently
' make that felt by every one; but I must beg leave
' to appeal to gentlemen's attention and humanity:
' What an insignificant, insufficient, totally inade-
' quate pittance, is two shillings a day for an officer

' who

'who bears the King's commission, to subsist up-
'on?---Is there a footman, is there a stable boy in
'any gentleman's family, who, from one consi-
'deration or other, has not more to maintain him-
'self?---Sir, it is too melancholy a scene to dwell
'upon.---I could lay before you many distressing
'scenes, but I will not take up your time, as bu-
'siness of such great consequence is now coming
'on: But, Sir, I believe scenes of the distresses that
'are suffered by these brave, deserving officers,
'are too frequent in every county of *England*, not
'to be known to every gentleman present, and
'make it evident, how necessary it is to give them
'some immediate and effectual relief.

'Sir, it was insinuated the other day, when I
'gave notice of this motion, that it would open a
'door to more representations, more claims and
'sollicitations of this kind; that there would be
'more applications, and that this might be of bad
'consequence. In the name of God, Sir, are these
'reasons founded on equity, compassion, or princi-
'ples of common justice?---Are such as these to
'invalidate what I have urged?---Shall we be afraid
'to-day of doing what we know to be an act of
'justice, lest we should be asked to do another act
'of justice to-morrow? I never heard such reasons
'in private life; I hope I shall not hear them se-
'riously urged in public life.---But, Sir, I will go
'further; I will be candid enough to say, that I
'do not mean to shut the door here: No, Sir,
'bring me any cases, similar to these I represent
'to you, and I will give all the assistance I can to-
'wards obtaining redress: But, Sir, I would en-
'deavour to avoid all comparisons; they are ever
'odious: but in this case they are particularly to
'be avoided.---But let gentlemen recollect that
'lieutenants in the navy are not, like mushrooms,
'to be bred in a night; they must be of a certain
'age before they go to sea; must be six years be-
'fore

'fore they can pass for lieutenants, and many of
'them many more before they can obtain a com-
'mission; and go through very hard service too,
'before they can be qualified or entitled to a rank
'that can make them of use. Sir, I take this
'corps, on a medium, to be upwards of ten years
'before they are lieutenants; and on the same cal-
'culation, they are one and twenty years before
'they can get on the two shillings and six-penny
'list, which consist of the 130 senior.---Tell me
'where the service is that equals this?---Sir, I will
'go no further; I honour and respect the gentle-
'men of the land service: I know the value of
'them, and am happy that I have been often a
'witness to their great unanimity and cordiality;
'and therefore whenever their distresses are proved
'to be as great as those I now represent, I shall be
'equally zealous and active in their behalf.---I think
'the necessities of the one may be pleaded, and the
'principles for redress supported, on principles
'very different from the other.

'Sir, I shall say no more at present, but hope
'for your indulgence to make a reply to any an-
'swer I may hear to this.'

This speech produced an address to his Majesty, That he would be graciously pleased to take the case of the lieutenants of his Majesty's navy, on half-pay, into consideration, and to make such further provision for *so useful and deserving* a corps, not exceeding one shilling a day, over and above their present half pay, as his Majesty in his wisdom shall think fit; and that the House would make good the same.

On *Friday* the 15th of *May*, 1767, Mr. *Fuller* having reported from the committee of the whole House, to whom it was referred, to consider of the several papers which had been presented to the House this session of parliament, relating to the

North *American* colonies—several resolutions, importing, That it appeared to the committee, that the House of Representatives of his Majesty's province of *New York*, have, in direct disobedience of the authority of the legislature of *Great Britain*, refused to make provision for supplying with necessaries his Majesty's troops, in such manner as is required by an act of parliament, made in the 5th year of his Majesty reign, intituled, ' An Act to ' amend and render more effectual, in his Ma- ' jesty's dominions in *America*, an Act passed in this ' present sessions of parliament, entitled An Act ' for punishing mutiny and desertion, and for the ' better payment of the army and their quarters.'

Also that it appeared to the committee, that an act of assembly hath been passed in the said province, for furnishing the barracks in the cities of *New York* and *Albany*, with fire-wood and candles, and other necessaries therein mentioned, for his Majesty's forces, inconsistent with the provisions, and in opposition to the directions of the said act of parliament.

Also, that it is the opinion of the committee, that until provision shall have been made by the said Assembly, for furnishing the King's troops, with all the necessaries required by the said act of parliament, the governor, council, and assembly, be respectively restrained and prohibited from passing or assenting to any act of Assembly, for any other purpose whatever;—and in consequence of these resolutions, a motion being made, that a bill be brought in upon the last of the said resolutions, Governor *Pownall* spoke as follows:

' Mr. Speaker,

Mr. Pownall.

' Having borne so great a share in the service of ' *North America*, I hope it will not be thought im- ' proper, that I take some share in the present de- ' bate. When matters are brought under consi-
' deration,

'deration, the facts and circumstances of which
'cannot be supposed to be fully known to this
'House, it becomes the duty of those whose ser-
'vice and station have rendered them duly cogni-
'zant of such circumstances and facts, to bear
'their testimoney of the state of things, and to
'give their opinion of the state of the business
'also.—However clear and distinctly these matters
'may lie in my own mind, in the strongest form
'of conviction, yet, being unaccustomed to speak
'in public, I am afraid I shall be unable so to dif-
'pose and explain them, as to exhibit that same
'distinctness, and to convey that same conviction
'to others. This being the first time I have pre-
'sumed to speak in this house, I feel that kind of
'awe in the presence of it, which every one must
'feel, who compares the little importance of his
'own sentiments, with the experience, the know-
'ledge, and the wisdom of so great an assembly;
'---so that, instead of finding myself master of my
'own sentiments and opinion, I feel as if I had
'arisen only to experience my own insufficiency.
'But the indulgence of the House gives me en-
'couragement, that they are willing to hear and
'receive what I can say on this subject. And in-
'deed, it is not only from the situation in general
'in which I stood, and the relation which I have
'borne to the business of America, which seems to
'render it proper that I should not give a silent
'vote upon this occasion---but the particular man-
'ner in which I have been concerned in this par-
'ticular business, does especially call upon me to
'give my opinion on the matter now under de-
'bate.

'As the present measure, now under considera-
'tion, is the proposal of a bill for enforcing an act
'of parliament, directing and regulating the quar-
'tering his Majesty's troops in *North America*, this
'matter will be best explained, by a plain narrative
'of

'of the rise of that act, and by comparing it with
'the circumstances and nature of the service, which
'it was meant to provide for; and also by compar-
'ing it with that province law, which it took (tho'
'mistook) for its model, on this occasion.

'It may be remembered, that the commander in
'chief of the King's forces in *North America*, ap-
'plied to government to furnish him with sufficient
'powers, whereby he might quarter the king's
'troops; and ideas of the necessity of quartering
'in private houses were suggested by some. A bill
'was formed on these ideas, and brought into this
'House.

'A measure so exceptionable and so alarming,
'must necessarily meet with opposition in this
'House.—There was an opposition made to it.—
'This opposition gave occasion to the minister of
'that day to recollect himself.

'I had heard accidentally of the state of this
'business, and thinking (as I did) the measure
'dangerous, and knowing that it was not neces-
'sary, I took the liberty to give this my opinion
'of it to that minister, and suggested a measure
'by which this business might have been done,
'and by which every thing, so contrary and dis-
'cordant to the constitution, might be avoided.
'I acquainted him, that there had passed, in the
'province of the Massachuset's-bay whilst I was
'Governor there, "An act for providing quarters
"for the king's troops,"---which, as it was adapt-
'ed to the nature of the country, and to the cir-
'cumstances of the people, so it was universally
'submitted to, and (during the war) constantly
'carried into execution. That, as I had been
'the author of this measure, and knew the effect
'of it, I was certain, that if that province law
'(adapted to the stated circumstances of the colo-
'nies in general) was made a clause in the act of
'parliament,

'parliament, allowing to the several provinces
'and colonies a proper latitude in the execution of
'it, it would answer every purpose required, could
'meet with no objection here, and would meet
'meet with no opposition in the colonies.

'I was desired to explain this measure to a cer
'tain office; but I am afaid I was so unhappy in
'the effect of my explanation, as to be totally
'misapprehended; because I see, that the act of
'parliament, which the proposed bill means to
'enforce, by its errors and defects, has mistaken
'and perverted every means of carrying the mea
'sure into execution; and has, from the tenor of
'it, been the natural occasion of all the confusion
'and misconduct which government now com
'plains of.

'The province law had in it every provision
'necessary for the carrying it into execution, and
'was accordingly constantly and invariably exe
'cuted.

'The act of parliament has neither any effec
'tual clause to enforce its execution, nor makes
'any sufficient provision for the expence incur
'red by the person who shall carry it into execu
'tion. It neither considers the various circum
'stances of the service in that country, as they
'arise and present themselves variously in various
'parts thereof; nor, as they must be perpetually
'changing, from time, in the same parts; but
'directs particular modes, and establishes regula
'tions to particular and special points, which must
'necessarily be incompatible with the nature of the
'country, and circumstances of the people in
'many parts, and on many occasions. It endea
'vours to lay down general rules, which can ne
'ver be applied to numberless particular cases that
'must arise; and, under this spirit of impractica
'bility, it allows no latitude in the execution
'thereof,

'thereof. And therefore, if there were full and
'effectual powers to enforce it, such powers could
'not produce an execution of this law, nor could
'produce any thing but confusion, so far as re-
'spects the law, and an arbitrary quartering of the
'troops contrary to law; of which, if you have
'not already had instances, you most certainly
'will have, whenever this law is attempted to be
'carried into execution.

'If you are determined to enforce this law, you
'ought, at least, to make it practicable. 1. Where
'the act directs, that the troops shall be quartered
'in barracks, provided for that purpose, you
'should, at least, direct the manner of that quar-
'tering, so that the barracks might answer the pur-
'pose thereof; and not first put the people under
'a kind of compact and agreement to the expence
'of building barracks; and then, after such are
'built, leave it in the power of the commanding
'officer of your troops, to judge, or to say, that
'these barracks do not answer the purpose of quar-
'tering: and under that decision, to demand quar-
'ters, either upon the inns or upon hired houses,
'even before any troops are quartered in such bar-
'racks as have been provided for them. 2. Where
'the act would mean to direct the quartering of
'the troops in inns, alehouses, &c. you should, at
'least, collect the peculiar circumstances of those
'inns and alehouses in that country, and whether
'they can answer the demands which the act makes
'upon them.

'You should consider, whether the officers
'which you direct to execute that business, can be
'required to do what is not practicable, and whe-
'ther your act has provided any means adequate
'to the inforcing them to do what they know is
'incompatible with the nature and circumstances
'of the country to perform. 3. Where the act
'directs that uninhabited houses, out-houses, &c.

' shall be hired for the accommodation and recep-
' tion of the residue of the troops, and provided
' with those special and particular articles, which
' the said act directs; you should, at least consider,
' whether there be any such uninhabited houses, and
' unoccupied out-houses; and whether your act con-
' tains any thing that shall oblige the people to lett
' them; or whether, when they are so hired, they
' will suit the purpose to which they are intended;
' or whether the circumstances of the people and
' country, where this service may be required to
' be performed, can supply those particular and
' special articles which you require of them.

' When the act requires a service, which (sup-
' posing it capable of being executed) engages the
' person who executes it in an expence, if you
' mean to enforce that act, you ought to provide
' effectually for his reimbursement: and in this
' instance, the act which you now propose to in-
' force, is, in every point of consideration, absurd
' and impracticable; as it neither provides itself
' for that reimbursement, nor puts the matter in
' any way of execution, that either can or will
' provide for it; but, on the contrary, entangles
' this business in a matter of controversy, which
' would of itself, if nothing else did, obstruct and
' stop it.

' The act of parliament for quartering his Ma-
' jesty's troops in *North-America*, directs, that the
' expence incurred by that measure, shall be pro-
' vided for by each respective colony, and raised
' in like manner, as the usual expences incurred
' by the province or colony are raised, that is, by
' an act of Assembly. This was an original error,
' which did prevent, and must for ever prevent,
' this act from being carried into actual execution
' as an act of parliament.

' If it be prudent and adviseable, that parlia-
' ment should charge any expence upon the colo-
' nies,

'nies, by way of tax, originated in this House;
'how shall it direct that charge to be levied and
'payed?---Shall parliament *direct the Assembly* of any
'province or colony, to make provision and sup-
'ply for it? Or shall parliament, directly and a-
'vowedly, imposing that sum upon the province
'or colony as a tax, settle the ways and means of
'levying it, and appoint executive officers to col-
'lect it? Or shall it direct the usual executive offi-
'cer of the colony to levy and collect that tax so
'imposed?———If the imposing by a direct tax be
'the proper political mode, the latter step is all
'regular, and but consequential of it---is conform-
'able to law.———The people having no share *in
'the will*, or in the *authority*, must submit to the
'*power* of the act, and have no duty left, but
'submission and implicit obedience.

'If parliament, the supreme legislature, shall
'order and impose a tax on a body of people, and
'shall order the legislative part of that body to
'provide for the payment of it, and to see it pay-
'ed, it must consider the members of that assem-
'bly merely as commissioners of taxes, appointed
'in such case to receive and register the act, to
'apportion and assess the tax. Yet surely this
'course is somewhat eccentric to the system of our
'happy constitution; it approaches, I am afraid,
'too near to the course taken by the arbitrary and
'despotic spirit of a neighbouring government,
'with the parliaments of its several provinces.
'This publishing the ordinance---this ordering a
'deliberative body to take it up as an act of its
'own will, and, as such, to register and carry it
'into execution, verges surely too near to that
'point which unites legislation and execution in
'the same body, to the utter destruction of poli-
'tical liberty. But I hope, and am willing to
'persuade myself, that I mistake this matter. It
'is impossible that, by any construction, this can

' be supposed to be meant; yet there is an use in
' that suspicion, which takes even a false alarm, as
' such alarm, when proved to be false, may lead to
' the conviction of truth.

' If on the other hand, we consider each of the
' assemblies of the provinces and colonies as what
' it is, as a legislative, deliberative body, as the
' will of that province or colony; it must have a
' right to deliberate, it must have a right to de-
' cide; if it has the free will to say *aye*, it must
' have the same power of will to say *no*. You may
' properly order an executive power to execute;
' but how, and with what propriety, can you or-
' der this deliberative body to *exert its will only in
' one prescribed direction*? If any supreme and so-
' vereign will shall pre-ordain what this inferior
' power of deliberation *shall will*, it will make the
' same confusion in practice, which the divines
' and metaphysicians have made in theory, between
' predestination and free-will absolute.---If you
' mean to try this experiment of reducing these
' absurdities and inconsistences to practice; if this
' bill must pass, and you have not yet predeter-
' mined on the title of it, it seems to me the bill
' may justly be intituled, *an act to render more ef-
' fectual predestination over free-will*. For as your
' measure now stands, if the assemblies of the
' provinces and colonies will not in every mode,
' article, and particular provision, decide *in their
' deliberative capacity*, as an act of parliament di-
' rects and pre-ordains, you consider the colonies
' as denying the sovereignty of *Great Britain*, than
' which nothing can be more unjust, unless it were
' possible to find any thing more absurd.

' Are you determined from hence to direct and
' regulate the quartering of the King's troops in
' *North America*?---Do it in a way that brings it
' home to the executive power there, to carry your
' directions and regulations into execution; ex-
' plain

'plain and amend your act: make it practicable;
'make it effective; and then you may fairly decide
'whether they deny your sovereignty or not. You
'will find they do not. If you think your way of
'making an adequate and certain provision for
'the charge of this service, is by the parliament's
'imposing a tax upon the people for that purpose;
'and that you have power, and it is adviseable to
'exert that power, to effectuate such supply, by
'such tax, you need not hesitate to avow it openly
'and directly; for the people of the colonies, from
'one end of the continent to the other, do inva-
'riably consider the clause in the act of parliament,
'directing how that charge shall be supplied, as
'an internal tax imposed upon them.---It is from
'this idea, that every act of obedience, as well as
'of disobedience to your act of parliament, must
'be construed and explained. Those whom you
'are willing to understand as having obeyed your
'act, have contrived to do it *in a mode* which nei-
'ther recognizes the act of parliament, nor sub-
'mits to the taxation---as such. And although
'you represent the assembly of the province of
'*New-York alone*, as having revolted against this
'power---believe me, there is not a province, a
'colony, or a plantation, that will submit to a tax
'thus imposed, more than *New-York* will. All
'have shewn their readiness to execute this service
'of quartering as an act of their own---all have,
'in their zeal to provide for it, by a grant of their
'own, provided a supply to answer the expence;
'---but not one single assembly has or ever will,
'act under the powers and provisions of this act,
'as acknowledging, and, in consequence thereof
'apportioning, assessing, and levying, the supply,
'as a tax imposed by parliament. They have ei-
'ther acted without taking notice at all of this act
'of parliament, or have contrived some way or
'other to vary in some particulars, sufficient to
'make the execution and the tax an act of their
'own.---

'own.---Try the conduct of every province and
'colony through by this rule, and you will find
'nothing particular in the case of *New York*———
'Don't fancy that you can divide the people upon
'this point, and that you need only divide to
'govern—you will by this conduct only unite them
'the more inseparably---you will make the cause
'of *New York* a common cause and will call up e-
'very other province and colony to stand forth in
'their justification--- while *New York*, learning
'from the complexion of your measure, how to a-
'void or evade the purport of your *enforcing bill*,
'will *suspend the force* of it, instead of it *suspending
'the assembly* of that province, against whom it is
'brought forward.

'But we are told, that there is something so pe-
'culiar in the spirit with which the House of Re-
'presentatives in *Boston* have opposed the autho-
'rity of this act of parliament, extending to the
'oppugning of all authority of parliament whatso-
'ever---that that particular case will demand the
'particular consideration of this House. We are
'told that they have charged the governor and
'council with unwarrantable and unconstitutional
'proceedings, for acting in consequence of an act
'of parliament.

'This is so total a misapprehension and misrepre-
'sentation of the case, as it doth actually stand, that
'a bare narrative of the circumstances and proceed-
'ings on the matter, will convince Ministry that
'they need not put themselves to the unnecessary
'and disagreeable pain of any further consideration
'of it, nor give this House any trouble about the
'affair. Some troops unexpectedly, and by acci-
'dent, put into the harbour of *Boston*—Some ex-
'pences arose in consequence of the necessity of
'providing for a temporary reception of them---
'The general assembly not having yet, from any
'occasion, been called upon to make provision for

'the

' the quartering of troops by an act of the province,
' and not being sitting at this particular time, the
' Governor, with the advice of council, incurred
' the expence. When the assembly met, the house
' of representatives considering, that the act of par-
' liament requires an act of the general court, in
' order to supply or reimburse any expence incurred
' by providing quarters, and so forth, and that no
' such act did as yet exist, and that therefore the
' Governor was not authorized, either *by any act of*
' *parliament*, nor as yet by an act of the province,
' to incur and supply such expence, did, with a
' jealousy and attention not unworthy even our i-
' mitation, object to the involving the treasury in any
' such charge, except what they authorized by their
' just power of appropriation. The Governor,
' with great prudence, founded in a knowledge an
' acknowledgment of the constitutional mode of
' proceeding, imputed the charge incurred to the
' necessity of the unforeseen occurrence, and apo-
' logized for his proceeding, as consonant to the
' usual practice in the like cases.———Although some
' of that ill-temper, which always mixes in with
' business when people are not well together, did
' mix in with this, yet here it ended; and from this
' plain narrative, I dare say, this House will never
' be troubled with any thing more about it. But
' to return:

' This clause in the quartering act, directing
' that the supply for reimbursing the expence of
' quartering the troops *shall be raised* by the respec-
' tive assemblies of the provinces or colonies---which
' is by all the people of *America*, considered as
' (and is indeed) a tax imposed by parliament, has
' brought, in fact, into discussion, that question of
' the right of taxation, which the cautious and
' (what I think) imprudent wisdom of many have
' endeavoured to keep wrapped up and suspended
' in theory.---What schemes of policy wished to
' hold

'hold in question---acts and deeds will bring into
'decision. You have, on one hand, by your de-
'claratory law, asserted your right and power of
'taxation over the colonies, and so far as this act
'goes, you have exerted that power. On the other
'hand, it is a fact which the House ought to be
'apprized of, in all its extent, That the people of
'*America*, universally, unitedly, and unalterably,
'are resolved not to submit to any internal tax im-
'posed upon them by any legislature, in which
'they have not a share by representatives of their
'own election.

'This claim must not be understood, as though
'it were only the pretences of party-leaders and
'demagogues; as though it were only the visions
'of speculative enthusiasts; as though it were the
'mere ebullition of a faction which must subside;
'as though it were only temporary or partial---it is
'the cool, deliberate, principled maxim of every
'man of business in the country.

'They say, that while we consider the nation,
'the realm, the government of *Great Britain*, col-
'lectively taken, *as the sovereign*, and the colonies
'*as the subject*, without participation in the deli-
'beration, or the will, bound *implicitly to obey* the
'orders of this sovereign, and implicitly to enact,
'register, and carry into execution *those grants*,
'which we by our *acts* have made of their property
'---they say, that this sovereign (however free
'within itself) is an absolute sovereign, an arbitrary
'lord, and that their obedience and subjection,
'without the interposition of their own free will,
'is (as to the subject so stated) absolute slavery.---
'We have by act of parliament declared our right,
'and thus their apprehensions feel the effect of it.

'They say, that supplies are *of good will*, and
'*not of duty*; are the *free and voluntary act of the
'giver*, having *a right to give*, not obligations and
'services to be complied with, which the subject
'cannot

'cannot in right refuse---they therefore maintain,
'claim, and insist upon, that whatever is given
'out of the lands or property of the people of the
'colonies, should be given and granted *by their
'own act*.

'They say that the true ground of justice, where-
'on the House of Commons grants supplies, and
'may lay taxes on the lands of themselves and
'their constituents, is, that they give what is their
'own, or that of others, for whom they are spe-
'cially impowered to consent; that they lay no
'taxes which do not affect themselves and their
'constituents; that therefore, they are not only
'the *proper givers*, but also the *best and safest judges*,
'as to the extent and the mode of the gift. But
'that where any legislature shall give and grant
'out of lands and property, in which they have
'no share or concern; where they have no tax im-
'posed upon others to supply that gift in ease of
'themselves and their constituents, the case la-
'bours with every effect, if not with every circum-
'stance of injustice.

'Thus this question is brought in issue, and
'must be decided; however much the policy of
'ministry may wish and labour to wave it, cases
'which constantly arise must bring it into discussion,
'and necessity will force it into decision.

'Is it the intent of government to exert the pow-
'er that it hath declared to be its right---is it de-
'termined to put this matter in contest---to put in
'contest the interest, the peace, and perhaps the
'being of this country---with the certain effect of
'ruin to our commercial interest---and to our co-
'lonies, as commercial accretions of the state?---
'Certainly no.

'Does ministry mean to propose the measure of
'imposing taxes on the colonies, and to force into
'execution the collection of them?---The whole
'system of the state, government, and interwoven
'interest

'interest of the colonies, is gone too far for that to
'be practicable.

' Does it mean by any *mode of policy*, to unite this
' system, which is *in fact* interwoven and incorpo-
' rated into the very being of the *British* empire?
' ---I am afraid not. Matters are not yet gone far
' enough to point out the practicability and ne-
' cessity of such political union.

' What then remains, but that we must return
' again, and re-establish the system of our politicks
' on that basis whereon they stood, before some late
' innovations in our system shook that basis?---
' What remains, but that we act, as to external tax-
' es, with that commercial spirit and prudence,
' which the wisdom of parliament hath always exer-
' cised towards the colonies, since their first esta-
' blishment: and that as to further supplies, when
' they become necessary, the colonies are properly
' applied to by requisitions in the old accustomed,
' known mode, which hath always succeeded and
' been found effectual.

' As this is my opinion on this question in ge-
' neral, so on the particular matter of this debate on
' the proposed bill, I will close what I wish to offer
' in recommending it to the House, either so to a-
' mend and explain its act, as that both the mode
' of quartering, and the act of making the supply
' for the expence of it, may originate with the peo-
' ple of the colonies, and be an act of their own as-
' semblies---in which case, this enforcing bill will
' become unnecessary---or let it be considered as a
' service which the crown requires of them, and for
' which, without the interposition of parliament,
' it makes the proper requisitions.

' This will restore peace, this will effect the bu-
' siness. The contrary measure of this enforcing bill
' will be the beginning of a series of mischiefs, and
' therefore I shall be against the bringing it in.'

This

This speech was followed by one from Sir *Thomas Sewell*, who was anſwered by the late Right Hon. *Charles Townſhend*; after whom ſpoke, in anſwer to what Governor *Pownall* had ſaid, Mr. Secretary *Conway*, Sir *Gilbert Elliot*, the Right Hon. *Hans Stanley*. The Right Hon. *George Grenville* aroſe on the ſame account, alſo the Right Hon. *Wellbore Ellis*, who were anſwered by Mr. Alderman *Beckford*. The bill however paſſed.

A remarkable Petition from New York, *deſerves to be noted in this place, though there were no proceedings upon it.*

Lord *Clare* (from the board of trade) informed the houſe that the board had received, incloſed in a letter from Sir *Henry Moore*, Bart. (his Majeſty's governor of *New York*) a petition of the merchants in the city of *New York*, addreſſed to the Houſe of Commons, which the governor ſays, he tranſmitted to the commiſſioners of trade and plantations, at the requeſt of a committee of merchants of *New York*.

This petition being brought up and read; ſet forth, ' that the commerce of the *North American*
' colonies is ſo ſeverely clogged and reſtricted by
' the ſtatutes of the 4th and 6th of his preſent Ma-
' jeſty's reign, as to afford a melancholy preſage of
' its deſtruction, the fatal effects of which, though
' firſt felt there, muſt be finally transferred to
' *Great Britain*, and center with her merchants and
' manufacturers: that an evil ſo extenſive, could
' not fail of alarming the petitioners, whoſe ſitua-
' tion expoſes them to the firſt impreſſion of this
' calamity; whence they think it their duty to im-
' plore the houſe to reſume the conſideration of the
' plantation trade, for effectual redreſs. It is the
' ſingular diſadvantage of the Northern *Britiſh* co-
' lonies, that, while they ſtand in need of vaſt
' quantities

'quantities of the manufactures of *Great Britain*, 'the country produces very little that affords a 'direct remittance thither in payment, and there'fore from necessity they have been driven to seek 'a market for their produce, and by a course of 'traffic, to acquire either money or such merchan'dize, as would answer the purpose of a remit'tance, and enable them to sustain their credit with 'their mother country: As the nature of the pe'titioners commerce, when free from the late re'straints, ought to be understood, they beg leave 'to observe, that their produce then sent to our 'own and the foreign islands, was chiefly bartered 'for sugar, rum, melasses, cotton, and indigo; 'that the sugar, cotton, and indigo, served as re'mittance to *Great Britain*, which the rum and 'melasses constituted essential branches of their 'commerce, and enabled them to barter with our 'own colonies for fish and rice, and by that means 'to pursue a valuable trade with *Spain*, *Portugal*, 'and *Italy*, where they chiefly obtained money, or 'bills of exchange in return, and likewise qualified 'them for adventures to *Africa*, where they had 'the advantage of putting off great quantities of '*British* manufactures, and of receiving in ex'change gold, ivory, and slaves, which last being 'disposed of in the *West India* islands, commanded 'money or bills: Rum was indispensable in their '*Indian* trade, and with *British* manufactures, pro'cured furs and skins, which both served for con'siderable returns to *Great Britain*, and encreased 'its revenue. The trade to the bay of *Honduras* 'was also of great importance, it being managed 'with small cargoes of provisions, rum, and *British* 'manufactures, which, while they were at liberty 'to send foreign logwood to the different ports in '*Europe*, furnished them with another valuable re'mittance. From this view, it is evident that su'gar, rum, melasses and logwood, with cotton and 'indigo,

'indigo, are the essentials of their return-cargoes, and the chief sources, from which, in a course of trade they have maintained their credit with *Great Britain*. That considering the prodigious consumption of the produce of the *West Indies* in *Great Britain*, *Ireland*, and the colonies on the continent of *America*; the rapid increase of those colonies; the vast accession of subjects by the late conquests; the utter incapacity of our own island to supply so great a demand, will, the petitioners presume, be out of all question; on the other hand, the lumber produced from clearing this immense territory, and the provisions extracted from a fertile soil, must raise a supply for exportation much greater than all our islands can consume; it seems therefore consistent with sound policy, to indulge those colonies both in the free and unrestrained exportation of all the lumber and produce they can spare, and an ample importation of sugar, rum, and melasses, to supply the various branches of their trade; since without the one the clearing of lands will be discouraged; and provisions, for want of vent, become of little profit to the farmer; without the other, the petitioners must be plunged into a total incapacity of making good their payments of *British* debts; their credit must sink, and their imports from *Great Britain* gradually diminish, till they are contracted to the narrow compass of remittances, in articles of their own produce; whence the colonies must, from inevitable necessity, betake themselves to manufactures of their own, which will be attended with consequences very detrimental to those of *Great Britain*.

'The petitioners having thus represented the nature of their commerce, humbly beg leave to point out the several grievances under which it labours, from the regulations prescribed by the two before-mentioned acts. The heavy embar-
'rassments,

'rassments which attend the article of sugar, is a capital subject of complaint; and, besides the absolute necessity of a great importation to sustain their trade, it often happens, that at the foreign islands a sufficient return-cargo, independent of sugar, cannot be procured, which renders trade precarious and discouraging; besides, the high duty of 5s. sterling a hundred, is found by experience to be so excessive, that it has induced the fair trader to decline that branch of business, while, to people less scrupulous, it presents an irresistible temptation to smuggling. That the pressure of this duty is not aggravated, the petitioners appeal to the officers of the customs of their port, who must confess that there have not been wanting instances where merchants have been driven to the disagreeable necessity of bringing their very plate into the custom-house to discharge it. The petitioners therefore most humbly entreat that a more moderate duty be laid on foreign sugars, which, they are assured, would not only greatly promote the prosperity both of those colonies and their mother country, but encrease the royal revenue far beyond what can be expected under the present restraints. The compelling merchants to land and store foreign sugars in *Great Britain*, before they are exported to other parts of *Europe*, is another expensive and dilatory restriction, without being of any material advantage to the revenue of *Great Britain*; for it puts it out of the petitioners power to meet foreigners at market upon an equal footing. That *British* plantation sugar exported from *North America*, should be declared *French* on being landed in *England*, the petitioners conceive may be justly classed among the number of hardships inflicted by those regulations, as in effect it deprives them of making a remittance in that article, by exposing them to the payment of the

'foreign

'foreign duty in *Great Britain*, which appears the
'more severe, as their fellow-subjects of the islands
'are left at liberty to export those sugars for what
'they really are, and a distinction is formed which
'the petitioners cannot but regard with uneasiness.
'That foreign rum, *French* excepted, is the next
'article which the petitioners most humbly pro-
'pose for consideration, as its importation, on a
'moderate duty, would add considerably to the
'revenue, prevent smuggling, encrease the sale
'of *British* manufactures, and enable the peti-
'oners to bring back the full value of their car-
'goes, more especially from the *Danish* islands of
'St. *Thomas* and St. *Croix*, where they can only
'receive half the value in sugar and cotton, and
'consequently rum alone can be expected for the
'other half, those islands having no spice but of a
'base kind. That it is with the greatest concern
'the petitioners observe, that foreign logwood is al-
'so made subject to the delay, hazard, and ex-
'pence of being landed in *Great Britain*; which
'with its low price, its bulk, and the duty with
'which it is now burthened, must totally destroy
'that valuable branch of the petitioners commerce,
'and throw it into the hands of foreigners unfet-
'tered with those heavy embarrassments. That
'their lumber and pot-ash, even when shipped for
'*Ireland*, where the latter is so necessary for the
'progress of their linen manufacture, and even
'provisions, though intended to relieve that king-
'dom from a famine, are subject to the same dis-
'tressing impediments; nor is flax-seed on the
'timely importation of which the very existence
'of the linen manufacture immediately depends,
'exempted: Yet both flax-seed, lumber, and pot-
'ash, may all be imported into *Ireland* directly from
'the Baltic, where they are purchased from fo-
'reigners under the national disadvantage of being
'paid for with money instead of manufactures;
'the

' the petitioners, therefore, humbly beg leave to
' express their hopes, that an evil so highly pre-
' judicial to them, to the staple of *Ireland*, and to
' the trade and manufactures of *Great Britain*, will
' not fail of obtaining the attention of the House,
' and an immediate and effectual redress. The pe-
' titioners beg leave further to represent, that the
' wines from the islands, in exchange for wheat,
' flour, fish and lumber, would considerably aug-
' ment the important article of remittance, was the
' *American* duty withdrawn on exportation to
' *Great Britain*: It is therefore humbly submitted
' to the House, whether such an expedient, calcu-
' lated at once to attach the inhabitants to hus-
' bandry, by encreasing the consumption of *Ame-*
' *rican* produce, to encourage *British* manufactures
' by enabling the petitioners to make good their
' payments, and to encrease the royal revenue by
' an additional import of wines into *Great Britain*,
' will not be consistent with the united interests
' both of the mother country and her colonies.
' The petitioners also conceive that the *North Ame-*
' *rican* fishery is of the highest national importance,
' since, by annually employing so great a number
' of shipping, it constitutes a respectable nursery
' for seamen, and is so advantageous in remittances
' in payment for *British* manufactures; whence the
' petitioners humbly presume it will be cherished
' by the House, and every impediment removed
' that tends to check its progress. The enlarging
' the jurisdiction of the admiralty is another part
' of the fourth of his Majesty's reign, very grie-
' vous to the trade and navigation of the colonies,
' and oppressive to the subjects. The petitioners
' beg leave to to express their warmest sentiments,
' of gratitude for the advantages intended by par-
' liament in the opening free ports in the islands
' of *Jamaica* and *Dominica*; yet, at the same time,
' cannot but lament their being so unhappy as to

' be

'be unable to reap the benefits, which, it was ima-
'gined, would flow from so wise a policy. The
'collecting great quantities of the produce of
'*Martinico, Guadaloupe,* &c. at the island of *Do-*
'*minica,* would be of real advantage to the colo-
'nies, were they permitted to take them in return
'for their lumber and provisions; but as they are
'now prohibited from taking any thing but me-
'lasses, the petitioners think it evident, that they
'can derive no substantial advantage under such a
'restraint, and are unable to discern the principle
'on which the prohibition is founded; for since
'sugar may be imported directly from the foreign
'islands, it seems much more reasonable to suffer
'it from a free port belonging to *Great Britain.*
'The petitioners, therefore humbly hope, that the
'House will think it equitable to adapt this trade
'to their circumstances, by granting them liberty
'to import into the colonies all *West India* produc-
'tions, in exchange for their commodities; and
'that, upon the whole, the petitioners, with the
'greatest anxiety, find themselves obliged to in-
'form the House, that although, at the last session,
'the necessity of relieving the trade of those colo-
'nies seems to have been universally admitted, and
'the tender regard of parliament for their happiness
'highly distinguished; nevertheless, experience
'has evinced, that the commercial regulations
'then enacted, instead of remedying, have en-
'creased the heavy burthen under which it already
'laboured. Hence, upon due consideration, no-
'thing can be more manifest, than that the ability
'of those colonies to purchase the manufactures
'of *Great Britain,* immediately depends upon,
'and is inseparably connected with the progress of
'their commerce; and that ability, by removing
'the necessity of home manufactures, would leave
'them at liberty to pursue agriculture, in which
'their true interest consists. The petitioners, there-

'fore, pray the house to take the above into con-
'sideration, and to grant such relief therein as
'shall be thought consistent with good policy,
'and the mutual interests of *Great Britain* and her
'colonies.'

This petition was ordered to lie upon the table: no other notice was taken of it.

The rest of the material business of this Session will be seen by the list of acts which were passed.

A List of the ACTS *passed this* SESSION.

AN Act *to punish mutiny and desertion.*

An Act *to continue, for a further limited time, the free importation of wheat and wheat meal, from any part of* Europe, *and to discontinue the duties payable on the importation of barley-meal and pulse.*

An Act *to discontinue the duties on the importation of tallow, hog's-lard, and grease.*

An Act *for granting an aid to his Majesty, by a land-tax, for the service of the present year,* (3s. *in the pound*).

An Act *for better regulating his Majesty's marine forces when on shore.*

An act *to apply the sum granted for the pay and cloathing of the militia, for* 1767.

An Act *to enlarge the term granted for building two new churches in the town of* Liverpool.

An Act *to enable the Earl of* Strathmore *to take the name of* Bowes, *pursuant to the will of* George Bowes, *Esq; deceased.*

An act *for the free importation of salted meat and butter into this kingdom.*

An Act *for establishing commissioners of customs in* America.

An Act *to continue several laws relating to the clandestine running of uncustomed goods, and to prevent frauds relating to customs, and for granting liberty*

to

to carry rice from Carolina *and* Georgia *to* America.

An Act *for the preservation of fish in rivers, so far as relates to the destroying of fish, and the damage done to sea banks.*

An Act *to render more effectual an act made in the eighth year of the reign of King* George II. *for the encouragement of the arts of designing, engraving, and etching, historical and other prints, and for vesting and securing to* Jane Hogarth, *widow, the property in certain prints.*

An Act *to continue so much of an act as relates to the free importation of cochineal and indigo, and for allowing the bounties on acts of parliament now in being upon the exportation of corn and malt, declared or made for exportation, and barley, &c. and entered at the Excise office.*

An Act *to render more effectual in his Majesty's dominions in* America, *the act for punishing mutiny and desertion.*

An Act *to prevent the fraudulent importation and wearing of* French *lawn.*

An Act *to encourage the trade and manufacture of the* Isle *of* Man, *and for the better supply of the inhabitants there with wheat-flour, barley, and meal.*

An Act *for raising* 1,500,000l. *by annuities and lottery.*

An Act *for laying an additional duty of* 3d. *an ell on linen cloth or sheeting, above a yard in width, imported from* Holland *and* Flanders, *except cloth of the manufacture of those countries.*

An Act *for allowing the free importation of rice, sago, powder, and vermicelli, from* America. [This immediately reduced the price of Rice to 2d. a pound.]

An Act *for redeeming the remainder of joint stock annuities, in respect of several navy, victualling, and transport bills, and ordnance debentures.*

An Act *for redeeming one-fourth part of the joint stock annuities, established by an act of his present Majesty, for granting several additional duties upon wines; and certain duties on cyder and perry.*

An Act *to explain an act of the 29th of* Q. Elizabeth, *to prevent extortion, in cases of execution.*

An Act *for extending the royalty of the city of* Edinburgh, *and for establishing a theatre in that city.*

An Act *for establishing a general hospital in the town of* Cambridge. (Adenbroke's)

An Act *for extending the navigation of the river* Hull, *from* Frodingham-Beck *to* Driffield, *in the East Riding of* Yorkshire.

An Act *to make* Codbeck *brook navigable, from the river* Swale *to* Thirsk, *in* Yorkshire.

An Act *for erecting a pier at St.* Ives.

An Act *for regulating the parish poor children within the bills of mortality.*

An Act *for compleating* Black-friars *bridge.*

An Act *for indemnifying persons who have omitted to qualify for employments.*

An Act *for granting certain sums out of the sinking fund; and for impowering his Majesty to permit the importation of corn, duty free, for a longer time.*

An Act *for taking off the duty of* 1s. *a pound on all black and Singlo tea, and for granting a drawback on teas exported to* Ireland *and* America.

An Act *for granting certain duties on foreign linen, and a premium for the encouragement of raising hemp.*

An Act *for restraining the assembly of* New York *from passing any act, till they had complied with the act of parliament for the furnishing his Majesty's troops with the necessaries required in that act.*

An Act *for putting the* American *duties into the hands of commissioners.*

An Act *for allowing a longer time for the enrollment of*

of deeds of papists, for relief of protestant purchasers.

An Act *for extending the window act to* Scotland.

An Act *for altering the duties on policies, and lessening the allowance for prompt payment of certain stamp duties.*

An Act *for granting certain duties in the* British American *colonies.*

An Act *for regulating the dividend of the* East India *company.* [By this act no dividend is to be made from the 24th of *June* but in pursuance of a vote carried on a ballot, in a general court summoned for the purpose seven days beforehand; nor any increase of dividend beyond 10 *per cent.* till the next meeting of parliament.]

An Act *for establishing an agreement between the government and the* East India *Company.* [By this agreement the Company are to pay the government 400,000l. yearly for two years, by half yearly payments, during which time the territorial possessions and revenues lately obtained are to remain in the Company's hands; but if dispossessed of any of them in the mean time by any foreign power, a proportional abatement is to be made in the annual payments; and money wrongfully paid to be refunded. The monies to be reserved for the disposition of parliament.]

On the Second of *July* 1767, the King put an end to this Session with the following Speech.

My Lords, and Gentlemen,

'THE advanced season of the year, joined to the
' consideration of the inconvenience you must
' all have felt from so long an absence from your se-
' veral counties calls upon me to put an end to the
' present session of parliament; which I cannot do,
' without returning you my thanks for your diligent
' application to the public business, and the proofs
' you have given of your affection for me, for my
' family, and for my government: And although,

' from

'from the nature and extensiveness of the several objects under your consideration, it could not be expected that all the great commercial interests should be compleatly adjusted and regulated in the course of this session, yet I am persuaded, that, by the progress you have made, a solid foundation is laid for securing the most considerable and essential benefits to this nation.

'As no material alteration has happened in the state of foreign affairs since your first meeting, I have nothing to communicate to you on that subject. The fixed objects of all my measures are, to preserve the peace, and at the same time to assert and maintain the honour of my crown, and the just rights of my subjects.'

Gentlemen of the House of Commons,

'I thank you for the necessary supplies which you have so chearfully granted for the public service; and my particular acknowledgements are due to you, for the provision you have enabled me to make for the more honourable support and maintenance of my family.'

My Lords, and Gentlemen,

'The great attention which you have shewn to the particular purpose for which I called you so early together, and the very wholesome laws passed for relieving my subjects from the immediate distress which the great scarcity of corn threatened to bring upon them, give me the most sensible pleasure. I rely upon you for the exertion of your utmost endeavours to convince my people, that no care has been wanting to procure for them every relief which has been possible; and that their grateful sense of provisions so wisely made for their present happiness and lasting prosperity cannot be so fully expressed, as by a strict observance of that order and regularity, which are equally necessary to the security of all good government, as well as to their own real welfare.'

DEBATES.

A. 1767.

The SEVENTH SESSION

OF THE

Twelfth Parliament of *Great-Britain*.

On the 24th of November 1767, *the King went to the House of Peers at* Westminster, *and opened this Session with the following Speech.*

My Lords, and Gentlemen,

'I Have chosen to call you together at this season of the year, that my parliament might have full deliberations upon all such branches of the public service, as may require their immediate attention; without the necessity of continuing the session beyond the time most suitable to my people, for the election of a new parliament: And I doubt not but you will be careful, from the same considerations, to avoid in your proceedings, all unnecessary delay.

'Nothing in the present situation of affairs abroad gives me reason to apprehend, that you will be prevented, by any interruption of the public tranquillity, from fixing your whole attention upon such points, as concern the internal welfare and prosperity of my people.

'Among these objects of a domestic nature, none can demand a more speedy or more serious attention, than what regards the high price of corn, which neither the salutary laws passed in the last session of parliament, nor the produce of the late harvest, have yet been able so far to re-
'duce,

'duce, as to give sufficient relief to the distresses
'of the poorer sort of my people. Your late re-
'sidence in your several counties must have ena-
'bled you to judge, whether any further provi-
'sions can be made conducive to the attainment of
'so desirable an end.'

Gentlemen of the House of Commons,

'I will order the proper officers to lay before you
'the estimates for the service of the ensuing year.

'The experience I have had of your constant
'readiness to grant me all such supplies, as should
'be found necessary for the security, interest, and
'honour of the nation (and I have no other to ask
'of you) renders it unnecessary for me to add any
'exhortations upon this head: And I doubt not
'but the same public considerations will induce you
'to persevere with equal alacrity, in your endea-
'vours to diminish the national debt; while, on my
'part, no care shall be wanting to contribute, as
'far as possible, to the attainment of that most es-
'sential object, by every frugal application of such
'supplies as you shall grant.'

My Lords and Gentlemen,

'The necessity of improving the present general
'tranquillity to the great purpose of maintaining
'the strength, the reputation, and the prosperity
'of this country, ought to be ever before your
'eyes. To render your deliberations for that pur-
'pose successful, endeavour to cultivate a spirit of
'harmony among yourselves. My concurrence in
'whatever will promote the happiness of my peo-
'ple you may always depend upon; and in that
'light, I shall ever be desirous of encouraging
'union among all those who wish well to their
'country.'

An

An addreſs was moved and ſeconded, in the uſual manner. After which Mr. *Conway* ſtood up, and ſupported the motion. He concluded with a panegyric on the late Mr. *Charles Townſhend*; having mentioned his talents, abilities, judgment, ſagacity, &c. he ſaid, ' that his dear lamented friend
' had engaged himſelf to prepare a plan to be ſub-
' mitted to parliament, for the effectual relief of
' the poor in the article of proviſions; and he had
' no queſtion that, if that great man had ſurvived,
' he would have been able to perform his promiſe;
' but, unfortunately for the public, his plan was
' loſt with him : that it was eaſy to find a ſucceſſor
' to his place, but impoſſible to find a ſucceſſor to
' his abilities, or one equal to the execution of
' his plans—The houſe ought not, therefore, to
' be ſurprized, that the King's ſurviving ſer-
' vants had not yet been able to deviſe any ſcheme
' for the relief of the poor, although a man of Mr.
' *Townſhend*'s ſuperior qualifications might have
' been fully equal to the taſk.'

Mr.*Conway*.

Mr. *Edmund Burke* then got up, and ſpoke nearly to the following purport. ' The condi-
' tion of this country, at the concluſion of the
' laſt ſpring, was ſuch as gave us ſtrong rea-
' ſon to expect, that not a ſingle moment of
' the interval between that period and our win-
' ter meeting would be loſt or miſemployed.
' We had a right to expect, that gentlemen, who
' thought themſelves equal to adviſe about the go-
' vernment of the nation, would, during this pe-
' riod, have applied all their attention, and exerted
' all their efforts, to diſcover ſome effectual remedy
' for the national diſtreſs. For my own part, I had
' no doubt that, when we again met, the admini-
' ſtration would have been ready to lay before us
' ſome plan for a ſpeedy relief of the people,
' founded upon ſuch certain lights and informa-
' tions

Mr. *Burke*.

'tions as they alone are able to procure, and di-
'gested with an accuracy proportioned to the time
'they have had to consider of it: but if these were
'our expectations, if these were the hopes con-
'ceived by the whole house, how grievously are we
'disappointed! after an interval of so many months,
'instead of being told that a plan is formed, or
'that measures are taken, or, at least, that mate-
'rials have been diligently collected, upon which
'some scheme might be founded for preserving us
'from famine; we see that this provident mini-
'stry, these careful providers, are of opinion, they
'have sufficiently acquitted themselves of their du-
'ty, by advising his Majesty to recommend the
'matter once more to our consideration, and so
'endeavouring to relieve themselves from the bur-
'then and censure, which must fall somewhere,
'by throwing it upon parliament. God knows
'in what manner they have been employed for
'these four months past. It appears too plainly
'they have done but little good—I hope they have
'not been busied in doing mischief; and though
'they have neglected every useful, every necessary
'occupation, I hope their leisure has not been spent
'in spreading corruption through the people.

'Sir, I readily assent to the laborious panegyric
'which the hon. gentleman upon the floor has been
'pleased to make on a very able member of the ad-
'ministration whom we have lately lost: no man
'had a higher opinion of his talents than I had;
'but as to his having conceived any plan for reme-
'dying the general distress about provisions, (as
'the gentleman would have us understand) I see
'many reasons for suspecting that it could never
'have been the case. If that gentleman had form-
'ed such a plan, or if he had collected such ma-
'terials as we are now told he had, I think it is
'impossible but that, in the course of so many
'months, some knowledge or intimation of it must
'have

'have been communicated to the gentlemen who
'acted with him, and who were united with him,
'not less by friendship than by office. He was
'not a reserved man; and surely, Sir, his col-
'leagues, who had every opportunity of hearing
'his sentiments in office, in private conversation,
'and in this house, must have been strangely inat-
'tentive to a man, whom they so much admired,
'or uncommonly dull, if they could not retain
'the smallest memory of his opinions on matters
'on which they ought naturally to have consulted
'him often. If he had even drawn the loosest
'outlines of a plan, is it conceivable that all traces
'of it should be so soon extinguished? To me, Sir,
'such an absolute oblivion seems wholly incredible.
'Yet admitting the fact for a moment, what an
'humiliating confession is it for an administration,
'who have undertaken to advise about the con-
'ducting of an empire, to declare to this house,
'that by the death of a single man, all projects for
'the public good are at an end, all plans are lost,
'and that this loss is irreparable, since there is not
'a leader surviving, who is in any measure capable
'of filling up the dreadful vacuum!

'But I shall quit this subject for the present;
'and, as we are to consider of an address in return
'to the speech from the throne, I beg leave to
'mention some observations occurring to me upon
'the speech itself, which I think I am warranted,
'by the established practice of this house, to treat
'merely as the speech of the minister.

'The chief and only pretended merit of the
'speech is, that it contains no extraordinary mat-
'ter, that it can do no harm, and consequently
'that an address of applause upon such speech is
'but a mere compliment to the throne, from
'which no inconvenience can arise, nor consequence
'be drawn. Now, Sir, supposing this to be a true
'representation of the speech, I cannot think it
'does

'does the adminiſtation any great honour, nor can
'I agree, that to applaud the throne for ſuch a
'ſpeech, would be attended with no inconvenience.
'Although an addreſs of applauſe may not enter
'into the approbation of particular meaſures, yet
'it muſt unavoidably convey a general acknow-
'ledgment, at leaſt, that things are, upon the
'whole, as they ſhould be, and that we are ſatisfied
'with the repreſentation of them, which we have
'received from the throne. But this, Sir, I am
'ſure, would be an acknowledgement inconſiſtent
'with truth, and inconſiſtent with our own interior
'conviction, unleſs we are contented to accept of
'whatever the miniſtry pleaſe to tell us, and wil-
'fully ſhut our eyes to any other ſpecies of evi-
'dence.

'As to the harmleſſneſs of the ſpeech, I muſt
'for my own part regret the times, when ſpeeches
'from the throne deſerved another name than that
'of innocent; when they contained ſome real and
'effectual information to this houſe,---ſome expreſs
'account of meaſures already taken, or ſome poſitive
'plan of future meaſures, for our conſideration.
'Permit me, Sir, to divide the preſent ſpeech in-
'to three heads, and a very little attention will
'demonſtrate how far it is from aiming at that
'ſpirit of buſineſs and energy, which formerly
'animated the ſpeeches from the throne: you will
'ſee, under the diviſion, that the ſmall portion of
'matter contained in it is of ſuch a nature, and ſo
'ſtated, as to preclude all poſſibility or neceſſity
'of deliberation in this place. The firſt article is,
"That every thing is quiet abroad." 'The truth of
'this aſſertion, when confirmed by an enquiry,
'which I hope this houſe will make into it, would
'give me the ſincereſt ſatisfaction; for certainly
'there never was a time when the diſtreſs and con-
'fuſion of the interior circumſtances of this nation
'made it more abſolutely neceſſary to be upon ſe-
'cure

'cure and peaceable terms with our neighbours:
'but I am a little inclined to suspect, and in-
'deed it is an opinion too generally received,
'that this appearance of good understanding with
'our neighbours deserves the name of stagnation,
'rather than of tranquillity; that it is owing not so
'much to the success of our negociations abroad,
'as to the absolute and entire suspension of them for
'a very considerable time. Consuls, envoys, and
'ambassadors, it is true, have been regularly ap-
'pointed, but, instead of repairing to their stations,
'have, in the most scandalous manner, loitered at
'home; as if they had either no business to do, or
'were afraid of exposing themselves to the resent-
'ment or derision of the court to which they were
'destined. Thus have all our negociations been
'conducted, and thus they have been dropped.
'Thus hath the *Manilla* ransom, that once favou-
'rite theme, that perpetual eccho with some gen-
'tlemen, been consigned to oblivion. The slight-
'est remembrance of it must not now be revived.
'At this rate, Sir, foreign powers may well per-
'mit us to be quiet; it would be equally useless
'and unreasonable in them to interrupt a tranquil-
'lity, which we submit to purchase upon such in-
'glorious terms, or to quarrel with an humble,
'passive government, which hath neither spirit to
'assert a right nor to resent an injury. In the di-
'stracted, broken, miserable state of our interior
'government, our enemies find a consolation and
'remedy for all that they suffered in the course of
'the war, and our councils amply revenge them
'for the successes of our arms.

'The second article of the speech contains "a
"recommendation of what concerns the dearness of
"corn, to our immediate and earnest deliberation."
'No man, Sir, is more ready than myself, as an
'individual, to shew all possible deference to the
'respectable authority under which the speech from

'the

'the throne is delivered; but, as a member of this
'house, it is my right, nay, I must think myself
'bound to consider it as the advice of the minister;
'and, upon this principle, if I would understand it
'rightly, or even do justice to the text, I must
'carry the minister's comment along with me.
'But what, Sir, has been the comment upon the
'recommendation made to us from the throne?
'Has it amounted to any more than a positive as-
'surance that all the endeavours of administration
'to form a plan for relieving the poor in the arti-
'ticle of provisions, have proved ineffectual? That
'they neither have a plan, nor materials of suffi-
'cient information to lay before the house, and
'that the object itself is, in their apprehen-
'sions, absolutely unattainable? If this be the fact,
'if it be really true that the minister, at the same
'time that he advises the throne to recommend a
'matter to the earnest deliberation of parliament,
'confesses in his comment that this very matter is
'beyond the reach of this house, what inference
'must we necessarily draw from such a text, and
'from such an illustration? I will not venture to
'determine what may be the real motive of this
'strange conduct and inconsistent language, but
'I will boldly pronounce, that it carries with it a
'most odious appearance. It has too much the
'air of a design to exculpate the crown, and the
'servants of the crown, at the expence of parlia-
'ment. The gracious recommendation in the
'speech will soon be known all over the nation.
'The comment and true illustration added to it by
'one of the ministry will probably not go beyond
'the limits of these walls. What then must be
'the consequence? The hopes of the people will
'be raised. They of course will turn their eyes
'upon us, as if our endeavours alone were want-
'ing to relieve them from misery and famine,
'and to restore them to happiness and plenty; and

'at

' at last, when all their golden expectations are dis-
' appointed ; when they find that notwithstanding
' the earnest recommendation from the crown,
' parliament has taken no effectual measures for
' their relief, the whole weight of their resentment
' will naturally fall upon us their representatives.
' We need not doubt but the effects of their fury
' will be answerable to the cause of it. It will be
' proportioned to the high recommending autho-
' rity, which we shall seem not to have regarded;
' and when a monarch's voice cries havock, will
' not confusion, riot, and rebellion make their ra-
' pid progress through the land? The unhappy
' people, groaning under the severest distress, de-
' luded by vain hopes from the throne, and disap-
' pointed of relief from the legislature, will, in
' their despair, either set all law and order at de-
' fiance; or, if the law be enforced upon them, it
' must be by the bloody assistance of a military
' hand. We have already had a melancholy ex-
' perience of the use of such assistance. But even
' legal punishments lose all appearance of justice,
' when too strictly inflicted on men compelled by
' the last extremity of distress to incur them. We
' have been told, indeed, that if the crown had ta-
' ken no notice of the distress of the people, such
' an omission would have driven them to despair;
' but I am sure, Sir, that, to take notice of it in
' this manner, to acknowledge the evil, and to
' declare it to be without remedy, is the most likely
' way to drive them to something beyond despair
' ---to madness; and against whom will their mad-
' ness be directed, but against us their innocent
' representatives?

' With respect to the third and last head, into
' which the speech may be divided; I readily agree
' that there is a cause of discord somewhere: where
' it is, I will not pretend to say. That it does exist
' is certain, and I much doubt whether it is likely

' to

'to be removed by any measures taken by the pre-
'sent administration. As to vague and general
'recommendations to us to maintain unanimity a-
'mongst us, I must say I think they are become
'of late years too flat and stale to bear being re-
'peated. That such are the kind sentiments and
'wishes of our monarch, I am far from doubting;
'but when I consider it as the language of the
'minister, as a minister's recommendation, I can-
'not help thinking it a vain and idle parade of words
'without meaning. Is it in their own conduct that
'we are to look for an example of this boasted
'union? Shall we discover any trace of it in their
'broken, distracted councils, their public disa-
'greements and private animosities? Is it not no-
'torious that they only subsist by creating divisions
'among others? That their plan is to separate par-
'ty from party? Friend from friend? Brother
'from brother? Is not their very motto *divide et
'impera?* When such men advise us to unite,
'what opinion must we have of their sincerity?
'In the present instance, however, the speech is
'particularly farcical. When we are told that af-
'fairs abroad are perfectly quiet, consequently
'that it is unnecessary for us to take any notice of
'them; when we are told that there is indeed a
'distress at home, but beyond the reach of this
'house to remedy; to have unanimity recom-
'mended us in the same breath, is, in my opinion,
'something lower than ridiculous. If the two first
'propositions be true, in the name of wonder, up-
'on what are we to debate? upon what is it pos-
'sible for us to disagree? On one point our advice
'is not wanted; on the other it is useless: but it
'seems it will be highly agreeable to the ministry
'to have us unite in approving of their conduct;
'and if we have concord enough amongst ourselves
'to keep in unison with them and their measures,
'I dare

' I dare say that all the purposes of administration
' aimed at by the address, will be fully answered,
' and entirely to their satisfaction. But this is a
' sort of union, which I hope never will, which I
' am satisfied never can prevail in a free parlia-
' ment like ours. While we are freemen we may
' disagree; but when we unite upon the terms re-
' commended to us by the administration, we must
' be slaves.'

The motion for an address was agreed to without a division; to return his Majesty the thanks of
this House for his most gracious speech from the
throne:

' To acknowledge his Majesty's goodness and
' attention to the convenience of his people, in call-
' ing his Parliament together at this time; and to
' assure his Majesty, that we will endeavour to im-
' prove the opportunity which the present happy
' state of peace and tranquillity affords, by exert-
' ing our utmost abilities in the prosecution of such
' measures as may most effectually promote the
' public welfare and prosperity:

' That we are equally sensible of his Majesty's
' paternal care, in the measures already taken by
' his Majesty to alleviate the distresses of the poor;
' and of his royal wisdom, in recommending the
' same interesting and important object to the con-
' sideration of his Parliament; and that we will not
' fail to take into our most attentive deliberation
' all such measures as shall appear conducive to the
' accomplishment of that great and most desirable
' end:

' To congratulate his Majesty on the late in-
' crease of his royal family, by the birth of a prince;
' and to assure his Majesty that we regard as an ad-
' dition to the happiness and welfare of this nation
' every increase of that illustrious house, under
' whose mild and auspicious government our reli-

'gious and civil liberties have been so happily
'maintained and protected:

'That it is therefore with equal grief and anxiety
'we reflect on the late untimely loss of his Maje-
'sty's royal brother, the Duke of York; whose
'early and ready zeal in his country's cause shewed
'him worthy of the heroic race he sprang from;
'and whose amiable virtues, in the more private
'scenes of life, must ever make his memory dear
'to all who had the happiness of approaching him.

'To assure his Majesty, that this House will,
'with a zeal and alacrity becoming the representa-
'tives of an affectionate and grateful people, rea-
'dily grant such supplies as shall be requisite for
'the support of his Majesty's government, for ad-
'vancing the honour and interest of this country,
'and effectually providing for the public safety:

'And that our regard to his Majesty's recom-
'mendation, as well as the indispensible duty we
'owe to those whom we represent, will make us
'earnestly attentive to the great object of dimi-
'nishing the national debt; being convinced that
'nothing can so effectually tend to add real lustre
'and dignity to his Majesty's government, or to
'give solid and permanent strength to these king-
'doms:

'That with these views, and in these sentiments,
'we will endeavour, with the utmost unanimity
'and dispatch, to promote the public service, and
'to deserve, by our sincere and unwearied labours
'for the general good, that confidence which it
'has pleased his Majesty to repose in us: not
'doubting of his Majesty's gracious disposition to
'confirm and perfect what our true zeal may sug-
'gest, for the lasting advantage and happiness of
'his people.'

The house being informed that the sheriffs of the city of London attended at the door, they were called in; and having presented to the House the

following

following petition from the lord mayor, aldermen and commons of the city of London in common council, withdrew. The said petition was then read; setting forth, 'that the present 'high prices of grain, and all other sorts of pro-'visions, particularly in the metropolis, forcibly 'call upon the petitioners, humbly to solicit the 'earnest attention of the House, to the distresses 'of the industrious poor, whose situation, whilst 'it excites compassion for the immediate sufferers, 'cannot but raise the apprehensions of the legisla-'ture, for the consequences thereof to the manu-'factures, trade, and population, and ultimately 'to the landed interest, of *Great Britain*; and that 'the petitioners most gratefully acknowledge the 'wisdom and goodness of Parliament, in the acts 'passed last session, for prohibiting the expor-'tation, and allowing the free importation, of corn 'and grain, and (in part) restraining the distillery; 'humbly trusting, that the House will be of opi-'nion, not to suffer those salutary regulations to ex-'pire, until the produce of the next year's harvest 'shall be clearly known, and the poor manufac-'turer, and labourer, secure of bread, at a mo-'derate price. That the dearness of flesh-meat, 'fish, and other necessaries, at this time, seem '(in the judgment of the petitioners) also to re-'quire some speedy and effectual relief; and there-'fore, they submit it to the wisdom of the House, 'whether the deficiency therein arising, partly from 'former calamities, not yet repaired, ought not, 'during the present exigency, to be supplied by a 'free importation. That the petitioners trust the 'House (after providing some immediate relief for 'the present urgent necessities) will turn their 'thoughts to more lasting and extensive regula-'tions, which (as far as human wisdom can) may 'prevent the like difficulties for the future. The 'petitioners think it a duty incumbent on them,

'humbly

'humbly to lay before the House such considera-
'tions as have occurred to them, on this import-
'ant subject. In the first place, the petitioners
'humbly conceive, That, although a moderate
'bounty on the exportation of corn and grain, in
'times of great plenty and cheapness, may be a
'wise and necessary encouragement to the cultiva-
'tion and encrease thereof, and the present bounty
'has, in fact, made them cheaper than they were
'before (some few unfavourable seasons only ex-
'cepted); and although the exportation of our
'surplus appears a necessary and highly beneficial
'trade to the nation in general; yet as the con-
'sumption of wheat is become much more general
'within this kingdom since the commencement of
'the bounty, the petitioners conceive it might
'now be good policy to reduce the highest bounty
'price thereof to a more moderate sum: And it
'appears probable to the petitioners, that if the
'bounty had some years ago been limited to what
'has been the average price since the year 1688;
'it might have preserved to this country all the
'wheat which has been exported at the interme-
'diate prices, and all the money that has been paid
'to re-place it with foreign corn, of a much in-
'ferior quality. Secondly, That the acts relating
'to the bounty are defective, in not expressly re-
'straining it to grain of the growth of this king-
'dom, the exporters from the out-ports (*Berwick
'upon Tweed* only excepted) not being called upon
'to make any proof thereof, whereby the inten-
'tions of parliament may, in some measure have
'been frustrated, and the public revenue defrau-
'ded. Thirdly, That the present method of ascer-
'taining the bounty price also appears defective in
'several particulars, which (in the port of Lon-
'don at least) might be remedied, by taking the
'average price, as weekly returned upon oath to
'the court of Lord Mayor and aldermen of the
                                            'said

' said city. Fourthly, That the market hours not
' being fixed by law, gives undue advantages to
' speculative and designing men, and tends to en-
' hance the price of the necessaries of life, to the
' consumer. Fifthly, That the present regulations
' in the assize of bread seem highly disadvantageous
' to the poor, who, as the petitioners humbly con-
' ceive, might be supplied cheaper, and better, if
' only one sort of bread was made assizeable.
' Sixthly, That the great increase in the breed of
' horses (owing partly to the growing practice of
' employing them, instead of oxen, in tillage, and
' partly to the great demands from abroad), has
' greatly contributed to diminish the number of
' cattle for slaughter, and necessarily tends to en-
' hance the price thereof, which the petitioners ap-
' prehend, might be corrected, by a duty upon
' the exportation of horses, and a small bounty up-
' on the use of oxen in tillage. Seventhly, That
' the scarcity of grown cattle, and consequently the
' dearness of flesh meat, are still farther increased
' by the unlimited destruction of ewe lambs, and
' cow calves, in all seasons of the year, merely to
' gratify the unreasonable appetite of the rich and
' luxurious. Eighthly, That the prevailing prac-
' tice of consolidating small farms not only tends
' to render many articles of provision and consump-
' tion scarce, but must, in time, depopulate the
' country of its most useful inhabitants, by de-
' priving the industrious poor both of labour and
' habitation. Lastly, That the misguided and
' often ill-grounded resentment of the common
' people, in times of public calamity (by prompt-
' ing them to destroy mills, corn, and other pro-
' visions, and to obstruct the removal of the latter
' from one place to another) is not only an injury
' to their fellow-subjects, but also to themselves,
' by aggravating the very evils they complain of;
' and therefore, for their sakes, as well as that of

'the public, ought to be timely and effectually
'prevented, or suppressed. And therefore pray-
'ing the House to take these important matters in-
'to their most serious consideration, and to pro-
'vide such remedies as their respective natures
'shall appear to require, or admit, and such as the
'House shall judge consistent with the real and
'permanent interests of the whole kingdom.'

This was followed by a petition of the mayor and burgesses of the *Devizes* in *Wiltshire*, complaining of the distresses of the poor from the dearness of corn and other provisions, and also of the high price of wool; praying the House to take the premises into consideration, and provide such remedies for the distresses of the poor, as should be thought prudent and fitting. These petitions were severally ordered to be referred to the consideration of the committee of the whole House, to whom it was referred to consider of the several acts passed in the last session of Parliament, relative to corn and provisions.

The consequence of these petitions, was a continuation of the acts passed last session, prohibiting the exportation of corn, &c. and allowing an importation from *America*.

Supplies *granted this* SESSION.

December 3.   *l.*   *s.*   *d.*
1. THAT 16000 men be employed for the sea service for 1768, including 4287 marines
2. That a sum not exceeding 4l. *per* man *per* month, be allowed for maintaining them, including ordnance for sea service - 832000   0   7
    December 8.
1. For the ordinary of the

navy

A. 1767.   DEBATES.   343

| | *l.* | *s.* | *d.* |

vy including half pay to sea and marine officers, for 1768 — 416403 0 11

2. That a number of land forces, including 2460 invalids, amounting to 17253 effective men, commission and non-commission officers included, be employed for 1768.

3. For defraying the charge of the said number of land forces for 1768 - - - 606221 12 10¾

4. For maintaining his Majesty's forces and garrisons in the plantations and *Africa*, including those in garrison at *Minorca* and *Gibraltar*, and for provisions for the forces in *North-America*, *Nova-Scotia*, *Newfoundland*, *Gibraltar*, the ceded islands and *Africa* for 1768 - 396950 4 6¾

5. For defraying the charge of the difference of pay between the *British* and *Irish* establishment of six regiments of foot, serving in the *Isle of Man*, at *Gibralter*, *Minorca*, and the ceded islands for 1768 - 7226 17 2½

6. For the pay of the general and staff officers in *Great-Britain* for 1768. - - 12237 7 3

7. For defraying the charge of full pay for 366 days for 1768, to officers reduced, with the tenth company of several battalions reduced from ten to nine companies, and who remained on half pay at the 24th of *December* 1765. - - 5227 14 0

8. For

	l.	s.	d.

8. For the charge of the office of ordnance for land service for 1768 — — — — 159328 11 6

9. For defraying the expence of services performed by the office of ordnance for land service, and not provided for by parliament in 1767. — — 68944 12 11

1672540 1 6¼

December 15.

1. That one third part of the capital stock of annuities after the rate of 4l. *per cent.* established by an act made in the third year of his Majesty's reign, which shall remain after the 5th day of *January* next, be redeemed and paid off on the 5th of *July* next after discharging the interest then payable in respect of the same

2. To enable his Majesty to redeem and pay off the said one third part — — — 875000 0 0

December 21.

1. Towards the buildings, re-buildings, and repairs of ships of war in his Majesty's yards, and other extra-works, over and above what are proposed to be done upon the heads of wear and tear and ordinary, for 1768 277954 0 0

1. To enable the trustees of the *British* Museum to carry on the execution of the trust reposed in them by parliament — 2000 0 0

January

	l.	s.	d.
	279954	0	0

January 26, 1768.

1. For paying the pensions to the widows of such reduced officers of his Majesty's land forces and marines, as died upon the establishment of half pay in *Great Britain*, and who were married to them before the 25th of *December* 1716, for 1768 — 1536 0 0

2. Upon account of the reduced officers and marines, for 1768. — — — — 132431 0 0

3. For defraying the charge for allowances to the several officers and private gentlemen of the two troops of Horse guards and regiment of horse reduced; and to the superannuated gentlemen of the four troops of horse guards for 1768 — 1715 13 0

4. Towards defraying the charge of out pensioners of *Chelsea* hospital, for 1768 — 109849 17 6

5. Towards defraying the extraordinary expences of his Majesty's land forces and other services, incurred to the 25th of *December* 1767, and not provided for by parliament — — 199988 4 2

444620 14 8

January 28.

1. Upon account for maintaining and supporting the civil establishment of *Nova Scotia*, for 1768 — — — 3895 1 11

	l.	s.	d.
2. Upon account for defraying the charges of the civil establishment of *Georgia*, and the incidental expences attending the same from the 24th of *June* 1767, to the 24th of *June* 1768	3986	0	0
3. Upon account for defraying the charge of the civil establishment of *East Florida*, and the incidental expences attending the same from the 24th of *June* 1767, to the 24th of *June* 1768.	4758	0	0
4. Upon account for defraying the expences of the civil establishment of *West Florida*, and other incidental expences attending the same from the 24th of *June* 1767, to the 24th of *June* 1768	4400	0	0
5. Upon account for defraying the expences of general surveys of his Majesty's dominions in *North America*, for 1768	2036	14	0
6. Upon account for defraying the charges of the civil establishment of *Senegambia*, for 1768.	5550	0	0
	24657	15	11

February 1.

For paying off and discharging the Exchequer bills made out by virtue of an act passed in the last session of parliament for raising a certain sum of money by loans or Exchequer bills, and

charged

	l.	*s.*	*d.*

charged upon the first aids to be granted this session - 1800000 0 0

February 4.

1. To replace to the Sinking Fund the like sum issued thereout, to make good the deficiency on *October* 10, 1767, of the fund established for paying annuities in respect of 3,500,000l. borrowed by virtue of an act of the third of his present Majesty, towards the supply granted for the service of 1763 - - 59322 16 10

2. To replace to ditto, the like sum paid out of the same, to make good the deficiency, on *July* 5, 1767, of the fund established for paying annuities in respect of five millions, borrowed by virtue of an act made in the 31st of his late Majesty, towards the supply granted for the service of 1758 - - 53480 17 8¾

3. To be employed in maintaining and supporting the *British* forts and settlements on the coast of *Africa*, under the direction of the committee of merchants trading to *Africa* - 13000 0 0

4. That provision be made for the pay and cloathing of the militia, and for their subsistence during the time they shall be absent from home on account of the annual exercise, for 1768.

5. Upon account to enable the Foundling Hospital to maintain and educate such children as

were

	l.	*s.*	*d.*

were received into the same on or before the 25th of *March* 1760, from the 31st of *December* 1767 exclusive, to the 31st of *December* 1768 inclusive, and the said sum to be issued without any deduction - - - 29000 0 0

6. Upon account, for enabling the said hospital to put out apprentice the said children, so as that the said hospital do not give with one child more than 7l. - 2000 0 0

                                156803 14 6¼

February 8.

1. To make good to his Majesty, the like sum issued by his Majesty's orders, in pursuance of the addresses of this House - 10500 0 0

2. To make good the deficiency of the grants for the service of 1767 - - - 392484 4 5¾

3. To replace to the Sinking Fund the like sum paid out of the same to discharge for one year and a quarter, ended the 25th of *December* 1767, the annuities after the rate of 4l. *per cent.* attending the remainder of the joint stock, established by an act of the third of his present Majesty, in respect of certain navy, victualling, and transport bills, and debentures, that have been redeemed, in pursuance of an act made in the last session, and the charges of management

during

A. 1767. DEBATES. 349

	l.	s.	d.
during the said term of the annuities - - -	88435	19	6½
4. To replace to ditto, the like sum issued thereout, to discharge from the 10th of *October* 1767, to the 5th of *January* following, the annuities attending such part of the joint stock established by an act made in the third of his present Majesty, for granting several additional duties on wines imported, and certain duties on cyder and perry, and for raising the sum of 3,500,000l. by way of annuities and lotteries, to be charged on the said duties as hath been redeemed in pursuance of an act made in the last session -	8750	0	0
5. To redeem and pay off the remaining parts of the said capital stock of annuities -	1750000	0	0
	2250170	3	11⅞
Sum total of the supplies granted in this session - -	8335746	11	2⅞

Ways and Means, *December* 7.

That the duties upon malt, mum, cyder, and perry, be continued from the 24th of *June* 1768, to the 24th of *June* 1769, and charged upon all the malt which shall be made, and all mum which shall be made or imported, and all cyder and perry, which shall be made for sale, within the kingdom of *Great Britain* 700,000l.

December 10.

That the sum of 3s. in the pound, and no more, be raised within the space of one year, from the
25th

25th of *March* 1768, upon lands, tenements, hereditaments, pensions, and personal estates, in that part of *Great Britain* called *England, Wales,* and the town of *Berwick upon Tweed*; and that a proportionable cess, according to the ninth article of the treaty of union, be laid upon that part of *Great Britain* called *Scotland* 1,528,568 l. 11 s. 11 d¾.

February, 9.

1. That the sum of 1,900,000 l. be raised in manner following; that is to say, the sum of 1,300,000 l. by annuities, after the rate of 3 l. *per centum,* to commence from the 5th day of *January* last, and the sum of 600,000 l. by a lottery, to consist of 60,000 tickets, the whole of such sum to be divided into prizes, which are to be attended with the like 3 l. *per cent.* annuities, to commence from the 5th of *January* 1769; and that all the said annuities be transferable at the Bank of *England,* paid half yearly, on the 5th of *July,* and the 5th of *January* in every year, out of the Sinking Fund, and added to, and made part of, the joint stock of 3 l. *per cent.* annuities, which were consolidated at the Bank of *England,* by certain acts made in the 25th and 28th years of the reign of his late Majesty, and several subsequent acts, and subject to redemption by parliament; that every contributor towards the said sum of 1,300,000 l. shall, in respect of every 65 l. agreed by him to be contributed for raising such sum, be intitled to receive three tickets in the said lottery, upon payment of 10 l. for each ticket; and that every contributor shall, on or before the 18th day of this instant *February,* make a deposit with the cashiers of the Bank of *England* of 15 l. *per cent.* in part of the monies so to be contributed towards the said sum of 1,300,000 l. and also a deposit of 5 l. *per cent.* in part of the monies so to be contributed in respect of the said lottery, as a security for making the respective future payments to the said cashiers,

on or before the times herein after limited; that is to say, on the 1,300,000l. 10l. *per cent.* on or before the 9th of *April* next; 10l. *per cent.* on or before the 7th of *June* next; 15l. *per cent.* on or before the 19th of *July* next; 15l. *per cent.* on or before the 20th of *August* next; 15l. *per cent.* on or before the 21st of *October* next; 20l. *per cent.* on or before the 25th of *November* next. On the lottery for 600,000l. 25l. *per cent.* on or before the 17th of *May* next; 30l. *per cent.* on or before the 28th day of *June* next; 40l. *per cent.* on or before the 8th of *September* next. And that all the monies so received by the said cashiers, be paid into the receipt of his Majesty's Exchequer, to be applied, from time to time, to such services as shall then have been voted by this house, in this session of parliament; and that every contributor who shall pay in the whole of his contribution towards the said sum of 1,300,000l. at any time, on or before the 17th of *October* next, or towards the said lottery, on or before the 25th of *June* next, shall be allowed an interest by way of discount, after the rate of 3l. *per centum, per annum,* on the sums so compleating his contribution respectively, to be computed from the day of compleating the same, to the 25th of *November* next, in respect of the sum paid on account of the 1,300,000l. and to the 8th of *September* next, in respect of the sum paid on account of the said lottery.

2. That, from and after the 5th of *April* next, the annuities, after the rate of 4l. *per centum,* attending the remainder of the capital stock, established by an act made in the third year of his Majesty's reign, entitled 'An act for granting to 'his Majesty several additional duties upon wines 'imported into this kingdom, and certain duties 'upon all cyder and perry: and for raising the sum 'of 3,500,000l. by way of annuities and lotteries, 'to be charged on the said duties,' be charged upon and made payable out of, the surplusses, excesses,

or

or overplus monies, and other revenues, composing the fund commonly called the Sinking Fund, until the redemption of the said capital stock, which is to be compleated on the 5th of *January* 1769.

3. That the duties, revenues, and incomes, which now stand appropriated to the payment of the said annuities, be continued, and be, from and after the said 5th of *April*, carried to, and made part of, the said fund, commonly called the Sinking Fund, towards making good the payment of the said annuities, and of the annuities after the rate of 3l. *per cent.* intended to be granted in respect of the said 1,900,000l.

4. That, towards raising the supply granted to his Majesty, the sum of 1,800,000l. be raised, by loans, or Exchequer bills, to be charged upon the first aids to be granted in the next session of parliament; and such Exchequer bills, if not discharged, with interest thereupon, on or before the 5th of *April* 1769, to be exchanged, and received in payment in such manner as Exchequer bills have usually been exchanged, and received in payment.

5. That towards raising the supply granted to his Majesty, there be applied the sum of 2,250,000l. out of such monies as shall or may arise of the surplusses, excesses, or overplus monies, and other revenues, composing the fund commonly called the Sinking Fund.

6. That a sum, not exceeding 70,000l. out of such monies as shall be paid into the receipt of the Exchequer, after the 2d of *February* 1768, and on or before the 5th of *April* 1769, of the produce of all or any of the duties and revenues, which, by any act or acts of parliament, have been directed to be reserved for the disposition of parliament, towards defraying the necessary expences of defending, protecting, and securing, the *British* colonies and plantations in *America*, be applied towards

wards making good such part of the supply as hath been granted to his majesty, for maintaining his majesty's forces and garrisons in the plantations, and for provisions for the forces in *North America*, *Nova Scotia*, *Newfoundland*, and the *Ceded Islands*, for the year 1768.

7. That such of the monies, as shall be paid into the receipt of the exchequer, after the 2d of *February* 1768, and on or before the 5th of *April* 1769, of the produce of the duties charged, by an act of parliament made in the 5th of his present majesty's reign, upon the importation of gum senega and gum arabic, be applied towards making good the supply granted to his majesty.

8. That the sum of 400,000l. which is to be paid within the present year, into the receipt of his majesty's Exchequer, by the united company of merchants of *England*, trading to the East-Indies, in pursuance of an act made in the last session of parliament intitled, ' An act for establishing an agreement for the payment of the annual ' sum of 400,000l. for a limited time, by the East-' India company, in respect of the territorial ac-' quisitions and revenues, lately obtained in the East ' Indies, be applied towards making good the sup-' ply granted to his majesty."

9. That the charge of the pay and cloathing of the militia, in that part of *Great Britain*, called *England*, for one year, beginning the 25th of *March* 1768, be defrayed out of the monies arising by the land-tax, granted for the service of the year 1768.

Feb. 22. That a sum not exceeding 106,358l. 17s. 8d. out of the sums received for provisions delivered to the troops serving in *North America*, and of certain sums charged on the pay of the forces serving at Minorca, the Floridas, and in Africa, and out of the balance of the 12d. in the pound deduction from the pay of the out pensioners of Chelsea hospital, from the 25th of *June* 1757, to the 4th of *December* 1767, and also out of the monies remaining in the hands of the Earl of *Kinnoul*, and the executors of the late Earl of *Darlington*, and of the late *Thomas Potter*, Esq; being part of the balances of the said Earls of *Darlington* and *Kinnoul*, and *Thomas Potter*, as paymasters general of his majesty's forces, be applied towards making good the supply granted to his majesty, towards defraying the extraordinary expences of his majesty's land forces, and other services, incurred to the 25th of *December* 1767, and not provided for by parliament.

Feb. 23. 1. That grey or scrow-salt, salt-scale, sand-scale, crustings, or other foul salt, be allowed to be taken from the salt works in England, Wales, or Berwick upon Tweed, to be used as manure upon payment of a duty of four pence *per* bushel only.

2. That all policies, by which the property of one person, or of a particular number of persons in one general partnership, or of one body politic or corporate, in any ship or cargo, or both, shall be assured, to the amount of more than 1000*l.* be stamped with two 5*s.* stamps.

3. That so much of an Act, made in the thirty-third year of the reign of his late Majesty, King *George* the second, intitled, 'An act for en-
' couraging the exportation of rum, and spirits of
' the growth, produce, and manufacture of the
' *British* sugar plantations from this Kingdom, and
' of *British* spirits, made from melasses, as directs
' that the rum, or spirits, of the growth, produce,
' and manufactures of the *British* sugar plantati-
' ons in *America*, which should be intitled to the
' allowance of the duty of custom, and freed from
' the duty of excise, on exportation thereof, should
' be proof spirits,' be repealed.

4. That

4. That upon the exportation of such rum, or spirits, there be an allowance, or drawback, of all the duties of customs payable upon the importation thereof; and that such rum, or spirits, be freed and discharged from all the duties of excise, though the same shall not be proof spirits.

These were the only resolutions of the committee of ways and means agreed to by the House, and with respect to the sums thereby provided for, that can at present be ascertained, they stand as follows:

	l.	*s.*	*d.*
By the resolution of December 7	700000	0	0
By that of December 10	1428568	0	0
By the first of February 9	1900000	0	0
By the fourth article of ditto	1800000	0	0
By the fifth of ditto	2250000	0	0
By the sixth of ditto	70000	0	0
By the eighth of ditto	400000	0	0
By the resolution of Feb. 22	106358	17	0
Sum total of such provisions as can be ascertained	8754626	17	8
Excess of the provisions.	419180	6	6

This being the last session, the attention of the members and of the nation was directed chiefly towards the approaching general election, and therefore very little material business was transacted this session.

One of the most remarkable occurrences of this session was an affair that related to a sum of money, which the magistrates of *Oxford* demanded of Sir *Thomas Stapleton* and the Hon. Mr. *Robert Lee,* who represented it, for their re-election in the ensuing new Parliament.

This corporation, it seems, was indebted in a considerable sum of money expended for its own public purposes, the interest of which made a very disagreeable diminution in its revenues, which were no way in a condition to pay the principal off.---Thus situated, several of the magistrates wrote a joint letter to their members, acquainting them with the state of their affairs, and offering to re-choose them at the approaching general election, provided they advanced such a sum as would be sufficient to extricate the city from its difficulties.

It is generally affirmed, and as generally believed, that the gentlemen who signed this letter to Sir *Thomas Stapleton* and Mr. *Lee* were wholly unactuated by any motives of self interest, and that they only meant to benefit the corporation in general by their request.---The gentlemen however did not chuse to comply with it: but complained to the House on the 26th of *January* 1768 of the letter. In consequence of which the magistrates who signed it were commanded to appear before the House on *February* the fifth, when they were all committed to Newgate, and the thanks of the House were given to Sir *Thomas Stapleton* and Mr. *Lee* for their conduct in this transaction.

On the 9th of *February* the magistrates petitioned the house, expressing a sincere contrition for their behaviour, and begging to be released from their confinement. In consequence of this petition they were ordered to be brought the next day to the bar of the House, to be reprimanded upon their knees.

The speech of the Speaker of the House of Commons, * when he reprimanded *Philip Ward,* late mayor

---

* The following observations on this speech were made by a well known gentleman, and are not undeserving a place in this Work.

' I beg you would re-print the noblest piece of modern elo-
' quence this country has produced. I mean the warm and pa-
' thetic harangue of the present Speaker, Sir *John Cust*, the *Ci-*
' *cero* of parliament, when he pointed all his thunders, red with
' uncommon

mayor of the city of *Oxford*; *John Treacher*, Sir *Thomas Munday*, *Thomas Wife*, *John Nicholes*, *John Philips*, *Isaac Lawrence*, *Richard Tawney*, all of the said City; *Thomas Robinson* and *John Brown*, late bailiffs of the said City; upon their knees, at the bar of the said House, upon *Wednesday* the tenth day of *February* 1768.

'Philip uncommon wrath, against the devoted heads of the poor, prostrate *Philip Ward*, late mayor of the city of *Oxford*, *John Treacher*, Sir *Thomas Munday*, *Thomas Wife*, *John Nichols*, *John Philips*, *Isaac Lawrence*, *Richard Tawney*, *Thomas Robinson*, and *John Brown*, who were lately brought, for the high crime of bribery and corruption, to the bar, not only of the most uncorrupted but the most uncorruptible assembly in the whole world. You will immediately know, Sir, that I can only speak of the *Lower House* of our Parliament, and that I allude to those three additional white, classic pages to the *Votes*, which are called there *The Speech of the Speaker of the House of Commons*.

' The *Journals* scarcely ever gratify the public with any speeches, except two at the beginning of each parliament, when the new Speaker is proposed. They are always professed panegyricks, and I will venture to promise every future Speaker, that all the virtues of *Onslow* himself he shall have in the *Journals*, although he has not from nature the strong abilities, nor from himself the wondrous accomplishments, of the excellent Sir *John Cust*. It was therefore peculiarly obliging in this gentleman, to enrich our *Journals*, and our language, by yielding to the earnest entreaties of his worthy brother members, whose happy efforts to overcome such almost invincible modesty we can never enough applaud. We see their joint detestation of bribery and corruption, and the stigma of infamy is now affixed to such enormous guilt. If so baneful a weed is not quite rooted out, it is at least blasted by the *afflatus divinus* of our *Cicero*, and, like the accursed fig-tree, will droop and wither. No man for the future shall ever dare to sign a bargain for 1500*l*. to bring his son into parliament. Should even a *future* Speaker venture on this, I hope to see him on his knees, and that an orator equal to Sir *John Cust*, if nature is not exhausted by this last perfect production, will pronounce him expelled, and add those awful words, I DO REPRIMAND YOU.

' This beautiful oration of Sir *John Cust*, I think, Sir, is not only striking in a general comprehensive view of it, but will likewise bear the nicest scrutiny. It is complete taken in the whole, and nicely finished in every minute part. It may be analysed to as much advantage as any thing in Tully. Although I feel that I am unequal to the task, I shall venture to attempt it, because it will be the occasion of my dwelling longer on a performance, which gives more pleasure, the more it is examined.

' I shall

'*Philip Ward, John Treacher*, Sir *Thomas Munday, Thomas Wise, John Nicholes, John Philips, Isaac Lawrence, Richard Tawney, Thomas Robinson, John Brown*; The offence of which you have been guilty has justly brought you under the severe displeasure of this House. A more enormous crime you could

'I shall first consider the oration itself, as branched out under the four general heads of

'Exordium
'Constitutio Causæ
'Infectatio
'Peroratio,

'and then I shall examine the four other accessory circumstances of the

'Personæ
'Tempus
'Locus
'Eventus.

'I begin with the *Exordium*. It is plain and simple, according to all the rules laid down by the antients. It contains only these words,

'*Philip Ward, John Treacher*, Sir *Thomas Munday, Thomas Wise, John Nicholes, John Philips, Isaac Lawrence, Richard Tawney, Thomas Robinson, John Brown*.

'No *Exordium* was ever built on so firm a foundation. It stands on the legal base of the baptismal register itself. I do not believe any thing happier could have been conceived, unless the great orator had taken Tully's own *exordium*, pro Archia poeta, *si quid est in me ingenii, quod sentio quam sit exiguum*, &c. but why are we to be charmed with any such false modesty in him, more than we are in his great model, Cicero?

'I must confess, with all my partialities about me, that the *Constitutio Causæ* is not so clear and full as I could wish. In the oration, it is only said, *the offence of which you have been guilty, has justly brought you under the severe displeasure of this house*. The title is only *The Speech of the Speaker of the House of Commons, when he reprimanded Philip Ward*, &c. *upon their knees*, &c. without saying for what crime. We are left to guess what it could be, and I own when I read at the beginning, that *a* MORE *enormous crime they could not well commit*, I did not directly think of bribery and corruption. Although I was a little doubtful *what enormous crime a man might* WELL *commit*; yet when I heard, that *a* MORE *enormous crime they could not well commit*, I own I was afraid that they had been guilty of murder, perjury, rape, incest, sodomy, or some other crimes, whose guilt I should imagine to be of a shade of black darker and deeper than this of bribery and corruption. I was a little relieved, when I found that this was not the case, and that there was even somewhat of honesty in their proceeding; that they were endeavouring to pay off old debts, by trying to get before-hand a part of the money, which such country-puts falsely imagine

'their

'could not well commit: since a deeper wound
'could not be given to the constitution itself, than
'by the open and dangerous attempt which you
'have made to subvert the freedom and indepen-
'dence of this House.

'their representatives afterwards make of them. I had heard too,
'that the price asked was considerably under the market price of
'boroughs; For, Sir, it can no longer be dissembled, that a
'share of the *British* legislature has in our times been bought
'and sold as publicly as a share in the New River Company, or
'York Buildings water-works, or either of the Theatres. I
'admired, however, in all this, the noble enthusiastick zeal of Sir
'*John Cust*, and the *verba ardentia*, the bold glowing expres-
'sions, in which that zeal was shewn, *a more enormous crime you
'could not well commit*. Yet I believed, that not many gentle-
'men in *England* will be quite so severe upon them. Few of my
'countrymen would keep company with a murderer, a man per-
'jured, &c. but I am apt to think, that before two months are
'past, we shall hear of some very respectable personages shaking
'by the hand, hobbing and nobbing, touching glasses, nay, per-
'haps, condescending even to cuckold these very *Philip Ward,
'John Treacher*, Sir *Thomas Munday, Thomas Wise, John Nicholes,
'John Philips, Isaac Lawrence, Richard Tawney, Thomas Robinson,
'and John Brown*. If I am rather uncharitable in the last ar-
'ticle, Sir, I beg pardon; but it may be, because as to the na-
'ture of crimes, I do not hold this modern gallantry to be quite
'so enormous a sin as some others, and as it is in the eye of
'*James Boswell*, Esq; of *Auchinleck*, in *Ayrshire*. That pri-
'mitive christian, that admirer of every thing opposite and con-
'tradictory, of *Pascal Paoli*, the true hero of liberty in his own
'country, and of pensioner *Samuel Johnson*, the old arch-enemy
'of it in our's, whom he wishes to bring together, for the fun,
'I suppose, of seeing them quarrel, like the two equally conge-
'nial spirits of *Hume* and *Jane Jacques*; that gentleman, as well
'as Sir *John Cust*, ventures on a new system of crimes. In the
'*account of Corsica*, page 217, he says, *better occasional murders
'than frequent adulteries*. Surely, Sir, never any but an Italian
'with the stilletto in his pocket, and a highlander with the dirk
'by his side, ever talked so lightly of murder. I therefore won-
'der at such an assertion from a gentleman, a man of humanity,
'and an *Englishman*, for so I call him, as he chose to be our
'countryman abroad, though not at home. "Upon my arrival,
"the captain of the guard came out, and demanded, who I was?
"I replied, *Inglese, English*." page 277. "When I told them that
"I was an *Englishman*," page 289. I hope Mr. *Boswell* did not
'advance such sentiments abroad as the sentiments of *English-
'men*.

'This new-fangled system however of crimes, and conse-
'quently of their punishment, broached by Sir *John Cust*, and
'*James Boswell*, Esq; is too deep a disquisition for the Political
'Register. It is not quite so humane as that of the great friend

'The freedom of this house is the freedom of
'this country, which can continue no longer than
'while the voices of the electors are uninfluenced
'by any base or venal motive. For if abilities
'and

'of man, the *Marquis Beccaria*; but whether *adultery* be worse
'than *murder*, or *bribery* worse than *murder* or *perjury*, I do
'not think proper questions for such a publication as
'your's, Sir. As to my own difficulties, I have stated them with
'modesty;

to swear
In such a case I shou'd be loth————
But PERRY CUST may take his oath.
The GHOST. Book 4.

'Two little circumstances of the cause should be mentioned
'under this head. It appears by the *Votes*, that a private letter
'had been sent to Sir *Thomas Stapleton*, and another to Mr.
'*Lee*. Now our ingenious orator finds this not only a *dangerous*,
'but an OPEN *attempt to subvert the freedom and independency of
'this House*, and in the second place declares they have *set the
'infamous example of prostitution in the most* PUBLIC *as well as
'daring manner*——by writing a *private* letter to two former
'friends.

'If a regard to truth, Sir, has obliged me to find the *Constitu-
'tio Causæ* rather deficient, I am glad the *Infectatio* can with jus-
'tice be said to be complete. It is touched with wonderful force
'and spirit, though I am afraid it will be another proof, that the
'townsmen of *Oxford* have always hated the University, if they
'chose in every thing to act the quite opposite part. I beg to quote
'the whole sentence, "Many circumstances concur to aggravate
'your offence. The place of your residence was a singular
'advantage. You had *at all times* the example of one of the
'most learned and respectable bodies in Europe before your
'eyes. Their conduct *in every instance*, but especially in the
'choice of their representatives in parliament, was *well worthy
'your imitation*." Now this is the true part of an orator, to
'advance bold, daring assertions, to support them with effrontery,
'and to leave cold, heavy, phlegmatic people afterwards to exa-
'mine into the dry matter of fact. *At all times—in every in-
'stance—and well worthy your imitation?* Let us then go to a few
'historical facts *in our own times*, since the accession of the house
'of *Brunswick*. I wish to know, if the overt acts of treason
'daily committed at *Oxford*, in 1715, did not force the go-
'vernment to send General *Pepperel* there, in the same military
'disposition, and with the same orders, he would have had in
'marching into *Dunkirk*. Was the conduct of *Oxford* at that
'time WELL *worthy our imitation?* I hope not, even in the opinion
'of Sir *John Cust*; because, I suppose, than treason, *a more
'enormous crime a man cannot* WELL *commit.* If the conduct of
'*Oxford* was then *well worthy of imitation*; the conduct of
'*George* I. was to the highest degree cruel and oppressive; but
'the sober page of history gives the lie to such oratorical declama-
'tions, even of Sir *John Cust* himself; and we now thank the
'memory

'and integrity are no recommendation to the elec-
' tors; if those who bid highest for their voices
' are to obtain them from such detestable consider-
' ations; this house, will not be the representatives
' of the people of *Great Britain*. Instead of being
'the

' memory of that great prince for so seasonable an interposition,
' so spirited an attack on Jacobitism in her strongest hold, her
' very citadel. When their chancellor, the Duke of *Ormond*,
' was attainted of high treason, was it *worthy of imitation*, that
' the University chose for his successor, a man equally disaf-
' fected, his own brother, the Earl of *Arran?* In the late reign,
' the conduct of the University, particularly of the vice-chan-
' cellor, in the affair of the students, who had publickly drank
' the Pretender's health *on their knees*, was so infamous, that the
' government could not wink at it. Even so mild a prince as
' *George* II. was at last forced to a severity painful to his nature,
' but which the public good rendered necessary, against the most
' inveterate enemies of his person and family. Was the conduct
' of *Oxford* then *worthy of imitation?* Methinks, Sir, I still hear
' the seditious shouts of applause given to the pestilent harangues
' of the late Dr. *King*, when he vilified our great deliverer, the
' Duke of *Cumberland*, and repeated with such energy the trea-
' sonable REDEAT. Was the conduct of the University, at the
' opening of the Ratcliffe library, by their behaviour to the
' known enemies of the Brunswick line, and their approbation of
' every thing, hateful to Liberty and her friends, *worthy of imi-
' tation?* When I was told of *all times*, and *every instance*, in
' which *Oxford* has been exemplary in her conduct, I have been
' led to consider those two instruments of slavery, the *Oxford*
' *decree* in the reign of *Charles* II. and the *Recognition* at the ac-
' cession of *James* II. either of which is a repeal of *Magna Char-
' ta*; but I would not go so far back, and I have said enough,
' Sir, to convince you, that I more admire the art of the orator,
' and the heavenly fire of his eloquence, than the mere mechanic
' part, the faithfulness of a memory, which in him is not quite
' exact.

' The *Peroratio* is alas! too short, but full of dignity, suited to
' the Majesty of the Commons of *Great Britain*. I DO REPRI-
' MAND YOU. The little word *do* is very emphatical here. This
' is not a case where, as *Pope* says, *feeble expletives their aid* DO
' *join*. How weak would the sense, and how poor the expression
' be, without it!

' The last words, *you are discharged, paying your fees*, I fear
' will to many suggest an idea beneath the dignity of parliament,
' and may make the world imagine, that the *fees* were an ille-
' gal claim, not recoverable by action, and that therefore Mr.
' *Speaker* took the short way of keeping in custody till his own
' and the clerks *fees* were paid. But for my part, I believe that as
' an orator he talked of the *fees* to add to the terror of the sen-
' tence, and the weight of the punishment.

' May

' the guardians and protectors of their liberties,
' instead of redressing the grievances of the sub-
' ject, this house itself will be the author of the
' worst of grievances: they will become the venal
' instruments of power to reduce this happy na-
' tion, the envy and admiration of the world, to
' the lowest state of misery and servitude. This
' is the abject condition to which you have at-
' tempted to bring your fellow-subjects.

' Many

' May I now venture to hint at a little omission in the Speech?
' There is not a word about *undue, unconstitutional influence* in
' elections, although it would so naturally have come in under
' the head of preserving the *freedom and independence of this house.*
' This too seemed the more necessary on so public an occasion,
' because an appeal had been made so lately to the world in the
' case of Mr. *Legge*'s Hampshire election, against the Favourite
' himself, when all the Whigs, as usual, appeared against a Stuart,
' and were victorious. But perhaps we are as much to admire
' the wisdom and prudence of Sir *John Cust* in what he has not
' said, as in what he has. In this case we should copy the fa-
' mous Monsieur *Omer Joly de Fleury*, The Sir *Fletcher Norton* of
' the French King, who speaking of the late *pragmatic sanction*
' for the expulsion of the Jesuits, says, " that he admires the
' reasons given by the King of Spain, and still more the rea-
' sons he has not given any man, but which are hid in his
' royal breast." Yet, after all, I wish we had got one sentence
' only on this subject from Sir *John Cust, because every thing must
' have the greatest weight, which falls from such a height.* Permit
' me, Sir, to use the fine imagery of the gentle, smooth, silver-
' tongu'd *Conway*, of all our generals confessedly *lingua melior*—

' Let us now, Sir, proceed to the other accessory circum-
' stances as they are called. The *Personæ* are plainly Mr.
' *Speaker* himself, in the chair speaking, the awful terrors of O-
' *lympian Jove* sitting on his majestic brow, three hundred mem-
' bers laughing and listening, the poor culprits, mace and train
' bearers, &c. affecting to be grave and solemn, with looks of
' meek submission, downcast and low, fix'd on the floor, lest they
' should be burnt up by the flashes of fire from the indignant eyes
' of the *Speaker*, but they are all *mutæ personæ*, except Sir *John
' Cust* himself, and therefore are beneath our further attention.

' For the *Tempus*, there is something singular to be remarked.
' The letters which contained the corrupt offer, are dated in
' the year 1766. One is of *May* 12, 1766. The first notice ta-
' ken of them in the House, is *January* 26, 1768, and the *Repri-
' mand* is *February* 10, 1768; yet we see in the votes, Veneris 5°
' die Februarii, 1768, " Resolved, that this House doth highly
' approve of the very *honourable* conduct of the *honourable Robert
' Lee*, and Sir *Thomas Stapleton*, Bart. *on their receipt of the said
' letters.*" This is rather hard of digestion. Why did not those
' gentlemen,

'Many circumstances concur to aggravate your
'offence. The place of your residence was a
'singular advantage. You had at all times the
'example of one of the most learned and respec-
'table bodies in Europe before your eyes. Their
'conduct in every instance, but especially in the
'choice of their representatives in parliament, was
'well worthy your imitation.

'You are magistrates of a great city. In such
'a station, it was a duty peculiarly incumbent
'upon you to watch over the morals of your fel-
'low-citizens; to keep yourselves pure from ve-
'nality;

'gentlemen, the first day of the sitting of the House, *after the
'receipt of the said letters*, make *themselves* a complaint to parlia-
'ment? Why was it left to be done by *another* so long after,
'and without their privity or consent? No complaint is made till
'near two years after the transaction; and as perhaps the finan-
'ces, no less than the consciences of the honourable *Robert Lee*
'and Sir *Thomas Stapleton*, Bart. were found not to suit with the
'offer, it will, I fear, be suspected, that pique and disappoint-
'ment seemed to have made them at last join in measures, which
'the *generous disdain* the *Speaker* mentions could not at first pro-
'duce.

'As for the *Locus*, Sir, it is the Chapel of St. Stephen, which
'formerly glowed with a holy zeal of religion, and afterwards
'with the bright flame of patriotism, while *William Pultney*, and
'*William Pitt*—but their names fill my eyes with tears—Virtue
'left them, and they the people. Dazzled with the lure of titles,
'places, and pensions, they fell into a rank apostacy, and their
'names now only remain a terror to all who would dare such
'guilt, to meet so vain, so unsatisfactory a recompence, while
'the liberty of *England* shall find firm and undaunted guardians,
'to the latest ages, within these sacred walls.

'As to the *Eventus*, it shall be told very short. An artful at-
'torney, an accomplice in the guilt, drew his associates into the
'snare, and then left them. One of the most amiable, and ex-
'cellent peers of this country, whose family have, for above a
'century, done very signal services to the city of *Oxford*, has by
'the treachery of those, who owe all to that bounty, and by
'the mean and artful contrivances of some *ignoble* persons of the
'first rank, lost his influence in a place, where honour is no lon-
'ger regarded. As for the rest, *Philip Ward, John Treacher,
'Sir Thomas Munday, Thomas Wise, John Nicholes, John Philips,
'Isaac Lawrence, Richard Tawny, Thomas Robinson* and *John
'Brown*, were discharged, paid their *fees*, went down to *Ox-
'ford*; and when they make any future libations *on their knees*,
'they will, I hope, although on the banks of *Isis*, drink *loyal*
'healths.'

'nality; and to prevent, by your influence, those
'under your government from being tainted by
'this growing and pestilential voice. How have
'you abused this trust! You yourselves have set
'the infamous example of prostitution, in the most
'public and daring manner.

'Surely you must have felt some remorse from
'the generous disdain with which your corrupt of-
'fer was rejected by your representatives. They
'thought, and justly thought, that a seat in this
'house, obtained by a free and independent choice
'of their constituents, was the highest honour to
'which a subject can aspire; and that discharging
'their duty, as such representatives, was the no-
'blest of services. Sorry am I to say, that these
'considerations do not appear to have had the
'least weight with you.

'However, you have at last acknowledged
'your guilt; and, by your petition yesterday, you
'seem conscious of the enormity of your offence.
'This house, in the terror of its judgments, al-
'ways thinks upon mercy; nor do they ever in-
'flict punishment but for the sake of example,
'and to prevent others from becoming the objects
'of their resentment.

'The censure passed upon you will, they hope,
'have that effect. You are now the objects of
'their mercy; and are brought to the bar to be
'discharged.

'May you be penetrated with a due sense of
'their justice and lenity! May you atone for your
'past offence, by your constant endeavours to
'make a right use of the invaluable privileges which
'you enjoy as electors! Consider these privileges
'as a sacred trust reposed in you. Discharge it
'with integrity.

'But, before you rise from your present posture,
'I do, in obedience to the commands of this house,
'REPRIMAND you.

'I am

A. 1768.   DEBATES.

' I am to acquaint you, that you are discharged,
' paying your fees.

On the 17th of *February* 1768, Sir *George Savile* moved for leave to bring in a bill for quieting the possessions of the subject, and for amending and rendering more effectual an act of the 21st of *James* I. entitled an act for the general quiet of the subject, against all pretences of concealment whatsoever.

This motion was seconded by Sir *Anthony Abdy*, Bart. but it passed in the negative by 134, against 114.

The following is a LIST *of the* GENTLEMEN
who voted for the motion.

Anson, Thomas	Litchfield
Abdy, Sir Anthony Thomas, bart.	Knaresborough
Adams, George	Saltash
A'Court, Lieut. Gen. William	Heytsbury
Aislabie, William	Rippon
Archer, Hon. Andrew	Coventry
Aufrere, George	Stamford
Bentick, Lord Edward	Lewes
Bentinck, Captain John	Rye
Bertie, Peregrine	Westbury
Barrow, Charles	Gloucester
Beauclerck, Hon. Aubrey	Thetford
Burdett, Sir Robert, bart.	Tamworth
Bromley, William	Warwickshire
Baker, Sir William	Plympton
Burt, William Matthew	Great Marlow
Burke, Edmund	Wendover
Burke, William	Bedwin
Bootle, Richard Wilbraham	Chester
Cave, Sir Thomas, bart.	Leicestershire
Cavendish, Lord George	Derbyshire
Cavendish, Lord Frederick	Derby
Cavendish, Lord John	Knaresborough
Cavendish, Richard	Wendover

Cocks

Cocks, Charles	Ryegate
Coke, Wenman	Oakhampton
Codrington, Sir William, bart.	Tewkſbury
Cholmondeley, Thomas	Cheſhire
Cholmley, Nathaniel	Aldborough
Carnac, General	Leominſter
Cornewall, Velters	Herefordſhire
Cotton, Sir John Hynde, bart.	Cambridgeſhire
Curzon, Aſheton	Clitheroe
Curwen, Henry	Carliſle
Craven, Thomas	Berkſhire
Clive, Richard	Montgomery
Darker, John	Leiceſter
Deleval, George, Shaftoe	Northumberland
Dempſter, George	Forfar, &c.
Downe, Lord Viſcount	Cirenceſter
Dummer, Thomas	Newport
Dolben, Sir William, bart.	Oxford Univerſity
Finch, Savile	Malton
Foley, Thomas jun.	Herefordſhire
Frankland, Sir Thomas, bart. Admiral	Thirſke
Fuller, Richard	Steyning
Gaſcoign, Bamber	Midhurſt
Grey, Lord	Staffordſhire
Garth, Charles	Devizes
Grenville, Right Hon. George	Buckingham
Grenville, James, junior	Thirſke
Groſvenor, Thomas	Cheſter
Hamilton, William Gerrard	Pontefract
Hardy, Sir Charles	Rocheſter
Hanbury, John	Monmouthſhire
Harley, Hon. Robert	Droitwich
Harris, James	Chriſtchurch
Heathcote, Sir Gilbert, bart.	Shaftſbury
Hervey, Hon. Auguſtus	Saltaſh
Hervey, Hon. William	St. Edmondſbury
Hewet, John	Nottinghamſhire
Hotham, Col. Charles	St. Ives
Honeywood, Philip, General	Appleby
Howard, Thomas	Caſtelriſing

Hunter,

A. 1768.   D E B A T E S.

Hunter, Thomas Orby	Winchelsea
Irwin, John, Major General	East Grinstead
Keck, Anthony James	Leicester
Kepple, Hon. Augustus, Admiral	Windsor
Ladbroke, Sir Robert	London
Lascelles, Edwin	Yorkshire
Lascelles, Daniel	Northallerton
Lascelles, Edward	ditto
Lawrence, William	Rippon
Legh, Peter	Newton
Lenox, Lord George	Sussex
Long, Sir James, bart.	Marlborough
Luther, John	Essex
Meredith, Sir William, bart.	Liverpool
Mills, Richard	Canterbury
Molesworth, Sir John, bart.	Cornwall
Manners, Lord Robert	Kingston
Morgan, Thomas, jun.	Monmouthshire
Morgan, Charles	Brecon
Murray, James	Wigtownshire
Newdigate, Sir Robert, bart.	Oxford University
Norris, John,	Rye
Offley, John	Orford
Osbaldeston, Fountayne	Scarborough
Orwell, Lord	Ipswich
Palmer, Sir John, bart.	Leicestershire
Palmerston, Lord Viscount	East Looe
Parker, John	Devonshire
Pitt, Hon. Thomas	Wareham
Prescott George	Stockbridge
Ridley, Matthew	Newcastle
Rushout, John	Evesham
Sackville, Lord George	Hythe
Seymour, Henry	Totness
Savile, Sir George, bart.	Yorkshire
Scawen, James	St. Michael
Shiffner, Henry	Minehead
Smith, Sir Jarret, bart.	Bristol
Tudway, Clement	Wells
Vansittart, Arthur	Berkshire
	Weddell,

Weddel, William	Kingston upon Hull
Way, Benjamin	Bridport
West, James	St. Albans
West, James, jun.	Boroughbridge
White, John	Retford
Winterton, Earl	Bramber
Whateley, Thomas	Luggershall
Walsh, John	Worcester
York, Hon. Charles	Ryegate
York, Hon. John	Higham Ferrers.

Tellers, Sir George Armitage, bart.
Frederick Montagu, Esq;

The following voted against the Motion.

Allen, Lord Viscount	Eye
Ashburnham, William	Hastings
Barrington, Lord Viscount	Plymouth
Barré, Isaac	Wycombe
Beauchamp Lord	Lestwithel
Beckford, William	London
Bertie, Lord Robert	Boston
Best, Thomas	Canterbury
Boscawen, Hon. George	Truro
Boscawen, Hon. Edward Hugh	ditto
Bradshaw, Thomas	Harwich
Bridgeman, Sir Henry, bart.	Ludlow
Brudenell, Hon. James	Hastings
Brudenell, Robert	Marlborough
Brudenell, George Bridges	Stamford
Bull, Richard	Newport
Buller, John	Eastlooe
Burghersh, Lord	Lyme Regis
Burrell, Peter	Launceston
Campbell Pryse	Nairn, &c.
Clare, Lord Viscount	Bristol
Conway, Right Hon. H. S.	Thetford
Corke, George	Middlesex
Cowper, Grey	Rochester
Coutts, James	Edinburgh

Crauford,

A. 1767.   DEBATES.

Crauford, Patrick	Renfrewshire
Dalrymple, Sir Hew, bart.	Dunbar, &c.
Delaval, Sir John Hussey, bart.	Berwick
Drummond, Adam	Lymington
Duncomb, Thomas	Newport
Dyson, Jeremiah	Yarmouth
Earle, William Rawlinson	Newport
Edmondstone, Archibald	Dumbarton
Elliot, Sir Gilbert, bart.	Roxburghshire
Ellis, Wellbore	Aylesbury
Fanshaw, Simon	Grampound
Fitzroy, Colonel Charles	Bury
Frederick, Sir Charles	Queenborough
Fuller, Rose	Maidstone
Gage, Lord Viscount	Seaford
Gilbert, Thomas	Newcastle
Gordon, Lord Adam	Aberdeenshire
Hope-Weir, Hon. Charles	Linlithgowshire
Herbert, Edward	Ludlow
Hopkins, Richard	Dartmouth
Howe, Lord Viscount	ditto
Howe, Hon. William	Nottingham
Huske, John	Malden
Jenkinson, Charles	Appleby
Jenyns, Soame	Cambridge
Jennings, George	Whitchurch
Lamb, Sir Matthew, bart.	Peterborough
Mackay, Alexander	Sutherlandshire
Mackenzie, Right Hon. James Stuart	Rossshire
Mount Stuart, Lord	Bossiney
Medlicott, T. Hutchings	Milbourne
Montgomery, Archibald	Air County
Middleton, Richard	Denbigh
North, Lord	Banbury
Paterson, John	Luggershal
Peachy, Sir James, bart.	Seaford
Pelham, Right Hon. Thomas	Sussex
Percy, Earl	Westminster
Philipson, Richard	Eye

Vol. VII.   B b   Pryse,

Pryse, John Pugh	Cardiganshire
Reynolds, Francis	Lancaster
Rigby, Right Hon. Richard	Tavistock
Robinson, Hon. Thomas	Christchurch
Rodney, Sir George Brydges, bart.	Penryn
Ryder, Nathaniel	Tiverton
Scott, John	Tain, &c.
Scudamore, Charles	Hereford
Sebright, Sir John, bart.	Bath
Selwyn, George	Gloucester
Sewel, Right Hon. Thomas	Winchelsea
Shelley, Right Hon. John	Retford
Stanley, Right Hon. Hans	Southampton
Staunton, Thomas	Ipswich
Thurlow, Edward	Tamworth
Touchet, Samuel	Shaftsbury
Townshend, Charles	Yarmouth
Townshend, Right Hon. Thomas	Whitchurch
Vane, Frederick	Durham
Villiers, Lord	Aldborough
Upton, John	Westmoreland
Wauchope, Henry	Buteshire
Warren, Sir George	Lancaster
Wood, Robert	Brackley
Wynne, Sir John	Carnarvon

Cum multis aliis.

A List of the ACTS *passed this* SESSION.

AN Act *To prohibit the exportation of corn, grain, meal, malt, flour, bread, biscuit, and starch, and also the extraction of low wines, and spirits from wheat and wheat flour.*

An Act *For allowing the importation of wheat, wheat-flour, barly, barley-meal, pulse, oats, oat-meal, rye, and rye-meal, duty free; and to allow the importation of wheat and wheat-flour from* America, *for a limited time, duty free.*

An act *For the free importation of* Indian *corn or maize;—to the qualification act.*

An Act *To explain the act for reducing into one act the several statutes for the preservation of the public highways.* [By this act, the clause, "That no waggon having the wheels bound with streaks, or tire of a less breadth than two inches and a half, when worn, or being set or fastened on with rose headed nails, shall go, or be drawn with more than three horses; and that every owner or driver of any such waggon shall forfeit all such horses above the number three, with all gears, bridles, halters, and accoutrements, to the sole benefit of any persons who shall seize the same, with a proviso next after the said clause, containing particular restrictions as therein mentioned," is repealed and made void to all intents and purposes.]

An Act 14 *and* 15 Hen. VIII. *for altering highways in the Weald of* Kent.

An Act 26 Hen. VIII. *entitled, a bill for the highways in the county of* Sussex, *which were repealed by the act of the last session,* (great benefit having arisen from them) *are revived, and to be in full force. And the several acts, previous to the recited act of the last session, relative to the surveyors, and to the cleansing, lighting, &c. the streets in* Bristol, *are to be in force, and fully executed.*

An Act *For the importation of salted provisions from* Ireland *and* America, *duty free.*

An Act *For a navigable cut from* Coventry *to the* Mersey.

An Act *For a navigable cut from* Severn *to* Droitwich.

An act *For licensing a playhouse at* Bath.

An Act *For granting an aid to his Majesty for disbanding the army, and other necessary occasions, as relate to the number of troops kept upon the* Irish *establishment.*

An Act *For better regulating his Majesty's Marine forces when on shore*

An Act For providing accommodations for Justices of the Great Session in Wales.

An Act For regulating the East India Company with respect to making of Dividends.

An Act For preventing delays in the transportation of offenders.

An Act For rebuilding and enlarging Coventry Goal.

An Act To amend and render more effectual, an act for supplying the town of Halifax with fresh water, and for other purposes.

An Act For making a navigable canal from Birmingham to Bilston, &c.

An Act For applying the sinking fund for the service of the present year.

An Act To raise money by loans on exchequer bills, for the same.

An Act To raise 1,900,000l. by annuities and lottery.

An Act For redeeming the remainder of the joint stock of annuities, established in the third year of his present Majesty's reign.

An Act To apply the sum granted for the pay and cloathing of the militia.

An Act For better paving and lighting the city of London, &c.

An Act To amend an act for regulating journeymen taylors.

An Act To amend an act of this session, for punishing mutiny and desertion in America, &c.

An Act To continue several acts for encouraging the whale fishery.

An Act For more effectually recovering the penalties relating to trade in America.

An Act To amend the laws touching the elections of knights of the shires in England.

An Act For converting Gresham College into an Excise-office.

An Act For allowing foul salt, taken from the salt works, to be used as manure.

An Act *For allowing the exportation of malt now in his Majesty's warehouses.*
An Act *To license a playhouse in* Norwich.
An Act *For better supplying* Dunbar *with water.*
An Act *For encouraging the trade to* Newfoundland, *&c.*

On the 10th of March 1768, *the King went to the House of Peers, and put an End to this Session with the following Speech.*

My Lords, and Gentlemen,

'The readiness with which you entered into the
' views I recommended to you at the opening of
' this session, and the assiduity wth which you have
' applied yourselves to the dispatch of the public
' business, give me great satisfaction. At the same
' time, the affectionate concern you have shewn
' for the wellfare of your fellow-subjects, by the sa-
' lutary laws passed for their relief in respect to the
' high price of provisions, cannot fail of securing
' to you their most grateful regard.

' I have nothing new to communicate to you in
' relation to foreign affairs. The apparent interests
' of the several powers in Europe, as well as the
' express assurances I have received from them,
' leave me no room to doubt of their disposition to
' preserve the general tranquillity. And on my
' part, you may rest assured, that every measure
' that is consistent with the honour of my crown,
' and the rights of my subjects, shall be steadily di-
' rected to that most salutary purpose.

Gentlemen of the House of Commons,

' Your chearfulness in granting the necessary
' supplies, and your attention to the ease of my
' good subjects in the manner of raising them, e-
' qually demand my acknowledgements. I see,
' with pleasure, that you have been able to prose-
' cute

'cute the diminution of the national debt, with-
'out laying any additional burthen upon my peo-
'ple.

My Lords, and Gentlemen,

'As the time limited by law for the expiration
'of this parliament now draws near, I am resolved
'forthwith to issue my proclamation for dissolving
'it, and for calling a new parliament. But I can-
'not do this, without having first returned you
'my thanks, for the many signal proofs you have
'given of the most affectionate attachment to my
'person, family, and government, the most faith-
'ful attention to the public service, and the most
'earnest zeal for the preservation of our excellent
'constitution. When, by the vigorous support
'which you gave me during the war, I had been
'enabled, under the Divine Providence, to restore
'to my people the blessings of peace, you con-
'tinued to exert yourselves, with equal alacrity
'and steadiness, in pursuing every method that
'could contribute to the public safety and tran-
'quillity; which you well understood could be no
'otherwise preserved, than by establishing, on a
'respectable foundation, the strength, the credit,
'and the commerce of the nation. The large sup-
'plies you have from time to time granted, and
'the wise regulations you have made for these im-
'portant purposes, will, I am persuaded, be found
'to have been productive of the most beneficial
'consequences.

'In the approaching election of representa-
'tives, I doubt not but my people will give me
'fresh proofs of their attachment to the true in-
'terest of their country; which I shall ever receive
'as the most acceptable mark of their affection to
'me. The welfare of all my subjects is my first
'object. Nothing therefore has ever given me
'more real concern, than to see any of them, in

'any

'any part of my dominions, attempting to loosen
'those bonds of constitutional subordination, so es-
'sential to the welfare of the whole. But it is with
'much satisfaction that I now see them returning
'to a more just sense of what their own interest, no
'less than their duty, indispensibly requires of
'them; and thereby giving me the prospect of
'continuing to reign over an happy, because an
'united people.'

On the 12th of *March* 1768, the Parliament was dissolved by proclamation, and writs were issued for electing a new Parliament returnable on the 10th of *May* 1768.

The following short observations on the conduct of this Parliament, were published a few days after its dissolution.

'It was the general and established rule to vote
'with the Treasury Bench; and as those who sat
'there, were frequently changed in these last seven
'years, the resolutions of the House became as va-
'rious and contradictory. No peace, that shall
'leave the two branches of the house of *Bourbon*
'united! says one minister: war everlasting! ec-
'choed the worthy representatives of the people.
'Peace on any terms! says the favourite minister:
'we are an undone bankrupt nation! cried the
'House. Cyder ought to be taxed! declared the
'same genius: double tax cyder by all means!
'answered the Parliament. It was a damned thing
'to tax cyder! exclaims the next dictator: aye,
'damn the cyder taxers, and all their friends!
'replied the commons of G. B. *America* should
'pay her proportion of her own expences; says
'the finance minister: nothing so reasonable!
'cries Parliament; we won't hear a word against
'it; stamp the dogs if they refuse to pay. *Ame-*
'*rica* pays too much already, is too beneficial to
'this country, by dealing with it *only*, take off
'their

'their taxes, and allow them to trade to other na-
'tions; were the opinions of the next in order:
'repeal, repeal, no taxes, no duties! and free
'ports for *America!* resounded through St. *Ste-*
'*phen's* chapel, during the whole Session.'

About the same time was also published the following.

A List of Ministers made and unmade by the Earl of Bute.

In *October*, 1760. He closed with the late King's Ministry.

In *March*, 1761. He pensioned off Lord *Holder-nesse*, and became himself Secretary of State.

In *October*, 1761. He removed Mr. *Pitt*, and took in a new set of men.

In *May*, 1762. He quarrelled with the Duke of *Newcastle*, and set himself at the head of the Treasury.

In *October*, 1762. He removed Mr. *Grenville*, and entrusted the conduct of affairs with Mr. *Fox*.

In *April*, 1763. He resigned in favour of Mr. *Grenville*, the Earls of *Halifax* and *Sandwich*.

In *August*, 1763. He advised the sending to Mr. *Pitt*, and negotiated with him a change, which, however, did not take place.

In *May*, 1765. He advised the making fresh offers to Mr. *Pitt*, which were considered to be *inadmissible*.

In *July*, 1765. He procured the dismission of Mr. *Grenville*, the D. of *Bedford*, and their friends, and advised the appointment of the Marquis of *Rockingham*, with a new set of men.

In *July*, 1766. He displaced the M. of *Rockingham*, and advised the sending again for Mr. *Pitt*, who was now created Earl of *Chatham*.

In 1767, He gave the reins to the Duke of *Grafton*, and obliged Lord *Chatham* to resign.

END OF VOL. VII.

Lightning Source UK Ltd.
Milton Keynes UK
UKHW031133300522
403723UK00007B/1851